The 220 Best Franchises To Buy

The 220 Best Franchises To Buy

The Sourcebook for Evaluating the Best Franchise Opportunities

Constance Jones

The Philip Lief Group, Inc.

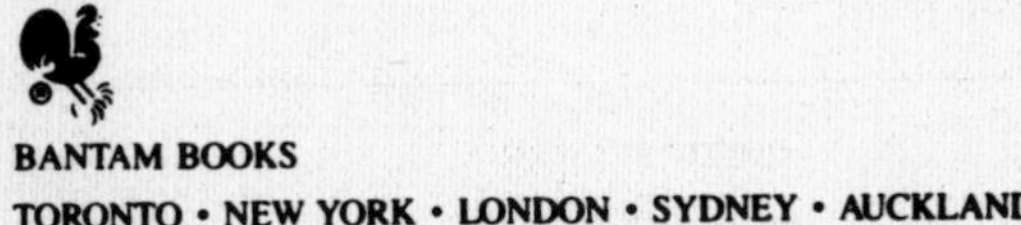

BANTAM BOOKS
TORONTO • NEW YORK • LONDON • SYDNEY • AUCKLAND

THE 220 BEST FRANCHISES TO BUY
A Bantam Book / May 1987

Produced by The Philip Lief Group, Inc.,
319 East 52nd Street, New York, NY 10022

Written by Constance Jones

Project Consultant: Gene Brown

Library of Congress Cataloging-in-Publication Data

Jones, Constance.
The 220 best franchises to buy.

1. Franchises (Retail trade)—United States.
I. Philip Lief Group. II. Title. III. Title: Two hundred twenty best franchises to buy.
HF5429.235.U5J66 1987 658.8'708 86-47887
ISBN 0-553-34385-8

Published simultaneously in the United States and Canada

Bantam Books are published by Bantam Books, Inc. Its trademark, consisting of the words "Bantam Books" and the portrayal of a rooster, is registered in U.S. Patent and Trademark Office and in other countries. Marca Registrada. Bantam Books, Inc., 666 Fifth Avenue, New York, New York 10103.

PRINTED IN CANADA

WC 0 9 8 7 6 5 6 4 3

Contents

PART III

Tables and Indexes

Introduction

The Franchising Boom

Franchising now accounts for more than one third of all retail sales. Total sales by franchised retailers topped $530 billion in 1985 and climbed to an estimated $576 billion in 1986. According to the U.S. Department of Commerce, franchising will sustain—or better—this annual 8.5 percent rate of growth in sales for years to come. As greater numbers of enterprising business people recognize the profits to be had through franchising, they purchase franchises in every field from automotive services to video cassette rental. The number of franchised units in operation expands at a rate of 6 percent annually, which is good news—for close to two thousand franchisors, who reap a percentage of their franchisees' gross sales; for half a million franchisees, who cash in on franchisors' good names and experience; and for over 6 million people directly employed in franchising. And new franchisors enter the arena every day, opening up even more opportunities for ambitious people who dream of owning their own businesses. *The 220 Best Franchises to Buy* contains descriptions of franchising giants with histories of phenomenal success, and of young companies with fresh ideas and aggressive strategies for growth.

A Little Bit of History

The term "franchise" comes from the Old French word *franc,* meaning "free from servitude." Its Middle English form, *fraunchise,* meant "privilege" or "freedom," and today *The American Heritage Dictionary of the English Language* defines "franchise" as a "privilege or right granted a person or a group by a government, state, or sovereign, especially . . . suffrage . . . the grant of certain rights and powers to a corporation . . . authorization granted by a manufacturer to a distributor or dealer to sell [its] products."

Since the 1850s, when the Singer Sewing Machine Company became the first to employ franchising as a method of distribution, independent business people have been enjoying unique privileges and freedoms as franchisees. In the first half of the twentieth century, franchising took the forms of automobile and truck dealerships, gas stations, and soft drink bottlers. These franchised businesses still make up three quarters of total franchise sales, but ever since McDonald's came on the scene in the 1950s, companies in virtually every industry have adopted franchising as a way of business. As the economic scene changes, franchising finds new and wider applications. And because franchising can be used to distribute just about any product or service, its potential seems almost unlimited.

What Is Franchising?

Though often referred to as an industry, franchising is actually a method of doing business. Franchisors use franchising as a marketing technique in order to expand their market share more rapidly and less expensively. Three distinct types of businesses make up the larger category known as franchising. The first, distributorships, involves the simple granting of the right to sell a product or products originated or owned by the parent company. The second, trademark or brand name licensing, gives licensees the right to use the company's trademark or brand name in conjunction with the operation of their businesses. This book is primarily concerned with the third type of business, the full business format franchise.

In a full business format franchise, the franchisor (licensor) sells to franchisees (licensees) the license or right to sell its goods or services and/or to use business techniques the franchisor has developed. Franchisees generally pay an initial fee to start up and thereafter forward a percentage of their gross sales to the franchisor at agreed-upon intervals throughout the term of the franchise contract.

In return for these payments, franchisees gain a combination of privileges, which may include the rights to sell a proven, recognized product, to use a set of business practices based on the parent company's experience in the field, to receive initial training, and to benefit from an assortment of ongoing support services. But franchisees also have responsibilities to franchisors—which go beyond the payment of fees and which they are contractually obliged to meet. Among these might be requirements to meet a variety of quality controls for products and services sold, restrictions on what they can sell or how they can operate under the company's name, specifications for their business location and site appearance, and prohibitions on the operation of any similar businesses during or after the term of the franchise contract.

Franchisees have a range of tools at their disposal that their small, nonfranchised competitors rarely have. Brand names, trademarks, copyrights, and patented trade secrets allow them to offer customers what no one else can. Uniform logos, storefronts, and interiors make their businesses more immediately recognizable to potential clients. By following the company's business practices and offering products that meet the company's standards, franchisees can consistently provide customers with quality goods and services.

Many franchisors are corporations with purchasing power that can save franchisees money. They often operate research and development divisions, which constantly test and improve products; marketing departments, which conduct regional or national advertising in a variety of media; and franchisee development programs, which offer comprehensive initial and refresher training to franchisees. And the franchisor's ongoing support system can supply franchisees with assistance in organization, site selection, construction, store opening, merchandising, management, sales, purchasing, and employee recruitment and training, among other things. As long as they keep up their own end of the franchise bargain, franchisees can reap the many advantages of operating their own businesses under the guidance of an experienced and recognized company.

Better Odds

As a franchisee, you can have the satisfaction of being in business for yourself, of making your own business decisions, and of seeing your own hard work pay off. But you need not feel that you're all alone out there. Before they franchise their businesses, good franchisors thoroughly test their products and methods. They make the mistakes, work the kinks out of the business, and establish a reputation. So if you're willing to work hard, pay a few fees, and conform to the franchisor's system, statistics show that you are more likely to succeed with a franchise than if you opened a nonfranchised business on your own.

According to the Small Business Administration, 30 to 35 percent of small businesses fail within the first year of operation. But less than 5 percent of all franchise units fail each year, says the U.S. Department of Commerce. Clearly, franchising increases your chances of success—but no one can guarantee your success. "The biggest problem with people getting into franchising is that they think it's easy," notes Linda Serabian, a Subway sandwich shop franchisee. "They think that they don't have to do anything. But it doesn't work like that. It takes a lot of hard work."

No franchise can offer instant wealth, and you should steer clear of any that make get-rich-quick promises. Most franchisees see very low income in the first couple of years of operation—indeed, some even lose money during the first year or two. But with enough elbow grease, the well-capitalized, motivated franchisee can expect to earn an excellent income after the rocky opening period.

A Franchise versus Your Own Small Business

Though owning a franchise may involve just as much work as running an independent small business, you can gain two advantages through franchising: When you operate a franchise, you generally offer a good or a service that people may buy more readily because of its recognized name, and you use previously tested and proven operating systems and business methods. It is easier to maintain a good reputation than to establish one, and you will save your energy and money by following established procedures rather than having to figure out, by trial and error, how best to run your business. "In order to set up this business on their own, a person would have to stumble around for three or four years," says Michael Webster of his Corporate Investment Business Brokers franchise. As a franchisee, you receive ongoing support and assistance from experienced professionals, but as a small business owner-operator, you have to figure out how to do everything yourself.

Why, then, doesn't every hopeful entrepreneur rush out to purchase a franchise? Because franchising involves two tradeoffs that not everyone is willing to make: fees and conformity. Many successful, satisfied franchisees, like Sherridan Revell, who owns an AAA Employment franchise, feel that "the only disadvantage to owning a franchise compared with running your own business would be giving up the royalties each week to the home office." While the vast majority of franchisees consider the security of a franchise and the expertise of the franchisor well worth the added expenses, some resent the requirement that they must continue paying royalties even when they no longer need the constant support or assistance of the parent company.

The initial franchise fee, the franchisor's requirements for the size and location of your facility, and its specifications for the equipment and supplies you must use can add up to higher start-up costs for franchisees than for business people who open similar businesses on their own. When it does, however, Sherridan Revell still feels that the advantages far outweigh the disadvantages. "It is well worth it to be part of an established company."

Franchisors have carefully determined what makes their businesses work, and therefore require franchisees to make the investment needed to implement their methods. In some cases, this results in a larger initial investment by the business person, but not always. Because the company's research and experience can decrease or eliminate some expenses that you would have to bear if you struck out on your own, and because many other costs (like those for advertising and product development) are spread over many franchisees, buying and operating a franchised business can end up costing you less.

Despite this, some prospective franchisees decide that the rights to sell a patented product or process or use prepackaged procedures, or the intangible benefits of an established company name, are not worth the amount they would have to pay in order to have access to them. All hopeful business owner-operators must decide: "Could I do just as well on my own?"

The second perceived disadvantage to being a franchisee is that "in exchange for security, training, and the marketing power of the franchise trademark, you must be able and willing to give up some of your independence," as Bruce Weldon, a Coustic-Glo franchise owner, puts it. Your own success depends in great part on the company's reputation, which in turn depends on your ability to maintain the company's standards. In order to succeed as a franchisee, then, you must follow company guidelines for offering uniformly high-quality products or services.

For mavericks, tinkerers, and incurable noncomformists, franchising can be a frustrating experience. Franchisees give up some of their business autonomy in exchange for the use of the franchisor's name, products, and techniques. "Only a fool would pay for tried-and-true methods and then not use them," says Jane Miller, an AAA Employment franchisee. Purchasing a franchise eliminates some of the risks associated with starting a business only if you take advantage of the franchising system—which means submitting to some controls. If you don't mind turning in reports, purchasing from designated sources, or allowing company personnel to check up on your operation, then you won't mind the relatively minor constraints involved in being a franchisee. But if you like to do things your own way, you may not be satisfied with reproducing someone else's success.

Should You Buy a Franchise?

Only you can determine if franchising is right for you. Deciding whether you should buy a franchise, which one to buy, and how to go about buying one is a complicated, sticky business. Part I contains detailed information on what you should consider when making what could be the most important investment of your life. Guidelines and checklists, arranged in a logical, step-by-step manner, will provide you with a starting point for your decision-making process.

Part I

Choosing and Buying a Franchise

Introduction to Part I

The Big Picture

Choosing which—if any—franchise to buy can be confusing, time consuming, and a little overwhelming. But you can make the process a lot easier by carefully determining what you need to know and do and then conducting your investigation in an organized way. Like Joyce Gump, a Precision Tune franchisee, almost any franchisee will recommend that you "thoroughly research the background of the business you are considering getting into." A decision based on a thorough, sound evaluation of your franchising opportunities will make good financial sense and will match your personal and professional goals and abilities.

No one can give you better advice on buying a franchise than a franchisee, who has gone through the experience of evaluating and selecting a franchise. Paul and Evy Hatjistilianos, who own a Merry Maids franchise, summarize what most franchisees have to say about choosing a franchise: "Compare the available franchise opportunities. Look at the company's track record on training, marketing, start-up support, and continuous growth and development support. Understand the contract with respect to royalty fees, contract renewal, and other short- and long-term commitments." Part I is, in effect, a step-by-step breakdown of the many details involved in analyzing yourself and the franchises in which you are interested. Clearly, each person and each situation is a little different, so you should adjust these guidelines to fit your specific needs and objectives.

Organizing Your Investigation

Your franchise will probably be the biggest investment (except, perhaps, your home) that you will make in your lifetime, and it will also entail an enormous legal commitment. As a career, a franchise will demand the lion's share of your time and energy for the next several years, if not for the remainder of your working life. Because of the significance of your franchising decision, you should do everything in your power to be thoroughly informed about your opportunities and obligations as a franchisee. Before you invest, you should:

1. Know yourself
2. Know the franchisor
3. Know the product and its market
4. Know about fees, expenses, and financing
5. Know about training programs, support, and assistance
6. Know your legal rights and the terms of the contract

Step by Step

You can find out what you need to know by following a straightforward, step-by-step process. Chapters 1–6, based on the list that follows, will guide you through the stages of investigating a franchise opportunity.

1. Before you contact franchisors, you should analyze your interests, abilities, and weak points, as well as your financial goals, capacity, and limitations.
2. Take a look at the product you would be selling as a franchisee. Analyze the market for the product in your region and determine if you can find a viable location for the franchise in your area.
3. Determine which franchise programs might suit you (based on your self-analysis) and contact the franchisors for further information.
4. After you receive the information you have requested, narrow down your list of possibilities to two or three companies, using a preliminary evaluation of the franchisors, their products and services, and their franchise programs.
5. Check outside sources of information— publications, government agencies, consumer groups, etc.—for more background on the franchisors.
6. Contact the companies you've singled out and indicate your interest to them. Submit the preliminary franchise applications to establish yourself as a serious prospect.
7. If any of the companies have not yet provided it, request detailed information on the financial and legal particulars of owning one of their franchises. Ask for a list of currently operating franchisees that you may speak with.
8. Consult with your accountant and lawyer to determine the feasi-

bility of investing in the franchises in which you are interested. Check franchisors' earnings claims (if they make any) and prepare profit projections for your potential business.

9. Speak with some of the companies' franchisees regarding their experiences with the franchisors. Learn all you can about the kinds of support the companies provide.
10. Meet with the corporate staff of each of the companies you are considering. Ask any questions you might have, and give the company an opportunity to interview you. Make your decision.
11. Have your accountant and lawyer review the standard franchise agreement that the franchisor has given you. Negotiate favorable terms before you sign the contract.

If you follow these steps, you should be able to make a wise decision regarding your investment in a franchise. Though franchise fraud has become relatively rare since the 1979 passage of laws that require all franchisors to disclose certain basic facts to potential franchisees, you can never be too careful. Don't rely solely on the information the company gives you, and verify financial data and earnings claims whenever you can. And remember: Franchise owners can be a most valuable source of information.

The hints and checklists that follow in Chapters 1–6 will help you make the most of the information contained in Parts II and III. Because you, your region, and each of the franchisors you are investigating have unique characteristics, you may want to tailor the guidelines to fit your situation. The checklists should simply provide a framework for your research and evaluation.

1. Know Yourself

1. Before you contact franchisors, you should analyze your interests, abilities, and weak points, as well as your financial goals, capacity, and limitations.

Although most prospective franchisees know it is wise to evaluate franchisors' performance and learn about a franchise before investing in it, many never think to sit down and take a good look at themselves. But self-analysis must play a vital role when making the right franchising decision. No matter how good an investment a given franchise might be, it can only bring headaches if you are ill-suited to the business itself, to franchising in general, or to running your own business in any form. As Gary Sollee, a Chem-Dry franchisee, puts it: "You will not succeed in any business unless you have a positive attitude and are willing to work your tail off and sacrifice for a few years. You'll only get out what you put in." And if you don't have an honest understanding of your financial capabilities, or realistic financial goals and expectations, you could get in over your head. To avoid making a costly mistake, determine whether or not you are cut out to be a franchise owner—both temperamentally and financially.

Franchisors frequently point to the following characteristics as key to the success of a franchisee: a willingness to work hard, take risks, and work within the franchisor's system. Your business and educational background, your management and sales abilities, and the support of your family will also play significant roles in your business. True, no two franchise owners are alike, but those who prosper share certain traits: enthusiasm, ambition, energy, organization, the ability to get along with others, adequate capitalization, and clear, realistic financial goals. When considering franchising, ask yourself:

- Do I enjoy hard work?
- Am I willing to work long hours?

- Am I willing to forfeit days off and vacation time?
- Am I motivated to succeed—whatever it takes?
- Do I have a lot of physical and emotional stamina?
- Will my family tolerate my long hours?

- Why do I want to own a franchise?
- Have I ever been self-employed? Did I like it?
- Am I enthusiastic about running my own business?
- Would I resent taking business problems home with me?

- Would I like to make my franchise my career?
- Can I dedicate years—or a lifetime—to my franchise?
- Will I run my franchise myself?

- Where will I get the money to finance my business?
- Do I have sufficient resources to tolerate low or negative returns for the first year or so of operation?
- Could I live with temporary financial uncertainty?
- Am I willing to forfeit income now to gain income later?
- Am I looking to get rich quick?

- Do I enjoy taking risks?
- Do I prefer the security of working for someone else?
- Do I enjoy making decisions?
- Am I self-reliant and self-motivated?
- Am I willing to accept responsibility for my actions?

- Do I have any business management experience?
- Am I an organized person?
- Can I handle lots of detail?

- Am I a good supervisor?
- Can I recruit and hire the right employees?
- Do I enjoy working with others?
- Can I deal effectively with customers?
- Do I enjoy sales?

- Am I willing to conform to the franchisor's system?
- Will I mind giving up some of my independence?
- Can I take orders and follow instructions?
- Can I deal effectively with authority?
- Can I accept help from others when I need it?

- Do my friends and family think I can succeed?
- Would they provide encouragement and support?

- What kind of business would I like to own?
- Do I have hobbies or interests which could become part of a business—a love of children, an interest in fashion, etc.?
- Do I have any special skills or talents that might be useful in my business? Can I repair cars, operate a computer, etc.?
- Do I have any pertinent work experience or education?
- What are my dislikes—do I hate paperwork, sales, or manual work, for instance?
- Do I have any particular weaknesses that might be a disadvantage in running my business; e.g, am I afraid of public speaking, am I bad with numbers, do I have a short temper, etc.?

If you think your answers to these questions indicate that you have a balanced combination of independence and team spirit, ambition and realism, experience and flexibility, then you are ready to take the next step in your search for the ideal business opportunity: researching the market demographics in your region.

2. *Know the Product and Its Market*

2. Take a look at the product you would be selling as a franchisee. Analyze the market for the product in your region and determine if you can find a viable location for a franchise in your area.

Your livelihood as a franchisee will depend upon your ability to sell your product to customers within your region. If you can't sell the product in your area—no matter how successfully it might sell somewhere else—you won't make any money. Do an honest evaluation of the sales potentials of the franchises that you are considering purchasing: Do they offer high-quality products that will appeal to your customer base? Will the products sell five years from now? What kind of competition can you expect? Can you find an appropriate location for your business in your area?

Check sales data of similar or related businesses in your region to get a feeling for how your franchise might do. Your Chamber of Commerce, local banks, and trade associations might be helpful in this regard, as will the Small Business Administration and the Department of Commerce. Consult national and regional business or trade publications to determine how the particular type of business—whether franchised or independent—has performed historically, both in your area and as a whole. Find out what industry analysts and government experts have to say about the future: industry trends, economic forecasts, and projections of future demand for the product you would sell as a franchisee.

As they recognize the potential profits of catering to the special needs of the baby boom generation, people purchase franchises designed to appeal to that market, especially those in the service industries. New business areas just now being tapped by franchising include upscale, sophisticated home and personal goods and services (like maid services and interior decorating); child care services; health/beauty/fitness goods and services;

convenience stores; and business services like banking, consulting, and financial planning.

Increasingly, small independent businesses convert to franchising to gain an extra edge in the marketplace, especially in the areas of home repair and construction, restaurants, business services, and nonfood retailing. These areas all promise to remain hot markets for some years to come, not only for conversion franchises but for franchisees starting from scratch. Additionally, experts like Andrew Kostecka of the Department of Commerce predict that the strong demand for recreation, entertainment, and travel-related products, as well as for automobile and truck rental and aftermarket services, will continue. Management consulting, tax services and accounting, computer-support services, and financial planning promise to be big sellers among the business service industries.

These forecasts provide only a general idea of where some of tomorrow's opportunities may lie. Use your own specific knowledge of your region when analyzing the local market for a given product. Note regional trends and tastes, and the economic condition and outlook for your area. If location will play an important role in the success of the particular franchise in which you are interested, check to see if you can find any viable locations available in your area. But most of all, make sure that the franchisor distributes products and services of the highest possible quality. As you consider the franchisor's product and its market, ask yourself the following questions:

- How long has the product been on the market?
- Is it a proven seller or a brand-new innovation?
- Could it become obsolete?
- Is it a fad or gimmick product?
- Will it sell a year from now? Five years? Ten years?
- Is it a necessity or a luxury item?
- Is the product's appeal seasonal?
- Does the product have broad appeal or a specifically defined market, e.g., tourists, children, senior citizens, the wealthy?
- Is the product manufactured by the franchisor or by a third party?
- What is the reputation of the manufacturer?
- Are the materials, products, and techniques I use and sell as a franchisee of a good quality?
- Are there warranties or guarantees on the product or service? Who backs them up?
- Who is responsible for the repair or replacement of faulty merchandise?
- Who pays for such repairs? Who is responsible for refunds?

- Are there government standards or regulations for the product or service?
- Are there any restrictions on its use?
- Is the product or service patented, copyrighted, or otherwise protected?
- Is the product exclusive to the franchisor?

- From whom do I purchase merchandise, materials, and supplies?
- Will I get a fair price?
- Can I count on reliable delivery and ready availability?
- Will I be able to sell the product at a competitive price?
- Who sets the price of the product to my customers?
- Who in my territory will buy the product?
- Will demand be strong enough to support my business, net a healthy profit, and meet any sales quotas the franchisor might set?

- What kind of competition will I face in my region?
- Do numerous companies already compete for the same business in my area?
- Do I know of any major competitor planning to enter the market in my territory?
- What is the franchisor's competition now, and will it change in the future?
- What is the franchisor's strategy for dealing with competition?
- What are the franchisor's views with regard to product diversification? Advertising and marketing?
- Will the franchisor's name attract customers to my business?

- Is the location of my franchise important?
- What kind of location will my franchise require?
- Are there any such locations available in my area?
- Is the purchase or lease price affordable?
- What kind of construction or improvements would be required?
- Would the franchisor approve the site I have in mind?

Many franchisors will conduct a demographic analysis of your region and study the traffic patterns of possible franchise sites once you make a formal application for a franchise. These studies can provide you with further information that you can use in evaluating your franchise opportunities.

Once you have taken a look at yourself and evaluated your region's marketplace, you should find out everything you can about your potential business partner—the franchisor.

3. *Know the Franchisor*

3. Determine which franchise programs might suit you (based on your self-analysis) and contact the franchisors for further information.

Do you have extensive sales experience? Do you enjoy working with children? Do you have an interest in fitness? Find out what franchising opportunities exist in your area of interest or expertise; then call or write to the companies that offer franchises that appeal to you. Most franchise departments will send you a package of materials containing information on the company, the franchise itself, requirements for becoming a franchisee, the estimated initial amount required to invest in a franchise, and the franchisor's training and support programs.

4. After you receive the information you have requested, narrow down your list of possibilities to two or three companies, using a preliminary evaluation of the franchisors, their products and services, and their franchise programs.

In order to conduct a meaningful investigation of your choices as a potential franchisee, you should explore more than one company in great detail. But you should limit your comparison shopping to no more than a few prospects. You don't want to be overwhelmed by a multitude of details. You may have sent an initial request for information to ten or fifteen companies, but you can't do an in-depth evaluation of all of them—and you won't need to.

In most cases, you can tell right off the bat whether or not you are really interested in knowing more about a given franchise program. By answering the following basic questions about each franchise that has immediate appeal for you, you will be able to pinpoint two or three real possibilities from among those you initially thought might interest you.

- Would you enjoy making a career out of running this franchise?
- Do you have the skills—or could you learn them—to operate this business?
- Do you have the resources to invest in and operate this franchise?
- Does it seem as if the returns of your investment in this franchise might be in line with your financial needs and objectives?
- Does the franchisor seem to be reputable, forthcoming, and the type of company with which you would enjoy a partnership?

Checking off the points on this list will help you decide which franchisors you would like to know more about. As you continue your investigation, don't rely solely on the information companies send to you.

5. Check outside sources of information—publications, government agencies, consumer groups, etc.—for more background on the franchisors.

Find out what the business press—newspapers, magazines, etc.—has to say about each company you are considering. Is it financially strong, well managed, and reputable? Are its officers well regarded in the business community? Has performance been good in the past year, and does it promise to remain so? What is the outlook for its franchise program? Does the company have good relations with its franchisees?

Government agencies like the Federal Trade Commission, the Department of Commerce, state consumer protection and securities divisions, and the Small Business Administration can be valuable sources of information on individual franchisors and franchising in general. They may keep on file disclosure statements of registered franchisors, which contain detailed information about all aspects of the companies' franchise programs.

Since 1979, when the Federal Trade Commission promulgated its disclosure rule, the law has required most franchisors to provide disclosure statements (also referred to as "offering prospectuses" and "offering circulars") to prospective franchisees. Additionally, many states have laws requiring the registration of companies that offer franchises for sale within their boundaries, and the disclosure of certain information to prospective franchisees. You should contact your state's securities division or consumer protection division. The Department of Commerce publishes a number of useful pamphlets and booklets on franchising, and the Small Business Administration can also provide you with information.

Check with consumer protection groups like the Better Business Bureau to find out if any complaints have been lodged by franchisees or customers against any of the companies you are investigating. Try to get a sense of how the public at large perceives each company and its products. Does the company provide high-quality goods or services? Does it make good on warranties and live up to its promises? Is there any indication that it might be fraudulent—a fly-by-night organization?

Franchising organizations can also provide background information on many franchisors. The International Franchising Association (IFA), a membership organization for franchisors, can provide a list of its members, who abide by a strict code of business ethics. The IFA also makes available various other publications useful to prospective franchisees. For information on franchisor/franchisee relations, and to get an idea of how franchisees feel about various franchisors, you can contact the National Franchise Association Coalition, a membership organization of franchisees from many companies.

You may also go to credit agencies or investor service firms like Dun & Bradstreet, Standard & Poor's, or Moody's for more detailed financial information on a franchisor. Does the company pay its creditors promptly? Is its operation highly dependent on debt financing?

Once you've gathered all the information you can about the franchisors and their operations, do a detailed analysis of each one:

- In exactly what type of business is the company engaged?
- What do its franchisees do?
- Does the company have a reputation for honesty and fairness?
- What can the franchisor do for you that you would not be able to accomplish on your own?

- How many years has the company been in business?
- How many years has it been franchising?
- How many units are in operation?
- How many of those does the company own?

- As a franchisee, would you be getting in on the ground floor of the business, or joining an established network?
- Would you be working within a highly structured system, one that is more loosely organized, or one that is still being developed? Which would you prefer?

- Is the company publicly held?
- Is it a corporation, a partnership, or a proprietorship?
- Is the company a subsidiary of any other company?
- What is the parent company's reputation and condition?
- Does the company have any business relationships or structural peculiarities that might have an adverse effect on its franchise program?

- What is the experience of the company's officers?
- Is the company's management stable, or is there excessive turnover among corporate staff?
- Does the company's success appear to depend on the efforts of a single person, or does the company employ a dedicated, well-trained, knowledgeable staff?
- If the founder, chairman, or other individual left the company, would its ability to function and thrive be materially affected?
- Is the company or its officers engaged in any lawsuits or bankruptcy proceedings?

- Has the company's rate of growth been healthy?
- Can the company support all of the new franchises it sells?
- Does the company seem to sell too many units in the same region?
- Is the company more concerned with selling franchises, or with offering the public a quality product?

- Does the company have a good relationship with its franchisees?
- What are the company's plans for its franchise operations?
- Has the company been buying out franchisees?
- Has another company or individual?
- Does the company compete with its franchisees for business?

- Have the company's franchises been consistently successful?
- Can you verify figures for average sales per unit?
- Can you verify figures for the company's system-wide sales?
- Has the company's overall performance been historically strong, and is this performance likely to continue?
- What is the company's financial condition?
- Does the company have a good credit rating?

- Does the company hold patents, trademarks, or copyrights?
- Can you verify them?
- Is the business based on an exclusive product or process?
- Is the company restricted in any way in its use of its patents, trademarks, or copyrights?
- Will the expiration of these rights materially affect the franchisor or its franchisees?

- Do the company's promotional efforts or image depend upon the participation of a particular celebrity?
- Would the company's marketing strategy be materially affected if it lost the right to use the celebrity name or image in its campaigns?

- Is the company forthcoming with information?
- In its dealings with you, is it employing high-pressure sales tactics?
- Is it complying with laws regulating the sales of franchises?
- Is it eager to investigate you carefully?
- Does the company appear to be ready to help you in every way possible once you become a franchisee?

Find out as much as you can about each franchisor and carefully determine what your findings mean. A poorly managed franchisor can be a franchisee's nightmare. Protect yourself by getting the complete picture of each company that you may one day have as a business partner. After you learn how the business community views each company you are investigating, get in touch with each one and make a more personal judgment.

6. Contact the companies you've singled out and indicate your interest to them. Submit the preliminary franchise applications to establish yourself as a serious prospect.

Your first meaningful contact with the franchisor can provide you with valuable data on the company— information that goes beyond the usual photos and figures in its promotional booklets and fact sheets. You will be able to get a reading of the franchisor's "personality" through even a short telephone conversation with the executive responsible for recruiting new franchisees. When you call the company, note if it seems well organized and if knowledgeable staff is accessible and willing to answer your questions. Determine if its employees seem unprofessional, uninformed, rude, or evasive. How does the franchisor respond to your expression of interest: with a flashy hard sell or with an attempt to get to know you better? Ask yourself: Would I like to work with this company?

Find out what kind of preliminary application the company requires franchise candidates to complete. Often this form will have been included in the package of information that the franchisor sent in response to your initial request. If the company does not require such an application, find out why. A franchisor that expresses little interest in your background or qualifications, and instead tries to pressure you into making a quick decision, may not be the kind of company that you want as a partner. Though it may make you feel a little uncomfortable at times, a franchisor's investigation of you indicates that the company licenses only qualified individuals. Such a company will be interested in establishing and maintaining a sound, mutually profitable relationship with you—not in taking your money and running.

Filling out the preliminary application at this stage of your investigation serves several purposes. First of all, it will give you a better idea of what the franchisor seeks in its franchisees. Secondly, by submitting the application, you formally express your serious intention to buy a franchise, thus opening communications between yourself and the franchisor. And finally, the company's evaluation of your application will determine whether you should spend more time and energy investigating the franchise.

Based on the application, the company will decide whether or not it considers you a viable candidate for a franchise. A rejection will free you to devote your time and energy to pursuing other franchises, and you can avoid wasting effort on pointless research. On the other hand, if the company decides that it would like to know more about you, then you should take several more steps to find out more about its franchise program.

7. If any of the companies have not yet provided it, request detailed information on the financial and legal particulars of owning one of their franchises. Ask for a list of currently operating franchisees that you may speak with.

The most complete source of information a franchisor can provide you is the disclosure document (offering circular or prospectus), which it has prepared in compliance with the trade regulation rule issued by the Federal Trade Commission (FTC). Some franchisors send this document along with their initial package of information, but most will not release it to you until they feel sure that you are very seriously considering the purchase of one of their franchises.

By law, you must receive a copy of the disclosure statement either at your first personal meeting with the franchisor (or its appointed agent) or at least ten business days before you either sign any agreement with them or pay any fees in relation to the purchase of the franchise. In addition, if your state regulates the sale of franchises within its boundaries, you may be able to review a copy of the franchisor's disclosure document at the state's consumer protection or securities division offices.

The disclosure document contains the following:

- The general disclosure statement, which includes information on the company and its franchise program: biographical data on company officers, descriptions of training programs, etc.
- A list of the names, addresses, and telephone numbers of currently licensed franchisees.
- A copy of the company's generic franchise agreement—the contract that contains detailed information on your rights and responsibilities as a franchise owner.

Additionally, some franchisors include earnings claims in their disclosure statements. Earnings claims are statements about the profitability of a company's franchises. The company must fully support these claims with documentation stating exactly how it arrived at the figures. But even when earnings claims appear to be well-founded, you should take them with a large grain of salt, because they may be based on assumptions that do not apply to your situation.

While the FTC requires franchisors to release disclosure statements to potential franchisees and indicates what types of information these documents must contain, it does not usually check them for accuracy. The FTC rule states that disclosure documents must be "complete and accurate," but leaves the definition of "complete and accurate" up to the individual franchisor. In the vast majority of cases, these documents are legitimate, but you should try to verify on your own any information vital to your analysis of the franchisor.

If a company does not seem willing to provide the hard facts you need to evaluate the franchise opportunity, try to determine if this indicates a genuine concern for the security of potentially sensitive material or if instead the company might be trying to hide something from you. You could probably complete your investigation without the disclosure statement, but that document is by far the most useful tool you can have at your disposal. Now that you have gathered all of the available data that you can find, use it to evaluate the franchise program itself.

4. Know about Fees, Expenses, and Financing

8. Consult with your accountant and lawyer to determine the feasibility of investing in the franchises in which you are interested. Check franchisors' earnings claims (if they make any) and prepare profit projections for your potential business.

In order to make a wise investment, you must have a thorough understanding of the many financial details involved in buying and owning a franchise. The various fees, royalties, and other costs of setting up and running your business, the cash and capital required, the financing possibilities, your sales and profit potential, and your financial liability as a franchisee deserve a close look. After all, profits are what it's all about, and if your franchise doesn't give you a healthy return on your investment—and a substantial reward for the risks you've taken in starting a business—then you'll have thrown away a lot of time, effort, and money.

Unless you have training as an accountant and as a lawyer, you should hire professionals to look over the franchise offering. Someone familiar with balance sheets and contracts can probably sift through the information better, to give you a more accurate assessment of which franchises are wise investments—and what would actually be involved in purchasing and running them.

A good rule of thumb to follow while you investigate the financial aspect of your franchise is that if the franchisor clearly spells out all of the financial details of the franchise, you can be fairly sure of the company's legitimacy. However, you should watch out for any hidden costs of the franchise. Quite often your actual investment can end up much greater than you expected because of miscellaneous added charges, the costs of "optional" items that the company effectively requires you to buy, or other expenses not in fact included in the fees. Make sure that you know exactly what you will have to spend: Your accountant can outline the expenses typically involved in starting up the kind of business the franchisor sells. Get specific answers from the franchisor about who pays how much for each item.

When you read through franchisors' disclosure statements or other sales material, you will have to decipher a lot of financial jargon. You will quickly discover that different companies use different terminology to refer to the same items. At the same time, they often use the same words to refer to different things. Carefully determine just what each company means when using terms like "initial investment," "total investment," and "total capital required." In order to make a valid comparison of franchising opportunities, you must make certain that you are, in fact, comparing comparable things.

The third consideration to keep in mind throughout your evaluation of fees and finances is your liability. If you or the franchisor encountered operating difficulties, you would doubtless have some responsibility to customers or to the company for losses incurred by you or the parent company. Find out exactly what responsibilities you would have, and also what rights you would have as a franchisee. Your lawyer's assistance can prove invaluable in this part of your investigation. Suppose your franchise failed? Suppose the franchisor decided to increase royalty rates? Suppose the franchisor went out of business? You could suddenly find yourself in an untenable financial and legal position. You may want to consider forming a corporation in order to limit your personal liability (in addition to reaping certain tax benefits). In any case, you would be unwise to invest without first investigating the issue of financial liability.

Buying a franchise involves some expenditures that you would not have if you opened a nonfranchised business, although savings in other areas often compensate franchisees for their added expenses. Regardless of this balancing effect, you should find out exactly what tangibles and intangibles you will get for your money. Franchise fees remunerate franchisors for the expertise they lend you, the years of research and development they have put into their products and methods, and your use of the company's brand name.

A large, nationally known franchisor will generally charge a higher license fee than a lesser known one, simply because of the better recognition its name will afford you. In some cases, a higher fee reflects the lower risk associated with your investment in an established company. Beyond a recognized name, the inital fee may cover the costs of training provided by the company, an opening stock of supplies, consultation on various details associated with opening for business, and other services. The next chapter, "Know about Training Programs, Support, and Assistance," will help you evaluate these aspects of your franchise.

You may find that the franchisor does not set one standard license fee for all franchisees. If the fee varies, find out on what basis the company determines individual fees. Common criteria determining variable license fees include the characteristics of your territory, the location of your store, and the projected sales volume of your business. Ask how the services provided by the franchisor differ with varying fees.

Keep in mind that you can in many cases pay the initial fee in installments. While many franchisors require full payment of the fee as a sort of down payment on your franchise, you can often arrange to pay one third down, one third after six months or so of operation, and one third after a year in business. Some franchisors will finance the fee themselves at a special rate of interest, while others leave the financing arrangements up to you.

Your start-up expenses will include a lot more than your initial license fee. You may have to make significant expenditures for real estate, equipment, inventory, supplies, and opening promotion, in addition to paying further fees to the franchisor for training or other start-up assistance. You should expect to make a substantial total investment—and do not underestimate just how substantial. To protect itself from your possible failure due to undercapitalization, the franchisor may require you to prove that you have a certain net worth or a certain amount of cash or other liquid assets. While this might seem restrictive, the company bases its requirement on its experience of the kind of investment it takes to start one of its units. You would do far better to overcapitalize your business than to come up short.

In calculating your total initial investment—your total start-up cost—take the following things into account:

- Does the franchisor charge an initial franchise fee?
- How much is the fee?
- Is the initial fee refundable?
- What services does the fee cover?
- Does the fee cover the cost of:
    - Start-up training tuition, room, board, and travel?
    - Site selection and construction aid?
    - Signs and fixtures?
    - On-site preopening and grand opening assistance?
    - Opening promotional and advertising help?
    - Opening inventory and supplies?

- How must you pay the fee? All at once? In installments?
- Will the franchisor finance the deferred balance of the fee?
- At what interest?

- What will be your additional expenses (if any) for:
  Purchase or lease of your business location?
  Construction or remodeling of your facility?
  Equipment and fixtures?
  Parts, materials, and supplies?
  Inventory?
  Training for yourself or your employees?
  Opening advertising and promotion?
  State or local licenses?

Have your accountant calculate your approximate total start-up cost, and compare it with the figure the franchisor has supplied. Once you've determined the probable range of your initial investment, estimate your ongoing operating expenses.

A fundamental component of your operating expenses as a franchisee will be another type of fee charged by the franchisor—the royalty (sometimes referred to as the franchise fee; do not confuse this with the *initial* franchise fee). Royalties both compensate the franchisor for the ongoing support it provides, and serve as one of its main profit centers. Most franchisors calculate royalties as a percentage of your gross monthly sales. In other cases, franchisees pay a fixed fee per month or week or per unit sold. Your royalty payments will constitute a significant portion of your ongoing operating expenses, so you should make sure that you consider them equitable in light of the support you will receive in return. In making your judgment, you may want to compare the franchisor's royalty requirements with those of similar franchisors.

Many franchisors charge an additional fee, known as the advertising royalty, which they apply directly to their company's national or regional advertising efforts or to the development of promotional materials that you can use in the operation of your business. This royalty can also take the form of a requirement that you spend a certain amount on your own marketing campaign. In some cases, you must pay both an advertising royalty to the company *and* spend an additional amount on your local promotions. Look at the company's marketing program to make sure that you'll get what you pay for.

Address each of the following points with regard to both royalties and advertising royalties:

- What royalty payments does the franchisor require?
- How are royalties calculated (as a percentage of gross monthly sales, as a flat fee per month, etc.)?
- If royalties are a percentage of sales, how are sales calculated?
- How often must you make royalty payments to the company?
- How do the franchisor's royalty requirements compare to those of similar franchisors?
- Does the franchisor require you to spend a set amount on your own marketing efforts in addition to paying advertising royalties?
- Will you pay the same royalties as other franchisees? If not, why not?

Some franchisors may not charge royalties in any recognizable form, but might instead require you to purchase certain products or services from them. By taking a percentage profit on everything you purchase from it, a company in effect collects a royalty payment from you. When a company both charges a royalty and requires you to purchase materials or supplies from it, you should adjust your calculation of royalty costs to reflect the additional profit the company may make.

Royalties will be just a part of your ongoing operating costs. As a franchisee, you will have most of the same costs that the independent small business owner/operator has. Some franchisors eliminate some of the direct costs of these items to their franchisees by including them in their ongoing support services. Many provide, free or at a reduced charge, accounting and bookkeeping assistance, offer insurance programs, or conduct advertising campaigns.

Have your accountant prepare an estimate of the ongoing costs of operating your business. This calculation should include:

- Royalties
- Advertising royalties
- Rent or mortgage payments
- Payroll and your own salary
- Insurance payments
- Interest payments
- Ongoing equipment purchase or rental
- Purchase of materials and supplies
- Plant and equipment maintenance
- Advertising
- Legal and accounting fees
- Taxes
- Licenses
- Utilities and telephone

Once you have an idea of what it will cost to run your business, have your accountant prepare projections of your sales and profit potential—for the first year or two of operation and for when your business has gotten off the ground. Your estimate of sales should take into account current (and probable future) market conditions of your region, demand for your product in your area, traffic patterns of your business location, and prospects for growth. Combine your sales and cost estimates to determine your potential profit, and compare these results with any earnings claims the franchisor may have included in its prospectus or any other sales material.

When looking over a franchisor's earnings claims, make sure you understand exactly how the franchisor calculated the profit projections:

- Are they based on the performance of the company's franchisees in markets similar to yours? On that of independent businesses in similar markets?
- Were the earnings used in the calculations those of long-time franchisees, or newcomers?
- Were the calculations made during economic boom times?
- How many franchisees actually earn as much as or more than the amount of the earnings claim?
- Do the figures take into account all operating expenses?

The franchisor must provide written substantiation for its earnings claims. If your accountant's estimate differs greatly from the franchisor's, try to determine why. And once you have actual profit projections in front of you, ask yourself whether or not the projected return on your investment of time and money would be high enough to make owning and operating the franchise worthwhile:

- Will my sales enable me to make enough to meet expenses and make a profit?
- Will I be able to meet any quotas the franchisor sets?
- In order to achieve the required sales volume, will I have to make an excessive investment?
- Do my estimated operating costs appear excessive?
- Will I make enough money to be satisfied?
- Does the risk seem worthwhile—will it pay off?

In your initial self-evaluation, you should have come to a basic understanding of your financial capabilities and goals. Now is the time to do a thorough analysis of your financial status and to compare your financial capability with the total initial investment you will have to make, the operating costs for your first year in business, and your short- and long-term personal and business goals, to determine how much of your operation you will need or want to finance.

Investigate possible sources of financing, and determine which lenders would best fit into your business plan. Many franchisors offer limited financing at special rates to their franchisors, and still more offer assistance in securing financing from third-party lenders. Others may actually require that you enter into some sort of financing arrangement with them. Other sources of financing include banks or other financial institutions, relatives, friends, or federal agencies like the Small Business Administration or the Minority Business Development Agency.

In order to obtain financing, you will need to present a personal financial statement and a business plan to the franchisor or other lender. You will need to determine your total net worth and how much of that is in liquid assets. For lenders other than the franchisor, you will also have to develop a business plan outlining the application of borrowed funds and the expected returns of your business. You should present loan applications before signing your franchise contract to find out if the strength of your credit rating and your business plan will allow you to borrow the money you'll need to start your franchise.

Will you be able to borrow enough to help you get started? Do you have the resources to purchase and operate your franchise for a year or more with low or negative returns? Are you likely to get too far into debt? Will a minor setback in your business have major repercussions on your ability to pay back creditors?

When you make any investment, you take a risk. Buying a franchise is no different from buying securities in that you need to decide whether or not to take a risk. It all comes down to one basic question: Is the return on your investment likely to make the risk worthwhile? Your return should be greater than that which you would receive on a less risky investment, like stocks. If you feel that the franchisor you have been investigating can offer the profits you seek, find out more about the franchise program itself: What kind of training and support programs will your license fees and royalties buy?

5. *Know about Training Programs, Support, and Assistance*

9. Speak with some of the companies' franchisees regarding their experiences with the franchisors. Learn all you can about the kinds of support the companies provide.

"Talk to existing franchisees as much as possible, in as many different locations as possible," recommends Del Garber, a Coast to Coast Stores franchisee. Richard Steht, who owns a Clentech/Acoustic Clean franchise, echoes Del Garber's advice and expands on it: "Check out the parent company beyond the references it supplies. Talk to a good long list of franchisees. Ask what the franchisor will do for you." According to franchisees and franchise experts alike, talking to franchisees should be the single most important aspect of your franchising investigation. No one can give you a clearer notion of what it is like to be a franchisee than a franchisee.

Your investigation of a franchisor will not be complete until you speak with active franchisees—those who have been in business a long time and those new to franchising; those who own many units and those who own just one; and those who have been successful and those who have not. Seek out franchisees who operate in regions with market characteristics similar to those of your region, and try to contact independent business people or franchisees of other companies similar to the ones you are evaluating. Both during your investigation of franchisors and once you have become a franchisee, you can learn as much from your fellow franchisees as you can from any other source. Take full advantage of this valuable—and free—resource.

Franchisees can supply insight into the real-life financial facts of franchise ownership, and they can advise you about other things to consider when looking at franchise opportunities. "Do not take a pie-in-the-sky approach," warns Robert Bonin, a Ground Round franchisee. "Do an analysis based on realistic sales projections for your location." But—"Don't just look at earnings," says Dale Strack, who runs a Help-U-Sell franchise.

Dale Strack recommends that you "talk to successful franchisees, and ones that aren't doing so well, in person if you can. You will be able to tell if problems lie with the franchisor or the franchisee. Compare yourself with the successful franchisees to see if you could succeed with the franchise. Ask if the company knows what it's doing. A franchise should be chosen on the basis of the training and follow-up support available. Confirm that the company does what it promises." You should speak with as many franchisees as possible, and ask:

- Do franchisees think the franchisor is honest, reliable, competent, and genuinely interested in the success of its franchisees?
- Do franchisees feel that the franchisor exercises too much control? Not enough?
- Does the franchisor give franchisees the freedom to make their own decisions regarding the control of their investment?
- How would franchisees characterize franchisor/franchisee relations?

- Is the franchisor accessible to franchisees?
- Does the franchisor provide enough support and guidance?
- Is the franchisor always willing to help?
- Has the training provided by the franchisor met franchisees' needs?
- Has the franchisor lived up to its promises regarding the training, support, and services it provides?

- Has the franchise been a good investment?
- Are the franchisor's estimations of the initial investment required accurate?
- Are its cost and profit projections on target?

- Can franchisees recommend the franchise to you?

Based on what you find out through your conversations with franchisees, as well as what you have learned by reading the material you have gathered about the franchise, determine just what kind of support and assistance you can expect to receive during the preopening, opening, and later phases of your operation. Between the time you sign the franchise agreement and the time you open your doors for business, you will probably receive some form of initial training—usually a comprehensive introduction to every aspect of your business—as well as assistance in site selection and preparing your premises for opening. Just before opening, you may receive help in ordering inventory, obtaining licenses, recruiting and training employees, and hundreds of other necessary details.

During your grand opening and first few weeks in business—the period that many franchisors consider crucial to the success of your business—a company representative may come to your location to provide general operational support. Once your business takes off, franchisors generally provide a number of services, which may include refresher training, bookkeeping services, periodic visits from company representatives, centralized ordering services (which can result in savings for you because of the company's purchasing power), company publications, and other forms of support. The franchisor's marketing and advertising efforts can also benefit you significantly.

Every franchisor supplies its own unique package of support services, and you will need assistance tailored to your particular needs and abilities. In order to make sure that the franchisor's capabilities fit with yours, you need to find out what kind of help the franchisor provides during each phase of your operation: before you open your doors, during your opening period, and for the term of your contract agreement. Make sure that the details of the training and support that the company will provide are clearly set down in your contract. Your success depends in large part upon whether or not you get the help you need in running your business.

The checklists that follow outline the points with which you should become familiar.

Site Selection and Premises Development

1. Will the company perform an analysis of the demographics within your region to help you find the best location for your business?
2. Will the company require you to use a designated location?
3. Who purchases or leases the site?
4. Are you required to purchase your land and building?
5. Will the company help you negotiate a lease?
6. Will the company purchase or lease the site and then lease it to you?

7. Who is responsible for the construction or refurbishing of your facility? Will the company build your facility for you?
8. Will the company supply you with plans and specifications for your facility?
9. What design or other requirements must your facility meet?
10. Does the company provide any construction assistance?
11. Will the company help you order fixtures and equipment and help you set it up?
12. Are you required to purchase signs, fixtures, or equipment through designated sources?
13. Will you get competitive prices on these purchases?
14. Is there any additional charge for site-selection and premises development assistance?

Initital Training

1. Is initial training available? Required? Optional?
2. Where does the training take place? At corporate headquarters, at your own unit, at an existing unit?
3. Can you train independently using self-study materials?
4. How long is the initial training session?
5. Is there any expense to you for training, e.g., for tuition, supplies, room, board, or transportation?
6. Who trains you? Corporate staff or active franchisees?
7. Who must complete the initial training? You, your management, all of your employees?
8. Does the training take place in a classroom or on the job?
9. Will you get hands-on experience before you open for business?
10. What does training cover? Does it cover:
    Specialized technical/trade knowledge?
    General operations?
    Management and administration?
    Employee recruitment, hiring, training?
    Accounting and bookkeeping?
    Planning and projections?
    Inventory control and merchandise ordering?
    Sales, merchandising, promotion, advertising?
    Customer service?
    Credit accounts management?
    Insurance?
    Legal issues?

Preopening and Opening Support

1. Will a company representative come to your location to provide assistance with your grand opening?
2. Will the company help you hire and train employees?
3. Will the company help you order inventory, materials, and supplies?
4. Will the company supply or help you with grand opening advertising or promotions?
5. Will a company representative accompany you on your first few sales calls (if applicable)?
6. Is there any cost to you for this initial support?

Ongoing Operational Assistance

1. Will you receive regular visits from a company representative?
2. Will support staff be available by phone for assistance?
3. Will field personnel come to your location at your request?
4. Is there any charge to you for these services?
5. Does the company provide you with a comprehensive operations manual?
6. Does the company publish newsletters, bulletins, or updates to your manual?
7. Is there a charge for these materials?
8. Does the company supply you with an accounting system and bookkeeping materials?
9. Does it provide bookkeeping services?
10. What are your reporting requirements?
11. Can you order inventory or supplies directly from the company?
12. Does the company offer merchandise, materials and/or supplies to you at a savings?
13. Will it extend a line of credit to you for your purchases?
14. Does it deliver orders promptly?
15. Does the company inspect your suppliers for quality?
16. Does it inspect your operation?
17. Does the company provide any other services or benefits, such as tax preparation assistance, insurance plans, legal advice, etc.?

Ongoing Training

1. Is refresher training available? Required?
2. Where does this training take place?
3. Is there any cost to you for participation?

4. What does this training cover?
5. How frequently is such training offered?
6. Will the company train any supervisory or other staff that you hire as the result of routine employee turnover?
7. Will the company charge you for this service?
8. Does the company hold an annual national convention?
9. Are there regional meetings?
10. Can you attend periodic seminars or workshops?

Advertising and Marketing

1. What kind of advertising and marketing policy does the company follow?
2. Does the company conduct national, regional, or local advertising? In what media—television, radio, magazines, newspapers, direct mail, outdoor?
3. Do its efforts benefit all franchisees and company-operated units equally?
4. Is its advertising/marketing program effective?
5. Does the company provide you with promotional material for your own local use—brochures, point-of-sale material, radio spots, yellow pages ads?
6. Does the company provide you with the results of its market research?
7. Will you receive merchandising, promotional, or advertising advice?
8. What will your advertising costs be—royalties only or significant personal expenditure?
9. Who directs the company's promotional operations—corporate staff or franchisees?
10. Exactly how are your advertising royalties spent?
11. Will you have any additional marketing expenses?

Franchisor-Franchisee Relations

1. Does the company have a realistic understanding of what it's like to operate one of its franchises?
2. Do franchisees have any voice in company policy and/or operational decisions?
3. Does an elected board of franchisees serve in an advisory capacity to corporate management?
4. How does the home office respond to suggestions and complaints from the field?

5. Can franchisees communicate with management through a formal suggestions/grievances procedure?
6. Have franchisees formed an active franchisee association?
7. What is the franchisor's relationship with the association?

If, after completing your research and speaking with franchisees, you feel confident that the franchisor provides the kinds of training and ongoing support that you need, and that franchisor/franchisee relations are good, you can now take the final step toward becoming a franchise owner: negotiating your contract.

6. *Know Your Legal Rights and the Terms of the Contract*

10. Meet with the corporate staff of each of the companies you are considering. Ask any questions you might have and give the company an opportunity to interview you. Make your decision.

These meetings should allow you to make a final judgment regarding the franchisor with which you would like to do business. A face-to-face meeting can reveal—as no telephone call or letter ever can—the real character of a company and its management. Personal discussion can also raise issues that you might otherwise have neglected. Such a meeting will also provide the franchisor with the opportunity to decide whether or not to accept you as a franchisee.

Finally, if both you and the franchisor have an interest in further pursuing a partnership, the "personal meeting" serves as the franchisor's legal cue to submit to you its disclosure document, if it has not already done so. According to the FTC's 1979 ruling, you must receive a copy of this document at your first personal meeting with a representative of the franchisor to discuss the purchase of a franchise, and at least ten days before you sign any agreement with, or make any payments to, the franchisor.

11. Have your lawyer and accountant review the standard franchise agreement that the franchisor has given you. Negotiate favorable terms before you sign the contract.

In many cases, a franchisor will present you with a standard contract, which protects its interests but not yours. You should not feel pressured to sign this contract, but instead must study it carefully with the advice of your attorney and accountant, and negotiate the most favorable terms that you can with the franchisor. Rarely will astute business people sign a standard franchise agreement without making some changes, so your franchisor should be willing to negotiate with you. It is vital that you get everything relating to your franchise in writing and spelled out in detail.

Although you may feel nervous about demanding certain concessions from a franchisor, any franchisor interested in having you as a franchisee will work with you to hammer out the fine points of an agreement you can both live with. You can negotiate almost any point of the franchise contract. Many franchisees don't realize that they can negotiate franchise fees. Just as the franchisor may vary fees based on its assessment of your individual franchise, so you can in many cases negotiate more favorable fees based on your evaluation of the franchisor-franchisee relationship.

Use your position as a potential buyer as leverage in winning concessions. As long as you have the cash, you have a valuable bargaining chip. Beware, however, the franchisor that seems too eager to give in to your demands—if the company easily bargains away clauses that protect its standards, it clearly has a less than complete commitment to maintaining a quality image.

When you consult your attorney and accountant regarding the franchise contract, you should make sure that its terms are both favorable to you and agreeable to any third party lender that might be financing your venture. Otherwise you might find yourself in the uncomfortable position of being bound to a legal commitment that you cannot honor because you don't have sufficient funds.

You might consider hiring a professional—perhaps your lawyer or accountant—to negotiate your contract for you. A professional has the experience and cool that you may lack, and can often win greater concessions from the franchisor. If you decide to negotiate your own contract, your lawyer should accompany you to the negotiations. During this phase of buying your franchise, you should deal directly with the franchisor. Sales agents or other interested (i.e., profit-taking) parties generally have more to gain from a quick closing than from your satisfaction as a franchisee.

The three most important things to remember when negotiating your contract are:

1. Get everything in writing. Verbal agreements and "understandings" are unenforceable.
2. Make sure every detail is spelled out in plain English. Rid your

contract of vagueness and legalese. After all, what does it mean that a franchisor cannot "reasonably refuse" to approve a supplier? What is "just cause" for the franchisor to terminate your contract? Make it clear.

3. Do not pay the franchisor any money until both you and the franchisor have signed the contract. Even if the company assures you that it will refund any down payments if necessary, you will find it very difficult to get your money back after it has left your hands.

The average franchise agreement contains twenty to twenty-five clauses, covering everything from the initial franchise fee to the disposition of your building and equipment at the end of the contract. When reviewing the document, ask yourself whether or not the franchisor's requirements seem excessively restrictive or lax, and whether or not you can live up to your end of the deal. Make sure that the training, services, and advertising support provided are commensurate with the fees and royalties you pay. And make certain that you are protected from the consequences of any mismanagement or poor judgment on the part of the franchisor.

You should be able to answer the following questions when going over the franchise contract:

- Does the contract specify the exact amount of all fees charged by the franchisor?
- What fees does the company require you to pay?
- How does the franchisor calculate fees? Can they be changed?
- How do you pay fees—in installments, as lump sums, etc.?
- When do you pay fees?
- Will the fees required wipe out your profit margin?
- Will the franchisor refund any fees? Under what conditions?
- Can you negotiate lesser fees?

- What rights do you have concerning use of the franchisor's patents, trademarks, and brand names?
- How are you restricted in this use?

- What financial reporting practices does the company require you to follow?
- When and in what form must you submit financial statements?
- Must you follow specific accounting procedures or use certain forms to report to the franchisor?
- Must you meet sales quotas?
- Will the company penalize you for falling short?

- May the company use collection agencies to enforce your payment of fees?

- Does the company require that you actively participate in the operation of your franchise?
- Must you keep certain business hours?
- Can you set the prices of the items you sell?
- What products must you offer for sale?
- Are you prohibited from selling particular items through your franchise?
- Must you maintain certain levels of inventory?

- What supplies and/or merchandise must you purchase from the franchisor?
- Does the company maintain a list of other approved suppliers from whom you must purchase?
- Do you receive these goods at a discount?
- Does the company profit from these sales?

- What standards does the company set for your business?
- Must your supplies, materials, products, and services meet standards of quality, uniformity, appearance, or type?
- Will the franchisor give you at least forty-eight hours notice before conducting inspection visits?
- What are the company's criteria for acceptable location, premises, equipment, fixtures, and furniture?
- Can it require you to refurbish your facility or purchase new equipment to meet its latest standards?
- How much would this cost you?
- What proscribed operating procedures, bookkeeping systems, and other controls must you follow?
- What kind of insurance must you carry? At what cost?

- Do you receive an exclusive territory?
- What does the franchisor mean by "exclusive"?
- How is your territory defined?
- Do you have the option to expand your territory?
- Do you have the right of first refusal if someone else wants to purchase territory adjacent to yours?

- What are the company's requirements for your location?
- What assistance will the company give you in selecting a site, purchase or lease negotiations, and construction?

- Must the franchisor approve your lease?
- Will the franchisor serve as your landlord? At advantageous terms?

- Exactly what kind of training—initial and ongoing—will the company provide?
- What other management assistance will you receive?
- What start-up assistance does the franchisor include in your franchise fee?
- Will a trained company representative come to your site and stay for as long as necessary during start-up?
- Will you receive a comprehensive operations manual?

- What kind of marketing support will the company provide in return for your contributions to the advertising fund?
- How does the franchisor allocate advertising funds?
- Will you receive advertising support commensurate with your contribution?
- Will the company require you to spend more on advertising than you think necessary or than you can afford?

- What is the length of the contract?
- Can you sell or transfer your franchise?
- What kind of notice must you give the company?
- Does the company have the right of first refusal?
- Does the company have the right to approve your buyer?
- Do you have any liability to the franchisor after you sell your franchise?
- Will the company require you to pay a fee to sell?
- Can your heirs inherit the franchise, or will the contract terminate upon your death?
- How are you protected if the franchisor goes out of business?
- Do you have any liability for misconduct on the part of the franchisor that results in injury to your customers?

- Can you terminate your contract? Under what conditions?
- How much notice must you give of your intention to terminate?
- What are your obligations to the company if you terminate?
- Can the company terminate your contract?
- What is just cause for the company to terminate your contract (e.g., nonpayment of fees, violation of contract terms, abandonment of your business, etc.)

- What rights do you have regarding contract renewal?
- Can the company refuse to renew your contract? For what reasons?
- If the company terminates or refuses to renew, does the contract obligate it to purchase your equipment and supplies?
- Who would determine the purchase price—and how?

- Does the contract contain a noncompete clause?
- Are you prohibited from engaging in similar business during or after the term of your contract?
- How does the clause define similar business?
- In what geographical areas does the clause prohibit you from competing with the franchisor? For how many years?

These questions outline the issues that you should study when reviewing most franchise contracts. Clearly, contracts differ from franchisor to franchisor, and some franchising opportunities may not fit the typical legal mold. But no matter how individual franchise contracts may vary, each one should set down in writing everything relevant to the franchise. In negotiating your agreement, leave nothing to chance, make sure the document leaves nothing out, and get it all in writing. While you have no guarantees that your franchise will live up to your expectations, your contract can help protect you from the relatively minor risks involved in being a franchisee.

Part II

The Franchises

Introduction to Part II

The 220 franchises described in the pages that follow represent a wide variety of franchise opportunities. Chosen to provide a sampling of the many types of franchises available in diverse industry categories, the franchises listed in *The 220 Best Franchises to Buy* range from industry giants with established track records, to recent success stories that promise to keep right on booming, to younger companies—some with uniquely innovative approaches to franchising—that have identified and begun to tap new markets.

The vital statistics that lead off each entry require some explanatory notes. The terms used in the first part of each listing can be defined as follows:

Initial license fee: The amount you pay to the franchisor in order to become a franchisee. A one-time expense.

Royalties: The amount you pay to the franchisor weekly, monthly, yearly, or at some other interval to cover the franchisor's expenses of maintaining you as a franchisee. Generally calculated as a percentage of gross revenues, but sometimes set at a flat periodic fee or a fee per unit sold.

Advertising royalties: A periodic amount paid toward the franchisor's advertising fund. Sometimes includes a requirement that you spend a minimum amount on your own local promotional program. Calculated as a percentage of gross or as a flat periodic fee.

Minimum cash required: The minimum amount of cash or other liquid assets the franchisor requires you to have available in order to qualify as a franchisee.

Capital required: The amount of capital, as estimated by the franchisor, that you will need to buy and start up your franchise operation.

Financing: Any financial assistance the franchisor provides to new franchisees.

Length of contract: The term of your franchise agreement.

In business since: The date that the company or its parent was founded.

Franchising since: The year that the company started franchising its business.

Total number of units: The latest available figure for the total number of business locations in operation.

Number of company-operated units: The total number of units operated by the company rather than by franchisees.

Total number of units planned, 1990: The company's projection of the number of units it hopes to have in operation by 1990.

Number of company-operated units planned, 1990: The number of units the company plans to operate itself in 1990.

Keep in mind that, in most cases, the statistics were obtained from the franchisors themselves and may have changed since the time of this writing. Whenever the notation "NA" appears instead of a number, the data was unavailable.

Each of the entries provides a brief description of the company and its franchise program. You should by no means consider these profiles complete—they only provide an overview of each franchisor's operation, which you can use to decide whether or not you would like to find out more about the company. And again, some of the information included in these descriptions may have changed by the time you read them. You should only use the information provided in these pages as a starting point for your investigation.

7. The Automotive Industry

Contents

Tune-Up and Lubrication

CAR–X Service Systems, Inc.
Grease Monkey International, Inc.
Jiffy Lube International, Inc.
Precision Tune, Inc.
Sparks Tune-Up

Muffler Services

Meineke Discount Muffler Shops, Inc.

Initial license fee: $25,000
Royalties: 8%
Advertising royalties: 10%
Minimum cash required: $45,000
Capital required: $45,000
Financing: Available for equipment
Length of contract: 15 years

In business since: 1972
Franchising since: 1972
Total number of units: 704
Number of company-operated units: 1
Total number of units planned, 1990: 1,176
Number of company-operated units planned, 1990: 1

Meineke knows it has company at the top of the muffler business, and that it must differentiate itself from the competition. The key is the "Discount" in the company name. Meineke employs several methods that enable it to offer consistent quality in products and service while competing on price.

Meineke keeps the lid on prices by specializing in exhaust repair service, although Meineke dealers also service and repair brakes, shocks, and struts. Confining its operations to three-bay facilities and running them at peak efficiency holds down land costs and has made it possible to convert many closed service stations to Meineke shops. Franchisees can also build their own shops, as well as lease or rent a currently standing building.

Meineke's especially efficient inventory system allows its dealers to fill 98 percent of orders for company products from stock. And the company offers a limited guarantee, designed to eliminate the added costs of a more elaborate policy on future repairs or replacements.

The company doesn't accept absentee owners. Meineke's management thinks your customers should be able to see and talk to you when they drive in. You don't need previous business experience; Meineke dealers come from many backgrounds, including teaching, the restaurant business, and engineering. You must have pride, ambition, and an intense desire to succeed, and be the kind of person who feels that everything that leaves your shop—both products and services—should be of the highest quality because it bears your personal imprint.

You don't need mechanical experience to buy a Meineke franchise, since the company will teach you the whole business. Your three-week training period in Charlotte, North Carolina, will include both classroom instruction and practical experience in a shop. The management curriculum includes advertising, sales techniques, shop organization, product guarantees and catalogs, inventory control, and the Meineke trade account and fleet programs. You will also study customer relations and personnel management. Hands-on instruction will include every product and service you and your staff will handle once you open your business.

Meineke franchisees receive ongoing help from their operations manager and from the Meineke Mobile Communications Center, training vans that periodically visit shops to familiarize franchisees and their employees with the company's latest products and services. Through the company's Dealer Advisory Council, you will also have the means to communicate your ideas about company policies and products to top management.

You can expect extensive bookkeeping help from Meineke and financial advice to help you maximize profits. Meineke will also give you weekly sales figures from all the units in the company so that you can see how your efforts stack up against those of your peers.

Meineke currently seeks to establish new franchises in the West, Midwest, and Canada.

For further information contact:
Ron Smythe, President, Meineke Discount Muffler Shops, Inc., 12013 Wilcrest, Houston, TX 77031, 713-879-1811

Midas International Corporation

Initial license fee: $10,000
Royalties: 10%
Advertising royalties: 10%
Minimum cash required: $75,000
Capital required: $170,000
Financing: The company will help with financing through Chicago banks.
Length of contract: 20 years

In business since: 1956
Franchising since: 1956
Total number of units: 1,508
Number of company-operated units: 40
Total number of units planned, 1990: NA
Number of company-operated units planned, 1990: NA

The elderly gentleman drives his ancient automobile up to the Midas shop and says to the service people: "Howdy, boys." Again he takes advantage of the Midas guarantee on its mufflers: "For as long as you own your car." It's a memorable commercial. The company's jingle, with the tag line, "Trust the Midas touch," also sticks in your mind. Because of advertising like this, according to the company, people in 85 percent of the households in this country think of Midas when they think of mufflers.

Thirty years ago this company consisted of one shop in Macon, Georgia. Today there are Midas shops in every state and on four continents. And Midas no longer confines its business to mufflers, having expanded into brake, suspension, and front-end repair. The company's plants in Connecticut, Wisconsin, Ontario, and Illinois turn out more than fifty-nine hundred parts that enable Midas dealers to satisfy its customers.

The company wants enthusiastic, foward-looking franchisees with previous business experience, entrepreneurs who can deal with people comfortably. It looks for people who can control expenses and inventory and keep organized records. If preliminary conversations between you and the company go well, it will invite you to a two-day orientation seminar in Chicago, where you and the company can decide if you make a good match.

If you and the company work well together, you will not have to worry about securing a location. In this franchise, the franchisor picks the spots, builds the facilities, and leases to franchisees for the length of the franchise agreement. You will train at "MIT"—the Midas Institute of Technology at Palatine, Illinois. There, you will take a concentrated two-week course covering shop organization, products and installation, and inventory control. In addition, you will spend at least two weeks in an operational shop to get practical experience for running your own business.

Your franchise agreement requires you to stock and sell Midas parts in your new business. Once you open your doors and wear the familiar yellow Midas shirt, you can expect continued support through the company's district manager and field personnel. The Midas staff will assist with your opening and help you with financial statement analysis, sales training, employee selection, and promotion.

For further information contact:

Midas International Corporation, Corporate Offices, 225 North Michigan Ave., Chicago, IL 60601, 312-565-7500

Painting and Rustproofing

Endrust Industries

Initial license fee: $30,000
Royalties: None
Advertising royalties: None
Minimum cash required: $30,000
Capital required: $30,000
Financing: None
Length of contract: Indefinite

In business since: 1969
Franchising since: 1969
Total number of units: 81
Number of company-operated units: 1
Total number of units planned, 1990: 130
Number of company-operated units planned, 1990: NA

Average Americans drive their cars 12,000 miles each year. More than half of that is in city traffic. Their cars, which as late as 1968 were likely to be less than five years old, are these days, on the average, about six years old. Except if they are kept covered when not in use, and driven only when the sun shines, in moderate temperatures, and in areas where there is no industrial pollution in the air, these average cars need protection from the elements.

Endrust Car Care Centers cater to the growing market of car owners who care about auto longevity. Franchisees either open businesses devoted exclusively to complete car care and reconditioning or run their units as a supplement to their already existing automotive businesses. Endrust services include rustproofing, undercoating, and sound deadening. They also sell Englaze exterior paint sealant, End-a-Stain fabric protection, and car detailing services.

Someone with minimal capital and a feeling that profits should not be drained off by the payment of royalties will find Endrust an interesting business prospect. The company's profits are based on the sale of products it makes, not on a percentage of what you charge to customers for the services you provide. As a franchisee you become part of Endrust's distribution network, selling its products, which you must buy from the company. If your needs match Endrust's, it could be a comfortable fit.

The company offers the standard assistance in picking a site and getting set up. Endrust will train you in sales, service, and administration at your location, so you don't even have the problem of paying for travel, food, and lodging for instruction at national headquarters. Postopening training is provided on an "as needed" basis, and the company says it will always be available for consultation as long as you're a franchisee. Once you're an Endrust dealer, you remain an Endrust dealer—if you continue to sell the company products. It's that simple.

Gary Slattery is the Endrust franchisee in Morgantown, West Virginia. He chose his franchise "by comparing the profit potential and opportunities of Endrust as opposed to other companies." He was impressed with the company's "excellent reputation," and, he feels, that reputation was proved by the support the company gave him as he put together and opened his business. The help the company gave him "was extremely beneficial and useful." According to Garry Slattery, "car care is a great business through which to meet people and make friends, as they come back on a continual basis."

For further information contact:
Gary B. Griser, Endrust Industries, 1725 Washington Rd., Suite 205, Pittsburgh, PA 15241, 412-831-1255

Maaco Auto Painting and Body Works

Initial license fee: $15,000
Royalties: 8%
Advertising royalties: $500/week
Minimum cash required: $45,000
Capital required: $134,900
Financing: None
Length of contract: 15 years

In business since: 1972
Franchising since: 1972
Total number of units: 405
Number of company-operated units: 5
Total number of units planned, 1990: 550
Number of company-operated units planned, 1990: None

Anthony A. Martino, president, chief executive officer, and chairman of the board of Maaco, has made an indelible mark on the automobile aftermarket. In 1959 he founded AAMCO Transmissions, reorganizing it into a franchising operation in 1963. When he founded Maaco in 1972, he took some of his colleagues from AAMCO with him. Three of them now hold top executive positions at Maaco.

With consumers keeping their cars longer than they used to, you can make good money in the repainting field. It only takes about 1.5 gallons of paint to cover the average car, but you make your profits in the body preparation and the skilled service provided in a professional job.

Your Maaco shop will occupy 8,000 to 10,000 square feet of space, probably in a light industrial or commercial zone. Maaco will offer advice on site selection and will inspect your chosen location for suitability before giving you the go-ahead to build. But finding the site is your responsibility.

Your four weeks of training, at Maaco's headquarters in King of Prussia, Pennsylvania, will stress management skills rather than actual shop work, although the company will familiarize you with the paints, solvents, and thinners you use in your operation. Subjects covered in your training will include sales, advertising and promotion, equipment and maintenance, safety, estimating, inventory control, personnel, customer relations, fleet accounts, record keeping, accounting, budgeting, and insurance. You will also receive on-the-job training at a nearby Maaco shop. The company covers the expense of your training-related transportation and lodging.

Maaco representatives will give you two weeks of assistance, before and during your opening, focusing on hiring and training your staff. Refresher training is available throughout the year at the company's home office and at regional locations. The company will also schedule product update training from time to time.

You can purchase equipment and supplies from Maaco, both for your initial inventory and ongoing operations, although you are free to buy them from other sources. If you buy from Maaco, the company will make a profit on the sale.

Maaco will design and place your yellow pages advertisement for you, although you will pay for the advertisement. The company will oversee a mandatory advertising and promotional campaign at the time of your opening, for which you will be billed $3,000. When you sign your franchise agreement, Maaco will also require you to deposit $6,500 with the company. It will redeposit that sum in your checking account when you open for business, Maaco's way of insuring that you have enough working capital when you begin operations.

All Maaco customers get a company warranty on work done on their car. You will have to honor the warranty even for work done at another Maaco shop. In that case, however, you will be reimbursed for this work.

Should you own three or more Maaco centers, you will be entitled to a royalty rebate. Currently, the rebate is 0.5 percent to owners of three centers and 1 percent to those with four or more.

Maaco also sells franchises for its Sparks Tune-Up business.

For further information contact:
Linda Kemp, Maaco Enterprises, Inc., 381 Brooks Rd., King of Prussia, PA 19406, 1-800-523-1180

Tuff-Kote Dinol, Inc.

Initial license fee: $4,000 to $11,000, depending on where your business is located
Royalties: 8%
Advertising royalties: 5%
Minimum cash required: $25,000
Capital required: $25,000 to $35,000
Financing: Franchise fees over the base of $4,000 can be financed.
Length of contract: 10 years, renewable at 50% of initial fee

In business since: 1964
Franchising since: 1967
Total number of units: 160
Number of company-operated units: 8
Total number of units planned, 1990: 223
Number of company-operated units planned, 1990: 12

Only certain areas of the United States are in the "rust belt"—the prime area for automobile rust, that is. Vehicles are constantly exposed to winter road salting, humidity, sea air, and industrial air pollution in these places. Unfortunately for automobile owners (but fortunately for Tuff-Kote franchisees), these areas constitute some of the most populous in the country—including the East and West coasts, the Gulf coast, and the upper Midwest. Tuff-Kote, part of the Axel Johnson Group conglomerate based in Sweden, especially wants to expand its franchise operations in the Mid-Atlantic, New England, and upper Midwest areas, as well as in the Ohio River Valley.

Tuff-Kote covers the automobile aftermarket market with a range of products, led by a special two-step rustproofing process. Other Tuff-Kote products preserve and enhance the value of a car with paint, carpet and upholstery protection; underbody sound deadening; body moldings and trim; sunroofs; security systems; truck and van running boards; slider windows; bedliners; siderails and racks; and used vehicle reconditioning.

This franchise could be part of an already existing automobile-related operation or a new business. The sales possibilities are threefold: private vehicle owners; new car customers buying the service from their dealer; and fleet owners such as contractors, government agencies, and delivery services.

Tuff-Kote franchisees take on a line with built-in appeal—and a reputation that goes back fifteen years. As one franchisee, Paul Bosley, of Euclid, Ohio, puts it, "T.K.D. is *the* name in rustproofing." The company claims that by using its process, you can rustproof a three-year-old car for the first time and still give the customer a warranty. It also claims that, unlike similar products, which only cover up the rust and allow corrosion to continue underneath the coating, Tuff-Kote's formula penetrates the rust and then seals the metal against further rusting.

Your ties with Tuff-Kote Dinol begin with a hands-on training program that covers both technical skills and sales and management. You bear the travel expenses to company headquarters in Detroit, where the classes are held. You will spend three and a half days on technical applications and installation of basic products, and a day and a half on sales and management—including instruction on how to train your employees. Tuff-Kote Dinol's technical staff will help you set up shop at your place of business, and its advertising department will provide you with a custom grand opening program. The company's sales advisors will even go with you when you make your first sales calls.

In addition to the franchise fee, you will pay about seven thousand dollars for initial stock and equipment. This package includes:

- Rustproofing material with application pumps and tools
- System-6 exterior glaze and application tools
- Inner-Kote package (fabric protection)
- Splash-Gard inventory and tools
- Showroom displays and promotional material

Tuff-Kote doesn't skimp on its after-opening support. One enthusiastic dealer, James B. Sullivan, had this to say: "When you buy a franchise you expect to receive 100 percent from them. You usually get 80 percent. In Tuff-Kote's case, they have given me 125 percent." A telephone hotline provides help from headquarters—"When I call, I get an answer," says Sullivan—and the company will train you in the use of new products and sales programs when necessary. Tuff-Kote Dinol also offers monthly refresher courses at company headquarters and at regional locations.

The color of your building and your brand identification must conform to Tuff-Kote Dinol standards. And you must buy supplies only from vendors who meet the company's specifications.

How do Tuff-Kote franchisees feel about their experiences with the company? Do they enjoy it and would they recommend it to others? "Yes, yes," says Paul Bosley. "Yes, yes, yes, yes, yes," says James Sullivan.

For further information contact:
William Wooton, Tuff-Kote Dinol, Inc., 15045 Hamilton Ave., Highland Park, MI 48203, 313-867-4700

Ziebart Corporation

Initial license fee: $15,000
Royalties: 8%
Advertising royalties: 5%
Minimum cash required: $50,000
Capital required: $50,000 to $60,000
Financing: None
Length of contract: 10 years

In business since: 1954
Franchising since: 1962
Total number of units: 371
Number of company-operated units: 14
Total number of units planned, 1990: NA
Number of company-operated units planned, 1990: NA

When E. J. Hartmann purchased the Ziebart company in 1970, he bought a business that was already well known for its automobile rust-protection service. But by 1975 he felt that Ziebart had to go beyond rust protection and develop a line of products and services that would offer a total appearance and protection package for customers' automobiles. Aware that his was not the only company that would try to develop this market—although Ziebart would be the first—he decided to think big, and rather than slowly building up this new product and service line, he bought an entire chemical company to give Ziebart an instant technical edge on the competition.

Ziebart continually expands its range of automotive protection services. It now sells a rust-eliminator system for used vehicles that already have problems with rust, and a radiator and air-conditioning service, all in addition to its standard line, which includes vinyl top, paint, and interior protection; chip stop; pinstriping; sunroofs; and splash guards.

The company helps you choose a location and advises you on any remodeling or construction that may be required for your Ziebart center. According to Ziebart, "Centers are placed at reasonable distances apart to avoid oversaturation of a given market." But they do not offer you an exclusive, protected territory.

Ziebart offers a three-week training program at the company's headquarters in Troy, Michigan. You pay for travel, lodging, and meal expenses for you and your employees. During the first week you study rust protection; during the second you learn about Ziebart appearance and protection services; and in the last week you deal with the business side of your operation, covering sales, marketing, budgeting, advertising, inventory ckntrol, and personnel. Should you choose to include Ziebart's new optional air-conditioning and radiator service in your business, you will take, at an additional charge, two weeks of training in that subject.

Your district sales manager continues to train you during your ongoing operations, instructing you on making outside sales and counseling you on all other aspects of your business. The company's manual will answer virtually any technical question you might have. The manual deals with over two thousand makes and models of vehicles. You can always consult a company expert if you encounter problems not covered by the manual. In addition, a technical specialist will visit your business periodically to make sure that your operation is up to par and to make specific recommendations to improve any deficiencies.

Your initial equipment and supplies are part of a package Ziebart requires you to buy. Currently, only Ziebart and its authorized vendors supply the products used in your business.

On the national level, Ziebart helps build business for you through its fleet program and national advertising. Locally, Ziebart dealers participate in cooperative advertising.

For further information contact:
Mark Bollegar, Ziebart Corporation, P.O. Box 1290, Troy, MI 48007-1290, 313-588-4100

Rental Services

American International Rent A Car Corporation

Initial license fee: $5,000 to $175,000
Royalties: 7%
Advertising royalties: None
Minimum cash required: $30,000
Capital required: $30,000 to $350,000
Financing: Discussed on a case-by-case basis
Length of contract: 5 years

In business since: 1969
Franchising since: 1969
Total number of units: 1,300
Number of company-operated units: None

Total number of units planned, 1990: NA
Number of company-operated units planned, 1990: None

The continuing demand for rental cars fuels an industry whose annual revenues are expected to reach $7 billion by 1990. This sustained growth can be attributed to increasing domestic air travel, growth in the primary car-rental market of twenty-five- to fifty-four-year-olds, and the rising costs of automobile ownership. While the rental-car industry is still dominated by the "big four"—Hertz, Avis, Budget, and National—smaller operators like American International Rent A Car have been driving away with a bigger and bigger share of the market.

Established as a franchise system in 1969, American International is one of the fastest growing "second-tier" passenger car-rental companies in the U.S. With locations in twenty-five countries, the company services customers at airport, downtown, and suburban locations. Committed to offering reduced prices on auto-rental service comparable to that offered by the big four, American International sacrifices none of the amenities that discounters often eliminate. "We've always emphasized the fact that our service is comparable to the majors and that our prices are significantly lower," says a company spokesman. "The key to our success has been making sure that the customer is number one."

Because every American International location is licensee-operated, the company's franchisees enjoy numerous benefits. American International's board of directors is elected annually from the ranks of active franchisees, and the system has the lowest royalty fee structure of all the large industry operators. The company designs its advertising and marketing efforts specifically to meet the needs of franchisees. Seeking to improve name recognition and distinguish itself both from the big four and discount renters, American International has in recent years aimed at travel professionals and business travelers.

When you buy an American International franchise, you have the opportunity to train at corporate headquarters or at an existing franchise, though you are not required to do so. If you elect to train, you will be instructed in all aspects of daily rental agency operations, including accounting, customer service, sales, and marketing. Company staff will help you select an appropriate location in a high-traffic area, arrange financing, obtain insurance, hire employees, place advertising, and set up your office.

Once your franchise is fully operational, you can receive refresher training at the home office or in the field whenever you feel you need it. This training covers fleet planning, revenue forecasting, sales, and marketing. Support staff is always available by phone to provide assistance. And American International holds regional meetings twice a year to help you keep abreast of developments in the car-rental industry.

For further information contact:
Marge Wavernek, Vice President, American International Rent A Car Corporation, 4801 Spring Valley Rd., Suite 120-B, Dallas, TX 75244, 214-233-6530

Budget Rent a Car Corporation

Initial license fee: $15,000 and up, depending on the population of your territory
Royalties: 5%; also a maintenance fee ranging from 2.5 to 5%
Advertising royalties: 2%
Minimum cash required: $250,000
Capital required: $250,000 to $750,000
Financing: License fee may be paid in installments.
Length of contract: 5 years, renewable

In business since: 1958
Franchising since: 1960
Total number of units: 3,100+
Number of company-operated units: 75
Total number of units planned, 1990: NA
Number of company-operated units planned, 1990: NA

The only thing small about this company is the "Budget" in its name. From one lot with twelve cars in 1958, the company has—through Budget Rent a Car International—expanded all over the world, with sites in over one hundred countries. In 1968 it was purchased by Transamerica Corporation, whose headquarters is the huge pyramid building in downtown San Francisco. In 1986 Gibbons, Green, van Amerongen Ltd., an investment bank, bought it in a leveraged buyout. Now fourth in market share among car-rental companies, Budget is closing in on the number-three position.

The heart of the rent-a-car industry is the business traveler. Typically, the rental-car customer has just gotten off a plane and is headed for an appointment. Budget Rent a Car does everything it can to see that this traveler heads for the Budget sign first. Its CorpRate sales department, the first of its kind in the industry, zeroes in on the commercial traveler by offering a commercial account featuring one rate with unlimited mileage on all cars. This part of the company's business is up by more than 25 percent in the last four years. It also customizes pricing plans for companies with frequently traveling personnel. One of Budget's most important customers—whose employees are often in transit—happens to be the biggest consumer of car-rental services in the world: the United States government.

Another strong point of Budget's business is its affiliation with Sears Roebuck. Budget has been operating Sears Car and Truck Rental for the past eighteen years. This concession is run through regular Budget Rent a Car locations. Budget franchisees thus have an opportunity to tap a market of 50 million people who have Sears credit cards.

This company takes maximum advantage of its size and reach. Budget's worldwide computerized reservation center in Carrollton, Texas, is staffed by over three hundred sales agents, who have instant access to any information a customer might need. Patrons may reach one of those agents through one of many 800 numbers. Major airline computer systems display Budget vehicle availability and rates, making travel agents an ally of Budget Rent a Car franchisees.

Many of the decisions involved in opening your Budget Rent a Car business will be your own, with the company acting only in an advisory capacity. You and your general manager—if you hire somebody else for that job—will be trained by the company in the Budget way of doing business. Training will take place either at your business site or at the company offices in Chicago. That training will include instruction on acquiring and maintaining vehicles, as well as standard business practices. You will probably begin business with a fleet of twenty to fifty cars and five to ten trucks.

Budget has a fairly elaborate organization called the Licensee Operations Field Staff, which is dedicated to helping its franchisees. Among the things it is likely to help you with are control and distribution of your fleet, revenue and expense forecasting, market analysis, and handling customer complaints. There is, incidentally, a national toll-free number that any Budget customer can use to register a complaint about any aspect of the company's service.

The company's Fleet Operations Department will help you purchase and sell your vehicles. Its "Fleet Operations Buying Guide" consolidates all relevant data between two covers. Budget will help you establish a line of credit through the company's Budget Vehicle Purchase Program.

Budget Rent a Car management stresses the importance of having up-to-date reports detailing the vital statistics of your business. For example, the company will provide you with figures comparing the performance of your business with that of similar franchisees. Budget will also give you data that will help you develop a profit plan, with forecasts of revenues and expenses. Your participation in these programs—including reporting financial data from your business so it can be included in the company's data base—is mandatory. You can also purchase the company's optional computerized accounting system—Best II—which will further assist you in controlling your finances.

Budget's nationwide marketing program notwithstanding, your local promotional efforts play an important part in bringing in business. Those efforts should generate about a third of your car rentals. The franchisor has extensive marketing capabilities to supplement your local efforts. Its yellow pages department, for example, will work with you to develop your phone book ad. That's a vital place for you to shine, since it's the source for about 80 percent of all rental business on the local level.

A big factor in your business will be Budget's marketing to the travel industry. The company participates in several airline promotions, including United's "Mileage Plus"; joint programs with tour operators; and cooperative activities with hotels, such as the Hilton chain. Budget Rent a Car also actively pursues the meeting and convention business.

For further information contact:
Eleanor Norman-Alvord, Coordinator, Franchise Department, Budget Rent a Car Corporation, 200 North Michigan Ave., Chicago, IL 60601, 312-580-5000

Dollar Rent A Car

Initial license fee: $150/1,000 population;$7,500 minimum
Royalties: 9%, less up to 5% of credit card fees
Advertising royalties: Included in royalties
Minimum cash required: $50,000
Capital required: $50,000 plus credit line of $0.5 to $1 million
Financing: The company will help franchisees obtain third-party financing.
Length of contract: Indefinite

In business since: 1966
Franchising since: 1969
Total number of units: 540
Number of company-operated units: 10
Total number of units planned, 1990: NA
Number of company-operated units planned, 1990: NA

"The demand for rental cars is virtually unlimited," according to Kermit Whyte, vice president of systems development for Dollar Systems, Inc. "As the population grows and more small- and medium-sized cities open airports, the market for rental cars grows. While our larger metropolitan franchises are sold out, we will keep expanding into mid-sized urban areas, particularly those served by airports." The Dollar

Rent A Car credo is to deliver full-service car rental at a discount. Its commitment to customer savings has allowed Dollar to grow rapidly, and it now offers a nationwide reservations system. Through an agreement with interRent, Europe's largest rent-a-car company, Dollar can also offer international travelers confirmed reservations at over seventeen hundred locations worldwide.

Dollar prefers to sell "master franchises," the right to develop a defined region, but it does have available some single-location franchises for nonairport units only. The company will help you select an off-airport location or gain entry to airport locations, and will sell you the appropriate indoor and outdoor signs for your business. According to Kermit Whyte, you don't need previous experience in the car-rental business to qualify as a Dollar franchisee, but you should have "any kind of business experience." Because air travel generates most rental-car business, the company is planning most of its expansion at airport sites, but it will approve downtown locations if they can bring in corporate business.

After the company helps you select and set up your site, it will prepare you through hands-on training at your site. Dollar staff will help you purchase your fleet—you can offer any make of car for rental as long as no car is more than two years old—and will train you in every aspect of rental operations, from car control to accounting procedures. In addition, the company will help you train your counter personnel and plan local advertising and promotions. To supplement your marketing efforts, Dollar conducts a national advertising campaign in airline and hotel magazines as well as newspapers. You may also take advantage of approved co-op advertising.

Periodic reviews ensure that your business operates as efficiently as possible, and the corporate office checks over your revenue reports, profit projections, and operating statements to catch and correct any problems that might crop up. Simplified accounting systems and forms will make your bookkeeping easier. You can puchase these forms from Dollar. With a proven record-keeping system and a detailed operations manual at your disposal, you will be well equipped to run your business. But if you should have any problems or questions, Dollar staff is only a phone call away.

Dollar regularly offers regional training for you and your employees. Through a variety of workshops and seminars, the company addresses the specific needs of its franchisees as well as general topics in car rental. The company meets another of your needs by making business insurance available to you at premium rates based on your revenue. Of particular advantage to you as a Dollar franchisee, though, are the material benefits of the company's nationwide reservations system, through which you can receive reservations from travelers around the country who are planning trips to your area.

For further information contact:
Kermit Whyte, Vice President, Systems Development, Dollar Systems, Inc., 6141 West Century Blvd., Los Angeles, CA 90045, 213-776-8100

Freedom Rent-A-Car

Initial license fee: $11,000
Royalties: 3.5%
Advertising royalties: 1% to 2%
Minimum cash required: $20,000
Capital required: $20,000 and up
Financing: Promissory note at 3% above prime available
Length of contract: 25 years

In business since: 1981
Franchising since: 1981
Total number of units: 130
Number of company operated-units: 2
Total number of units planned, 1990: 600
Number of company-operated units planned, 1990: None

Achieving success in many service businesses often means more than just picking the right product and the right time to introduce it. Frequently it comes down to targeting a segment of the market not adequately served in your area by the "big guys." A thin slice of the pie can go a long way if you don't have to share that slice with too many other entrepreneurs. One way of doing that is to offer a no-frills, "plain vanilla" service. Leaving out the fancy touches enables you to compete on price, something that many customers really appreciate.

Freedom Rent-A-Car is one of these operations. Its president, Neil Wilderom, perfected its system in his own company before he founded Freedom Rent-A-Car with several associates. He decided to concentrate on renting late-model used cars, putting together a fleet of cars ranging in age from new to five years old, which made for lower depreciation and interest rates. Lower costs enabled him to charge lower rates to his customers.

A business like this offers to potential franchisees the freedom to make the enterprise really their own. The important element is the basic company concept, not a prescribed way of doing everything. Freedom Rent-A-Car's franchisees have to use the company logo, and they must buy the franchisor's numbered rental agreement forms and make use of the company's national reservation system, but after that they make most of the decisions. The company will offer its guidance on choosing a site for your business, but you have the final say—as long as the location is within the postal zone that marks off your exclusive territory. You must display approved signs, but you can furnish and decorate your place of business according to your own tastes.

The company trains new franchisees in Bartlesville, Oklahoma. You pay for your own travel and lodging expenses for the three days of training. Using the company operating manual as a text, your instructors will cover vehicle preparation and maintenance, forms, accounting and bookkeeping, placing local advertising, telephone applications, sales, and customer service. By keeping class size small, the company can tailor the instruction to the particular needs of its franchisees, thus enabling you to have your instructor concentrate on any area in which you feel weak. Periodic visits from the company's staff to your place of business will back up your training and help you cope with specific problems.

Freedom Rent-A-Car franchisees also influence the company's advertising policy through their representatives on the National Advertising Committee, which controls the national advertising budget. Franchisees elect five of the committee's nine members.

For further information contact:
Peter D. Fritz, Vice President, Operations, Freedom Rent-A-Car, P.O. Box 2345, Bartlesville, OK 74005, 918-336-0562

Holiday-Payless Rent-A-Car System

Initial license fee: $12,000 to $75,000
Royalties: 5%
Advertising royalties: 3%
Minimum cash required: $35,000
Capital required: $35,000 to $125,000
Financing: None
Length of contract: 5 years

In business since: 1971
Franchising since: 1971
Total number of units: 150
Number of company-operated units: None
Total number of units planned, 1990: 295
Number of company-operated units planned, 1990: 5

Holiday-Payless is the product of the 1982 merger of the Payless Car Rental System and Holiday Rent-A-Car. The company now serves markets in Canada, the Caribbean, and England, as well as in this country.

As rent-a-car franchises go, this company does not require a huge investment by its new franchisees. It keeps costs down by specializing in the rental of economy cars at off-airport locations, where site costs are minimized. The lowest franchisee fee secures a location in a market of fewer than one hundred thousand people, while the highest is for major airport markets, such as Chicago and Atlanta.

Franchisees train to run their business at the company's headquarters in Saint Petersburg, Florida, paying their own travel and living expenses for the five days of the course. Among the subjects covered in the training are counter and office procedures, sales calls and business development, vehicle procurement and maintenance, staffing, and customer qualification and selection. You can obtain supplementary training on request, for a reasonable fee.

The company advises its new franchisees on site selection, and it works with them to make sure they pick the right mix of vehicles for their beginning fleet. Franchisees can purchase the company's optional computerized accounting system, and they can also take advantage of Holiday-Payless' volume purchasing of supplies.

One of Holiday-Payless' strongest points is merchandising, on the local as well as the national level. In fact, as soon as the franchisee's business opens, the company literally walks its franchisee through the process of establishing important local contacts. During that period, a company representative accompanies the new franchisee on visits to insurance adjusters, repair shops, hotels, motels, and major industries to make contacts and drum up business. Holiday-Payless also promotes itself on the national level with advertising and its Passport Club card, with which business people can rent an economy car at any company location in the country at a special rate.

The company obtains even more business for its franchisees through its computerized connection to major airline reservation systems, such as United's Apollo and Eastern's Sabre. Holiday-Payless' own computerized national reservation system not only links customer needs to available vehicles, it also compiles information on each of its franchisees' operations and comparative data on their competitors, which it supplies to franchisees monthly.

The company points out that its franchisees can profit from activities related to their main business. Some units also rent trucks, although the company suggests that new franchisees put their business on a sound footing before venturing into this area. Other sidelines include used-car sales, putting together tour packages, arranging for drivers to drive cars across country for businesses and private clients, and the establishment of lease lines.

For further information contact:
Les Netterstrom, Holiday-Payless Rent-A-Car System, 5510 Gulfport Blvd., St. Petersburg, FL 33707, 813-381-2758

Rent-A-Wreck

Initial license fee: $5,000 to $50,000
Royalties: 6%
Advertising royalties: 2%
Minimum cash required: $75,000
Capital required: $75,000 to $250,000
Financing: The company will finance licensing fee and help you apply for vehicle financing.
Length of contract: 5 years

In business since: 1969
Franchising since: 1980
Total number of units: 350
Number of company-operated units: 3
Total number of units planned, 1990: 1,510
Number of company-operated units planned, 1990: 10

The Rent-A-Wreck story began on a used-car and truck lot in Los Angeles, when the owner, David Schwartz, thought up the tongue-in-cheek name for the service he had added to his regular business. The cars and trucks, though used, weren't really wrecks, which enabled Schwartz to rent them at low rates. Soon he had a thriving sideline and numbered among his customers Henry Fonda, Richard Gere, and Kathleen Turner.

The entrepreneurial flair that Rent-A-Wreck needed to turn a good idea into a nationwide enterprise was supplied by Geoffrey Nathanson, Rent-A-Wreck's current CEO. Before joining Rent-A-Wreck he started America's first FM rock station and its first pay cable television station. He built Rent-A-Wreck into the country's first major used-car-rental service—and the fastest growing car-rental company of any kind, according to the company. Initially, Rent-A-Wreck specialized in customers who did not have expense accounts, renting them well-kept cars of an average of two to six years old. But while many units still do that, others now rent new cars, often to corporations seeking a lower price for their rental-car needs.

The Rent-A-Wreck licensing fee depends on the population of your market, not the size of your fleet, which can be as few as five cars. About 85 percent of Rent-A-Wreck franchisees have added the franchise to automobile businesses they operated previously, like car dealerships or taxi fleets. Adding Rent-A-Wreck as a component to your business will not put you under somebody else's thumb. Rent-A-Wreck insists that your fleet be clean and in good shape and that you give your customers good service, but it won't tell you how to arrange your lot, what prices to charge, or require you to wear a uniform. You will have to provide maintenance for your cars, including customer access to twenty-four-hour repair service.

Rent-A-Wreck conducts a four- to five-day mandatory training program for its franchisees in Los Angeles. Subjects covered include personnel, automobile purchasing, maintenance, insurance, advertising and promotion, rates, developing sources of referrals, qualifying customers, telephone sales procedures, budgeting, security, and renting trucks and vans. Rent-A-Wreck also gives regional refresher courses five times a year, and a representative of the franchisor periodically visits each unit.

The Rent-A-Wreck franchise package contains an initial supply of forms for rental agreements, maintenance records, rental history, accident reports, and reservations. Advertising and promotional aids are also included.

For further information contact:
Franchise Sales Director, Rent-A-Wreck, 10889 Wilshire Blvd., Suite 1260, Los Angeles, CA 90024, 1-800-421-7253

Thrifty Rent-A-Car System, Inc.

Initial license fee: $9,000
Royalties: 3%
Advertising royalties: 5%
Minimum cash required: $10,000
Capital required: $10,000 to $75,000
Financing: None
Length of contract: NA

In business since: 1962
Franchising since: 1964
Total number of units: 491
Number of company-operated units: 1
Total number of units planned, 1990: NA
Number of company-operated units planned, 1990: NA

Thrifty, which ranks fourth among off-airport car-rental services, has carved out a niche in its highly competitive field through constant innovation. One of the first rent-a-car companies to locate on airport perimeters (to avoid high rents), Thrifty was also the first to offer customers a choice between cars rented to smokers and nonsmokers.

The company's business strategy puts an accent on high-level service, typified by the chauffeured limousine that transports customers between the airport and the Thrifty lot. The chauffeur takes care of passengers' luggage, and Thrifty staff heats or cools the rental car, depending on the season, while the customer fills out the rental form.

Thrifty trains franchisees at its headquarters in Tulsa, Oklahoma. The training course combines classroom work and hands-on experience at the company's own active rental center in Tulsa. Back at your place of business, the company's regional director will help you select a site for your business and assist you in procuring vehicles and arranging financing for your fleet. Your regional director will also help you train your staff and will offer ongoing support for your operations, advising you on insurance, sales and marketing, and counter and operational procedures, as well as making quality control inspections. Regional seminars will give you an opportunity to exchange ideas and experiences with other franchisees.

The company maintains a fleet department at its headquarters to inform you about new automobile manufacturer programs, and it acts as a liaison between you and the automobile companies. Since 1984 Thrifty has offered franchisees many special deals involving Chrysler cars, including rebates, incentive programs, and promotional allowances. It has also negotiated special leasing rates for the Chrysler limousines that most units use to chauffeur customers to and from the airport.

The company's reservation system, which handles over eighty thousand calls a month, will bring in the bulk of your business. Thrifty's advertising, administered by a committee of which franchisee representatives constitute the majority, appears in travel, tour, consumer, and trade publications. The company's Tour and Travel Department also promotes your business through the exhibits it stages at more than twenty annual trade shows.

For further information contact:

Brett Thomas, Thrifty Rent-A-Car System, Inc., P.O. Box 35250, Tulsa, OK 74153-0250, 918-665-3930

Tires and Parts

Champion Auto Stores, Inc.

Initial license fee: None
Royalties: None
Advertising royalties: None

Minimum cash required: $70,000
Capital required: $130,000
Financing: None
Length of contract: Indefinite

In business since: 1956
Franchising since: 1961
Total number of units: 113
Number of company-operated units: 10
Total number of units planned, 1990: NA
Number of company-operated units planned, 1990: NA

Franchising opportunities with Champion appear most promising in Kansas, Illinois, Missouri, and Michigan. This chain of do-it-yourself auto parts supermarkets, spread over nine states in the Midwest and West, has grown by 30 percent in the past three years. The franchisor claims that its business is immune to dips in the business cycle. In fact, it says it has achieved its greatest growth during recessions.

The automobile parts business got a boost from the oil price shocks of the 1970s. Large numbers of gas stations closed, and many of the surviving stations turned to a self-service, gas-only mode of operation. With repairs less readily available, many car owners finally got up the courage to start fiddling around under the hood. For many people, it started with the feeling that they were capable of changing their own oil. After that, there was no turning back.

Champion store design divides a large expanse of space into neat rows of fixtures, with auto parts either stacked on shelves or hanging from hooks. Radiator belts hang high on the wall. As in a supermarket, numerous signs call attention to sales items or new products. Customers do their shopping with supermarket carts or baskets.

Champion emphasizes that it wants the people who own and run these stores to concentrate on service and sales volume without getting bogged down in details that could be better handled by company professionals. The company notes that many of its franchisees are first-time entrepreneurs. It therefore tries to take on many of the burdens that go with running the business, such as choosing stock. Champion sums up its intent to assist and encourage franchisees in its franchising slogan: "On your own, but not alone."

It's not that you won't be making decisions. You will, for example, have a say in what you stock and how much of it you keep on hand, but the franchisor has a staff of specialists in each product area who buy in quantity at maximum discounts, and you are likely to want to take their advice. Champion also manufactures many parts under its own brand name, which you will stock as a matter of course. You will receive a weekly delivery of your regular stocking order, although anything can be special-ordered at any time. The company fills your orders on a two-day turnaround schedule.

The company will choose your location and lay out your store subject to your approval. You will have to train for eight to ten days in the Minneapolis area, where instruction will take place in one of the company stores as well as in a classroom. Should you desire, the training period can be lengthened. Some of your instructors in Minneapolis will be company store managers, whose knowledge of their field is a good deal more than theoretical.

Champion will help you choose your start-up inventory and put together your first annual sales and expense forecast and monthly budget. The franchisor guarantees that each store, no matter what its size, will pay the same price for all merchandise. The special company computerized accounting system will evaluate how well you do with that merchandise. You can draw on that system at any time for an analysis of any part of your operation.

Champion franchisees must attend the company's semiannual marketing conferences, where they will discuss new products, promotions, and services in a seminar atmosphere. And there will be plenty of promotions to discuss. In fact, Champion runs its own advertising agency. The company does extensive TV and radio advertising, and it will also mail ten 8-page, 4-color circulars a year to your customers. In addition, the circulars appear as inserts in newspapers.

Perhaps the most interesting promotional tool the company uses is its in-store Video Tech Center. This laser disc-based audiovisual device will teach your customers the basics of doing their own repairs. Ordinarily, a programmed sequence of "tech tips" will be displayed on the screen, but customers can interrupt it by using a search control to find the topic most interesting to them. Champion's vice president, Dene Billbe, has observed that customers need a visit or two before they become comfortable with this machine. But, like a video game, it does grab their attention, and "by their second or third visit, they go right to the machine."

For further information contact:

Dene E. Billbe, Champion Auto Stores, Inc., 5520 North County Rd. 18, New Hope, MN 55428, 612-535-5984

Goodyear Tire Centers

Initial license fee: None
Royalties: 3%
Advertising royalties: None

Minimum cash required: $65,000
Capital required: $65,000
Financing: Long-term note-line and open-account credit available
Length of contract: 10 years

In business since: 1898
Franchising since: 1968
Total number of units: 610
Number of company-operated units: None
Total number of units planned, 1990: 1,000
Number of company-operated units planned, 1990: None

Children growing up in this country in recent years probably think that no important ceremony held outdoors—especially major sporting events—can begin without two rituals: the singing of the "Star Spangled Banner" and the passing overhead of the Goodyear Blimp. The airship, now something of an institution, to the point where comedians make good-natured jokes about it, has helped Goodyear achieve household-name status. Its franchisees count it among the many benefits of opening their own Goodyear tire center.

As a Goodyear franchisee, you trade a certain amount of independence to use the most familiar name in the tire industry. Goodyear will sublease a location to you and outfit your unit with the equipment and fixtures you need. You lease most of that equipment from the company. Goodyear is the only source for the products you sell, and it will also supply you with equipment for supplementary services like wheel alignments, brake jobs, and tune-ups.

In addition to the use of a heavily advertised brand name, you will also receive some of the most thorough training given by any franchisor. The company picks up all expenses for this training, except your transportation. Goodyear requires that new franchisees take a full three months of training at its Akron, Ohio, headquarters. The training includes eight weeks of classroom instruction and four weeks at an operating tire center. The company takes particular pains to make sure that business people who lack familiarity with the tire industry get a thorough grounding in all that a Goodyear dealer needs to know.

Your Goodyear business counselor and area and district sales managers, your follow-up contacts with the company, call on you regularly at your business to provide merchandising advice and deal with any problems that might arise in your ongoing operation. Your staff will receive supplementary training as needed in regional schools. The company also supplies various in-store training aids, including flip charts and videotapes. You will not need a specialized accounting system. Goodyear processes your daily reports, which include invoice, check, and cash records, with its computerized dealer management system, making available to you an analysis of your sales, profits, and expenses. The company's computers also generate your inventory records, as well as all other figures that an accounting system usually produces.

Goodyear facilitates customer credit through an arrangement with Citibank. Citibank handles your customer's billing; and it issues them special Silver Cards, with quick credit clearance. You can also solicit business by direct mail through this Citibank operation.

Goodyear knows what it takes to make a successful franchisee. The company seeks people who already have business experience, supervisory ability, and an aggressive sales personality.

For further information contact:
H. M. Harding, Goodyear Tire and Rubber Company, 1144 E. Market St., Akron, OH 44316, 216-796-3467

Uniroyal Goodrich

Initial license fee: None
Royalties: None
Advertising royalties: None
Minimum cash required: $50,000
Capital required: $100,000
Financing: The company assists you in obtaining financing from local sources.
Length of contract: 1 year

In business since: 1870
Franchising since: 1920
Total number of units: 2,200
Number of company-operated units: None
Total number of units planned, 1990: NA
Number of company-operated units planned, 1990: NA

In 1870 a doctor started this company because he feared that he would not be able to support his wife on his doctor's income. Often thought of today as the company without the blimp, Goodrich tries to make the most of it. The company's franchised dealers like to think of themselves as "The Blimp Busters." But blimp or no blimp, Goodrich can take pride in having chalked up several notable firsts: the first pneumatic automobile tire, the first commercial tubeless tire, and the first American radial tire. The first American astronauts wore space suits made by Goodrich.

If you decide to join the company, you could run either a Goodrich Broadline dealership, carrying a full line of passenger and light truck tires, or a dealership specializing in radials. In either case, the company promises to supply your inventory with maximum efficiency at minimum prices.

Goodrich coordinates its tire shipments to dealers through its National Order Processing Center, or NOPC. You can always get up-to-the-minute information about the status of your order from NOPC via a toll-free number. The company points out that this will aid your cash flow and give you maximum control over your inventory.

The company also has a net pricing program notable in the industry for its simplicity. All dealers are in one pricing category. You can earn extra discounts for large-volume purchases and another discount if you have the capacity to pick up large orders at the warehouse rather than having them delivered by the company. Dealers receive annual volume and cash discounts, and since Goodrich makes its profits from your inventory purchases, you also save by not having to pay royalties.

Your new business can also take advantage of special opening-order premiums. With certain minimum opening orders, you will receive extra promotional aids, slide projectors, and training films, and special assistance in obtaining fleet accounts.

As a Goodrich franchisee, you will have considerable freedom to select and develop the site for your business as you wish. Your company training, which covers sales technique, product knowledge, servicing techniques and business management, will take place at your site. A company representative will provide you with a market analysis and suggest an inventory stocking pattern, as well as help with your grand opening.

Each year the company gives formal refresher training seminars, and you may also request additional informal training at your place of business. Training takes several forms, including lectures, audio/visual aids, and hands-on experience. Topics covered in supplementary training include sales technique, product knowledge, and market and customer analysis. Your district manager will give you further sales assistance if you need it.

Goodrich has a cooperative advertising program for its dealers. The company also promotes its merchandise through national advertising and encourages steady patronage by issuing its own credit cards. Franchisees can take advantage of a special dealer insurance plan the company has worked out with Liberty Mutual. Dealers are also eligible for travel and merchandise incentive programs.

For further information contact:

Drew Banas, Uniroyal Goodrich, 0636/24D, 600 South Main St., Akron, OH 44318, 1-800-321-1800

Transmission Services

AAMCO Transmissions, Inc.

Initial license fee: $25,000
Royalties: 9%
Advertising royalties: variable
Minimum cash required: $42,000
Capital required: $100,000 to $110,000
Financing: None
Length of contract: 15 years

In business since: 1963
Franchising since: 1963
Total number of units: 920
Number of company-operated units: None
Total number of units planned, 1990: 1,000
Number of company-operated units planned, 1990: None

America's continuing love affair with the automobile sustains one of the nation's largest industries: the auto aftermarket. With millions of automobiles on the road, the market for automotive products and services is enormous. New-car prices continue to climb, so car owners want to make sure their cars last. Demand for transmission service will remain strong for years to come.

AAMCO can help you get in on a good thing with its established reputation and proven methods. The company is seeking franchisees throughout the United States and Canada, and you can become an AAMCO franchisee even without any prior experience in auto mechanics. More important, according to the company, is experience in business management. The company will augment your experience by training you in both technical and business skills, preparing you to run your own transmission-repair and servicing shop. Your AAMCO shop will be able to handle just about any vehicle.

New franchisees are required to complete AAMCO's training program in Bala Cynwyd, Pennsylvania. The five-week course will qualify you as a transmission mechanic as well as train you in sales, marketing, production, and administration. Throughout the term of your franchise agreement, AAMCO will provide supplemental training in the form of courses and seminars offered monthly in major metropolitan areas across the country. In addition to formal instruction, you will receive on-site operational and technical assistance from AAMCO's consulting and operations department at no extra charge.

During the term of the fifteen-year contract, you are free to conduct your business as you see fit, as long as the service and products you offer meet AAMCO's standards and specifications. You may lease or purchase your site, provided the company approves the location, and you may purchase your equipment and supplies from any source, as long as they are of suitable quality. You are, however, prohibited from operating another transmission shop while your contract with AAMCO is in effect, and within a ten-mile radius of your AAMCO shop location, for one year following termination of the franchise agreement.

For further information contact:
AAMCO Transmissions, Inc., Franchise Sales Dept., One Presidential Blvd., Bala Cynwyd, PA 19004, 215-668-2900

Interstate Automatic Transmission Company, Inc.

Initial license fee: $20,000
Royalties: 6%
Advertising royalties: Minimum of $250/week
Minimum cash required: $73,000
Capital required: $88,000
Financing: Available
Length of contract: 15 years

In business since: 1973
Franchising Since: 1974
Total number of units: 69
Number of company-operated units: 2
Total number of units planned, 1990: 130
Number of company-operated units planned, 1990: None

The evolution of the automobile aftermarket, strangely enough, resembles the development of modern medical practice. At one time there was the general "practitioner," the mechanic who took care of your car from headlights to exhaust pipes. But the industry has long since passed into the age of the specialist. If, for example, your transmission starts to fail, you take it to a transmission repair shop, where specialists are familiar with each of the transmission's five hundred or so parts. No longer would you consult an independent all-purpose garage or new-car dealer.

Interstate thinks you should take your transmission to one of its shops, and it has at least one good argument to offer on its own behalf: "We're Nationwide . . . So Is Our Warranty," the company's slogan goes. An unaffiliated transmission repair shop couldn't offer its customers that kind of protection out of town. Interstate franchisees also give one-day service and will tow you in for free if you can't drive in.

With the average age of cars increasing and the use of automatic transmissions proliferating, the company estimates that one of eight cars on the road now needs its services. Automatic transmissions often need repairs after about two years of driving or 30,000 miles. In fact, according to the company, some kind of work on the transmission is usually needed every year. That produces a business that amounts to almost $2 billion a year for the industry.

Don't let the complexities of automatic transmissions discourage you out of hand. Interstate claims that fewer than 20 percent of its franchisees have worked with transmissions before taking their training. Jeff Claus, whose Interstate franchise is in Corpus Christi, Texas, substantiates the company's reassurance that you don't have to be an expert. Claus says "We were totally ignorant when we purchased—they taught us everything."

Mandatory franchisee training includes a week of classroom and a week of hands-on instruction at the company training site in Michigan. You pay for your own and your managerial employee's living and traveling expenses. The training covers advertising, insurance, personnel selection, accounting and, of course, the technical side of the business. The company encourages its franchisees to pursue fleet service, an aspect of the business covered in the training. You and your managers may also take refresher courses from time to time.

The company supports and monitors your operations fairly closely. Company representatives make periodic field visits, and you have to file weekly reports. However, the company will give you plenty of room to breathe. Bob Reuwer, who owns two franchises in Michigan, reports that Interstate is "not overbearing in any respect." And Jeff Claus originally picked this company rather than another one in the same field because franchisees of the other company said it resembled a "dictatorship."

Interstate dealers get an "Equipment and Supply List" from the company with suggestions for purchase. The franchisor can get you good prices on many items, but the final decision on what and from whom to buy is yours.

For further information contact:

Aaron A. Reavis, Interstate Automatic Transmission Company, Inc., 29200 Vassar Ave., Suite 501, Livonia, MI 48152, 313-478-9206

Lee Myles Associates Corp.

Initial license fee: $20,000
Royalties: 8%
Advertising royalties: $300 to $400/week

Minimum cash required: $45,000
Capital required: $75,000 to $78,000
Financing: The company will finance purchase of equipment.
Length of contract: 15 years

In business since: 1947
Franchising since: 1964
Total number of units: 140
Number of company-operated units: None
Total number of units planned, 1990: 225
Number of company-operated units planned, 1990: None

Average drivers spend at least $450 a year on repairs for their vehicles. According to the National Highway Traffic Safety Administration, there's a good chance that as much as 40 percent of that goes toward unnecessary or even fraudulent repairs. It stands to reason, then, that unless a person knows a skilled mechanic whom they trust implicitly with their car, they will look for a familiar name when something as complicated and expensive as its transmission needs work. And that's why Lee Myles maintains a steady presence in radio and television commercials in each of its markets. Lee Myles wants to be the name that people automatically think of when they think of transmissions.

While Lee Myles has so far confined its operations to nine states, its market is, for the most part, in areas with high concentrations of people and businesses: New Jersey, New York, Connecticut, Massachusetts, Rhode Island, Pennsylvania, Florida, New Mexico, and Arizona. The areas that currently offer the greatest opportunities for prospective Lee Myles franchisees are Pennsylvania, Florida, Massachusetts, Connecticut, and upstate New York.

If you buy one of these businesses, Lee Myles will teach you the basics in a three-week session of formal classroom instruction at its corporate office in Maywood, New Jersey. The curriculum includes the setting up of your transmission center, and personnel, financial planning, advertising, inventory control, and sales programs. Your license fee includes tuition for this instruction as well as transportation and lodging, but you will have to pay for your food. The company will also give you a week of on-the-job training at your business when you open.

Lee Myles will advise you on selecting a site for your business—most likely a leased location—although you actually find the location and execute your own lease. To get you off to a good start, the franchisor will supply you with an advertising program for the first thirteen weeks of your operations. Periodic visits from the Lee Myles operations manager will give you an opportunity to discuss your problems and get valuable advice about how to make your business grow.

All the equipment you will need to run your business—from joggle jacks to creepers—and a starting parts inventory are included in your franchise package. Stationery and forms bearing the Lee Myles logo are also part of the material you will receive from the franchisor, material that you can reorder only from Lee Myles. You can, however, buy extra equipment and replenish your parts inventory from whomever you wish, with Lee Myles' approval.

For further information contact:
Bert Stadtman, Director of Franchise Sales, Lee Myles Associates Corp., 25 East Spring Valley Ave., Maywood, NJ 07607, 201-843-3200

Mr. Transmission

Initial license fee: $19,500
Royalties: 8%
Advertising royalties: 10%
Minimum cash required: $35,000
Capital required: $103,000
Financing: The company may assist you in obtaining financing through the Small Business Administration.
Length of contract: 20 years

In business since: 1962
Franchising since: 1978
Total number of units: 207
Number of company-operated units: 2
Total number of units planned, 1990: 512
Number of company-operated units planned, 1990: None

"To start with, I was a company manager at a company-owned store," says Rodney Randall, whose Mr. Transmission franchise is in Hixson, Tennessee. "I knew it was a great opportunity." Rodney Randall went from employee to entrepreneur in a chain of shops that started over a quarter of a century ago in Nashville with a rebuilt-transmission center called the Automatic Transmission Company. Today, according to Mr. Transmission, it is the fastest-growing chain of transmission shops in America.

Mr. Transmission centers usually occupy 2,000 to 4,000 square feet on 7,000- to 10,000-square-foot plots, and house three to eight bays. The company will help you find and develop a site, but you have primary responsibility for these tasks. Among the criteria for site selection are an area's traffic volume, population, and zoning; location of other retail businesses; and local competition.

Training is an essential part of your preparation as a Mr. Transmission franchisee. You will pay any transportation, food, and lodging costs incurred during your three- to four-week period of instruction in Nashville. Your classroom training will cover management techniques, technical procedures, legal forms, customer service, personnel, inventory control, advertising, and cash management. Training places emphasis on the management of your business rather than on installation and repair of transmissions.You do not have to be a mechanic to run one of these franchises, and Mr. Transmission won't teach you how to be one. The manager of your center, who will handle the technical end of your business, will receive one week of specialized training in Nashville.

Mr. Transmission will help you organize your parts department and install your equipment. Company staff will also help you hire mechanics and a manager and schedule your preopening and postopening advertising. A Mr. Transmission representative will remain on the premises during your first week in business, assisting you in applying your training to actual business conditions.

Mr. Transmission emphasizes its postopening support for franchisees. In fact, Gary Rickles, the president of the company, makes himself available to any franchisees who want to come to company headquarters and talk over their problems with him: "I will see you any day, any time, at your convenience." Mr. Transmission will support you in other ways. Each week you will get a call from corporate headquarters to discuss your sales volume, and you will be able to get in touch with the company over its toll-free line. Company field personnel will visit your location periodically. You can get retraining if you need it, and Mr. Transmission offers sales and technical seminars several times a year to update you on new programs and products.

While you do not have to buy from Mr. Transmission's parts subsidiary, US Transparts, the company thinks you will probably want to, since through volume purchasing it can save you money on supplies and equipment as well as on transmission parts.

You may sell other products and services at your Mr. Transmission center, but only with the written permission of the franchisor.

For further information contact:

Debbi Parker, Mr. Transmission, P.O. Box 111060, Nashville, TN 37222-1060, 1-800-251-3504

Tune-Up and Lubrication

Car–X Service Systems, Inc.

Initial license fee: $12,500
Royalties: 5%
Advertising royalties: 5% to 10%
Minimum cash required: $40,000
Capital required: $150,000
Financing: The company will help you secure local financing.
Length of contract: 10 years

In business since: 1971
Franchising since: 1973
Total number of units: 101
Number of company-operated units: None
Total number of units planned, 1990: 250
Number of company-operated units planned, 1990: None

CAR–X Service Systems, Inc., a chain of automotive specialty shops, deals primarily in exhaust systems, shock absorbers, and brakes. Part of the auto aftermarket industry—manufacturers and dealers of automotive parts and services—Car–X shops service the growing number of car owners who want their cars to last longer. CAR–X recruits shrewd business people who realize that the market for automotive services is still wide open, and who want to establish a partnership with an experienced, growing company in order to tap this market. The company offers prime regions throughout the U.S. to individuals who are willing to work hard and can deal effectively with customers and employees.

The company must approve your location before you can become a CAR–X franchisee; they will then provide you with a list of contractors who can help you develop your site. Your initial training consists of instruction at the company's Chicago, Illinois, headquarters and company involvement in the opening of your shop. You will learn about auto parts and products, equipment used in servicing cars, and service center management. CAR–X will supply you with an invaluable operations manual and make sure your shop gets off to a running start.

Throughout your career as a CAR–X franchisee, the company will be available at all times for telephone consultation. Company representatives will work as troubleshooters on specific business problems you might encounter, and other staff will answer any technical questions that might arise. In addition, the company will conduct refresher training for you whenever they feel it is necessary, so you will be able to keep up to date on every aspect of the automotive service industry. All of the equipment and supplies that you use must meet CAR–X specifications. Once the company approves your suppliers, you may purchase directly from them with no further supervision by CAR–X.

If you have previous experience in some capacity in the auto aftermarket, you will be that much better prepared to own your own auto service shop. But CAR–X does not require that prospective franchisees have any previous technical knowledge. You will learn everything you need to know about the nuts and bolts of auto repair in the CAR–X training program. The company does, however, stress the importance of management skills in the successful operation of its franchises, so it seeks out franchisees with backgrounds in administration.

For further information contact
Joseph Marley, Director, Franchise Sales, CAR–X Service Systems, Inc., 444 North Michigan Ave., Suite 800, Chicago, IL 60611, 312-836-1500

Grease Monkey International, Inc.

Initial license fee: $20,000
Royalties: 5%
Advertising royalties: 4%
Minimum cash required: $80,000
Capital required: $80,000 to $160,000
Financing: Some offered by suppliers
Length of contract: 10 years

In business since: 1978
Franchising since: 1978
Total number of units: 63
Number of company-operated units: NA
Total number of units planned, 1990: NA
Number of company-operated units planned, 1990: NA

Grease Monkey International, Inc., is not afraid of a light touch. Its house newsletter is called *Monkey Talk*, and the company logo is a grinning simian holding a lube gun. But a few years ago, anyone with a financial interest in this company would not have been amused. Nineteen eighty-three found the young company on the skids, slipping on its own banana peel. The culprit was poor management. However, Arthur Sensenig, formerly a banker with the Western National Bank of Denver, rescued the company. He took over as president, cleaned up the mess, and put the company back in good financial shape.

"We're selling convenience," Sensenig says, "where a car owner can drive in, have a complimentary cup of coffee, and drive away ten minutes later with an oil change, new filters, lube, fluids topped, windows washed, and floors vacuumed." Or, as Harry Blankenship, Grease Monkey's first franchisee, characterizes the operation: "The fast-lube business can be referred to as the fast-food phenomenon of the auto industry."

These days more than half of all car owners still hire others to do their routine maintenance. Match that with the fact that for the decade 1973–1983, the number of full-service stations providing lubricating services dwindled from 194,000 to 110,000, and you have fertile ground for a business just like Grease Monkey. In 1985 there were about 1,500 quick-lube centers, Grease Monkey included. By 1990, according to industry giant Pennzoil, there could be as many as 6,000.

Grease Monkey franchises come from just about every kind of background, including real estate, civil service, the military, fast food, and sales. Some people even come out of retirement to buy one of these businesses. And they're not all men. In the Denver metropolitan area, for example, nine of the twenty-two Grease Monkey units are either run or owned by women.

If you join this group, Grease Monkey will have to approve the site you choose. The company will give you blueprints so your building can meet its specifications. At its Denver training location, Grease Monkey will train you in all aspects of the business in a one- or two-week course, depending on how much you need to learn. The course covers accounting, advertising, business management, and promotion, as well as technical services. Field representatives will provide follow-up help at your business when you open.

Grease Monkey won a coveted "Alfie" award for radio advertising aimed at selling its service to working women. The company wants its name—and by extension, yours—before the public. Toward that end, it will deliver its message in any form that works, including: "We lube you truly."

For further information contact:
Roger D. Auker, Grease Monkey International, Inc., 1660 Wynkoop, Suite 960, Denver, CO 80202, 303-534-1660

Jiffy Lube International, Inc.

Initial license fee: $35,000
Royalties: 5% the first year; 6% thereafter
Advertising royalties: 8%
Minimum cash required: $35,000
Capital required: $84,000
Financing: Available for real estate and construction
Length of contract: NA

In business since: 1979
Franchising since: 1979
Total number of units: 262
Number of company-operated units: 15
Total number of units planned, 1990: 1,000
Number of company-operated units planned, 1990: NA

Jiffy Lube has high hopes for the growth of its franchised operations. Reaching its goal of 1,000 units by 1990 would be a considerable achievement for the company, which began with one service center in Ogden, Utah, in 1973.

Jiffy Lube's reputation is based on fast, quality service. In ten minutes, and without an appointment, your customer can have his or her car's oil changed; a new oil filter installed; chassis lubricated; differential, transmission, brake, power steering, and window washer fluid checked and refilled; battery checked and refilled; air filter and wiper blades checked; tires inflated to the right pressure; interior vacuumed; and windows washed.

Unlike some franchisors, who either choose a site for their franchisee or do most of the work in picking the right location, Jiffy Lube wants you to act as a full partner in the site selection and building process. The company's real estate division will train you in site selection and then work with you to pick the right place. Jiffy Lube will also train you to do construction bidding and monitoring. You will have your choice of building layouts: two 2-car bays, three 1-car bays, or three 2-car bays. Once in operation, you can expect to handle an average of about forty vehicles a day. If zoning permits and marketing research suggests it's likely to be profitable, your business could also have a car wash.

You and your service center manager will receive two weeks of training at a Jiffy Lube training center. A company representative will assist you with preopening work and your grand opening. Ongoing assistance for your business will come in the form of financial and marketing analyses by a Jiffy Lube representative. The representative will evaluate your inventory levels and controls, staffing, fleet account acquisitions, and promotional efforts. Through Jiffy Lube, you will have the opportunity to purchase at a discount the supplies and equipment you will need to run your business.

You can choose to spend your advertising fee in one of two ways. You can spend it on your own, sending the company proof of your purchases, or you can choose to advertise in cooperation with nearby Jiffy operators, in a program organized by the company.

According to the company, the best opportunities for opening new

Jiffy Lube operations are in Louisiana, Michigan, Texas, and Washington State.

For further information contact:
Judith L. Bungori, Manager, Franchise Sales, Jiffy Lube International, Inc., 7008 Security Blvd., Suite 300, Baltimore, MD 21207, 301-298-8200

Precision Tune, Inc.

Initial license fee: $15,000
Royalties: 7.5%
Advertising royalties: 9%
Minimum cash required: $35,000
Capital required: $102,000 to $118,000
Financing: None
Length of contract: 10 years

In business since: 1976
Franchising since: 1977
Total number of units: 295
Number of company-operated units: 2
Total number of units planned, 1990: NA
Number of company-operated units planned, 1990: NA

"I wanted a business of my own and needed a proven system to be successful," reasoned Joyce Gump, who chose to enter a partnership with Precision Tune, the country's largest auto tune-up franchising system. Most Precision Tune franchises are in the eastern half of the United States, with concentrations in the upper Midwest, Ohio, and Texas, where the chain opened its first unit. Joyce Gump's service center is in Rockville, Maryland, and she describes her relationship with the franchisor as "very lucrative."

According to the company, its line of business is preferable to other opportunities in the automobile aftermarket because of its low start-up costs, the possibility of fitting its operations into an existing service station, and the minimal staff of three to six it takes to run it. Precision also stresses the repeat-customer aspect of the business, the all-cash basis of the enterprise, and the continued increase in stringent emission control standards that will create further demands for the services it offers.

Most of the company's franchisees have not had previous experience in an automotive business. Their backgrounds range from accounting to sales to medicine to civil service. Many of them—34 percent, according to the latest company statistics—end up buying more than one franchise.

The company's required training takes place either at the franchisor's home base in Beaumont, Texas, or at a subfranchisor's headquarters, if one operates in your area. You absorb the travel-related costs, but the company includes tuition in its franchise package. Precision's training, geared for beginners, includes standards, methods, procedures, and techniques of performing auto tune-ups and managing the business. It was "most informative and useful," according to Joyce Gump. You can get advanced training in sales, operations, and management in Beaumont and in regional seminars. Precision Tune also offers to its franchisees videotaped instruction on how to run an advertising campaign.

Precision Tune's ongoing support includes field visits to your business by a company representative and weekly technical bulletins to keep you up to date. You will also have access to a film library covering various aspects of management, operations, and the nuts and bolts of doing auto tune-ups. In addition, you can use the company cost-control system, supplemented by consultation on your profit-and-loss performance.

The company will provide you with building plans for your station and review your progress as you build it. You can purchase equipment and supplies from vendors of your own choosing, provided they meet company approval. Precision Tune does, however, maintain a subsidiary from whom you may purchase your inventory: PAC Manufacturing and Distributing Company.

Optional services you may offer at your station include computerized engine-control-system and carburetor-repair services, for which the company has an advanced training program. Precision Tune will also sell you a portable lift for about four thousand dollars should you decide to do oil change and lubrication.

Precision Tune gives its customers a six-month or 6,000-mile warranty on parts and labor. To make sure that you do your part to provide the services on which the company bases its warranty and reputation, your customers will get "We Care" cards to fill out, permitting them to evaluate the service you have given them.

For further information contact:
Precision Tune, Inc., New Center Development, 755 S. 11th St., Suite 101, Beaumont, TX 77701, 1-800-231-0588; in Texas: 409-838-3781

Sparks Tune-Up

Initial license fee: $20,000
Royalties: 7%
Advertising royalties: $420/month

Minimum cash required: $32,000
Capital required: $120,000+
Financing: None
Length of contract: 15 years

In business since: 1980
Franchising since: 1981
Total number kf units: 120
Number of company-operated units: None
Total number of units planned, 1990: 450
Number of company-operated units planned, 1990: None

Many franchise owners say they chose to go into business for themselves through franchising because they didn't want to "reinvent the wheel." They wanted an already proven business concept, operational procedures that had been worked out, a training program with the kinks ironed out, and the marketing savvy based on extensive experience in the field that a beginner couldn't possibly have. Sparks Tune-Up had that when it started in business. It was founded as a subsidiary of Maaco, which had established itself in the automotive aftermarket as the leading specialist in auto painting and bodywork, and had perfected the use of franchising within its industry. The management of Sparks Tune-Up feels the company is where Maaco was in the mid-seventies—already achieving considerable penetration in the market and primed for growth.

Sparks Tune-Up keeps its business simple. A Sparks shop will change your oil and give your car a lube job, but it specializes in tune-ups. Sparks keeps prices down, and charges the same price for most cars. The service takes no more than forty-five minutes, includes all parts and labor, and begins with a computerized analysis of your car's engine and exhaust. Then Sparks mechanics "road-test" the vehicle with a dynamometer. They make any needed adjustments and guarantee the work for 6,000 miles or six months, whichever comes first.

George and Sally Mader, Sparks franchisees in Royal Oak, Michigan, opted to buy their franchise because of the "past performance of Maaco." They found Sparks' training "excellent," one of the best parts of their purchase. You will take that training at company headquarters in King of Prussia, Pennsylvania. It covers sales, finances, and business management, as well as procedures involved in running a Sparks Tune-Up shop. While you are at headquarters, you'll have an opportunity to speak with various company specialists about your plans and strategy for your business.

The company assists you in choosing and leasing a site—high-traffic only—for your operation, negotiating the lease and doing whatever construction may be necessary. It also advises you on supplies and equipment, which you can buy from the vendor of your choice. A Sparks Tune-Up technical-operations trainer will come to your place of business to help during the week before and the week after you open, as you set up the business system you learned at King of Prussia, and will train your crew in the techniques they will use as Sparks mechanics. The Sparks marketing director will also confer with you to assist you in planning your initial advertising.

For further information contact:

Barbara Campbell, Sparks Tune-Up, 381 Brooks Rd., King of Prussia, PA 19406, 1-800-523-1180; in Pennsylvania: 1-800-331-4303

8. *The Business Services Industry*

Contents

Accounting and Financial

H & R Block, Inc.

Initial license fee: Refundable deposit
Royalties: 50% of first $5,000; then 30% of everything over
Advertising royalties: None
Minimum cash required: $1,500
Capital required: $1,500 to $3,000
Financing: None
Length of Contract: 5 years

In business since: 1946
Franchising since: 1958
Total number of units: 9,000
Number of company-operated units: 4,100
Total number of units planned, 1990: NA
Number of company-operated units planned, 1990: NA

Each year in late winter, as sure as death and taxes, the H & R Block commercials begin to appear on television. A comfort to many people who can't or don't want to deal with the rigors of wading through income tax forms, Block has carved a unique niche for itself in the U.S. economy. It prepares about 10% of all federal income tax returns filed, each with a written guarantee. In addition, it pledges to be available to answer questions from its customers year-round and to accompany them to an audit, if necessary, to explain how their taxes were calculated.

The company runs offices in major population areas and serves smaller communities through its satellite franchising program. If you think such a franchise would do well in your own area, or in a neighboring community, look in the phone book. If you can't find a listing for H & R Block, or if the company seems underrepresented relative to the population of your area, you may have the opportunity to start a good business.

You will need a thorough knowledge of taxes to operate this business. Your training takes place in the region where you will open your office. You will pay for the travel and lodging expenses related to your training. The company uses a variety of instructional techniques, including video and audio cassettes and role-playing, in addition to formal classroom instruction. Subjects covered include accounting, marketing, sales, staffing, and management. Your ongoing business will receive support from a regional office, and the company will update you with bulletins and other communications about any changes in the tax laws and company procedures. You can receive refresher training virtually any time at corporate headquarters and regional locations.

H & R Block supplies, without charge, everything necessary for you to run your operation, aside from the stationery and office machines usually found in an accounting office. As long as your office appearance meets the company's minimum standards, its specific location is up to you.

For further information contact:
Christopher Meck, Director of Franchise Operations, H & R Block, Inc., 4410 Main St., Kansas City, MO 64111, 816-753-6900

Marcoin Business Services

Initial license fee: $20,000
Royalties: 6.5% plus $100/month
Advertising royalties: 0.5%
Minimum cash required: $11,000
Capital required: $11,000 to $30,000
Financing: Available for part of the license fee
Length of contract: 15 years

In business since: 1952
Franchising since: 1956
Total number of units: 151
Number of company-operated units: 15
Total number of units planned, 1990: NA
Number of company-operated units planned, 1990: NA

It seems absurd for a business that is doing well to fail because of poor bookkeeping. But it happens. Many professionals and entrepreneurs simply don't keep track of what they do with their money, and when they realize something is wrong, they are already too deep in a financial morass to pull themselves out.

Some simple businesses can make it by having an accountant periodically go over their records. A larger company will have its own accounting and finance department. But millions of small businesses, too big to function with just the occasional visit from an accountant but not big enough for an accounting department, need the kind of services provided by Marcoin franchises.

As a Marcoin business management consultant, you will help small businesses with financial controls; sales, expense, and profit goals; monthly profit-and-loss statements; and tax planning. To adequately do this job, you should already have some expertise in taxes, and accounting, business management, or other finance experience.

The franchisor will train you for three weeks at its Atlanta headquarters and at field offices near your location. You pay for your travel expenses. Part of this training will involve actual experience in soliciting business. You will also create accounting reports from data supplied by a current company client. The classroom instruction includes advertising and public relations, client-prospecting techniques, personnel management, business organization. The company will also instruct you in the basics of your work for clients: processing and analyzing clients' data, record-keeping systems, payroll taxes, and counseling.

Follow-up training, important in this franchise, is required. By the end of your first year in business, you will have taken Marcoin's Advanced Financial Management Seminar, a five-day course concentrating on counseling and management techniques. In addition, franchisees must attend at least one national, regional, or district meeting a year at their own expense.

At your option, you can buy special computer software—written for the IBM PC—for processing your clients' financial information. Sometimes new businesses use the computer systems owned by other franchisees to process data. Marcoin has its own EDP department to refine the software and deal with any problems that come up.

The company's district manager spends a week with new franchisees at their locations, helping them to develop their lists of clients. Marcoin pays special attention to how its new units do in the first year, offering assistance when it seems called for. The company also helps you get your franchise under way with printed announcements of your new business, which you can send to prospective clients. At any time, you can tap the knowledge of Marcoin's Tax Advisory Service to help you over rough spots in your clients' taxes.

Marcoin franchisees do not have to buy any supplies from the company. However, the company does issue detailed specifications about the appearance of the forms you use, and you will need written permission to buy supplies from outside sources. Marcoin reserves the right to charge you a fee for the expenses it incurs in checking such outside suppliers.

For further information contact:
Franchise Department, Marcoin Business Services, 1924 Cliff Valley Way, Atlanta, GA 30329, 404-325-1200

Mifax Service and Systems, Inc.

Initial license fee: $16,340 for a Class I dealership; $22,150 for a Class II dealership
Royalties: None

Advertising royalties: None
Minimum cash required: $8,500
Capital required: $20,000 to $30,000
Financing: The company will finance part of the franchise fee with a two-year note; it also offers financing to hire salespeople.
Length of contract: Continuous

In business since: 1969
Franchising since: 1979
Total number of units: 68
Number of company-operated units: None
Total number of units planned, 1990: 100
Number of company-operated units planned, 1990: NA

Mifax is a franchised dealership through which you can sell health-care professionals a variety of pegboard posting and accounts receivable systems, microfilm billing statement services, and other forms and systems made by the Control-o-fax company. The franchise is exclusively for the sale of these products, and you will not be permitted to sell any other products or services in your business.

The market for these products has expanded rapidly in recent years. There are now over 400,000 doctors in America providing daily patient care (between 1963 and 1981, the number increased by about 75 percent). Since 1978 there has been an increase of approximately 75,000 physicians with office-based practices. Medicare, and the expansion of private insurance plans, have created a glut of paperwork for these doctors—and for the 126,000 dentists who treat 231 million patients annually—cutting into the time and attention they have available to practice medicine.

Control-o-fax has been making products to deal with doctor's administrative problems since 1948; today it is the leading manufacturer of these systems. Control-o-fax products help physicians keep records, improve their cash flow, and reduce their accounts receivable. In addition to those Control-o-fax items, Mifax Service and Systems also provides doctors and dentists with monthly financial statements and computerized management reports, as well as insurance, collection, and aged account reports.

James Firmender, a Mifax franchisee in Fairfield, Connecticut, had become familiar with Mifax while working at 3M and decided to buy a franchise. The people at Mifax, he had heard, had "a reputation of being hard-working, honest people."

Your own accounts receivable will also be simplified, since Mifax will bill your clients and then pay you. However, you will receive payment from the company when the clients are billed, not when they pay, so you will not risk suffering a cash flow crunch due to delinquent accounts.

The two franchise fees cover territories of different sizes. Class I territories contain fewer than 1.5 million people, while Class II covers all larger areas. There is a possibility that your territory will not be exclusive. Although no other franchisee can sell Control-o-fax products in your area, the Control-o-fax company has other distributors besides Mifax franchisees, and they are not necessarily bound by your franchise agreement. Control-o-fax also has its own retail outlets.

You will train to sell these products both at the Mifax headquarters in Waterloo, Iowa, and in your market area. Your training begins with a brief period of field training in your territory to get you oriented to the nature of your business. Then the company flies you to Iowa for a one-week sales seminar, covering products, sales, and knowledge of the market. You will spend an additional week in a sales management seminar, learning how to choose and train salespeople. Since a basic technique for increasing sales in this business is telephone marketing, you will also take a telemarketing seminar. All seminar work will be enhanced by video taping, which will show you how you might be perceived by a client.

Six months after you begin your business, you will take the second weeks of both the sales and sales management seminars, in which you will cover practical applications of sales techniques and the supervision and motivation of your salespeople. This training takes place in the field.

Mifax regional managers serve as business advisors to franchisees in the field. Managers also help you set up your office and make sales calls. Your regional manager will have responsibility for no more than twenty-five franchisees and will be available for consultation at any time.

All Mifax franchisees must buy or lease a Recordak RP-1 microfilm camera, which costs over four thousand dollars. You need the camera for the billing statement service you will sell.

For further information contact:

Deanne DeLange, Mifax Service and Systems, Inc., Box 5800, Waterloo, IA 50704, 319-234-4896

Money Concepts International, Inc.

Initial License Fee: $10,000
Royalties: 8% to 10%
Advertising royalties: 2%
Minimum cash required: $7,000
Capital required: $20,000 to $28,000

Financing: The company waives course fees for franchisees for full curriculum of financial-planning courses at its school.
Length of contract: Indefinite

In business since: 1979
Franchising since: 1982
Total number of units: 319
Number of company-operated units: 1
Total number of units planned, 1990: 2,113
Number of company-operated units planned, 1990: None

John P. Walsh got the idea for Money Concepts while serving as president of American Bankers Life. Financial planning was just hitting its stride as a growth industry. Clients wanted access to a wide variety of investment and insurance options, but, Walsh noticed, "agents were finding it difficult to compete with the financial supermarkets because they didn't have the resources to be all things to all people."

The company he started makes it possible for independent agents running their own businesses to compete with the financial behemoths. Franchised financial brokers have some weight behind them. "If I have a problem, I have a team of people to turn to for help," says David Gullidge, owner of the San Jose, California, Money Concepts franchise. "I don't have to spend a lot of time researching products or figuring out how to market them. I've got people working for me that I don't have to pay out of my own pocket."

The typical Money Concepts franchisee is an insurance or real estate agent, tax practitioner, or broker who might want to supplement an ongoing business or make a move into the world of entrepreneurship. Such a person has ambition and the willingness to work hard, but needs connections to extensive information resources, expertise, and experience.

Money Concepts appeals to entrepreneurs both because of its products and the method the company has developed to sell them. The products include a broad spectrum of insurance, mutual funds, real estate investments, and collectibles. Money Concepts, through its franchisees, can offer more than four hundred products from fifty different financial services.

You market the service through financial seminars on any one of about thirty topics, which you offer in your community. The company trains you in giving these scripted seminars and provides (at a cost) the audio-visual equipment needed to make them effective in cultivating clients who have small businesses.

Money Concepts prefers that its franchisees offer clients complete financial planning in an office that bespeaks professionalism. So when your level of business permits, the company suggests that you acquire a suite with a reception area, two executive offices for consultation, a computer center, and a seminar room. For use in your computer center, the company supplies special software for analyzing your clients' needs and options.

Money Concepts sells its franchises the same way its franchisees sell services to prospective clients: through a seminar. If you're interested in the company, it invites you to attend its day-long seminar in the area closest to where you live. You can also take Money Concept's three-day franchise implementation seminar before deciding whether to buy a franchise to get a feel for the operation. If you decide to buy, the seminar is free.

The company will train you at its North Palm Beach, Florida, headquarters, where you will undergo three days of intense instruction in the Money Concept business system and five days of operation and management training. Just as important, the company will expect you to continue your training once you open for business, preferably until you reach the level of Certified Financial Planner. Toward that end, you will take specialized courses in financial planning (no tuition for you) offered frequently at either North Palm Beach or a location in San Jose, whichever is more convenient for you.

For further information contact:
Jerry R. Darnell, Vice President, Franchise Acquisition, Money Concepts International, Inc., One Golden Bear Plaza, 11760 U.S. Highway One, North Palm Beach, FL 33408, 305-627-0700

National Financial Company

Initial license fee: $18,000
Royalties: Fee sharing
Advertising royalties: None
Minimum cash required: $18,000
Capital required: $18,000
Financing: None
Length of contract: 4 years

In business since: 1970
Franchising since: 1970
Total number of units: 101
Number of company-operated units: 1
Total number of units planned, 1990: 200
Number of company-operated units planned, 1990: None

Finding capital to finance a business venture can be as simple as using a computer dating service. Leonard vander Bie, formerly with the All-state Mortgage and Investment Company, borrowed the concept of using a computer to match two people who have not been able to find suitable dates and applied it to the search for investment capital. He assembled a data base of potential investors and lenders that people seeking capital may tap for a fee—and an additional commission if they find an investor or lender through his service.

The company's data base contains more than fifteen thousand sources of capital, with a description of the types of businesses they will consider funding. Investors and lenders include financial and insurance companies, pension funds, leasing companies, brokers, and others. Among the types of funds available are venture capital, accounts receivable, financing, purchase lease backs, mortgages, and start-up capital. Clients might be able to locate some of these sources on their own, but it would take a lot of time and money to track down possible sources and make a presentation to each.

Not only do entrepreneurs get access to possible sources of funding through a National Financial outlet, they also get the services of a financial consultant who will help them prepare a proposal, summarize it for computer matching, and then print and mail the proposal to investors whose interests match theirs.

The company emphasizes that typical clients have unusual investment proposals that have not attracted funding from banks, insurance companies, and other conventional sources. In fact, National Financial will not accept as a client anyone who has not exhausted ordinary sources first. Leonard vander Bie points out that since clients pay both a fee to the company and a commission, if successful, they should not use the service if they can secure funding in ordinary ways. "We are a court of last resort," says vander Bie, "and if a client has a good idea, but is unsophisticated, about financial matters, he would be angry if we charged him all these fees and then found he could have gotten the money for less from a more conventional source."

The company is careful to make sure clients realize that, at best, they might get about eight positive responses to their proposal, which only means that an investor or lender wants to hear more and will at least consider it. More often than not, they get no response. But at least this gives the client the satisfaction that they have tried every last possibility. As the company puts it: "Give the capital source a chance to say no."

Getting into this business, if you have "a well-rounded business background" and the money to invest, is as simple as the concept that underlies the enterprise. National Financial Company will train you for three days at your office, which could be in your home. You train hands-on, working with actual clients who need to find lenders or investors. And any additional help you may need at any time is available by phone from National Financial Company.

For further information contact:
Leonard H. vander Bie, National Financial Company, 7332 Caverna Drive, Hollywood, CA 90068, 213-856-0100

Advertising

Homes & Land Publishing Corporation

Initial license fee: $7,500
Royalties: 6% to 9%
Advertising royalties: None
Minimum cash required: $7,600
Capital required: $7,600
Financing: None
Length of contract: 10 years

In business since: 1973
Franchising since: 1984
Total number of units: 208
Number of company-operated units: None
Total number of units planned, 1990: NA
Number of company-operated units planned, 1990: None

In the real estate boom of the 1980s, people have found scores of ways to make money from the buying and selling of buildings and land, often by investing "other people's money." The bookstores feature many how-to titles on the subject, and late-night TV runs countless advertisements for audio cassette courses that teach people to become real estate millionaires.

Of course, many people still make a living in this field the old-fashioned way—they earn it by working as real estate agents and brokers. Now, Homes & Land Publishing Corporation provides still another way an ambitious person can make it in real estate—with a little hard work. You can publish one of those real estate magazines given away in banks, supermarkets, restaurants, and other public places. The magazine contains listings from local brokers, with photographs of the houses that are for sale. There are about ten such multiregional magazines currently in circulation, but *Homes & Land Magazine* is the biggest, with local editions in more than one hundred eighty locations in thirty states.

Homes & Land Publishing Corporation calls its franchisees associate publishers—a fancy title for real estate advertising salespeople. Your work involves convincing brokers in your community to place their listings in the local edition of *Homes & Land*. Usually, real estate brokers rely on newspaper advertising, on-site signs, referrals, and a multiple listing service to get listings and make sales. The company therefore has to provide its associate publishers with good arguments to use in convincing brokers to place their advertisements in its magazine.

According to the franchisor, people who want to sell their home are more likely to list with a broker who advertises in the magazine because people like to see a picture of their house in an advertisement. The magazine sweetens this appeal with an offer to brokers to photograph houses if they don't have good pictures. People also tend to retain the magazine longer than a newspaper, and there is thus more time for them to react to an advertisement—perhaps having second thoughts about a house they initially passed up.

Franchisees selling advertisements can offer brokers another special service. The magazine lists the locations of its other local editions. A reader thinking of moving to one of these places can call a toll-free number listed in the magazine to get a free copy of the publication in that area. Thus local brokers who advertise can reach a potential buyer in another town. In addition, brokers in the communities from which people have called receive the names of those people. People thinking of moving may have a house to sell, and the broker in their area can use this as a lead for new listings.

Who qualifies to be a Homes & Land associate publisher? "They are established, participating residents of their communities and bring with them a successful record of growth and productivity in other facets of business," according to company president W. R. "Jerry" Lunquist. And they have a "strong desire to be independent." Currently, the prospect for openings is best in the upper Midwest.

Franchisees must go to Tallahassee, Florida, for their training. You pay for your own transportation, but the company will pick up part of the expense for your lodging. Training lasts a week and includes instruction on photographing houses, as well as sales training and a tour of the company's facilities. Annual sales meetings include follow-up sales training. District sales managers act as liaisons between the company and its associate publishers, providing ongoing support for franchisees.

For further information contact:

Ken Ledford, Vice President, Sales, Homes & Land Publishing Corporation, P.O. Box 13409, Tallahassee, FL 32317, 904-385-3310

TV Focus, Inc.

Initial license fee: $2,500
Royalties: $90 to $250/week
Advertising royalties: None
Minimum cash required: $5,000
Capital required: $2,500 to $7,500
Financing: None
Length of contract: 25 years

In business since: 1980
Franchising since: 1980
Total number of units: 190
Number of company-operated units: None
Total number of units planned, 1990: 300
Number of company-operated units planned, 1990: None

Owning a *TV Focus* franchise, even though it is one of the simpler and less expensive franchises to start, would nevertheless require you to work as hard as you would in any other business to achieve success. The work involves publishing a free local TV listings magazine—a product that has only existed for about fifteen years. You would devote most of your energies to selling spare advertising in the magazine, as advertising serves as your only source of profits. But your responsibilities would also include distributing copies of the publication to the banks, supermarkets, apartment buildings, and variety stores that permit you to leave it for consumers to pick up. The company prints the magazine and ships it to you (you pay for shipping) ready for distribution: You don't take an active role in producing and printing the publication. But you pay for the company's services, so you must sell enough advertising space to cover the cost of the publication plus the company's royalty fee—and still make a profit.

TV Focus blends gossip and recipe columns, interesting facts, horoscopes, crossword puzzles, and similar features with local broadcast and cable TV listings. The remainder of the magazine consists of advertising from major retail chains and other businesses, as well as small local operations. Toyota, Burger King, Panasonic, London Fog, Sony, Simmons, Goodyear, and RCA are among those who have advertised in *TV Focus*.

When you apply for the franchise, you must pay a fee of fifty dollars to cover market research, which will determine the feasibility of publishing *TV Focus* in your area. If you buy the business, the company credits this amount toward your franchise fee, but refunds it if you don't. They say they do this to avoid frivolous applications. The market study takes only a week, and if everything goes well, you could start your business a month after you sign the franchise agreement.

You need neither previous experience nor special equipment—other than a car and telephone—to open this business. The company requires no formal training program, but it does send you a manual that covers every aspect of the operation. Topics covered in the manual include recruiting salespeople, telephone sales, credit and collections, and selecting distribution points. For help with specific problems, you call the company's hotline number.

You can operate this business part-time, by yourself or with a staff, and it does not require an office other than space in your home. You can purchase forms for bookkeeping, invoicing, and other purposes from the company.

For further information contact:
Louis C. Fernandez, Publisher, TV Focus, Inc., P.O. Box 133, One Anderson Ave., Fairview, NJ 07022, 201-945-2800

Consulting and Brokerage

Corporate Investment Business Brokers, Inc.

Initial license fee: $22,500 to $35,000
Royalties: 6%
Advertising royalties: 2%
Minimum cash required: $50,000
Capital required: $80,000
Financing: The company will finance a portion of the franchise fee.
Length of contract: 10 years

In business since: 1979
Franchising since: 1982
Total number of units: 169
Number of company-operated units: None
Total number of units planned, 1990: 400
Number of company-operated units planned, 1990: None

"Never in my entire life have I made more money," says Michael Webster, a Corporate Investment Business Brokers franchisee in Las Vegas, Nevada. He read about CIBB in an airline magazine and "became intrigued with the idea of selling businesses." Today, just a few years later, he's happy he took that flight and happier still that he took the risk of becoming his own boss. "My CIBB franchise has been an excellent investment."

CIBB is a franchisor of business brokerage firms that specialize in brokering the sales of companies offered for $50,000 to $10 million.

Other divisions of the company focus on mergers and acquisitions, franchise development, and insurance, providing additional profit centers to franchisees.

CIBB prepares you to manage your own business brokerage firm with two weeks of classroom training at its Phoenix, Arizona, headquarters. Initial training in business brokerage techniques and management is "very strong, very helpful," according to Michael Webster. "They even came to Las Vegas to give me on-site training." CIBB provides all franchisees with preopening assistance at their locations, which it follows up with bimonthly refreshers in management and problem solving, also at the franchisee's location. The company will give you constant updates on brokerage techniques, tax laws, and other economic developments that affect your business, and will supply training tapes for you and your staff. In addition, CIBB publishes listings that you can use to find your clients the business prospects they're looking for.

Michael Webster is happy he decided on a CIBB franchise. "In order to set up my own business brokerage firm, I would have had to stumble around for three or four years. But CIBB gives me full support. I recommend it highly."

For further information contact:
Patrick McHenry, Corporate Investment Business Brokers, Inc., 1515 East Missouri Ave., Phoenix, AZ 85014, 1-800-382-8240

General Business Services, Inc.

Initial license fee: $24,500
Royalties: 7%
Advertising royalties: None
Minimum cash required: 3 to 6 months of living expenses
Capital required: See minimum cash required.
Financing: Some financing possible
Length of contract: 5 years

In business since: 1962
Franchising since: 1962
Total number of units: 700
Number of company-operated units: None
Total number of units planned, 1990: 1,260
Number of company-operated units planned, 1990: None

Do the more than 17 million small businesses in this country need business counseling? The ones that survive their first eighteen months in business—and only half of those who start a small business make it that far—probably do. The other half definitely needed it.

It's hard enough for a new business to attract and please customers. But many small businesses go under simply because they can't negotiate the paperwork—legally required records that deal with a multitude of details, from sales income and cash to credit and personnel. Failure to do this adequately, according to the U.S. Small Business Administration, causes many businesses to flounder.

General Business Services, through its franchised counselors, offers small businesses a complete package of services and advice to help them prosper. GBS counselors provide clients with organized financial records and profit development counseling as well as tax planning. They help their clients formulate a business plan and project cash flow, show them how they stack up against the competition, and guide them toward making budget projections. GBS counselors help clients with the big things, such as determining goals and priorities, but if necessary, they will also help with details such as showing clients how to keep accurate books.

As a GBS counselor you will most likely service such businesses as owner-operated enterprises and professional offices with twenty-five or fewer employees and no more than $1 million in gross sales. The top ten GBS client categories, in descending order of sales volume, are: auto repair, food, general contractors, restaurants, automotive, furniture/home furnishings, manufacturing, doctors, printers, and beauty shops.

GBS counselors often begin by working out of their homes, opening an office only when cash flow permits, so a GBS franchise requires a relatively small initial investment. Franchisees usually have a college degree. Typically, GBS counselors have finance, management, or sales experience. They also get along well with people.

Your introductory training will be just the start of an intensive, ongoing effort by the company to teach you what you need to know. You will receive your basic training at national headquarters in Rockville, Maryland. For the first three months of your business, a company representative will give you field training as you begin to learn from experience. Then you will return to Rockville for advanced training. In all, you will spend thirty days of your first year as a business consultant in company training. You can also take advanced seminars, offered frequently throughout the year, to improve your skills.

Your clients pay you for the services you render, and you pay GBS when these services involve tapping the company's resources. Available company resources include the Advisory Research Service, which offers advice on incorporation. The Tax Preparation Service—staffed by specialists in all tax fields—will do all of your clients' taxes and guarantees its work for accuracy. Your clients will also receive *Washington Alert*, the company's tax newsletter.

You can also offer complete record-keeping systems customized to your clients' needs, whether they require a simple manual system or full automation through GBS' computer service bureau. That bureau will also give you recommendations to pass along to your clients concerning computer hardware and software that could be helpful.

GBS directly serves you with a monthly billing service for your clients, a lending library of materials dealing with various business topics, and specialists whom you can hire by the day to help with particularly difficult problems.

How does all this work in practice? W. Paul Woody has been a GBS franchisee in Oklahoma City since 1972. He counts on GBS to help him give tax advice: "I do a lot of research for my small business clients. That is, they will ask me to check into how to handle a particular tax strategy, and I will go to GBS, Inc., for their output. This is very helpful because it allows me to give the correct answers to my clients without having to 'shoot from the hip.'"

W. Paul Woody has already renewed his franchise twice. He says he "could never have earned the kind of income I am generating today if I had remained with the large company I was employed by when I purchased the franchise. And the independence, along with the excellent earnings potential, has allowed me to spend more time either on vacations or being active with my family."

Howard Marco is a GBS counselor in Shawnee Mission, Kansas. After eleven years with the company, he says he's "done quite well." "Without the support of the company and its franchisees, I believe that I would not have made it."

For further information contact:
Marketing Department, General Business Services, Inc., 20271 Goldenrod Lane, Germantown, MD 20874-4090, 1-800-638-7940

Direct Mail Marketing

American Advertising Distributors, Inc.

Initial license fee: $19,500 to $34,500
Royalties: $163/$10,000
Advertising royalties: None

Minimum cash required: $10,000
Capital required: $10,000 to $50,000
Financing: None
Length of contract: 10 years

In business since: 1975
Franchising since: 1977
Total number of units: 92
Number of company-operated units: 2
Total number of units planned, 1990: 156
Number of company-operated units planned, 1990: 6

Since its birth just ten years ago, local cooperative direct mail marketing has rapidly grown to a $60 million dollar industry, and 46.6 percent of leading retailers consider direct mail the best medium for target marketing. Over 150 billion advertising coupons are mailed each year. American Advertising Distributors, Inc., mails 1 million of those coupons each week and is looking for ambitious entrepreneurs throughout the U.S. to help its cooperative direct mail program grow.

AAD franchisees operate their own advertising agencies specializing in direct mail. Each franchisee has an exclusive territory of about eighty thousand households plus all of the businesses in that area. They sell the AAD direct mail service to businesses and coordinate with the AAD home office in mailing their clients' advertising coupons to households in their region. Because AAD charges a flat-fee royalty per envelope mailed, franchisees can make mailings highly profitable by including more clients' coupons in each envelope.

Many businesses—particularly smaller local businesses—have found that direct mail marketing, in which they include a coupon advertising their services in mailings with other advertisers' coupons, is one of the most effective and least expensive means of advertising. Rural areas, suburban regions, and large cities are fertile markets for direct mail advertising services.

As an AAD franchisee, you will receive four weeks of start-up training, all expenses paid. For the first two weeks you will be at the AAD home office in Mesa, Arizona, where you will learn management and administration, sales techniques, and production, as well as being introduced to the company's corporate staff and plant production system. Following this period of classroom instruction, you receive on-the-job training at an existing AAD franchise, where you will learn sales prospecting, presentation and closing techniques, and day-to-day operations. The fourth week of your training consists of working in your own territory with an AAD field-training specialist, who will help you get your business running.

Once an AAD franchisee himself, Vice President of Sales John D.

Alig believes in the importance of networking among AAD owners as a part of AAD's ongoing franchisee support system: "I ask all of the more experienced franchisees to seek out the new franchisees to welcome them and offer their assistance." You will also receive assistance in the form of standardized office supplies, sales aids, sample materials, price schedules, and training manuals supplied by AAD. Specially designed AAD profit analysis forms, which allow you to show prospective clients the sales and profit results AAD can have on their businesses, are a valuable selling tool. And home office target marketing studies and marketing analysis reports can help you evaluate opportunities in your region and find the most profitable prospects.

AAD's Franchise Sales and Service Division produces a number of newsletters and promotional programs, as well as providing national account coordination and health insurance. Twice a year each of the five U.S. AAD regions holds sales seminars to give franchisees an opportunity to share ideas, problems, and successes. The annual national convention provides a forum to review the past year, meet with other AAD owners from across the country, and learn about industry developments and new marketing tools and techniques. Between seminars, you can get help with anything relating to your business through the company's toll-free WATS line.

Essential to your success as an AAD franchisee are your own dedication, enthusiasm, self-motivation, and ability to develop accounts. Though the home office and other AAD owners will assist you in every way possible, your own ability to sell AAD's direct mail advertising services will determine the profitability of your business

For further information contact:
John D. Alig, Vice President, Sales, American Advertising Distributors, Inc., P.O. Box AAD 16964, Mesa, AZ 85201, 1-800-528-8249

Money Mailer, Inc.

Initial license fee: $15,000 to $150,000
Royalties: None
Advertising royalties: None
Minimum cash required: $4,500
Capital required: $17,000 to $200,000
Financing: Available
Length of contract: Perpetual

In business since: 1979
Franchising since: 1979
Total number of units: 102

Number of company-operated units: None
Total number of units planned, 1990: 265
Number of company-operated units planned, 1990: None

Direct mail advertising has grown faster than the American economy in the past decade, and Money Mailer feels it is well positioned to take advantage of this growth industry. The company itself has been growing at the rate of 200 percent a year, and now has a client base of 20,000 advertisers, for whom it delivers about 200 million pieces a year. In 1984 and 1985 *Entrepreneur* magazine rated Money Mailer the number-one direct mail franchise. Money Mailer's president, Kris O. Friedrich, says that his company "will soon be the largest direct mail marketing company in the nation."

Money Mailer mails packages of discount coupons to local consumers about six times a year. An A. C. Nielsen survey reported that 72 percent of people who received coupons in the mail used them, a powerful argument that Money Mailer's franchisees emphasize when persuading clients to include their coupons in the program. Local merchants provide much of Money Mailer's business, but nationwide companies have also participated in these mailings. Major accounts have included BFGoodrich, Burger King, Fotomat, McDonald's, Pizza Hut, Shell Oil, Taco Bell, and Volkswagen.

The company is organized in a three-tiered structure. Franchisees like you form the basis of the operation, selling the company's advertising service to businesses in your area. The franchise fee is based on the number of mailable addresses in your area. For an area with a population of 30,000 to 40,000, the fee falls at the low end of the range. At the next level is a regional franchisor, whose territory covers a minimum of 180,000 homes and who is responsible for overseeing franchisee operations within his or her territory. The regional franchise fee is also based on the number of mailable addresses in the territory. The company itself occupies the third tier of the organization.

You will identify your prospective clients using several resources, including the yellow pages and various business publications. By showing potential customers samples of coupons prepared for other companies in the same business as theirs, and by pointing out in your presentation that the cost of doing their own mailing could be as much as six times greater than the amount Money Mailer charges, you can sell your service to a substantial number of clients.

Using an Apple Macintosh personal computer, which you must either lease or buy, you will then design a coupon for your client based on the information the client gave you during your sales presentation. This task is easier than it sounds. With Money Mailer's special design software and the Macintosh's "mouse," a device that literally permits you to point to what you want the computer to do, you can design the coupon and store the design on a diskette. Then you will send the diskette to your regional franchisor, who uses a laser printer to run off a proof of the coupon. You get back the proof, show it to the client to secure final approval, and send the design to Money Mailer in California, where the coupons are printed and mailed.

Money Mailer's training program lasts three weeks. In the first week, you will work with your regional franchisor, receiving an introduction to the business. The second week takes place at corporate headquarters in Huntington Beach, California, where through role-playing and hands-on computer study, as well as classroom lectures, you will learn management, accounting, product preparation, merchandising, sales techniques, and marketing and advertising. During the third week, you will apply what you've learned in an ongoing Money Mailer operation either near corporate headquarters or in your own region.

The company keeps franchisees up to date on new products and methods through printed materials, and offers refresher training through field courses, in addition to formal classes at its headquarters. Your regional franchisor will act as your liaison with Money Mailer, consulting with you and helping you with such matters as sales training and computer output design. Regional franchisors also conduct periodic meetings of franchisees in their regions.

You can operate your Money Mailer franchise from your home using the supplies you receive in your franchise package, which you can reorder through Money Mailer.

For further information contact:
Money Mailer, Inc., 15472 Chemical Lane, Huntington Beach, CA 92649, 1-800-MAILER-1; in California: 714-898-9111; in Oregon: 619-437-1651

TriMark Publishing Company, Inc.

Initial license fee: $24,900
Royalties: None
Advertising royalties: None
Minimum cash required: $7,000
Capital required: $7,000
Financing: None
Length of contract: No set term

In business since: 1969
Franchising since: 1978
Total number of units: 96

Number of company-operated units: None
Total number of units planned, 1990: 200
Number of company-operated units planned, 1990: None

TriMark, a direct mail marketer specializing in cooperative direct mail programs, sent 184 million advertising coupons to 27 million households in 1985. As a franchisee, you sell the company's services to businesses in your territory, which pay to have their advertising coupons inserted in the semimonthly mailings, and you keep a percentage of the billing.

You can also solicit orders for business-to-business mailings and custom solo mailings for companies that do not want its messages mixed with those of other firms. And you can sell mailings that extend beyond your exclusive franchise territory. TriMark also pursues national accounts, and franchisees benefit when coupons from national advertisers go out in their mailings.

"They make their money after we make ours," says Harold E. Kinch, a Colorado franchisee, referring to his satisfaction with the company's franchise operation. The lowest franchise fee buys you the rights to a territory with up to 150,000 mailable homes (low-income families are excluded from the count). The fee rises with the size of the territory, reaching $33,900 for an area with 251,000 to 300,000 mailable homes.

Your training consists of a week of classes at company headquarters in Wilmington, Delaware, where you study mailing cycles, office setup, advertising copy and layout, business planning and management, sales, personnel recruiting, bookkeeping, and promotion. You also receive audio cassettes summarizing all aspects of your operations. In addition, a TriMark representative will spend a week giving you on-the-job training in your own territory. This help includes accompanying you to your first sales presentations and constructively critiquing your technique. Frequent memos and newsletters keep you current on the latest marketing information, and the annual convention allows you to communicate directly with other franchisees and company officers.

TriMark will supply you with customized computer software for accounting and office tasks like word processing, in addition to software that will assist you in laying out customer advertising coupons and transmitting them to headquarters. You also receive a supply of stationery and contract and invoice forms.

The company helps get you started with a mailing to 1,000 businesses in your territory. It will also give you an additional 4,000 names, printed on labels, for your own mailing after you follow up on the first 1,000. Further, to make sure you don't encounter a cash flow crisis in the early days of your business, TriMark does not charge you for your first mailing of 20,000 pieces to the homes in your area (you pay for postage), permitting you to retain the entire billing.

For further information contact:
Franchise Sales Director, TriMark Publishing Company, Inc., P.O. Box 10530, Wilmington, DE 19850-0530, 302-322-2143

Miscellaneous

Chroma International

Initial license fee: $5,000
Royalties: 5%; with a minimum of $100/month
Advertising royalties: 2%
Minimum cash required: $16,000
Capital required: $16,000 to $18,000
Financing: None
Length of contract: 10 years

In business since: 1983
Franchising since: 1983
Total number of units: 77
Number of company-operated units: 1
Total number of units planned, 1990: 220
Number of company-operated units planned, 1990: 2

Success in their careers is a priority for millions of people. As competition in the business world grows fiercer each year, an entire industry has developed to help people gain the edge they need to get ahead: the consulting industry, which includes businesses that teach everything from how to interview for a job, to how to negotiate for a raise, to how to dress for success. CHROMA International provides image-consulting services to businesses and individuals concerned with enhancing their own personal appearance or that of their employees.

First impressions play as important a role—perhaps even more important—in business as they do in personal life, and physical appearance has been shown to play the most significant part in people's reactions to one another. CHROMA has developed a complete system of visual image classifications that its consultants use to advise clients on how to improve dress and grooming. CHROMA consultants tailor recommendations to meet clients' personal and professional needs and objectives—to enhance an individual's self-esteem, productivity, promotability, and, ultimately, income. In addition to consulting,

CHROMA franchisees offer services like personal shopping, wardrobe reconstruction, and appearance seminars for businesses and civic organizations. The company also offers clients an expanding line of clothing and accessories.

CHROMA requires all new franchisees to attend fourteen days of training at its Salt Lake City, Utah, office. "CHROMA training is very professionally done, and it is quite intensive," recalls Zelda Wade, a CHROMA franchisee in Los Alamos, New Mexico. Working with up to eight client-models, you will gain valuable experience in color analysis, wardrobe planning, and reading the messages that physical appearance projects. In seminars you will learn clothing, fashion, and marketing skills. Your initial training includes materials that you will use in your operations, and an advertising kit. CHROMA also provides you with a step-by-step program for developing your client base.

"Providing the CHROMA service takes a lot more initiative than just opening the doors to a store," says franchisee Jillaine Hadfield of Salt Lake City. To help your motivation pay off, the company will contribute all of its experience and know-how to your business. Zelda Wade finds it "very helpful to be able to make a phone call and have any questions answered." Each month CHROMA publishes a newsletter filled with suggestions from the field (which the company welcomes), sales and marketing tips, advertising ideas, discussions of policy and procedure topics, and a calendar of events.

The company's annual UpDate seminar, which Jillaine Hadfield calls "very useful" and Zelda Wade cites as "essential," is made up of workshops on the year's theme topic and plenary sessions covering new techniques developed by CHROMA's research and development team. You will learn about current and upcoming fashion trends and hear ideas top-producing franchisees have developed in the field. Throughout the year, you can attend any refresher courses that you feel would be useful to you as a franchisee.

Most of your business supplies will be available only through CHROMA, but you may purchase supplies from other sources if they meet the company's standards. Because you will conduct most of your business at clients' locations, you can establish your office anywhere that fits the CHROMA image. Some franchisees operate out of their homes.

Both Jillaine Hadfield and Zelda Wade note that a CHROMA franchise is a people-oriented business. "You need good people skills, which some people have and some people don't," says Jillaine Hadfield. Also essential to a successful CHROMA franchise, according to both consultants, are your personal marketing skills. If you have a talent for both marketing and human interaction, a CHROMA franchise could offer you the right opportunity, like it has Zelda Wade: "I like having the tools to help people change their lives. I have access to terrific materials that I could never develop on my own. I like belonging to the group and enjoy learning from the other consultants. I couldn't ask to work with better people.

For further information contact:
Marlene B. Jones, CHROMA International, Suite 300, 5 Triad Center, Salt Lake City, UT 84180, 801-575-6556

*ISU International

Initial license fee: $3,000
Royalties: $300/month
Advertising royalties: $500/month
Minimum cash required: $10,000
Capital required: $10,000
Financing: None
Length of contract: 1 year

In business since: 1979
Franchising since: 1980
Total number of units: 465
Number of company-operated units: None
Total number of units planned, 1990: 2,000
Number of company-operated units planned, 1990: 1,000

"They're all over the country," a Citibank executive once said about Merrill Lynch, "they're aggressive, and they've got the smarts." Merrill Lynch has a substantial investment in *ISU, a conversion franchisor for independent insurance agents. In fact, on the board of directors of *ISU are: Harry B. Anderson, former vice chairman of the board at Merrill Lynch; David E. Rosenthal, Merrill Lynch vice president and director of corporate development; and Dennis J. Hess, Merrill Lynch's director of individual investor's services and a senior vice president.

The incentive for converting your present insurance business to an *ISU franchise, of course, is that there is strength in numbers. But by emphasizing its ties to Merrill Lynch, *ISU says something more: There's strength in experience. Add to that *ISU's program of national advertising on television and in the print media, and you have a strong enticement to surrender a little independence for some good connections.

It stands to reason that you can secure a bigger slice of the $250 billion insurance market if you have more to offer your clients, and through *ISU, you will have more insurance products to offer than other independents or "captive" agents. You can offer these products by using *ISU's Network Brokerage and computerized AnswerLine system. Access to these services will enable you to customize insurance policies to any client's needs, no matter what type of business he or she may be in.

The company requires its franchisees to have an "impeccable reputation" in their current insurance business. If you qualify, the company will train you at a regional location, for a modest fee, in its exclusive *ISU/1084 sales and marketing system. *ISU presents the system, consisting of seven training modules, in seminars supplemented by self-study courses based on printed material and audio tapes. Both you and your sales staff will benefit from this training, according to *ISU. In fact, the company feels that training the sales staff of an independent agency is the single most valuable contribution it makes to that business, since independent agents usually don't have the time to train their own sales personnel thoroughly. The company will keep you up to date on new products and services through the same training methods.

Once you are a franchisee, *ISU maintains an 800 number for consultation on any matter related to the services it offers.

Although *ISU is currently selling conversion franchises only, in the future it may add a full business format franchise for those wishing to open their first insurance agency.

For further information contact:
Mark Lefenfeld, *ISU International, 633 Battery St., Suite 450, San Francisco, CA 94111, 415-788-9810

Video Data Services

Initial license fee: $14,950
Royalties: $500/year
Advertising royalties: None
Minimum cash required: $16,950
Capital required: $16,950
Financing: None
Length of contract: 10 years

In business since: 1980
Franchising since: 1981
Total number of units: 142
Number of company-operated units: 2
Total number of units planned, 1990: 600
Number of company-operated units planned, 1990: NA

Video Data provides many of the same services professional photographers sold in the past, replacing still photography with video taping. Currently, law firms and insurance companies provide the most business for these franchises. Lawyers often need a taped statement from an out-of-town witness. Video data franchisees can make the tape and then edit out any portions of the testimony a judge would not want the jury to hear. Insurance companies hire franchisees to inventory property. Additionally, many people add a video tape to their will. A tape cannot take the place of a written will, but it can give them the chance to tell survivors a thing or two after their death.

The company constantly comes up with new ideas for drumming up business, and franchisees share their own ideas on developing new markets through Video Data Services publications. Among new markets recently suggested are corporate seminars, store promotions, body builder shows, and beauty pageants. Weddings provide steady business; some people even pay to have the funeral of a loved one taped.

You don't need any experience in the field. Most people begin on a part-time basis, using their home as an office. Many franchisees are retired people seeking a part-time business. Your franchise fee pays for the half-inch industrial-grade VCR, camera, color monitor, lights, and editing equipment. You will need an extra VCR to make copies. Because Video Data Services began as a company that sold video equipment and continues in that business, it can provide you with supplementary equipment at bargain prices. The company even makes it possible for you to sell VCRs in your community at prices that undercut even discount stores.

Your franchise will cover a territory with a population of about one hundred thousand. The company has no rules regarding your office or the purchase of supplies. You—and one other person, if you wish—can receive your required training in either Rochester, NY, or San Diego, CA. You bear the expense of travel and lodging for the three-day session, which covers all you need to know about the business. Should you need a refresher in this intensive course, the company invites you back for another session. Shirley Porter, a Video Data Services franchisee in Bloomfield Hills, Michigan, took advantage of the offer, and she found it "a real strong point" of the company.

Frequent company newsletters and the annual meeting keep you up to date on the latest technical and business information in the field. Video Data Services will also advise you on specific problems. "The home office has been very supportive," notes Shirley Porter. "They always answer any technical questions that I have." And yet, "they take no active role in managing my company, which is the way I want it."

Video Data Services emphasizes direct mail marketing as a way of bringing in new business. It runs frequent cooperative advertising programs with franchisees, stressing the systematic development of vertical markets, such as legal firms, rather than the scatter approach of going after every type of customer at once.

For further information contact:
Stuart J. Dizak, Video Data Services, 24 Grove St., Pittsford, NY 14534, 716-385-4773

Postal and Shipping

Mail Boxes Etc. USA

Initial license fee: $15,000
Royalties: 5%
Advertising royalties: 2%
Minimum cash required: $50,000
Capital required: $50,000 to $65,000
Financing: The company leases certain equipment to franchisees at terms varying with interest rates.
Length of contract: NA

In business since: 1980
Franchising since: 1980
Total number of units: 205
Number of company-operated units: None
Total number of units planned, 1990: NA
Number of company-operated units planned, 1990: NA

An all-cash business involving a moderate investment and a small inventory, tapping both the consumer and small business markets, is something to look into. *Venture* rated Mail Boxes Etc. USA, a convenience business, forty-sixth among the most profitable franchises in America and thirty-fourth among the fastest growing in 1985.

Mail Boxes Etc. began simply as a store offering mail box rentals—which it still does—with twenty-four-hour access. Gradually, it added ancillary services related to personal and business communication. Today, businesses can secure a mailing address with a street and suite number, not just a P.O. number, and receive information by phone about whether mail has accumulated in the box. When customers come for their mail, they can also buy postage stamps (and, for that matter, rubber stamps) and mail letters and packages via several carriers, including UPS, Purolator Courier, and Federal Express, all in one place. Mail Boxes Etc. will even help the customer decide which carrier to use and will, for a small fee, pack the item to be shipped. The stores also offer facsimile transmission, and they can send Western Union telegrams, cablegrams, telex messages, and mailgrams.

Mail Boxes Etc. will even play the role of office temp for a small business, taking telephone messages and doing typing, word processing, filing, and similar tasks. The stores will also take passport photos, make keys, process film, and have flowers delivered anywhere in the country. This enterprise has already test-marketed these services for you, and the combination apparently works. Mail Boxes Etc. will teach you how to make it work for you as a franchisee. At its corporate headquarters in San Diego, you will spend five days in the classroom and five days in an operating store learning the company system. Once in business, you can get any help you may need from the company simply by calling, twenty-four hours a day.

Mail Boxes Etc. works with you to choose and secure a good lease for the right location for your business and will custom design your space (usually about one thousand square feet) for maximum efficiency and attractiveness. The company's in-house advertising and public relations agency can supply you with any kind of material you need to promote your business, and the company will also arrange cooperative advertising.

Other advantages to a Mail Boxes Etc. USA, franchise are the help you get when setting up accounts with the various carriers you will use and use of company accounting forms, which, Mail Boxes Etc. says, will reduce your paperwork. In addition, Mail Boxes Etc. offers you discounts through its volume purchasing of equipment and supplies.

The company also sells area rights, or subfranchises. These franchises grant you a territory in which you sell franchises to others and take responsibility for training and supporting those franchisees. In return, you keep a percentage of the new franchisee's licensing fee and the royalties they pay to the company. However, you must sell a specified number of franchises within your territory according to a schedule or else you will lose that territory and part of your investment.

For further information contact:
Mail Boxes Etc. USA, 5555 Oberlin Drive, San Diego, CA 92121, 619-452-1553

Packy the Shipper

Initial license fee: $995
Royalties: $.50/package
Advertising royalties: Co-op; the company matches you at rate of $.05/package shipped.

Minimum cash required: $995
Capital required: $995 to $1,295
Financing: None
Length of contract: Perpetual

In business since: 1976
Franchising since: 1981
Total number of units: 800
Number of company-operated units: None
Total number of units planned, 1990: 3,500
Number of company-operated units planned, 1990: None

"Our store had a very bad reputation prior to our takeover," Jerry Breen says of his hardware business in Lowville, New York. "Changing the attitudes and buying habits of the customers was hard. Packy helped us from the first day we had it. Our Christmas sales were the largest out of the fourteen Sentry Hardware Stores in our district. We attribute the success to Packy the Shipper. . . ."

The originators of Packy—a subsidiary of PNS, Inc.—spotted a customer need and figured out a way to fill it cheaply and conveniently. UPS, the best way to ship packages, gears its service to the needs of commercial shippers of large numbers of packages. The customer who wants to send a gift, or even an occasional business item, has to find an appropriate carton, pack the item, and then locate a UPS office—a time-consuming and inconvenient procedure for many people.

The Packy solution, the installation of a shipping service at locations that people frequent in their everyday activities, offers the customer the option of having a franchisee pack their object for a small fee and arrange to have it shipped by UPS. For the store owner who actually runs the service, Packy offers a small business on the side that generates traffic yet requires little space and relatively little time and attention. According to the company, almost 18 percent of customers who use Packy the Shipper had not previously patronized the store providing the service, and about 44 percent of all customers buy something else while in the store to ship a package.

Packy even handles the onerous paperwork involved in a shipping operation. "Their program takes out all the hassle involved with customer complaints regarding damages and/or tracers," claims Sharon Wassberg, who runs a hardware store in Manitowoc, Wisconsin. "All we need to do is take down the information and pass it on to them; they handle it from there. The customer is always satisfied."

Packy means to spell convenience for its franchisees as well as for its customers. The company audits and pays shipper's bills, insures packages at no expense to the franchisee, absorbs UPS wrong address charges and the charge for a weekly pickup. It also takes care of Interstate Commerce Commission paperwork.

Don't worry about the training either. The company comes to you at your convenience and takes less than two hours to teach you how to pack and ship. The cartons come from your own inventory—the cartons that your regular store stock came in. "I trained our store manager in half an hour," says Jerry Breen. "I watched him do a few, and that was it."

If a problem should come up, it won't get out of hand because "support is just an 800 number away," notes Jerry Breen. "All questions are always answered, even if it means a visit from a representative who lives 350 miles away."

You purchase sales contracts and shipping labels from the company. Packy also offers an optional scale at a discount.

For further information contact:
R. W. Harrisson, President, PNS, Inc., 409 Main St., Racine, WI 53403, 414-633-9540

Pilot Air Freight

Initial license fee: $10,000 to $30,000
Royalties: 13%
Advertising royalties: 1%
Minimum cash required: $25,000
Capital required: $30,000 to $50,000
Financing: None
Length of contract: 10 years

In business since: 1970
Franchising since: 1978
Total number of units: 58
Number of company-operated units: 1
Total number of units planned, 1990: 82
Number of company-operated units planned, 1990: None

"You tell us where and when. It'll be there then" is Pilot's slogan. This air freight forwarder, a company whose growth has been fueled by the deregulation of the industry, doesn't own a single plane. It further distinguishes itself from competitors like UPS, Federal Express, and Emery by being the only air freight forwarder to franchise its operations. John Edwards, Pilot's founder, says of his company's experience: "Franchising allowed us to grow without investing a lot of capital. We were able to recruit better and more experienced people who would work twenty-eight hours a day and who knew their local market and how to handle it."

Pilot looks for franchisees who already have some experience in the industry. Some of Pilot's competitors fear what they call raids on their staffs. In its search for experience, Pilot even recruited a few competitors' vice presidents as new franchisees. As a Pilot franchisee, you manage an operation whose biggest customer, the federal government, currently supplies about 8 percent of the company's business. But your customers will come from almost any industry, and your days will be far from predictable. As a Pilot district manager recently commented: "When we open the doors, we don't have any business. Then people start calling. You're moving everything from inbound surgical supplies to major league umpire's equipment and you have to be ready if the game lasts fifteen innings."

The licensing fee, $10,000, $20,000, or $30,000, varies with the size of your market. At the time of this writing the company was most interested in setting up franchisees in Miami, Indianapolis, and Salt Lake City, each a major market requiring a payment of $30,000. Royalties also vary; for instance, the fee is 30 percent on profits from international cargo.

In this franchise the franchisor maintains close supervision of the business. Pilot will do your billing and pay you after deducting its royalties. The company will also specify which kinds of pickup and delivery vehicles you may use, what your office hours will be, and the kind of insurance you must carry. Every cartage agent you use must be approved by Pilot. If you hire a manager for your operations, Pilot must approve him or her.

Your office and warehouse must be located near an airport, probably in leased premises. You'll need about five hundred square feet of office space and fifteen hundred square feet for a warehouse. In addition, the facility should have at least two bay docks for loading. Pilot will not help you locate your place of business, but it must approve your choice.

You and your manager will be trained at Pilot's Lima, Pennsylvania, headquarters and at the company's terminal in Philadelphia. The two-week course includes customer services, financial reporting, business management, and sales. While tuition for this training is included in the franchise package, subsequent training for other personnel in your operation may involve a fee.

Pilot makes a profit on office supplies and business forms that it sells to its franchisees, but you can go elsewhere for this material. However, you may have to buy serially numbered air bills and buy or lease computer equipment and software from the company, but that will be at cost. You also must take out a yellow pages advertisement, with the size and content specified by Pilot.

The franchisor has established minimum levels of outbound freight business for each of its three market area types. If you generate less than the amount of revenue required for your size market in a six-month period, Pilot can terminate your franchise. Currently, those figures for the first six months of business are $150,000, $300,000, and $450,000, respectively.

For further information contact:

Chet Spencer, Pilot Air Freight, Route 352 , P.O. Box 97, Lima, PA 19037, 215-565-8100

9. The Education Industry

Contents

Academic

Sylvan Learning Corporation

Initial license fee: $20,000 to $30,000
Royalties: 8% to 10%
Advertising royalties: 4%
Minimum cash required: $25,000
Capital required: $49,550 to $107,000
Financing: None
Length of contract: NA

In business since: 1979
Franchising since: 1982
Total number of units: 136
Number of company-operated units: 3
Total number of units planned, 1990: NA
Number of company-operated units planned, 1990: NA

A steady stream of newspaper articles, magazine stories, and special television reports in recent years have focused on American children's declining scores on standardized academic tests. Many parents, government officials, and education experts are concerned that, because of inadequate public schooling, many American children will fall a step behind in an increasingly competitive society. And because they see public schools as overcrowded places, where even dedicated teachers simply don't have the time to devote to children who need special attention, many parents gladly pay for services that promise improved academic progress for their children.

Sylvan Learning Centers make that promise. According to John Gellatly, the company's executive vice president, "For every thirty-six hours of instruction" at a Sylvan facility, "students gain one to one and one-half years of academic growth, although not all students progress at the same rate." Sylvan Learning Centers operate after school, generally from 3 P.M to 8 P.M., and full-time during the summer. Most of its students are in elementary school, although high school students preparing for the College Boards and adults who have literacy problems also attend. The staff of each center consists of a director, an assistant director, and part-time instructors, usually moonlighting teachers. With a maximum faculty-student ratio of 3:1, Sylvan guarantees individual attention for its students. Sylvan professionals customize curriculums to help students overcome learning problems or to supply educational enrichment that can give youngsters an advantage over their peers.

Centers operate in areas with a middle-class student population of at least 25,000. Many students' parents are professionals who are predisposed to enroll their child in an enrichment program. Sylvan Learning Centers test children when they enter the program to see if they have any learning disabilities, and retest them regularly throughout their stay at the center to measure their progress. Most students take the center's one-hour classes twice a week for eighteen weeks. Using positive reinforcement, Sylvan centers motivate children to learn. Tokens, given to students when they master a new level of the curriculum, can be redeemed at a "store" on the premises for toys, games, and other rewards.

Although many Sylvan Learning Centers are owned by educators, doctors, lawyers, and business people have also bought franchises. The company will help you pick a promising location, usually in a medical/dental building or office park, and will give you standardized specifications for laying out your operation. The company sells two franchise packages, geared to the size of a region's potential market. One is designed for a space of 700 to 800 square feet, the other for an operation encompassing 1,200 to 1,600 square feet. Sylvan provides much of your furniture and forms, as well as all tests, motivational, and promotional materials.

Sylvan assists you in hiring your full-time staff. The training program for you and your staff lasts two weeks, and the company will help inaugurate your business three to six weeks after your actual opening with an open house and a complete advertising and promotional campaign. Thereafter a field representative will make periodic visits to help you improve your operation, and regional conferences and an annual meeting provide a forum for further enrichment.

For further information contact:
Sylvan Learning Corporation, 2400 Presidents Drive, P.O. Box 5605, Montgomery, AL 36103-5605, 205-277-7720

Gymnastics

Sportastiks

Initial license fee: $20,000
Royalties: 8% up to $300,000 gross sales; 6% over $300,000
Advertising royalties: 2%
Minimum cash required: $30,000
Capital required: $70,000
Financing: The company helps you apply for a loan package.
Length of contract: NA

In business since: 1979
Franchising since: 1985
Total number of units: 50 "pilot programs"
Number of company-operated units: 1
Total number of units planned, 1990: NA
Number of company-operated units planned, 1990: NA

Gymnastic activities for children began to spread beyond school-required physical education in the 1970s with the opening of private gymnastic centers. Parents enrolled their children in these programs more to see improvement in their children's physical fitness than to make them expert gymnasts. Bev and Yoshi Hayasaki, who in 1979 started their gymnastic centers, Sportastiks, have developed a program that focuses on general fitness and coordination and provides training modules for kids who show promise in the field. Yoshi Hayasaki provides the gymnastics expertise. The holder of twenty national gymnastic titles himself, he is currently head gymnastics coach at the University of Illinois. Bev Hayasaki, an expert in child psychology and physical education, developed the curriculum.

The Hayasakis developed their franchise system over a period of six years through the operation of fifty pilot programs. In order to give each new franchise sufficient attention, they have decided to limit their growth to ten new franchises per year.

Sportastiks centers typically enroll students ranging in age from one year old to eighteen years old in structured classes. Guided by a system of lesson plans, boys and girls participate in activities that begin with basic psychomotor conditioning exercises and proceed all the way up to formal training classes for possible future gymnastic champions. Children perform their workouts, carefully supervised, on a carpeted area of about sixteen hundred square feet.

While you should have some business experience before you buy this franchise, you need no background in gymnastics. Sportastiks will help you select a site for your business and purchase equipment, train you to run your center, help you hire and train your teachers, and advise you on pricing and marketing. A company support representative, assigned to you as soon as you buy a franchise, provides ongoing support in your operations—daily, if necessary. Because of Sportastiks' notable safety record, you will enjoy lower insurance rates than many other companies in the field.

For further information contact:
Sportastiks, 510 Staley Rd., Champaign, IL 61821, 217-352-4269

Preschool Activities

Gymboree

Initial license fee: $7,000 to $14,000
Royalties: 6%
Advertising royalties: 2%
Minimum cash required: $20,000
Capital required: $20,000 to $38,000
Financing: Available
Length of contract: 10 years

In business since: 1976
Franchising since: 1980
Total number of units: 201
Number of company-operated units: 5
Total number of units planned, 1990: 500
Number of company-operated units planned, 1990: 15

Ten years ago, Joan Barnes invented a product she couldn't find but strongly felt she needed: a developmental center for her two young daughters. "As a young mother," she recalls, "I wanted a positive environment where I could be with other like-minded moms for support, and I wanted my child to be with other kids."

The resulting program involves forty-five-minute once-a-week sessions in rented churches, synagogues, and community centers, in which parents join with their children in a systematic session of play, exercise, and song. Special equipment and decorations create a stimulating multicolored environment. Today, about thirty-five thousand kids across the U.S. and Canada participate in the program.

The Gymboree centers work because they meet a need that most parents share. More and more attention is being focused on the psychomotor and emotional development of children under the age of five. The time demands of dual-career families and the simultaneous desire of couples not to pass up the experience of parenthood puts a premium on whatever "quality time" parents can spend with their children. Add to that the growing interest in physical fitness and parent's concerns about not pushing young children into competitive atmospheres, and you have Gymboree.

At Gymboree kids as young as three months old gather with at least one of their parents in a room chock-full of soft and colorful play equipment, including bouncers, balance beams, and slides. In the middle of the room is a real multicolored parachute. The kids roll, touch, move, stretch, crawl, and jump, depending on their age. They also chant and sing. The sessions are usually structured around a warm-up exercise period with background music, a directed period of various kinds of movement on the equipment, and a final period of games and singing. Gymboree encourages parents to get right in there with their kids and play.

The point of all this, Barnes says, is "to build a child's self-confidence," while at the same time offering an opportunity for "self-discovery and exploration." Another benefit is an improvement in the children's self-image. Just as important—maybe even more important in terms of marketing—is what the program gives parents. They gain "greater confidence in how to parent and . . . a more positive feeling about their parenting ability and their relationship with their child."

Barnes obviously tapped into what many parents think, because Gymboree has received write-ups in *The Wall Street Journal, The New York Times, The Atlanta Journal, Time, Newsweek, Ms.*, and many other newspapers and magazines. *The Wall Street Journal* said: "Parents contend the program improves the child's balance, coordination, and social skills. *Newsweek* wrote: "Kids are also encouraged to play independently. As the children climb on diminutive jungle gyms or roll around on huge foam rubber logs, the classroom rings with laughter." "Good Morning America" and other network shows have also featured Gymboree.

Typical Gymboree franchisees are former business people or teachers in their late twenties and early thirties. Several of them became interested in running one or more Gymborees (the company encourages franchisees to operate multiple units) when they entered their own children in the program.

Franchisees participate in a nine-day training period at the company's headquarters in Burlingame, California. There is no extra charge for the instruction, but you have to pay for lodging and some meals. Optional annual seminars at headquarters ($100 fee) and regional training sessions ($25) update and reinforce the basic instruction.

If you become a franchisee, the company will give you guidelines for choosing a site, but you make the actual selection. You must purchase a package of program aids and equipment, although some additional material is optional. The company tests all Gymboree material at the five company owned centers before releasing it for use in other units. Gymboree also has a cooperative advertising program.

Recent developments will make the Gymboree name even more widely known. Karen Anderson, a company vice president, now writes a syndicated column on child care carried in more than two hundred newspapers. Major manufacturers have released Gymboree records and video and audio cassettes, and a series of Gymboree children's books is soon to be published.

Helen Thorpe, who owns Gymboree of North Central, New Jersey, feels that her decision to connect with the company was the right one. She told us she especially likes the combination of company assistance and the freedom to shape her business according to her own ideas. "I bought a franchise in order to have control over my own business," she says. "This is, in actuality, what does happen. I submit quarterly reports, but day to day operation is my decision."

For further information contact:
Robert Jacob, Gymboree, 872 Hinckley Rd., Burlingame, CA 94010, 415-692-8080

Playful Parenting

Initial license fee: $12,500
Royalties: 6%
Advertising royalties: 3%
Minimum cash required: $7,500
Capital required: $20,000 to $25,000
Financing: The company will give you guidelines for applying for a bank loan.
Length of contract: 15 years

In business since: 1971
Franchising since: 1984
Total number of units: 79
Number of company-operated units: None
Total number of units planned, 1990: 956
Number of company-operated units planned, 1990: 6

Playful Parenting franchisee Mary Drozda feels she has "the best of both worlds." A former physical education teacher, she now runs a Playful Parenting franchise in Landisville, Pennsylvania, a vocation in which she can express two important sides of her personality: "I get to dress up and be the successful business entrepreneur—and I get to get down on my knees and play."

The business that has provided a creative outlet and a financial opportunity for Mary Drozda began in 1971 when two teachers, Priscilla Hegner and Rose Grasselli, each the mother of infants, met at a children's birthday party and decided to form a play group. The play group grew, eventually moving to a local Y. Hegner and Grasselli read all they could about physical activities for young children and augmented their research with equipment and play routines they bought or developed while running the group. Before long, they found themselves conducting formal classes in children's play for kids and their parents and attracting the attention of professional educators. Hegner and Grasselli's 1981 book, *Playful Parenting,* further publicized their work and led to the current franchising operation.

Playful Parenting classes accept children from six weeks to five years old and limit the children-to-teacher ratios to ten or fifteen children per teacher. Gearing psychomotor activities to the proper age level, classes emphasize the participation of parents. Parents receive lesson plans and instruction in how to interact physically with their child, so the experience teaches effective parenting as well as providing directed play for kids. Playful Parenting's target market are the parents of infants, toddlers, and two-year-olds, particularly first-time parents. Client parents generally have college educations and come from middle- or upper-middle-income families.

Many Playful Parenting franchisees previously owned gym and dance schools, health and fitness clubs, or child care centers. They already had space (ideally, about 2,000 square feet; a minimum of 1,000) and equipment that they could put to profitable use when their regular clientele was not using it. Most were already employed or had easy access to teachers interested in supplementing their incomes. But you do not have to fit this profile to become a Playful Parenting franchisee, nor do you have to work full-time on your business. An established business, with a good manager on the job, would require no more than about fifteen hours a week of your attention. And you can house your facility in a Y, church, recreation center, or similar building in which you could rent suitable space.

If you buy this franchise, you will train for three days in Reading, Pennsylvania, in general business management and the Playful Parenting system. Teachers, who must have previous teaching experience, also come to Reading for five days of training in the system or may receive their instruction at a more convenient regional location. Your clients will evaluate your teachers as part of Playful Parenting's program of annual teacher recertification.

Playful Parenting will help you pick a site for your business and will offer advice on advertising, marketing, and public relations to help you get off to a fast start. A company field representative will visit you every three months, and your center must pass an annual recertification evaluation.

Your franchise package will include about five hundred pieces of play equipment, and you can purchase additional supplies and equipment from any supplier approved by Playful Parenting. The franchisor has a promotional and marketing relationship with several large companies like Johnson & Johnson, from which you will benefit indirectly through increased recognition of the Playful Parenting name.

For further information contact:
Gary Seibert, Director of Franchise Development, Playful Parenting, 60 Shillington Rd., Sinking Spring, PA 19608, 215-678-0232

10. The Employment Industry

Contents

Permanent Placement

AAA Employment

Initial license fee: Varies from state to state, with a base fee of $3,000, and an additional fee ranging from $2,000 to $10,000 depending on population
Royalties: 10%
Advertising royalties: None
Minimum cash required: $4,000
Capital required: $7,000 to $18,000
Financing: AAA will finance, at no charge, the deferred balance of the franchise fee after the down payment.
Length of contract: 10 years

In business since: 1957
Franchising since: 1977
Total number of units: 121
Number of company-operated units: 88
Total number of units planned, 1990: NA
Number of company-operated units planned, 1990: NA

Sherridan Revell, owner of an AAA Employment franchise in Roanoke, Virginia, calls the AAA franchise fail-safe: "If any qualified franchisee operates an agency according to the training and policy guides, that person cannot fail. The company's methods have been tested and proven many, many times." One AAA policy, that of applicant-paid placement, under which those placed by the agency generally pay about two weeks' salary to AAA, has made the company popular with employers nationwide. By providing a free service to employers for more than thirty years, AAA has become the largest privately owned employment agency in the United States. AAA agencies place people in all kinds of employment, from professional and executive to domestic help, in both temporary and permanent positions. The company is recruiting new franchisees in every state except Florida, Georgia, Alabama, and Mississippi.

AAA has developed a complete set of policies and procedures for agency owners and offers an optional two- to four-week training program at the home office in St. Petersburg, Florida. Almost all franchisees take advantage of this comprehensive program, in which they received intensive training in agency operation. Topics covered include bookkeeping, advertising, controls, budget, collections, taxes, payroll, hiring, and all other phases of day-to-day agency operation. The highly recommended sessions are free, except for the cost of travel, lodging, and meals.

In addition to its training program, AAA will provide you with support during every phase of preopening. The company will help you select a site for your agency, negotiate a lease, obtain the necessary licenses, furnish your office, hire and train employees, and set up procedures for advertising, budgeting, and bookkeeping. During your first week or two of operation, an experienced agency operator will work with you at your office. When you feel ready to go it alone, the company will allow you all the freedom you desire to make all of your own management decisions. And the operations manual will prove to be an invaluable resource to you as an independent business person.

If, like Jane Miller, an AAA franchisee in Pittsburgh, Pennsylvania, you enjoy owning your own business but "don't have the money to run it by trial and error," you will benefit from the regular visits that company field representatives pay to all AAA franchisees. In special circumstances, your representative will visit you upon request to assist with unusual problems. You can attend the semiannual seminars for updates on policy changes, industry information, and improvements in techniques and procedures, and read the weekly AAA newsletter for business tips and information on franchise activities.

The training and support that AAA provides franchisees make it "well worth the royalties paid to the franchise home office to be a part of this company," in the estimation of Sherridan Revell. As an AAA owner, you have the independence to make your own business judgments, your only obligation to the company being the payment of the 10 percent royalty. Operating franchisees, however, recommend that you stick fairly closely to AAA guidelines to increase your chances of success, and, Jane Miller notes, "you own your own business and are paying to use AAA's business methods. You should be making your own decisions, but you would be foolish not to follow proven procedures."

For further information contact:
Carolyn Weathington, Vice President, Operations, AAA Employment Franchise, 5533 Central Ave., St. Petersburg, FL 33710, 813-343-3044

Bryant Bureau

Initial license fee: $29,500
Royalties: 7%
Advertising royalties: 1%
Minimum cash required: $19,000
Capital required: $37,000 to $55,000
Financing: The company will accept a $15,000 down payment on the franchise fee and accept payment of the balance due on an installment plan, for which it charges interest.
Length of contract: NA

In business since: 1977
Franchising since: 1977
Total number of units: NA
Number of company-operated units: NA
Total number of units planned, 1990: NA
Number of company-operated units planned, 1990:

The American economy has seen radical changes in the past decade, changes that will continue to move the job market toward more highly specialized jobs. With the shift toward an information-based society, service industries are quickly replacing manufacturing as the major employers. And employers are seeking more white-collar employees, from word processors to engineers to management personnel. Snelling and Snelling, an employment industry pioneer, created Bryant Bureau to apply placement techniques and systems ideally suited to meet business' need for specialized personnel.

Both a member of the service industry and a specialist in serving that industry, Bryant Bureau is preparing for a period of substantial growth. As the job market becomes increasingly competitive, with more highly trained people competing for spots with increasingly demanding employers, job seekers and employers alike turn to employment agencies. Employment services now handle almost 20 percent of all job changes, placing over 4 million people a year. Today, Bryant Bureau offers prime franchises throughout the country. If you like sales work, particularly telephone sales; if you enjoy working with people to help them find the job that's right for them; and if you want to go into business without making an enormous investment; then you're cut out for the employment service profession.

Bryant Bureau applies its highly specialized experience to help you select your office location, negotiate a lease, lay out and install office equipment, and obtain the right telephone system. The company will train you in its unique systems for two weeks. Carefully designed recruiting techniques, interviewing methods, marketing campaigns, and other procedures make up the Bryant Bureau Placement Cycle, which will be the key to your successful operation. Experienced staff will make sure you have a firm grasp of these concepts before you complete your classroom training.

A National Marketing Consultant will come to your site to continue your opening training program and will be in constant contact with you during the first ninety days of your operation. Following this crucial period, you will continue to receive whatever support you need to reach your goals. Bryant Bureau also conducts a continuing series of training seminars in locations throughout the country. The seminars cover ongoing developments in the topics covered in your initial training. And each franchisee receives a complete set of manuals, including the "Staffing Specialist Manual," the "Director Manual," the "On-Line Training Manual," and others. Video cassettes and training guides provide current information on specific topics like career consultation and reference checking. Though ongoing support is generally free of charge, you may incur occasional expenses for travel or manual updates.

In addition to educational materials and programs, Bryant Bureau provides its franchisees with various operational support programs. The company offers a variety of services designed to relieve you of some of the miscellaneous administrative duties that come with running a business. Standard promotional materials, business forms, and stationery are conveniently prepackaged for you, but you are not required to purchase any of these items from the company.

The Bryant Bureau national insurance program and benefits trust offer various types of protection at group rates. Another benefit of being a Bryant Bureau franchisee is the recognition program, through which franchisees and their staffs are awarded for excellent performance. Newsletters and a national referral newspaper link you with Bryant Bureaus and Snelling and Snelling agencies across the U.S., tying you into a truly national organization.

For further information contact:
Bryant Bureau, A Division of Snelling and Snelling, Inc., 4000 South Tamiami Trail, Sarasota, FL 33581, 1-800-237-9497; in Florida: 813-922-9616

Dunhill Personnel System, Inc.

Initial license fee: Full service, $25,000; office personnel and temporary systems, $15,000
Royalties: Full service and office personnel, 7%; temporary systems, 2.5% of first $500,000, 2% of next $500,000, 1.75% of everything over $1 million
Advertising royalties: Full service and office personnel, 1%; Temporary Systems, 0.5%
Minimum cash required: Full service, $30,000; temporary systems, $53,000 to $116,000; office personnel, $17,500
Capital required: Full service, $30,000; temporary systems, $53,000 to $116,000; office personnel, $17,500
Financing: Part of the franchise fee may be paid in promissory notes at 8% interest.
Length of contract: 10 years

In business since: 1952
Franchising since: 1961
Total number of units: 284
Number of company-operated units: 2

Total number of units planned, 1990: 332
Number of company-operated units planned, 1990: 10

Word processors and duplicating machines have revolutionized corporate recruiting. Job applicants flood personnel departments with their resumes. That means corporate personnel departments are often overwhelmed by masses of paper. It also presents a golden opportunity for placement services. Personnel agencies now handle about two thirds of corporate professional recruiting (these search firms fill 15 percent of all job openings). Dunhill has a big share of that business. Last year their 1,200 recruiting specialists, working out of over 300 offices in the United States and Canada, placed 20,000 professionals with over 5,000 companies.

But it doesn't stop with professionals. Corporate demand for help in finding full-time office workers and temps is also growing. The same computers that enable job applicants to send out scores of resumes simultaneously have also made office jobs more highly skilled and thus more difficult to fill. According to the Department of Labor, American companies are only able to find qualified secretaries to fill 80 percent of their job openings. Meanwhile, those companies have 600,000 temporary jobs to fill every day. That's a $6 billion industry, growing at the rate of about 20 percent a year—one of our country's fastest-growing fields, according to the Department of Commerce.

All the signs bode well for the placement business. As the nation moves further toward a service economy, jobs in most industries become more specialized and potential employees need to have more advanced training and education. If a company makes the wrong hiring choice, rehiring and training to fill a position will be expensive. So there's greater emphasis on making the right choice the first time. And that means a greater need for professionals with specialized skills in personnel placement for picking these people in the first place. Even large corporations with big human resources departments can't do that for every kind of job.

And that's where you come in. A Dunhill franchise is one way to get a piece of this action. What will you be doing as a Dunhill franchisee? As the company puts it: "Searching, contacting, screening, qualifying, probing, questioning, answering, consulting, checking, verifying, selecting, negotiating, processing, interviewing, and facilitating." If you like interacting with people and think you're a good judge of people—and are willing to work hard and pay close attention to detail—this could be the business for you.

Dunhill is as proud of its specific programs in the placement field as it is of its high name recognition. One of its special programs is the Relocation Management Program, which enables a corporation to recruit personnel from all parts of the country with the understanding that neither the company nor its new employees will have to worry about the details of employee relocation. Dunhill takes care of the sale of the employee's old house, purchase of a new one, and arrangements for the move itself.

You don't need prior experience in this industry to get into the Dunhill system. One of the thirty offices the company expects to open this year could be yours even though you don't have a placement background. And you will have the opportunity to pick one of three franchise categories that seems to best fit in with your investment needs, your interests, and your abilities: executive placement, office personnel, or temps. As you can see from the license and royalty figures, the full service agency represents the largest initial investment.

The company will help you pick a location and plan your office layout. As a Dunhill franchisee, you'll take your training at company headquarters in Carle Place, New York, at your own expense. There you can expect a rigorous course of hands-on training. Not only will you receive regular classroom instruction, you will also work in a simulated office where you will get a real feel for the business and see what daily life will be like in your new career.

Dunhill will help you throughout the life of your business. They will assist you with your opening, and a company representative will be at your office for a posttraining help period. "There is constant phone communication" between franchisees and area managers, the company notes. The Dunhill Operations Team will always be there to advise you on difficult placement situations. And the company offers refresher training courses at the rate of twenty to twenty-five a year, nationally and on a regional basis. Also helpful—and unusual—is the company lending library of video cassette training tapes.

You can get your supplies from Dunhill, but you're not obligated to do so. If you purchase computer hardware and software from the company, you will save money and gain access to the National Exchange Network, a system that will allow you to match job seekers with corporate personnel needs across the country. This is especially valuable when you're dealing with a highly skilled applicant or a company that needs to fill a position requiring very specialized skills.

Individualized computer packages also allow you to perform services for clients that would not ordinarily be possible—at least not as efficiently and cheaply. This hardware and software will, for example, allow you to bill specific departments and cost centers in large corporations and to customize your invoices to suit your clients' specifications.

Computerization of such transactions will also permit you to deal easily and instantly with questions and problems related to billing.

For further information contact:
John Leddy, Dunhill Personnel System, Inc., One Old Country Rd., Carle Place, NY 11514, 516-741-5081

F-O-R-T-U-N-E Franchise Corporation

Initial license fee: None
Royalties: 7%; minimum of $25,000
Advertising royalties: 1%
Minimum cash required: $60,000
Capital required: $50,000
Financing: Up to 40% of the franchise fee
Length of contract: 20 years

In business since: 1959
Franchising since: 1973
Total number of units: 37
Number of company-operated units: None
Total number of units planned, 1990: 85
Number of company-operated units planned, 1990: None

People change jobs more often than they used to—sometimes as often as every three years on the middle management and executive level. Since management jobs command the highest salaries, it stands to reason that placement services will make their greatest profits filling these positions. Fortune confines its activities exclusively to this area. It points out that typical fees for filling these jobs run something like this: $9,000 for a position paying $30,000; $12,000 for one paying $40,000; and $18,000 for a job at the $60,000 mark. At these high figures, closing a few placements a month can result in a substantial income.

An employment agency has no inventory, so start-up costs can be kept down. However, you may find you make up for low start-up costs with the extra investment of energy you'll need to hustle up an "inventory" of jobs to offer. That involves a different type of selling: selling corporate personnel on why they should use your company, which you will be doing constantly. As Dennis Inzinna, the company's vice president of operations recently commented, "Obtaining jobs is a daily effort you cannot afford to neglect."

Fortune feels it has special features to offer both in organization and procedure. The company's placement people are called consultants.

Rudy Schott, Fortune's president, sees them as "experts whose advice is necessary for required solutions." Fortune's consultants are organized by specialties that parallel the organizational chart of a corporation: electronic data processing, sales and marketing, and accounting and finance, for example. Seating within the office is by groups of four consultants, to encourage mutual support and creative interaction.

At Fortune, placements are often closed through in-house interviewing. In this procedure, the hiring executive comes to the Fortune office and sees several qualified applicants, one after the other. Fortune feels this facilitates the closing of a greater percentage of placements in an efficient manner. Fortune consultants show corporate executives that it is better for them to travel to the Fortune location and spend half a day interviewing in a setting with no distractions than it is to spend parts of several days doing the same thing less effectively in their own office.

Fortune offices have been opened recently by a former manager of delivery operations for a large corporation, the director of management information services for an electronics division of Motorola, a plant manager for the huge Schlumberger oil company, and an assistant vice president of systems and programming at the United States Trust Company.

If you have a similar background and buy a Fortune franchise, you will get strong support. You don't need experience in the placement field. Fortune will train you with two weeks of classes at its New York City headquarters. Instruction includes actual experience in searching out positions and filling them. When you return to your office, the company will advise you on staffing your operation.

Not only does the company help you find a site for your office, it also helps with the layout and other details, such as phone installation. Fortune also helps you get insurance and qualify for your license.

In your first week of operation, somebody from Fortune will remain with you, helping to train your people. Even after you're well under way, the New York office will keep close tabs on your progress and you can consult the company on a daily basis if necessary. Joseph A. Genovese, a Fortune franchisee in Boston, says of the franchisor's support program: "I always have access to all of the people in the franchise when I have a special problem. They have never refused a request for help and in many cases have offered help when I didn't think I needed it."

That doesn't necessarily mean that Fortune will cramp your entrepreneurial style. As Genovese puts it: "The company has been very excellent in providing guidelines for the management of my business. Within those guidelines they have become more or less active depending upon my needs and my requests for assistance. I have been very pleased with the arrangement."

For further information contact:
Michael Meyerson, F-O-R-T-U-N-E Franchise Corporation, 655 Third Ave., Suite 1805, New York, NY 10017, 1-800-221-4864; in New York: 212-697-4314

Sales Consultants International

Initial license fee: $16,000 to $25,000
Royalties: 5%
Advertising royalties: 0.5%
Minimum cash required: $35,000
Capital required: $18,000 to $36,000
Financing: None
Length of contract: Minimum of 5 years

In business since: 1957
Franchising since: 1965
Total number of Units: 111
Number of company-operated units: 24
Total number of units planned, 1990: 205
Number of company-operated units planned, 1990: 50

Peter Cotton, a Rhode Island Sales Consultants franchisee, says his relationship with his franchisor is in keeping with the spirit of his enterprise. "Ours is a very personal business—placing people in careers and working with companies to help them find the best people becomes highly personal and intimate," he says. "Our organization is just the same way." On the other hand, the relationship is not so close as to preclude independence. "We are autonomous," he notes, "and have the ability to make decisions regarding the operation of our business as if it was our own without any franchisor's supervision."

The franchise involves finding and recruiting sales management, sales, and marketing personnel on an employer-paid contingency basis. Sales Consultants, a division of Management Recruiters International, stresses training as a key to your success in this business. The training—"the most intensive and best available for our industry," according to Peter Cotton—begins with a three-week session at company headquarters in Cleveland. The company uses a variety of techniques to teach you its business, including video and audio tapes, role playing, and actual hands-on search-and-placement projects, for which you earn a fee.

Peter Cotton describes Sales Consultants' preopening assistance: "A vice president of the company was extremely helpful in site selection, office design and layout, securing of telephone equipment, furniture, deposits and lease arrangements for the rental of office space, etc. Additionally, the corporate legal staff did all the paperwork necessary for opening the office prior to my arrival in the area. They made application to all the appropriate state departments and had all of the necessary paperwork in order for my signature upon the execution of my franchise agreement, saving me an enormous amount of time and money."

Sales Consultants sets you up in business with all the supplies you will need for the first three months. It also supplies a VCR, television set, and twenty-one video cassettes for you to use in training your account executives. Further, personnel from Sales Consultants' regional office spend about three weeks at your office, providing additional training for you and your staff as you begin operations.

Ongoing support is also extensive. During your first year of operations, you will receive an additional six visits from the regional staff, giving you twelve to eighteen days of training and consultation beyond your initial training. More contact with the franchisor will come through regional and national meetings and phone consultation. Field personnel will also visit your office on request to consult on any matters you wish to bring up. "We generally request a visit twice a year," says Bob Bakker of Sales Consultants of Northern Jersey. "These two-day visits are basically to critique the operation and point out to the manager ways to improve."

Sales Consultants also conducts a special one-week training course at headquarters for account executives who have been promoted to manager. Topics include: hiring and firing account executives, management information systems, time management, and public relations.

For further information contact:

Douglas G. Bugie, Director, Franchise Marketing, Sales Consultants International, 1127 Euclid Ave., Suite 1400, Cleveland, OH 44115-1638, 1-800-321-2309; in Alaska and Ohio, call collect: 216-696-1122

Snelling and Snelling

Initial license fee: $29,500
Royalties: 7%
Advertising royalties: 1%
Minimum cash required: $35,400
Capital required: $35,400 to $45,300
Financing: The company will finance $14,500 of the initial license fee.
Length of contract: NA

In business since: 1951
Franchising since: 1955
Total number of units: 445
Number of company-operated units: None
Total number of units planned, 1990: NA
Number of company-operated units planned, 1990: NA

If you buy this franchise, you will become part of the world's largest employment service. Robert and Anne Snelling started the company in Philadelphia in 1951. An innovator in employment service procedures and techniques over the years, Snelling and Snelling instituted the industry's first national insurance program for franchisees and pioneered the use of video tape for training programs.

Snelling and Snelling is bullish on the future of the employment service business. It points out that only about 15 percent of jobseekers today use an employment service. According to the company, that places the profession in a position much like that of real estate broker around 1900, when most people sold their houses themselves. As more people turn to employment agencies in their search for jobs, Snelling and Snelling's management sees the outlook for employment services as one of steady growth.

Training for Snelling and Snelling franchisees takes place at the company's headquarters in Sarasota, Florida. The company does not charge an extra fee for the two-week course, although you must absorb related travel costs. Curtis L. Nabors, owner of a franchise in Morristown, New Jersey, recalls he was impressed with the company's "excellent training." He still feels that way: "Four years later I realize how much it contributed to my success." As an additional benefit, you can tap this training program for your new employees as often as you need to without ever having to pay a fee. Company representatives will come to your office to train your employment counselors and your receptionist/administrative assistant when you are ready to open your service. The company also offers periodic field training and holds annual management conferences.

The company stresses the importance of employee morale to the success of its operations. To boost morale, it sponsors awards programs, which include the distribution of pins, tie clasps, and other such recognitions of achievement. Cathy Searby, a Palo Alto, California, franchisee, appreciates this aspect of company policy. There's "lots of recognition for me and my staff," she says. She also likes the policy of help "when you need it" and of being "left alone when you don't need it."

Snelling and Snelling advises you over the phone and by mail on how to select an office site, negotiate a lease, and furnish the premises.

Its comprehensive supply package includes everything you will need to open your business, from letterheads and business cards right down to pens and pencils. You don't have to order supplies from the company, but it will give you a supply catalog from which you can buy at a discount if you choose.

Snelling and Snelling stays at the top of the industry through an extensive advertising program. Its advertisements have appeared in: *Business Week, Reader's Digest, The Wall Street Journal, Saturday Evening Post, U.S. News and World Report, TV Guide, McCall's, Cosmopolitan*, and *Time*. Franchisees usually supplement the company's national campaigns by spending about 5 percent of their revenues on local advertising.

Snelling and Snelling is also a presence in the lucrative temporary employment field. The Snellings originally got into this side of the business in 1954 when they bought a Kelly Girl franchise. Eventually they launched their own temps operation, PARTIME, which they sold in 1976. Since 1984, however, Snelling and Snelling has reentered the field with Snelling Temporaries, and currently sells franchises for this business.

For further information contact:
Franchise Sales, Snelling and Snelling, Inc., Snelling Plaza, 4000 South Tamiami Trail, Sarasota, FL 33581, 813-922-9616

Temporary Placement

Norrell Services

Initial license fee: None
Royalties: 60%
Advertising royalties: None
Minimum cash required: $45,000
Capital required: $35,000 to $65,000
Financing: The company will help you put together a loan application.
Length of contract: 15 years

In business since: 1961
Franchising since: 1967
Total number of units: 252
Number of company-operated units: 160
Total number of units planned, 1990: 424
Number of company-operated units planned, 1990: 200

Norrell, a nationwide temporary-help service marketing clerical, office automation, and light industrial job personnel to client companies, operates in a growth field. The company's growth figures compare well with the rest of the industry: Since 1976 Norrell has more than quadrupled its revenues and tripled the number of offices in operation.

Norrell's marketing emphasizes that temporary workers can play a permanent role in its clients' personnel plans. Norrell points out that both big and small businesses should consider using temporary help—not just to fill in for absent workers, but to deal with specific situations that arise again and again. Such situations might include any projects in which staffing needs fall outside a business' normal capabilities; peak periods in cyclical operations; and repetitive, unchallenging work for which a company finds it difficult to motivate full-time employees over an extended period of time.

To ensure a good match between Norrell and its franchisees, the franchise application procedure includes three interviews. You pay your travel expenses to the first, in Atlanta. For the second meeting, a company representative comes to your area, and a final meeting in Atlanta, at company expense, will serve to introduce you to corporate personnel responsible for the company's ongoing franchise support.

Norrell advertisements, which have appeared in *Business Week, Time,* and *Newsweek,* stress the thoroughly trained staff that stands ready to serve client companies. Your training will consist of a week at company headquarters in Atlanta, where you will study operations and sales. A self-study course on company operations and field workshops throughout the year supplement the initial training. Your personnel will also receive extensive instruction, including more than eighty-four hours of classroom work annually.

The company will advise you on site selection and the leasing and equipping of your office. Its preopening team will assist you with recruiting, laying out your office, direct mail marketing, sales calls, and establishing payroll procedures. A district manager, who oversees no more than twelve franchisees, will provide a link between you and Norrell. The manager will assist you with hiring and training new staff, developing a business plan, budgeting, and procuring major accounts.

Norrell, and each of its franchisees, promises clients that it will respond to their requests for personnel within forty-five minutes of receiving their call. If you can't supply the right person, you will have to call a competitor to fulfill the client's need. At least twice a year the company will conduct an operations review of your business, and client and employee opinion surveys will give you another measure of your business' performance.

As part of your franchise package, you will receive enough supplies for three to six months of operations. Your subsequent purchases can come from any vendor whose products meet Norrell specifications.

For further information contact:
Dennis Fuller, Franchise Manager, Norrell Services, 3092 Piedmont Rd., Atlanta, GA 30305, 1-800-334-9694

Personnel Pool of America

Initial license fee: $15,000
Royalties: 5%
Advertising royalties: None
Minimum cash required: $80,000
Capital required: $100,000 to $200,000
Financing: None initially, but growth loans are available
Length of contract: 5 years

In business since: 1946
Franchising since: 1956
Total number of units: 381
Number of company-operated units: 103
Total number of units planned, 1990: NA
Number of company-operated units planned, 1990: NA

Personnel Pool of America, since 1978 a subsidiary of H & R Block, is the largest temp agency in America supplying medical and nursing services to individuals and health-care institutions. Personnel Pool also remains active in its original line of business: finding skilled industrial and office temporary workers for client companies. The company's operations as a whole rank it third in the country as a provider of temporary workers.

The company sells temp services through two divisions: Medical Personnel Pool and Personnel Pool. As a Personnel Pool of America franchisee, you may have your choice of which services you want to offer, or you could opt for both industry and clerical and medical services. However, your choice will depend on availability of franchise territory and the size of your market.

Clerical and industrial temporary services have changed substantially since Personnel Pool of America first opened its doors. In the last five years alone, the company's service mix has gone from 10 percent office and 90 percent industrial to an equal concentration on each. And within the industrial area, the emphasis has changed from heavy industry to semi- or paratechnical operations.

Allen Sorenson, the company's CEO, said recently of the office temps industry: "It has finally become recognized as an economical and convenient way to have a flexible work force to meet what every business and office has—variable workload." Temps available from your franchise might include convention personnel, demonstrators, market surveyors, micrographic personnel, and samplers, as well as clerks and word processors. Through your Law Services Division, which Personnel Pool franchisees have featured since 1976, you will provide law firms with digesters, indexers, paralegals, cite checkers, and proofreaders.

Medical Personnel Pool's business has expanded rapidly in the 1980s. The recent emphasis on decreasing the length of hospital stays and increasing home care has created a burgeoning demand for these services. When confronted by a sudden need for a registered nurse, homemaker, physical therapist, or companion, many families don't know where to turn. Your Medical Personnel Pool will ease their burden. Your operation will handle client calls around the clock, every day of the year. Your service will work with the family's physician to make sure that clients receive the kind of care they need. And you will bill for all services with one consolidated, itemized invoice. All told, this division of Personnel Pool serves 15,000 patients daily and employs 80,000 health-care professionals.

Personnel Pool of America franchisees come from diverse backgrounds. They have worked as aeronautical engineers, CPAs, professional athletes, bankers, and dentists. What they have in common, the company points out, is the success they have achieved.

Should you purchase a franchise, the company will reimburse you for your travel expenses to its headquarters in Fort Lauderdale, Florida, for a meeting that allows you and the company to determine if you would like to go into business together. Later, you will receive a site selection guide and phone guidance from Personal Pool of America as you set up your office.

The company will also pay for your travel expenses and your lodging for another trip to Fort Lauderdale for two weeks of training in sales, marketing, and operations. Your training period in Florida will include time in a company-run Personnel Pool of America office. You will also receive ten days of on-site instruction during the first four months of your business.

Personnel Pool of America gets you started in business with a direct mail marketing campaign in your area and an advertising allowance that you can use to attract potential employees for your business. The company offers postopening help continually by phone or through visits from field consultants. The franchisor sells the equipment and supplies you need, but you can buy it anywhere you wish.

For further information contact:

Hampton M. Miles, Personnel Pool of America, Inc., 303 S.E. 17th St., Ft. Lauderdale, FL 33316, 1-800-327-1396; in Florida: 305-764-2200

Western Temporary Services, Inc.

Initial license fee: $10,000 to $50,000
Royalties: Variable
Advertising royalties: Variable
Minimum cash required: $10,000
Capital required: $10,000+
Financing: None
Length of contract: 5 years

In business since: 1948
Franchising since: 1984
Total number of units: 236
Number of company-operated units: 145
Total number of units planned, 1990: 353
Number of company-operated units planned, 1990: 190

Western Temporary Services provides its franchisees a level of assistance that some entrepreneurs might find confining. But a close working relationship, especially with a company that has developed so much expertise in the field, might be just the thing for someone starting their first business.

You may find that Western will sell you that business in an area close to your home. The company, which has offices in Australia, Mexico, New Zealand, the United Kingdom, Norway, Denmark, and Switzerland, seeks franchisees in many areas of the United States. If you have a location in mind, it must gain company approval, and Western will require you to establish an office with a "professional" atmosphere, but beyond that, you will have the responsibility of setting up your place of business.

Your training, a two-week program, begins with a week at the company's headquarters in Walnut Creek, California. Here you will study payroll, invoicing, credit, applicant screening, and customer relations. Corporate staff will introduce you to Western's national contracts program and the methods of effective bidding that have made these contracts a cornerstone of company operations. During the second week, you go to work in an operating Western office. Under the tutelage of an experienced office manager, you will test, interview, screen, and place applicants. You will also take job orders from company's seeking temps.

Back at your own place of business, a company representative will help you develop a sales strategy tailored to your market and may also go with you as you make your first sales visits to major companies in your area. A substantial part of Western's business in the past has come from companies like IBM, Xerox, Rockwell, General Dynamics,

Lockheed, and General Electric. Western management feels that its history of supplying such corporate giants with temps will stand you in good stead when you solicit accounts in your territory. The company will assist you in those efforts, and you may also benefit from local business generated by national accounts negotiated by Western.

Western will mail grand opening announcements to 500 of your prospective customers and will arrange for and absorb the cost of your phone installation, get you started with an ample shipment of office supplies, and even pass up its share of your gross profits for the first six months so that you can more easily establish a good cash flow position.

You don't have to worry about accounting because Western will handle most of it for you. The company will pay your temps weekly and take care of payroll taxes, insurance, and workers' compensation. Western will pay you regularly, based on your billing, regardless of whether your customers have paid the company. In effect, the company finances your payroll and accounts receivable. You will receive a weekly report covering all this activity.

Western puts a great deal of stock in image promotion. For example, it garners a considerable amount of publicity every year by supplying Santas to such stores as Marshall Fields and Macy's. The company will supply you with press releases for any local promotions you plan, and it may provide further publicity assistance by sending in personalities like Betty Baird, a Western temp and the company's "national typing ambassador." Betty Baird travels around the country demonstrating her 166-words-per-minute typing skill.

On the national level, Western advertises in such periodicals as *The Wall Street Journal*, *Forbes*, *Business Week*, and *Money*, as well as in many trade journals. During every four-week accounting period, you will receive a local advertising allowance of 8 percent of your gross profit, up to a limit of $700. In some areas, the company currently uses outdoor advertising to promote Western business.

For further information contact:

Terry Slocum, Western Temporary Services, Inc., P.O. Box 9280, Walnut Creek, CA 94596, 1-800-USA-TEMP

11. The Food Industry

Contents

Ice Cream and Yogurt

Baskin-Robbins Ice Cream Company
Ben & Jerry's Ice Cream
Bressler's 33 Flavors, Inc.
Gelato Classico Italian Ice Cream
International Dairy Queen, Inc.
Swensen's
Tastee-Freez International
TCBY (The Country's Best Yogurt)

Pizza and Italian Fast Food

Domino's Pizza, Inc.
Mazzio's Pizza
Noble Roman's Pizza
Pizza Inn, Inc.
Round Table Pizza
Sbarro
Shakey's Pizza Restaurant

Restaurants

Benihana of Tokyo
Bob's Big Boy Restaurant System
Cuco's Restaurantes
El Chico Corporation
International House of Pancakes
K-Bob's, Inc.
Po Folks, Inc.
Rax Restaurants
Village Inn Pancake House Restaurants

Sandwiches

All American Hero
Arby's, Inc.
International Blimpie Corporation
Subway Sandwiches and Salads

Specialty Foods

Frontier Fruit & Nut Company
Hickory Farms of Ohio, Inc.
The Peanut Shack

Steakhouses

Bonanza Restaurants
The Ground Round, Inc.
Ponderosa Steakhouses
Sizzler Restaurants International, Inc.
Western Sizzlin Steak House
Western Steer Family Steakhouse

Tacos and Mexican Fast Food

Del Taco, Inc.
Taco Bell, Corp.
Taco John's International
Taco Time International, Inc.

Baked Goods

David's Cookies

Initial license fee: $25,000
Royalties: None
Advertising royalties: None
Minimum cash required: $25,000
Capital required: $125,000
Financing: None
Length of contract: NA

In business since: 1979
Franchising since: 1983
Total number of units: 176
Number of company-operated units: 1
Total number of units planned, 1990: NA
Number of company-operated units planned, 1990: NA

David Liederman is something of a phenomenon in the cookie industry. His mother swears the first word he ever said was "cookie," and that word has proven to be his password to success. In 1979 Liederman perfected a cookie formula that has since helped him turn $35,000 into almost $30 million and nearly two hundred David's Cookies shops worldwide. David's Cookies makes its products from good, basic ingredients like Lindt chocolate imported from Switzerland (the largest single importer of Lindt chocolate, the company uses five tons a week), raisins grown without commercially produced chemicals, pure vanilla extract, and ripe pecans purchased directly from a farm in Georgia. Baked before the customers' eyes in each store, David's Cookies are always fresh, both because the cookies sell so fast and because store owners may not sell cookies more than three hours old.

David's Cookies franchisees do not pay royalties, but they must purchase cookie dough and all other items they offer for sale from the company's plant in Long Island City, New York (the company makes a profit on these sales). David's uses only premium ingredients, prohibiting chemicals in any of its specialty foods, which include ice cream, brownies, frozen yogurt, muffins, french bread, and various beverages. Store owners purchase the cookie dough in fifteen-pound slabs (the minimum order for dough is around twenty-five hundred pounds) and hand form the cookies on their premises. Baked in special idiot-proof conveyor belt ovens, the cookies always have the same delicious David's taste. The fifteen cookie flavors David's has developed so far include Chocolate Chunk, Macadámia Chocolate Chunk, Walnut Raisin Chocolate Chunk, Chocolate White Chocolate Chunk, and No Chunk.

David's has developed a simple but highly effective merchandising technique: Stores are located in areas with heavy foot traffic whose passersby can smell the baking cookies. Drawn to the store by the aroma, they can watch cookies coming fresh out of the oven, which is situated in the store's front window. This strategy brings more customers into the store than any advertising could. And once inside, they can choose from a variety of specialty foods in addition to the cookies. One of the specialties, David's Ice Cream, has been selling well among David's customers like Mayor Ed Koch of New York, who after devouring a pint at a City Hall function honoring Liederman, leaned over to him and asked, "Listen, do you sell franchises?" Computerized ice cream machines in the stores mix David's Ice Cream with chocolate bars, fruits, nuts, or cookies, according to customer's tastes.

When you buy a David's Cookies franchise, you must come to the company's offices in New York City to spend time working in a company store to gain retail and operational experience and to learn about the company's operations at the cookie-dough plant. A David's Cookies store is a relatively simple operation, offering a limited number of items (all of which you purchase from a centralized source) and involving only easy-to-learn, standardized production at the store level. You don't have to mix the dough or second-guess your oven—if you follow the David's system, you will produce the same cookies that have made so many David's stores successful. Because you purchase dough by the pound and sell cookies by the pound, your inventory controls are just as simple.

Historically, cookie stores have been able to make $500,000 selling cookies alone, but David's Cookies foresees a decline in the potential of large, single-item shops. In response, the company has adopted a policy of selling more diversified products in smaller units. The company's management team has developed a kiosk that franchisees can set up in malls, department stores, or other high-rent areas. A maximum of 120 square feet in size, the kiosks still have the capacity to offer the full line of David's specialty foods. The company hopes to franchise several hundred of the units in the near future as it goes for a bigger bite of the $50 billion cookie industry.

For further information contact:

Director of Franchise Sales, David's Specialty Food Products, 12 East 42nd St., New York, NY 10017, 212-682-0210

Dunkin' Donuts of America, Inc.

Initial license fee: $30,000 to $40,000
Royalties: NA
Advertising Royalties: NA
Minimum cash required: $39,000
Capital required: $110,000 to $544,000
Financing: The company provides some financing for real estate, equipment, and signs.
Length of contract: 20 years

In business since: 1950
Franchising since: 1950
Total number of units: 1,350
Number of company-operated units: 65
Total number of units planned, 1990: 2,000
Number of company-operated units planned, 1990: NA

Dunkin' Donuts is a huge presence in this country—on TV, with its clever commercials (the only donut chain to go national with TV ads), as well as on roadsides, with its ubiquitous orange and raspberry signs. You've probably been in a Dunkin' Donuts shop. It's hard to get beyond the donuts, muffins, and French pastries with your will to resist still intact.

Dunkin' Donuts knows that about one out of every five Americans who eats breakfast out eats a donut. But the company is not in business simply to service the same sleepy-eyed commuters time and again. It is constantly doing market research and adding new products to expand its customer base as well as to get already loyal patrons to do more of their eating at Dunkin' Donuts. Muffins, brownies, cookies, soups, and, naturally, croissants are some of the examples of products that have been added to the mix.

Dunkin' Donuts franchisees invest varying amounts of capital, depending on whether they purchase or lease the land on which they build their store, or buy a company-developed site. In recent years, over half of new franchisees in this country have decided to own their own land and buildings. In any case, of course, Dunkin' Donuts must approve all decisions you make, from site selection to construction details. The cost of buying into the chain also varies by region. Some regions have been reserved for multiunit operators, who own more than 32 percent of the company's stores.

Franchisees attend a six-week semester at the Dunkin' Donuts University in Braintree, Massachusetts. The course includes production techniques as well as traditional business practices. You can borrow any of the training films you see here once you've set up your store.

You will also receive a set of manuals to use for reference in your business.

The company's district sales manager is the liaison between you and your franchisor. The district sales manager has a checklist of everything that needs to be done before your first customer comes through the door. That sales manager will guide you through your grand opening and be there for you whenever you need advice.

Dunkin' Donuts does not produce the ingredients for the products that you will produce and sell. You buy them from company-approved suppliers. That approval doesn't come easily, and the chain periodically monitors the suppliers to maintain quality control. Company inspectors check your end products at least as carefully. You must meet detailed specifications for everything you sell. The company has, for example, fifty pages of specifications for coffee alone.

While the franchisor doesn't manufacture its own ingredients, it does try to assist its franchisees in purchasing them at the lowest price possible, and it tries to insure that distribution channels are set up so that no store ever runs short of anything. Volume purchasing keeps prices low and steady. The company is also in the process of setting up regional distribution centers in cooperation with franchisees to hold down the costs of distribution.

Because of the company's size, requests for information about becoming a franchisee are handled by regional offices.

For further information contact the office closest to you:

Dunkin' Donuts
220 Forbes Rd., Braintree, MA 02184, 617-848-6800

825 Georges Rd., North Brunswick, NJ 08902, 201-846-1600

4380 Georgetown Square, Suite 1005, Atlanta, GA 30338, 404-451-5461

1550 Northwest Highway, Park Ridge, IL 60068, 312-296-1151

Campbell Forum, Suite 200, 801 East Campbell, Richardson, TX 75081, 214-783-8237

In Canada:
10620 Côte de Liesse, Lachine, P.Q., Canada H8T 1A5, 514-636-5165

Mister Donut

Initial license fee: $15,000
Royalties: 5.4%
Advertising royalties: 3%
Minimum cash required: $60,000

Capital required: $150,000 to $300,000
Financing: The company may help finance the purchase of equipment.
Length of contract: 20 years

In business since: 1955
Franchising since: 1956
Total number of units: 704
Number of company-operated units: 2
Total number of units planned, 1990: NA
Number of company-operated units planned, 1990: NA

This wholly owned subsidiary of Multifoods Corporation (acquired in 1970) has been turning out donuts since Eisenhower was president. They have, in their own words, "refined the art of donut making to the point where our donuts exceed the industry standard." In fact, Mister Donut has sold more than just donuts for some time. Its shops also feature a full line of pastries, including such delectables as brownies, cookies, muffins, pecan rolls, and turnovers. Other recent additions include bagels, croissants, and soup. And the company is quick to state that its "fresh-ground coffee is equally renowned."

The Mister Donut system is a fully packaged operation, from the appearance of its shops, emblems, and signs to the preparation of its products. According to the company, its "shop layouts are based on a 'quick-serve' concept, with customers purchasing their donuts as they would in a bakery, rather than 'ordering' them as they would in a restaurant. Booths have replaced counter seating. And drive-up windows add a new dimension to the convenience aspect of the shops."

At present, Mister Donut is the third-biggest donut chain in the United States and second in average sales volume per unit. That, says the company, makes it "one of the best-known names in the fast-food industry." It is adding new units at the rate of about eighty per year, some of them in Canada, where there are already fifty-six Mr. Donut shops, forty-seven of them in Ontario.

Mr. Donut works with you from the word "go." It begins by discussing site selection with you. Once you see a spot you like, the company analyzes its accessibility and visibility, zoning, and demographics. Whether you've chosen a freestanding building, a storefront, or a shopping center location, Mister Donut works with you to bring your store up to company specifications.

You don't need experience to become a Mister Donut franchisee, but before you open your doors for business, you have to take the company's four-week training program, which it gives at its headquarters in Saint Paul, Minnesota. This intensive training runs the gamut from cost and quality control to purchasing. Your traveling and living expenses during this period are your responsibility.

As you launch your new enterprise, Mr. Donut personnel help you to choose and train employees and build your inventory. They also vigorously promote your grand opening. Once in business, you can take advantage of company marketing aids, such as media tapes and on-site promotional material, and cooperative advertising campaigns. Should you run into problems with any aspect of your franchise, you can get advice from your district manager.

"When you use the Mister Donut name and trademark, you cash in on the benefits of an enormous amount of carefully built goodwill," says the company. And it means to keep its good name, for your benefit and its own. The company expects you to keep your business up to par as far as its standards are concerned. That means regular inspections of your business practices and products. In addition, Mister Donut will permit you to purchase only from approved vendors.

For further information contact:

In the United States:
Director of Franchise Development, Mister Donut of America, Inc., Multifoods Tower, Box 2942, Minneapolis, MN 55402, 1-800-328-8304, Ext. 3477

In Canada:
Mister Donut of Canada, Ltd., 1111 Finch Ave. West, Suite 206, Downsview, Ontario, Canada M3J 2E5 416-665-8846

The Original Great American Chocolate Chip Cookie Company

Initial license fee: $20,000
Royalties: 7%
Advertising royalties: None
Minimum cash required: $115,000
Capital required: $115,000 to $140,000
Financing: None
Length of contract: NA

In business since: 1977
Franchising since: 1978
Total number of units: 288
Number of company-operated units: 39
Total number of units planned, 1990: NA
Number of company-operated units planned, 1990: NA

This company's name is almost as big a mouthful as its product. Arthur Karp, one of the founders of The Cookie Company (as its store sign reads), says that "chocolate chips originated with the Indians who had to chop up chocolate with a knife." Therefore, he asserts, "the chocolate chip cookie is the only baked good indigenous to this country."

Karp has written that "the American dream is a dream of being your own boss, of owning your own business, of working hard at something you care about, and earning profits that can mean the good life for you and your family." His dream started in a garage, with himself, Michael Coles, an associate from the clothing business, and their wives trying to come up with an irresistible recipe for chocolate chip cookies. They found it in one handed down from Karp's wife's great-grandmother.

They sold their first cookies at the Perimeter Mall in Atlanta in 1977. Within a decade, the product had made The Cookie Company the biggest cookie retailer in the country. The company has continued to seek locations in malls, and gauges its operation's reputation as a solid business by the fact that it now numbers among its franchisees several of the top shopping mall developers in the United States.

In addition to the main product, The Cookie Company sells Pecan Chocolate Chip, Double Fudge Chocolate Chip, Oatmeal, and Macadamia Coconut cookies, as well as brownies. Its Double Doozie cookie sandwich has icing in the middle. Giant Message Cookies, a specialty of the shops, feature an inscription printed in icing, birthday cake-style. The company makes fresh batter daily for all these products at its plant in Atlanta and ships it by refrigerated truck to each store.

Wood, brass, hand-painted tiles, mirrors, and indirect light give a fresh look to Cookie Company stores. Cookies are displayed in the store's lighted showcases, and revolving ovens offer visual proof of a freshly baked product. If that doesn't draw customers, the odor of the just-baked cookies, wafted into the surrounding area by a fan, surely does the job.

The typical in-line store occupies about 600 square feet of space. In malls where such a store is not available, franchisees can take advantage of available space to install a kiosk, with 250 square feet and a small remote storage and cleaning facility. In some large malls, franchisees put in a satellite unit of 30 to 80 square feet, just big enough to display and sell cookies baked at the main, in-line unit. This covers traffic that might not pass the main location.

Franchisees do not need prior experience in the food business, and the company accepts absentee ownership. The Cookie Company helps new franchisees secure a good location and trains them in Atlanta, supplementing classroom lectures with on-the-job experience. The company helps you to get your business going with assistance in the hiring and training of your employees. It will back you up with a full program of on-site promotions, including a special grand opening promotion and ongoing advertising.

The Cookie Company stresses quality in its product above everything else. As company cofounder Michael Coles put it: "We better be good, because we're selling a product that's more expensive than steak."

For further information contact:
The Original Great American Chocolate Chip Company, Inc., 4685 Frederick Drive, S.W., Atlanta, GA 30336, 404-696-1700

Fried Chicken

Church's Fried Chicken, Inc.

Initial license fee: $15,000
Royalties: 5%
Advertising royalties 5%
Minimum cash required: $100,000
Capital required: $200,000
Financing: The company extends a line of credit to cover any unforeseen costs of restaurant opening.
Length of contract: 15 years

In business since: 1952
Franchising since: 1952
Total number of units: 1,445
Number of company-operated units: 1,218
Total number of units planned, 1990: 1,665
Number of company-operated units planned, 1990: 1,343

Franchisee Michael Gardner of Nashville, Tennessee, calls his relationship with Church's Fried Chicken, Inc., "an exceptionally good marriage." That's not surprising, because the company has had plenty of practice as a franchisor. And Church's plans to repeat its success on an even greater scale through expansion both in the U.S. and abroad.

"I was looking for a business opportunity that would allow me to manage my own investment," recalls Michael Gardner. Church's helped him make his decision by providing information on the financial condition of existing franchises and the corporation, and by arranging a fact-finding trip for him along with a tour of the company's facility. Impressed not only by the business but by Church's "concern with people," he decided to purchase his franchise after meeting with the complete franchise team, which included the chairman of the board, the president, and vice presidents.

New franchisees attend a five-week training school in San Antonio, Texas. You will receive intensive training in Church's cooking techniques and restaurant operations. The three weeks of classroom instruction and two weeks of on-the-job experience will thoroughly prepare you to manage your fast-food fried chicken store. Then a Church's field team will come to your site to assist you until you feel confident on your own. The company will also extend a line of credit to cover any unforeseen costs relating to your fledgling operation.

Church's maintains strict criteria for store locations. Once the site review board approves your location, field orientation staff will prepare you to negotiate the purchase or lease of the real estate. You will then meet with company construction experts to learn about construction issues like how to deal with contractors. And as your location nears completion, you will attend a preopening meeting to prepare for your grand opening.

Refresher training offered in stores near your location covers a variety of topics, such as new products, marketing promotions, and procedures. And, as Michael Gardner notes, "everyone needs to attend a refresher course on maintenance occasionally." For two people per store, this training is free of charge, though you will be responsible for employees' expenses and salaries while they attend. Church's is "very helpful as an information agency and helpful in maintaining our overall wholesale price structure," according to Michael Gardner. By reviewing and approving suppliers for its franchisees, Church's helps them get the best prices for the best materials. The company will also help you keep your books and will perform audits to ensure you manage your funds as efficiently as possible.

Michael Gardner feels that his Church's franchise has been a good investment because "I enjoy making decisions and I have the freedom I want. I have control of my own investment." He reflects that, like any good marriage, his relationship with Church's is based on mutual respect and support. "They practice what they preach and are concerned about me as a franchisee. They work hard to help me succeed. The Church's Fried Chicken management team is concerned about success. I am proud to be a member of this family."

For further information contact:

George N. Samaras, Vice President, Franchising, Church's Fried Chicken, Inc., P.O. Box BH001, San Antonio, TX 78284, 512-735-9392

Kentucky Fried Chicken

Initial license fee: $10,000
Royalties: 4%
Advertising royalties: 2%
Minimum cash required: $360,000
Capital required: $360,000
Financing: Available only through a special program to help minorities become franchisees
Length of contract: 20 years

In business since: 1930
Franchising since: 1952
Total number of units: 8,200
Number of company-operated units: 1,800
Total number of units planned, 1990: NA
Number of company-operated units planned, 1990: NA

As company legend has it, Colonel Harland Sanders discovered the Kentucky Fried Chicken secret formula in 1939. The Colonel began to sell franchises in 1952, but business didn't really take off until 1955, when he started to collect his pension from Social Security. Since then the company has changed hands several times, although the Colonel himself stayed on as a goodwill ambassador until his death in 1980, at which time the venerable white-suited gentleman with the goatee earned $225,000 a year to embody the old-fashioned, "finger-lickin'" goodness of the company's main product.

Pepsico, the most recent owner of Kentucky Fried Chicken, also owns Pizza Hut and Taco Bell. With its purchase of the chain, the company-owned stores switched from Coke to Pepsi, and Pepsico urged franchisees to do the same.

Kentucky Fried Chicken maintains a uniform appearance for its restaurants throughout the chain. Your free-standing store, therefore, probably seating about one hundred, must follow the company's specifications for construction and decoration, and you may have to remodel the premises from time to time, at your expense, in accordance with changes in the chain's look.

Franchisees take their Kentucky Fried Chicken training at the Louisville, Kentucky, company headquarters. The company requires the course for franchisees and recommends it for other key personnel. Kentucky Fried Chicken pays $150 toward the living expenses of two people during the training period. Subjects covered in the course include sanitation, product preparation, safety, inventory control, equipment maintenance, sales projection, staffing, and accounting.

For $1,800, you can buy a special Kentucky Fried Chicken Store

Training and Rating System (STAR) for training your employees. The system, based on the use of videotapes and workbooks, allows employees to learn at their own pace.

Franchisees must make all items on the menu according to specifications in the franchise manual, with supplies purchased from company-approved sources only. The fabled seasonings that enable the company to brag that "we do chicken right," for example, are made only by the Stange Company of Chicago.

Unfortunately, those wishing to buy one of these franchises will have to get on line. Previous franchisees have taken most of the market areas, and Kentucky Fried Chicken has reserved others for the development of company stores. When an area does become available, the company must offer it to the nearest franchisee already in business. Franchisees usually jump at the chance to buy additional units. So about the only thing you can do, if you're still interested, is to qualify as a franchisee and then wait for the opportunity to buy an existing franchise. However, there is already a waiting list of people who intend to follow that course of action.

For further information contact:
Becky Lynch, Franchise Sales, Kentucky Fried Chicken, P.O. Box 32070, Louisville, KY 40232-2070, 502-456-8647

Pioneer Take Out Corporation

Initial license fee: $25,000 to $150,000
Royalties: 5.9%
Advertising royalties: 3.9%
Minimum cash required: $75,000
Capital required: $150,000 to $300,000
Financing: The company will help you get a loan from the Small Business Administration.
Length of contract: 20 years

In business since: 1961
Franchising since: 1961
Total number of units: 300
Number of company-operated units: 45
Total number of units planned, 1990: 515
Number of company-operated units planned, 1990: 100

Pioneer promotes its Pioneer Chicken restaurants with advertising and public relations personal appearances featuring both former football star O.J. Simpson and a seven-foot chicken. The menu of the predominantly free-standing fast-food restaurants features fried chicken, although several other dishes have supplemented chicken in recent years. Patrons can now order spicy rice, soup, and seafood, and many shopping mall locations contain salad bars. In 1983 Pioneer began to make buttermilk biscuits a highlight of its menu, and it redesigned its plans for new restaurants to accommodate special baking areas.

Pioneer, which has made a profit in every year of its existence, has concentrated its restaurants in the West, with recent expansion to Indonesia. However, the company now feels ready to move into the eastern half of the United States, with Washington, D.C., Baltimore, Philadelphia, and selected areas of New Jersey targeted for its expansion. The company bases its licensing fee on the population of the territory granted.

Pioneer usually selects a site for franchisee restaurants and builds the unit itself. You will lease your building from Pioneer and buy your restaurant equipment from the company's subsidiary, PSI Equipment Corporation.

Pioneer's Los Angeles training program, one of the most extensive in its industry, is accredited by the American Council on Education for six college credits. You will start off with three weeks in a Pioneer restaurant, where you will receive an overview of the unit operations. There you will get experience in cooking, maintaining equipment, and customer service. Next you will take three weeks of classroom instruction, covering accounting, cash flow, ordering from suppliers, inventory and cost control, scheduling, sanitation and fire regulations, employee relations and training, and communications skills. The training concludes with a four-week management internship at a Pioneer restaurant, where you get a chance to apply what you've learned.

Just before the opening of your unit, Pioneer's opening team will spend seven days on the premises, training your crew and helping you with last-minute preparations. After your opening, Pioneer will keep in close touch with you, sending a company representative to your store once a month to spot any problems, answer your questions, and fill you in on the latest advertising campaign.

Pioneer restaurants use an enormous amount of food each year, including 30 million pounds of chicken and 2 million pounds of North Atlantic cod. While you may purchase much of your food and other supplies from any company on the list of company-approved vendors, you must buy certain items from a single authorized source. For example, you will buy the special batter with which you will make fried chicken, and Pioneer's Orange Whip soft drink, from company affiliates. And required purchases include a number of specially formulated foods like barbecue sauce, coleslaw dressing, barbecue beans, gravy mix, and seasonings available only from a limited number of wholesale grocers. Paper goods and uniforms imprinted with the Pioneer trademark fall in the same category.

For further information contact:
Pioneer Take Out Corporation, 3663 West Sixth St., Los Angeles, CA 90020, 213-738-0600

Popeyes Famous Fried Chicken & Biscuits

Initial license fee: $25,000 for first unit plus $10,000 option fee for each of the four other units you must purchase, for a total of $65,000
Royalties: 5%
Advertising royalties: 3%
Minimum cash required: $65,000
Capital required: $1,500,000
Financing: None
Length of contract: 20 years

In business since: 1972
Franchising since: 1976
Total number of units: 333
Number of company-operated units: 170
Total number of units planned, 1990: NA
Number of company-operated units planned, 1990: NA

"We're the most copied fried chicken franchise in the world today," claims Al Copeland, the founder of Popeyes. "We're responsible for bringing taste back to fast food," says Bill Copeland, the company's executive vice president. They base their claims on the franchisor's peppery Cajun recipe for chicken and rice, the "dirty rice" now available at competing restaurants.

Popeyes, the restaurants with the red roofs and orange-and-yellow signs, sells chicken by the bucket and by the piece. In addition to Cajun rice, which comes with chicken dinners along with Popeyes' buttermilk biscuits, side orders on the menu include red beans and rice, onion rings, french fries, cole slaw, chicken tacos, peppers, and corn on the cob. The restaurants serve two desserts: pudding and hot apple pie.

Popeyes sells franchise territories rather than individual franchises. This means you have to commit yourself to buying a minimum of five units, which can range from walk-up stands to 100-seat restaurants with elaborate interior decorating schemes. The company will not sell franchises to a corporation. After purchasing a territory, you can request that Popeyes assign ownership to a corporation, but you must own at least 51 percent of it.

You must secure land and construction services for your units, but

Popeyes will assist you with the negotiations. The more than twenty interior decoration plans available from the franchisor provide considerable flexibility for adapting your restaurants to their local markets and allow you to have some influence on what the appearance of your establishments will say about your business.

The franchisor requires that you and at least three managers from each of your restaurants attend the Popeyes Institute of Polytechnics, held either at corporate headquarters in New Orleans or at a district office. You pay for traveling and lodging expenses and, of course, the salaries of your personnel. Your six- to seven-week training will cover finance, real estate, operations, management, purchasing, marketing and advertising, and employee counseling.

A Popeyes "Pro-Crew" will come to your restaurants to help train your employees and get your business off to a prosperous start. The company's Biscuit College provides additional training for your staff. A Popeyes field consultant will work with you thereafter, visiting each of your businesses frequently. The company points out that it has the highest ratio of field consultants to restaurants in the industry: one for about every fifteen units.

You may purchase equipment and food from any company-authorized vendor, although the franchisor has its own purchase-and-distribution system, which, it says, offers some purchasing advantages to franchisees.

For further information contact:
Franchise Division, Popeyes Famous Fried Chicken & Biscuits, One Popeyes Plaza, 1333 South Clearview Parkway, Jefferson, LA 70121, 504-733-4300

Convenience Stores

Convenient Food Mart, Inc.

Initial license fee: $5,000 to $15,000, determined by regional franchisor
Royalties: 4.5% to 5%
Advertising royalties: None
Minimum cash required: $45,000
Capital required: $60,000
Financing: Some regional franchisors offer financial assistance to franchisees.
Length of contract: 10 years

In business since: 1958
Franchising since: 1958
Total number of units: 1,276

Number of company-operated units: 10
Total number of units planned, 1990: NA
Number of company-operated units planned, 1990: NA

From apples to aspirin, from milkshakes to motor oil, and from tin foil to tabloids, you can find almost anything at a Convenient Food Mart store. Founded on the idea that people would patronize "supermarkets in miniature," where they could find whatever they needed—Band-Aids, birthday candles, or bananas—at hours convenient to them, Convenient Food Mart now operates throughout the United States and worldwide. Located in strip shopping centers and urban storefronts, or established independently as freestanding stores, Convenient Food Marts serve high-traffic areas with a mix of merchandise designed to meet the needs of each specific community. Some offer gasoline, others sell alcoholic beverages, and still others operate full-service delicatessens. But all have in common a dedication to customer service.

The Convenient Food Mart system is actually a network of licensed regional franchisors who sell franchises to individual store owners. Independent business people obtain licenses to operate as regional franchisors and commit to a plan for developing an agreed-upon number of stores in their region within a given time frame. These regional franchisors in turn recruit franchisees and oversee franchisee operations in their region. Convenient Food Mart's strategy of decentralized operations ensures that the particular demographics of each region are more closely taken into account in the operation of stores in that region. At the same time, the company sets forth highly standardized requirements for store image and the methods by which stores are operated, in order to help franchisees repeat the success of Convenient Food Mart stores worldwide.

In addition to standardization, Convenient Food Mart strongly believes that the efforts of individual store owners play a vital role in the company's success. As Robert Risberg, president and CEO, puts it, "the people in our system are the strength of our enterprise. Our most important assets are our regional licensees and their store owner-operators." The company discourages absentee ownership and part-time management, and makes sure that franchisees receive all of the training and support they need to help make their stores a success.

Starting with site selection and store construction, your regional franchisor will help you meet your goals. The franchisor will research the demographics and traffic patterns of locations you are considering and will provide you with the best possible judgment of the potential of a given site. The ultimate selection is up to you, however, and when you start construction of your new store you must meet time-tested specifications intended to provide your Convenient Food Mart with the friendly, clean, and efficient image maintained by stores throughout the system. The company will provide you with an equipment package chosen specifically for your store and will help with interior design and store layout.

Your step-by-step training covers everything that goes into daily convenience store operation from the time you open your doors in the morning to the time you close them at night. You will learn how to read statements, keep records, maintain your store and equipment, manage employees, and promote your business. Your training continues after your store opening, as merchandising experts pay regular visits to your store to evaluate your operation and offer guidance on inventory, efficiency, and cost controls. You will also be given a manual of operations, which you can use as a daily reference.

Your regional franchisor will make initial arrangements for your inventory—arrangements that will continue to save you time and money throughout your years as a franchisee. The company will help out with advertising on a regional basis and provide you with a bookkeeping system based on the latest accounting technology.

Each day, franchisees complete reports that regional franchisors analyze. From these reports, your regional franchisor will be able to provide you with profit-and-loss statements and other valuable management reports. National franchisor analysts will periodically visit your store and furnish you with an analysis of your operations. Their reports will help you evaluate your product mix and inventory turnover, and make changes that can mean higher profits.

For further information contact:
Convenient Food Mart, Inc., National Executive Offices, World Headquarters, 9701 West Higgins Rd., Suite 850, Rosemont, IL 60018, 312-692-9150

7-Eleven

Initial license fee: $30,000
Royalties: 50%
Advertising royalties: None
Minimum cash required: $30,000
Capital required: $37,300
Financing: The company may finance part of your investment.
Length of contract: NA

In business since: 1927
Franchising since: 1964
Total number of units: 7,323
Number of company-operated units: 4,526

Total number of units planned, 1990: NA
Number of company-operated units planned, 1990: NA

Southland Corporation, 7-Eleven's parent company and America's seventh-largest retailer, got into the convenience store business almost as an afterthought. Its original business was selling ice. Bread, eggs, and milk entered the picture only when customers at one of its stores asked the manager to carry the items as a convenience to them. It turned out to be convenient for the company, too, which now serves 8 million customers a day in forty-one states and has stores in several foreign countries, including 2,592 in Japan.

While 7-Elevens have replaced mom-and-pop grocery stores in many neighborhoods, it would be inaccurate to think of them simply as franchised grocery stores. Despite the name—from the original store hours: 7 A.M. to 11 P.M.—most units stay open twenty-four hours a day. They serve sandwiches and hot coffee, and customers can also buy gasoline from the stores' self-service pumps. In fact, Southland, which purchased Citgo a few years ago, is the world's biggest independent gasoline retailer.

7-Eleven stores may not be the ideal franchise for every entrepreneur. The company makes most of your important business decisions, after you have decided what kind and level of service you will provide. In return for the company's expert assistance in every area of your business, you will pay a 50 percent royalty fee, but the 7-Eleven name makes it highly probable that your store will be profitable. And unlike many of the other big name franchisors, 7-Eleven charges you very little up front for the license to use its name.

7-Eleven provides you with a turnkey operation. It selects a site, builds the store, and stocks and equips it. Much of your royalty fee goes toward the rent the company charges. You establish the prices in your store and reorder inventory from company-approved vendors, some of which are 7-Eleven affiliates or subsidiaries of Southland. The company will do your bookkeeping for you. You will deposit your daily receipts, from which 7-Eleven will pay for your purchases and operating expenses and make out your payroll checks.

The company's training program includes work at a training store. You supplement this practical experience with a week of classroom work at a regional training center. After completing instruction, you hire and train the employees who will work in your store. Although often run as family operations, 7-Eleven stores generally require additional employees.

Every retail store owner thinks at least occasionally about the possibility of being held up. A few years ago stickups plagued many

7-Eleven stores, but the company helped reduce them substantially by taking the advice of its special security consultant, Ray Johnson, whose twenty-five years in prison for a series of holdups had well qualified him to speak on the subject. 7-Eleven improved store lighting, moved the cash register to a place easily visible from the street, instructed clerks to deposit large bills in a safe, and lowered display racks to improve visibility throughout the store.

The presence of its stores in so many places has kept 7-Eleven in the public eye, and it runs a good deal of national advertising to reinforce its high name recognition. It also promotes itself through an extensive program of public relations on the local and national level based on the image of "A Concerned Corporate Citizen." In keeping with this image, 7-Eleven is a sponsor of the Muscular Dystrophy Association and the Jerry Lewis Labor Day Telethon to raise money to fight the disease. It was also a sponsor of the 1984 Olympic Games and built the Velodrome for the Games' cycling events.

Currently, franchises are available only in the areas listed, and you should get in touch with the regional office of the area in which you have an interest.

For further information contact:

Arizona:
Zone Manager, 7-Eleven Zone Office, 1414 West Broadway Rd., Suite 101, Tempe, AZ 85282, 602-968-8728

Northern California; Reno, Nevada; San Joaquin Valley, California:
Franchise Liaison Manager, 7-Eleven Zone Office, 655 University Ave., Suite 110, Sacramento, CA 95825, 916-929-7700

San Fernando Valley, California:
Zone Franchise Coordinator, 7-Eleven Zone Office, 27201 Tourney Rd., Suite 225, Valencia, CA 91355, 805-254-7711

Inland Empire, California:
Zone Franchise Coordinator, 7-Eleven Zone Office, 9375 Archibald Ave., Suite 307, Rancho Cucamonga, CA 91730, 714-980-6290,

Central Los Angeles, California:
Zone Franchise Coordinator, 7-Eleven Zone Office, 27201 Tourney Rd., Suite 225, Valencia, CA 91355, 805-254-7711

Western Los Angeles, California:
Zone Franchise Coordinator, 7-Eleven Zone Office, 460 Carson Plaza Drive, Suite 207, Carson, CA 90745, 213-516-6710

Southern Los Angeles, California:
Zone Franchise Coordinator, 7-Eleven Zone Office, 13517 Fairview St., Garden Grove, CA 92643, 714-750-7711

San Diego, California:
Franchise Coordinator, 7-Eleven Stores, 7839 University Ave., La Mesa, CA 92041, 619-465-2101

Nevada (except Reno):
Zone Manager, 7-Eleven Zone Office, 1900 East Flamingo Rd., Suite 272, Las Vegas, NV 89119, 702-735-3178

Idaho, Oregon, and Washington:
Patsy Coffman, Administrative Superior, 7-Eleven Stores, 1035 Andover Park West, Tukwila, WA 98188, 206-575-6711

Northern Maryland (Greater Baltimore area):
Zone Manager, 7-Eleven Zone Office, 8605 Old Harford Rd., Baltimore, MD 21234, 301-665-7885

Southern Maryland; Shenandoah, Virginia (Greater Charlottesville area); Washington, D.C.:
Zone Manager, 7-Eleven Zone Office, 111 Massachusetts Ave., N.W., Suite 500, Washington, D.C. 20001, 202-682-1510

Southern New Jersey and Eastern Pennsylvania:
Division Training Manager, 7-Eleven Stores, 2711 Easton Rd., Willow Grove, PA 19090, 215-672-5711, Ext. 210,

Northern New Jersey, Connecticut, Massachusetts, Southern New Hampshire, New York, Rhode Island:
Flo Orlando, Secretary to Division Manager, 7-Eleven Stores, One West Red Oak Lane, White Plains, NY 10604, 914-694-4800

Illinois and Indiana:
Zone Manager, 7-Eleven Zone Office, 1995 Hicks Rd., Rolling Meadows, IL 60008, 312-991-8711

Michigan:
Zone Manager, 7-Eleven Zone Office, 26533 Evergreen Rd., Suite 508, Southfield, MI 48076, 313-356-0830

Hamburgers and Fast Food

A & W Restaurants, Inc.

Initial license fee: $10,000
Royalties: 4%
Advertising royalties: 4%
Minimum cash required: $100,000
Capital requried: $450,000
Financing: None
Length of contract: 20 years

In business since: 1919
Franchising since: 1925
Total number of units: 515
Number of company-operated units: 7
Total number of units planned, 1990: 633
Number of company-operated units planned, 1990: NA

Think of A & W, and you think of a big frosty mug of root beer topped with a rich head of foam. But A & W is more than root beer: The company likes to call its menu "upscale fast food." A & W currently sells "A & W Great Food Restaurant" franchises, which offer a full line of quality fast food, from one-third-pound hand-packed hamburgers to old-fashioned hot dogs, chicken, onion rings, and french fries.

A & W, one of the oldest fast-food chains in the United States, operates internationally as well. Many A & W units now include White Mountain Creamery Ice Cream, which is made on the premises according to a patented formula. White Mountain Creameries also operate as independent franchises. Because A & W has franchised since 1925, it has fully developed its training and support systems and has refined its time-tested franchise system, as well as the products themselves. The company hopes to continue expanding and improving its franchise program with new franchises throughout the United States.

When you buy an A & W franchise, the company will train you in all the skills and procedures essential to the successful operation of your restaurant. Every franchisee must complete the two-week training program, either at corporate headquarters in Dearborn, Michigan, or at a regional training center. Covering all points of your business, from equipment maintenance to inventory control, the classroom portion of your training includes special work in accounting. After you've completed the program, you get hands-on experience at a company-operated restaurant. For four to six weeks, franchisees work at an established A & W Restaurant to sharpen their skills on the job. You will learn all about what it takes to run an A & W Great Food Restaurant on a daily basis, whether it's how to grill the perfect hamburger or when to order new supplies.

A & W provides all its franchisees with comprehensive preopening support. The company will help you select a site and must approve the location you choose. During lease or purchase negotiations, construction, and equipment layout, a franchise coordinator works with you to make sure everything runs as smoothly as possible. And as your grand opening approaches, the company will advise you on hiring employees and advertising your restaurant.

Once your franchise is in operation, your franchise coordinator will continue to help you in any area in which you feel you need support.

In addition to responding to specific requests from A & W owners, franchise coordinators make periodic visits to units in their territories, assisting with operations, marketing, and equipment maintenance, and making sure that everything meets A & W's high standards. Owners can also attend refresher training whenever they feel they need it, and must attend at least once every five years. Conducted by A & W staff, these refresher sessions cover basic operations and update franchisees in policy and procedures. The training is free, but you must pay for your own travel and lodging. Between refresher sessions and visits from field representatives, you can rely on A & W's comprehensive operations manual to answer almost any question you might have about running your restaurant.

Because the company's reputation—and your own—rests almost entirely on the quality of the food served in your restaurant, A & W requires that you purchase A & W label supplies through company-approved sources only. You must carry A & W root beer in your restaurant, and you are expected to meet all of the company's criteria for food and service quality. Despite these and other common restrictions placed on you as a franchisee, the A & W franchise contract is unusual in that it does not prohibit you from putting the skills you have gained as a franchisee to work in operating your own non–A & W restaurant, as long as you don't violate certain patents on White Mountain Creamery Ice Cream.

For further information contact:

Paul E. Nierzwicki, Vice President, Franchise Operations, A & W Restaurants, Inc., One Parklane Blvd., Suite 500 East, Dearborn, MI 48126, 313-271-9300

Bojangles'

Initial license fee: $25,000 to $35,000
Royalties: 4%
Advertising royalties: 5%
Minimum cash required: $120,000
Capital required: $694,000 to $858,000
Financing: The company will recommend sources of financing.
Length of contract: 20 years

In business since: 1977
Franchising since: 1979
Total number of units: 360
Number of company-operated units: 169
Total number of units planned, 1990: NA
Number of company-operated units planned, 1990: NA

Tired of the same old burger-and-fries fast food? Consider Bojangles'. Founded in response to growing consumer demand for fresher, more nutritious fast food, Bojangles' concept is to serve made-from-scratch products in a fast-food setting. The Bojangles' menu is unique in the fast-food industry, consisting of fresh biscuits filled with a variety of ingredients and spicy Cajun-style fried chicken served with Cajun gravy, "dirty rice," and Cajun pintos. Serving three meals daily to eat-in, take-out, and drive-thru customers, Bojangles' is most popular among breakfast diners. By offering an alternative to standard fast-food fare and by maintaining its commitment to convenience and quality, Bojangles' has prospered, and the company hopes to share that prosperity with more franchisees in the eastern U.S., from New York State to the Florida keys.

Bojangles' offers single- and multiple-unit franchises. In a multiunit development agreement, the franchisee and company agree upon a plan whereby the franchisee will develop a specified number of Bojangles' restaurants within a certain time frame in a given geographical region. Franchisees must have a net worth of at least $500,000 and liquid assets of $120,000 for each unit to be developed. The franchise fee for the first unit in a territory is $35,000, and for subsequent units in the territory it is $25,000. The manager responsible for daily operation of the restaurant, if not a sole owner-operator, must have at least 25 percent of equity in the franchise.

Your site must meet the approval of Bojangles', and your building must be constructed according to Bojangles' specifications. With its distinctive design and colorful signs, your restaurant will be instantly recognizable. The company will assist you in every way possible during construction. Some of the equipment that you will use in your restaurant is unique to Bojangles', so you must purchase it from designated sources. You may purchase all other equipment and supplies from specified suppliers or from any other sources that the company approves.

Before opening your Bojangles', you and your management staff must attend a comprehensive six-week training program at the company's Charlotte, North Carolina, headquarters. Designed to mold your staff into a team of well-trained, highly motivated restaurant professionals, the program is divided into two sections: four weeks of on-the-job training in an existing Bojangles' restaurant and two weeks of basic management training at the Bojangles' Learning Center. You will learn work station operations, general procedures, labor and inventory management, profit-and-loss analysis, employee relations, and local restaurant marketing.

Following this, a Bojangles' franchise field service representative will come to your site to help you hire and train your restaurant crew and assist with all other phases of preopening. A Bojangles' "master biscuit maker" will join you seven days before opening to train your biscuit makers. The field representative will held with your grand opening and will then continue to visit regularly to make sure your restaurant operates at peak efficiency.

During the term of your franchise contract, the company requires you to participate in refresher training, generally held quarterly in franchise regions and sometimes conducted at corporate headquarters. Providing updates on new products, and equipment and marketing techniques, refresher training is designed to keep you on the cutting edge of the fast-food industry. Your advertising royalties will support the marketing fund, which provides market research, local media support, promotional materials, and national advertising. And Bojangles' test kitchens continually develop new products designed to make your Bojangles' even more profitable. Bojangles' also provides purchasing assistance and offers the purchasing power of a large organization, allowing you to buy quality products at the lowest prices.

For further information contact:
William Thelen, Vice President, Franchising, Bojangles' Corporation, P.O. Box 240239, Charlotte, NC 28224, 704-527-2675

Captain D'S Seafood Restaurants

Initial license fee: $10,000
Royalties: 3%
Advertising royalties: 2%
Minimum cash required: $122,000
Capital required: $122,000
Financing: None
Length of Contract: NA

In business since: 1969
Franchising since: 1975
Total number of units: 484
Number of company-operated units: 270
Total number of units planned, 1990: NA
Number of company-operated units planned, 1990: NA

The trend in this country toward a lighter diet has broadened the appeal of fast-food fish restaurants over the past two decades or so. Doctors and nutritionists have been warning the public to lower its risk of heart disease by cutting down on fats and cholesterol. One way to accomplish this, they keep saying, is to eat less red meat and more fish.

And Americans have been listening. Consumption of fish is up by more than 20 percent since 1969.

Combine the increase in fish eating with the fact that about 90 percent of Americans eat at a fast-food restaurant at least once a month, and it is clear that there's a lot of money to be made serving fish fast-food style. Shoney's, Inc., a company that operates several kinds of restaurants, knows it. Its Captain D's chain—"a great little seafood place"—seeks to exploit eating trends with its simple fast-food, limited menu restaurants. Combination seafood platters and clam, oyster, fish fillet, and shrimp dinners are the heart of its fare. But there are also chicken and burgers for the nonfish eaters. The restaurants sell beer where locally permitted.

The typical 74-seat Captain D's is located in an area with a population of about 30,000 people, at least 6,000 of whom live or work within a mile of the unit. The company places its restaurants on main traffic arteries, where they are visible from all directions, with no hills, curves, stop signs, or traffic lights nearby to distract attention or clog traffic. The decorative scheme of each establishment features stained wood for a rustic touch and other design elements that suggest a nautical spirit. Construction and layout provide for take-out and drive-thru service as well as on-premises dining.

Training for franchisees takes place in Nashville, Tennessee. The company requires four weeks of hands-on store training for the owner, manager, and assistant manager of each restaurant, and the manager and owner must also take an additional week of classroom instruction. A major subject covered in this training is the accounting system customized for Captain D's.

The company provides on-site help for your opening and initial days of operation. Regional franchise meetings, held several times a year, facilitate communication between franchise owners and the company and aid in solving any problems that may have arisen. Through its field marketing staff, the company will help you with any type of promotion you want to run.

You must use the special recipe fish batter prepared by the company. For other materials, you can choose your own suppliers, as long as they meet with Captain D's approval. You will also get an opportunity to take advantage of purchasing savings through national supply contracts negotiated by the company. Periodic unannounced inspection visits insure your compliance with Captain D's quality standards.

For further information contact:

Ronald E. Walker, Director, Franchise Operations, Captain D's, 1727 Elm Hill Pike, Nashville, TN 37210, 615-361-5201

Carl's Junior Restaurants

Initial license fee: $35,000
Royalties: 3% to 4%
Advertising royalties: 4%
Minimum cash required: $175,000
Capital required: $850,000
Financing: The company offers interim financing for real estate and construction when a third-party lender has committed to take over financing before the restaurant opening.
Length of contract: 20 years

In business since: 1956
Franchising since: 1984
Total number of units: 458
Number of company-operated units: 381
Total number of units planned, 1990: 708
Number of company-operated units planned, 1990: 454

Americans eat out more frequently than ever before, thanks to demographic shifts that include an increase in the number of single-person households and a steady rise in the number of mothers who work outside the home. The mothers of more than 60 percent of the nation's children have entered the work force so far, and that percentage continues to grow. Most of these women have little time to cook for their families, so eating out is no longer reserved for special occasions. In order to cash in more effectively on these trends, long-established Carl Karcher Enterprises recently adopted franchising as part of its strategy for expanding Carl's Junior Restaurants.

Serving moderately priced high-quality food in comfortable surroundings, Carl's Junior Restaurants feature a menu of hamburgers, specialty sandwiches, a salad bar, and a variety of desserts. The fast-service family restaurants also offer complete breakfasts. Carl's Junior franchisees can benefit from the many years of experience and the recognized name of Carl Karcher Enterprises, long known as a purveyor of good food.

Starting with one week of classroom instruction in the principles and techniques of running a restaurant, your preopening training as a new franchisee is thorough and comprehensive. The most important part of your training, though, takes place in an operating Carl's Junior unit. There you will gain the hands-on experience you need to learn daily restaurant operation. The company will provide you with the full complement of preopening and grand opening support services, from assistance in developing your site to help in training your employees.

Carl Karcher Enterprises offers ongoing operational assistance, marketing support, and help in human resources development, accounting, and other aspects of running your business. As needed, you can participate in the company's training program, which is held in the field or at the company's training facility in Anaheim, California. Some of this training is specialized, providing instruction in multiunit management and retail issues such as administrative controls. More general topics covered include new developments in menu, equipment, and procedures.

For further information contact:
Holli Ringgenberg, Director, Franchise Development, Carl Karcher Enterprises, Inc., 1200 North Harbor Blvd., Anaheim, CA 92801, 714-774-5796

D'Lites of America, Inc.

Initial license fee: $35,000
Royalties: 4%
Advertising royalties: 4%
Minimum cash required: $150,000
Capital required: $740,000 to $1.06 million
Financing: FFCA financing available
Length of contract: 20 years

In business since: 1981
Franchising since: 1982
Total number of units: 110
Number of company-operated units: 35
Total number of units planned, 1990: 1,000
Number of company-operated units planned, 1990: NA

"Just what America needs," D'Lites' motto sums up the company's concept of offering lower-calorie fast food to an increasingly health-conscious public. By 1990 Americans will eat three of every five meals outside the home, and the demand for fast food will be greater than ever. At the same time, diners will continue to seek an alternative to traditional fast food—a more nutritious, lower-calorie alternative. A multibillion dollar industry has already grown up in response to Americans' concern with healthier food, making "lite" a household word and manufacturing everything from "lite" frozen entrées to "lite" beer to "lite" cheesecake. D'Lites was founded to satisfy the tastes of the broad majority of consumers interested in lighter eating.

D'Lites restaurants offer a selection of hamburgers, chicken sandwiches, soups, salads, and desserts all designed for flavor and nutrition. The menu also includes a variety of side dishes and beverages carefully selected to meet the company's health guidelines. D'Lites prepares a number of the items, like the quarter-pound D'Lite Burger and its

Soup D'Lite, specifically to comply with the American Heart Association's dietary recommendations. Its sandwich buns, both the lite white sesame bun and the "lite" multigrain bun, are high in fiber and 25 percent lower in calories than other fast-food buns; its lite cheese and lite mayonnaise contain 50 percent less fat; and its frozen yogurt, in addition to being all natural, has 40 percent fewer calories and 75 percent less cholesterol than ice cream.

Doug Shelley, a former Wendy's franchisee and the D'Lites of America founder and chairman, believes that "success is very often affected by timing, and we have demonstrated that the time has arrived for our concept. I am particularly excited about the opportunity we have to make a positive impact on the fast-food industry and on the American consumer."

If you decide to offer your region "more of a good thing. And less," D'Lites will grant you exclusive franchise rights to the area. The company will furnish you with four sets of plans and specifications and will provide a layout for your approved site (which you can either purchase or lease). You can purchase signs, equipment, and furnishings either from D'Lites or from a supplier that meets the company's approval. D'Lites requires that your restaurant, and the products that you sell there, meet strict standards. Once your restaurant opens, other approved suppliers offer significant savings on materials and equipment because of D'Lites' national account purchasing.

Held at the company's Atlanta, Georgia, headquarters, the six-week initial training program will fully prepare you to operate your restaurant. You will learn the D'Lites system, from the company's quality criteria and corporate structure to the methods, procedures, and techniques of running a D'Lites restaurant. You and two managers from each of your restaurants must complete a total of more than 350 hours of training before you open for business.

Every one or two years, you can brush up on management, labor relations, operations, and equipment at advanced classes. And in between these classes, D'Lites will provide operational assistance by telephone. Company personnel will pay you personal visits at your site, and operations managers will oversee your restaurant's quality control. You will have access to confidential D'Lites business policies and practices through your operations manuals and other training aids, and you can keep up to date via regular newsletters and bulletins.

D'Lites field marketing managers will help you plan your promotional efforts. The 4 percent advertising royalty, rather than going to the company, is simply a requirement that you spend that amount of your monthly gross sales on local and regional advertising. To help you get the most out of your advertising budget, your marketing manager will advise you on media planning, promotions, community involvement programs, and specialized advertising materials. D'Lites is currently planning a national advertising program, which, when instituted, will require that you contribute an additional 1 percent of your gross to a national advertising fund.

D'Lites wants to attract franchisees capable of financing, constructing, and operating four to twenty units in a defined region. The company has particular interest in making an impact on major metropolitan areas. Doug Shelley challenges entrepreneurs to "join me in making that impact and achieving our leadership goals."

For further information contact:
Frank M. Montano, Vice President, Franchising, D'Lites of America, Inc., 6075 The Corners Parkway, Suite 200, Norcross, GA 30092, 404-448-0654

Everything Yogurt

Initial license fee: $20,000
Royalties: 5%
Advertising royalties: None
Minimum cash required: $80,000
Capital required: $165,000 to $450,000
Financing: None
Length of contract: 10 years

In business since: 1976
Franchising since: 1982
Total number of units: 70
Number of company-operated units: 18
Total number of units planned, 1990: NA
Number of company-operated units planned, 1990: NA

"*House Salad*—A healthful combination of romaine lettuce, fresh carrots, cucumbers, and tomatoes topped with alfalfa sprouts and seasoned croutons. *EY's Chef Salad*—An exciting array of 100% white chicken meat marinated in our mustard and poppy seed dressing, assorted cheeses, mixed vegetables and romaine lettuce, delicately tossed for a healthy low calorie lunch." You can find these light, tasty items on the menu at Everything Yogurt, a fast-food chain of health food restaurants.

Clearly, there is more than yogurt at these restaurants. But yogurt (they use Colombo) is also much in evidence on the menu. Frozen yogurt is Everything Yogurt's forte, the draw that gave the company its initial success. But there were many chains selling frozen yogurt in the 1970s, and this is one of the few that survived. The reason, according to the company, is that yogurt is part—and often the heart—of a full meal at Everything Yogurt, not just a dessert.

The company obviously tries to appeal to the desire of so many people in recent years to eat lighter, healthier food. Indeed, the slogan on the menu is: "THE FOOD YOU'LL NEVER FEEL GUILTY ABOUT. IT'S SO GOOD FOR YOU."

While the menu attracts many customers, the appearance of an Everything Yogurt restaurant goes a long way toward selling people on eating there. Everything Yogurt restaurants generate their ambience by making fresh fruit and flowers a very visible part of their decor. The dishes on the menu are displayed and lit to maximize their inherent visual appeal. Richard Nicotra, cofounder of the chain, is frank about the company's methods. "We're in show business, not the food business," he says. "We do everything in front of the customer, and we spend a lot of money on the way the store looks."

Contrary to what you might think, frozen yogurt sales do not decrease in the winter. Most of the franchises are in shopping malls. And, as Nicotra points out, "malls are indoors, they're warm, and they're full of shoppers who like to stop for something to eat."

Should you decide to open an Everything Yogurt store, the company will also give you and your customers an opportunity to go Bananas. Bananas is the sister enterprise—a smaller sister—to Everything Yogurt. These kiosks, which often share a mall location with an Everything Yogurt franchise, feature light snacks including shakes made from fresh fruit. Here, too, the emphasis is on catching the eye, with large quantities of fresh fruit displayed behind glass.

The franchise fee for a Bananas franchise, $15,000, drops to $5,000 when you buy it together with an Everything Yogurt franchise. Indeed, the company encourages such pairings. At its company-owned sites, often located in "food court" areas of malls, where there are concentrations of fast-food outlets, Everything Yogurt itself "multiplexes" its operations by running several franchises of other fast-food chains alongside its own. As Nicotra says, "Because of the costs in a mall, you get a much better return on investment if you do at least two operations, and three or four makes the return even better because one manager manages all of them."

Should you purchase an Everything Yogurt franchise, the company will help you set up your business. Company staff will help you pick the site and design and build the store. Training consists of a fifty-hour apprenticeship at a company training store. During your training you will be instructed in food display, inventory control, and buying procedures. Follow-up help is available if you need it. The company also gives franchisees advice on conducting local promotions.

You are required to buy your food from the company's approved list of suppliers.

For further information contact:
Everything Yogurt, Franchise Division, 304 Port Richmond Ave., Staten Island, NY 10302, 718-816-7800

Hardee's Food Systems, Inc.

Initial license fee: $15,000
Royalties: 3.5% first 5 years; 4% next 15 years
Advertising royalties: 5%
Minimum cash required: $150,000
Capital required: $675,000 to $1,303,800
Financing: Third-party financing available
Length of contract: 20 years

In business since: 1960
Franchising since: 1962
Total number of units: 2,546
Number of company-operated units: 875
Total number of units planned, 1990: NA
Number of company-operated units planned, 1990: NA

Hardee's ranks fifth among all fast-food chains in market share and third in the fast-food/hamburger market. The company, started by two businessmen in North Carolina, absorbed the Sandy's chain in the 1970s and Burger Chef in 1982. In 1981 Hardee's became part of the huge Imasco Limited holding company of Canada, whose other businesses include food products, retailing, and tobacco. Hardee's has expanded steadily, with management maintaining the ratio of franchise locations to company-owned restaurants at three to two.

Hardee's takes pride in its pioneer role in adding a breakfast menu—it is built around "made-from-scratch" biscuits—to a hamburger chain. Diners who come in later in the day can choose from a menu that has shifted gradually away from a concentration on the simple hamburger. It currently features specialty sandwiches like Hot Ham 'N' Cheese, Big Roast Beef, and Mushroom 'N' Swiss Burger, as well as hamburgers and regular cheeseburgers. Desserts include Apple Turnovers and Big Cookies.

Hardee's is one of the few big fast-food chains with substantially untapped territory, according to the franchisor. Currently, the company wants to expand in Texas, Ohio, New York, Pennsylvania, Louisiana, Michigan, and Colorado. However, while Hardee's licenses franchisees who want to run one unit, it would prefer multiunit operators. In fact, much of its growth comes from franchisees who already own at least one operation. Two of its biggest franchisees, Boddie-Noell Enterprises, Inc., and Spartan Food Systems, Inc., operate restaurants in more than one state.

Although the company specifies construction materials and designs that franchisees must use in building Hardee's restaurants, the entrepreneur does have an opportunity for some self-expression in the appearance of the establishment, especially in the interior. Typically, locations have 165 feet of frontage and are 210 feet deep.

Training consists of a four-week management internship at one of the company's regional learning centers. Franchisees receive hands-on restaurant management experience in the course, as well as classroom instruction. An operational supervisor will come to your site ten days before you open and will stay with you for a period after you begin your business. The company offers advanced training in the form of frequent seminars and workshops on assertiveness training, time management, and other subjects. There may be a nominal tuition charge for some of this training.

Hardee's management stresses the importance of accounting and financial controls in the fast-food business. It offers franchisees help in setting up a computerized accounting system, including point-of-sale terminals to provide up-to-the-minute inventory information. Multi-unit operators can tie these terminals into a central system to provide a comprehensive picture of business at all their locations at any given time.

Hardee's spends about $80 million a year on advertising. Franchisees participate in marketing campaigns through cooperative ads with other regional franchisees and have input into the company's general marketing policy through their representatives on the company's marketing advisory review council. For marketing advice, franchisees can also consult a field marketing executive in one of the six area offices.

Franchisees purchase food—except for perishables—from Hardee's distribution company: Fast Food Merchandisers, Inc. This company employs 1,100 people in its nine distribution centers in the East and Midwest. Its trucks travel over 9 million miles a year, delivering more than 38 million pounds of hamburger meat and 17 million pounds of boneless breast of chicken, among other products.

For further information contact:

Franchise Development Department, Hardee's Food Systems, Inc., 1233 N. Church St., Rocky Mount, NC 27802, 919-977-2000

Jack in the Box

Initial license Fee: $25,000
Royalties: 4%
Advertising royalties: 4%
Minimum cash required: $160,000
Capital required: $190,000
Financing: The company helps franchisees find sources of financial assistance.
Length of contract: 20 years

In business since: 1950
Franchising since: 1982
Total number of units: 813
Number of company-operated units: 671
Total number of units planned, 1990: 1200
Number of company-operated units planned, 1990: NA

Jack in the Box, a subsidiary of Foodmaker, Inc., has concentrated its fast-food restaurants in the West. Among major fast-food chains, it was the first to offer drive-thru service, tacos as well as hamburgers, breakfast sandwiches, and a wide-variety menu—including "Chicken Supreme" sandwiches and salads-to-go—that moved away from hamburgers. The company's marketing targets twenty-two- to forty-four-year-olds, an age group that eats out frequently. These potential customers now constitute 32 percent of the population, but will grow to 36 percent by 1990, thereby expanding the market for Jack in the Box products.

The company seeks franchisees with previous business experience who have the ability and the financial resources to run multiunit operations. Jack in the Box will consider partnership applications, but you must designate one partner the "operator," and that person must take responsibility for hands-on management of the business. In fact, Jack in the Box stipulates that this person must live within an hour's drive of the first restaurant built by the partnership. The company does not permit absentee ownership.

Jack in the Box offers extensive franchisee training. It begins with a three-day evaluation period in a Jack in the Box restaurant. After passing this test, you and your manager will take the company's full training program at the Foodmaker Management Institute in San Diego. The company includes tuition in the cost of the franchise, but you pay for transportation and living expenses for the forty- to fifty-day training period.

Jack in the Box training, a combination of classroom and on-the-job restaurant instruction, covers food preparation, crew training and scheduling, equipment use and maintenance, restaurant opening and closing procedures, accounting, inventory control, business management, quality control, customer service, sanitation, safety, marketing, financial management and taxes, and security.

The company will also help you train your other employees. The franchise operations consultant, your liaison with the corporate office as long as you remain a franchisee, will assist you with that task, and Jack in the Box will provide further instruction through its interactive laser disc training system and employee brochures. You can also choose to have any management-level employee trained at company headquarters "at cost."

If you build your restaurant, Jack in the Box will help you hire a contractor, and secure the necessary permits and inspections, and will supervise construction. Your royalties as the operator of a new Jack in the Box will start at 2 percent for the first two years and rise to 4 percent in the third year and thereafter. If you choose to buy an existing Jack in the Box restaurant, you will lease your premises from Foodmaker, with a lease not to exceed 8.5 percent of your monthly gross sales.

You can supply your restaurants from an approved list of vendors or buy from the company to take advantage of Jack in the Box's mass purchasing power and extensive distribution network.

For further information contact:
Franchise Department, Foodmaker, Inc., P.O. Box 783, San Diego, CA 92112, 619-571-2288

Long John Silver's Seafood Shoppes

Initial license fee: $15,000
Royalties: 4%
Advertising royalties: 5%
Minimum cash required: $76,000
Capital required: $76,000
Financing: None
Length of Contract: 25 years

In business since: 1969
Franchising since: 1970
Total number of units: 1,378
Number of company-operated units: 838
Total number of units planned, 1990: NA
Number of company-operated units planned, 1990: NA

This fast-food fish chain, with units in thirty-seven states and two foreign countries, prides itself on changing with the times. In keeping with the recent trend away from fried foods, it has emphasized lighter fare, with new broiled and baked items in the offing. Recently it added to its repertoire of shrimp, clam, oyster, and scallop dishes a new lighter-battered fish dish and chicken nuggets.

Computers play a big role in the operation of these restaurants. Computerized time monitors keep tabs on the right cooking time for each dish and also track postcooking holding times. Employees discard as stale anything that overstays its welcome in the holding area.

The elaborate Long John Silver computerized communications system uses sophisticated electronic cash registers. Every night, the system automatically transmits data accumulated at each terminal in every store in the chain to mainframe computers at the Lexington, Kentucky, company headquarters. The company sends marketing and operational information back to store managers over the same lines.

There is nothing extraordinary about the site selection and building of Long John Silver's franchise units. You will do the actual work in keeping with the company's guidelines, with all major details subject to Long John Silver's approval. But the required training is special.

Jerrico, Inc., the company that owns Long John Silver's Seafood Shoppes and the smaller Jerry's Restaurants chain, maintains an elaborate training facility on the campus of Transylvania University at the company's home base in Lexington. Employees at various levels of management in the chain take courses here. The staff of the training center, who must spend two weeks a year working in a company restaurant just to keep in touch with operations, also help create the in-store training, which is administered by regional training centers. Some students use courses at the center for college credit.

You will receive some of your training in Lexington and the rest at your location. The subjects covered will include operational procedures, equipment handling, repair and maintenance, cleaning procedures, customer service, products, advertising, and marketing. Company personnel will assist you with opening preparations and the start-up of your operation.

You will buy Long John Silver's proprietary items through the company's food distribution system. At your option, you may also purchase other food, beverages, paper goods, and equipment through the system.

Currently, the company has franchise openings in Alabama, Michigan, California, North Dakota, Idaho, Minnesota, Wisconsin, North Carolina, Montana, Delaware, New York, Connecticut, Massachusetts, Rhode Island, and Maine.

For further information contact:
Eugene O. Getchell, Vice President, Franchising, Long John Silver's, Inc., P.O. Box 11988, Lexington, KY 40579, 606-268-2000

McDonald's Corporation

Initial license fee: $12,500
Royalties: 11.5%
Advertising royalties: 4%
Minimum cash required: $200,000
Capital required: $400,000
Financing: None
Length of contract: 20 years

In business since: 1955
Franchising since: 1955
Total number of units: 8,500
Number of company-operated units: 2,500
Total number of units planned, 1990: NA
Number of company-operated units planned, 1990: NA

Many people would like the opportunity to own and operate a McDonald's franchise. McDonald's has made its 1.6-ounce hamburger on a 3.5-inch bun—and its Big Mac variation—an integral part of culture. Not content to rest on its laurels, the company has added Chicken McNuggets and the McD.L.T. to its menu, as well as prepared salads. By the time you read this, McDonald's may also be selling McPizza. McDonald's has a seller's market when it comes to recruiting new franchisees, and the company knows it.

This multibillion-dollar corporation, the biggest food service organization in the world, won't provide you with any financing, and it will require that you serve a brief internship in order for management to determine whether you qualify for training at Hamburger University. Should you qualify, you will probably have to run an operation at a location selected by McDonald's. The company requires that you participate in civic and charitable activities, and it will not even consider permitting absentee ownership. Yet, despite the requirement that franchisees run the business its way, McDonald's does not lack for applicants.

Of course, McDonald's did not start at the top. In fact, it really started at the end—the end of Route 66, in San Bernardino, California, that is. There Ray Kroc discovered the McDonald brother's hamburger stand, decorated with golden arches, in 1954. Kroc sold milkshake machines, and on a visit to the stand to sell his product (which he did), he noticed that the brothers had a thriving business. He asked them to sell him a franchise. Richard and Maurice McDonald had already sold six franchises in the state, and they figured that McDonald's had reached its natural limit of growth. But Kroc won them over, and in 1955 he opened his business in Des Plaines, Illinois. In 1960 he bought out the brothers for $2.7 million, and today you can buy Big Macs every place in the world where people eat fast-food hamburgers.

If you want to sell Big Macs, you and McDonald's management must first meet to see if you can establish a working relationship. If you can, you must then spend about fifty hours working part-time in a company restaurant for further evaluation. Hamburger University, near Chicago, is the next step. It might have a funny name, but the American Council on Education gives college credit for some of its courses.

The program at Hamburger University, which may last as long as two years, involves a combination of classroom study and periods of work in a McDonald's restaurant near you—where you get to use equipment like the french fry computer, the world's first. You pay for your own expenses during the part-time, unpaid, fifteen- to twenty-hours-a-week training period. The company warns that it has the right to wash you out at any time, and it therefore advises you to continue at your present job during training. If you make it through the rigorous training, McDonald's will offer you a franchise.

The company chooses the site for your franchise and builds the restaurant. You will equip and decorate it to company specifications. McDonald's doesn't have its own food plants, but it has a staff on the premises of each independent supplier to enforce the company's stringent quality standards.

McDonald's spares nothing to make its units successful. You and your staff will receive all the supplementary training necessary, and the company will advise you about particular problems. The company's laboratories constantly develop new products to stay ahead of the competition, and the chain spends literally hundreds of millions of dollars a year to make sure nobody forgets the place with the golden arches.

For a chosen few of its best candidates who are long on talent but short on funds, McDonald's has a business facilities lease that enables the franchisee to start an operation with a cash outlay of about $65,000. After two or three years, the lease holder has the option to buy the business and run it as a full franchise.

Obviously, a McDonald's franchise is not for everybody—certainly not for entrepreneurs who want the right to make most of the decisions affecting the conduct of their enterprise themselves. But for those who want the advantages of tremendous marketing clout and almost universal name recognition, the sacrifice of some personal independence can really pay off.

For further information contact:
Licensing Department,
McDonald's Corporation,

At the location nearest you:

300 Day Hill Rd., Windsor, CT 06095, 203-683-2200

1 Computer Drive, Albany, NY 12205, 518-459-6900

Suite 500, 5901 C Peachtree Dunwoody Rd., Atlanta, GA 30328, 404-399-5067

3707 FM 1960 West, Suite 300, Houston, TX 77068, 713-580-3322

One McDonald's Plaza, Oak Brook, IL 60521, 312-575-5124

Suite 500, 11880 College Blvd., Overland Park, KS 66210, 913-469-4200

10960 Wilshire Blvd., Suite 600, Los Angeles, CA 90024, 213-477-2961

5200 Town Center Circle, Suite 600, Boca Raton, FL 33432, 305-391-8003

Orange Julius

Initial license fee: $17,500
Royalties: 6%
Advertising royalties: You must commit 1% of your sales to local advertising.
Minimum cash required: $110,000
Capital required: $110,000 to $160,000
Financing: None
Length of contract: 10 years

In business since: 1926
Franchising since: 1963
Total number of units: 768
Number of company-operated units: 33
Total number of units planned, 1990: NA
Number of company-operated units planned, 1990: NA

The exact formula that forms the basis for Orange Julius' orange and other fruit drinks remains a secret that is embodied in a mysterious powder made of "pure food ingredients," says the company. This "devilish good drink," as the company slogan goes, was created in 1926. Bill Hamlin, a chemist, had a friend who had opened an orange juice stand in Los Angeles. Hamlin thought he could help the friend, whose name was Julius, increase sales by developing a formula for an extra-special orange drink. It worked, and they started opening other outlets to cash in on its success. Today, Orange Juliuses in Canada, Japan, Puerto Rico, the Philippines, the Netherlands, Hong Kong, Malaysia, and Australia, as well as all over the United States, continue to serve the popular drink.

The company maintains flexibility regarding what you can serve at your Orange Julius outlet. The fruit drinks are mandatory; in fact, you can operate a store with these as your only product. However, within certain guidelines, you can follow your own entrepreneurial instincts and put together the menu that you think will do best in your area. That could include hot dogs, hamburgers, french fries, chili, and whatever else you think will appeal to local tastes.

The typical location for an Orange Julius is in an enclosed shopping mall, although the company will consider other sites. As well as placing the operation in an area of high customer traffic, mall locations allow franchisees to pick up sales from mall employees—customers who account for about 25 percent of sales for each mall store, according to the company.

The company's real estate experts will pick out a location for you in a major regional shopping mall. The most recent list of available locations included sites in West Virginia, Pennsylvania, South Carolina, and Tennessee, but this list changes periodically. Orange Julius leases the site from the developers and then subleases it to you, adding a $100-per-month lease service fee to the terms of the original lease. Since it is always developing new locations, the company may have a store all set up, waiting for you when you apply for your franchise. Orange Julius will also consider a site for which you have obtained a lease.

The company's designers adapt each store to its particular location. They use materials like wood paneling and brick, with bright lighting that gives off a slightly orangish glow. Each store prominently displays the company logo with its red devil, and also includes a large display of oranges.

Orange Julius trains franchisees for ten days at a location designated by the company. Franchisees absorb the cost of travel, food, and lodging. The course includes—in addition to food preparation and equipment operation—management controls, employee and customer relations, inventory control, and work scheduling. The company also demonstrates the simplified accounting system you will use to track the performance of your new business. You can get supplementary training at regional meetings and seminars. District managers call on you periodically, both to assist you with any problems that arise and to make sure that your operation meets company standards.

For further information contact:

Orange Julius, 2850 Ocean Park Blvd., Suite 200, Santa Monica, CA 90405, 1-800-421-7127; in California: 213-450-2933

Primo's Delicafes and Jan Drake's Garden Cafes

Initial license fee: $20,000
Royalties: 6%
Advertising royalties: 1.5%
Minimum cash required: $46,200
Capital required: $132,000 to $216,000
Financing: None
Length of Contract: NA

In business since: 1972
Franchising since: 1976
Total number of units: 119
Number of company-operated units: 16
Total number of units planned, 1990: NA
Number of company-operated units planned, 1990: NA

In 1972 Tony Brunetti, Primo's president, spotted an important opportunity that other fast-food franchisors had missed. As he put it: "What's been largely overlooked in the fast-food industry is good old American fare—soup, sandwich, and salad—the food people have been eating for lunch for a hundred years and will be eating for the next one hundred years." Industry analysts seem to agree with him, and Primo has sold multiple franchises of its restaurants to investment bankers and securities specialists, as well as to people with less specialized business backgrounds but just as much drive and desire to succeed.

For the same licensing fee you can buy a franchise for either a Delicafe or Garden Cafe, although the Garden Cafes involve higher total costs. Both Primo restaurants serve sandwiches and salads. Neither needs a kitchen, which keeps space and labor requirements to a minimum and also permits these establishments to locate in places like office buildings, where rental agents frown on greasy fast-food cooking. Each restaurant features food made to order before customers' eyes, adding a bit of entertainment to the product mix.

The Delicafes, typically located in shopping mall food courts, average about 800 square feet and seat 60. Even at the peak of the lunch rush period, these units require no more than four employees. Menus emphasize New York-style cold cuts like pastrami. The 100-seat, 2,000-square-foot Garden Cafes, whose five- to seven-minute table service appeals to office workers, feature colorful and enticing salads, quiche, and croissants. The sandwich that the Delicafe menu calls "Hot Pastrami," the Garden Cafe's bill of fare refers to as "Peppercorn Cured Pastrami"—the same thing, and just as good by any name. But the Garden Cafe serves it in bright and airy establishments featuring exposed brick, oak and brass trimming, and hanging plants, while the Delicafes feature more of a fast-food, utlitarian look.

Primo will give you close support in locating and building your restaurant. It will pick a site that you approve, help you choose a contractor, give your architect or contractor floor plans, secure bids from national equipment suppliers, and help you get in touch with local suppliers to set up delivery patterns. You can achieve considerable savings by ordering many of your supplies through vendors with whom Primo has negotiated national contracts.

You and your manager will train for a week at Primo's Phoenix, Arizona, headquarters. Your pay only for travel and living expenses. The curriculum includes food preparation and service, ordering and inventory, equipment operation, merchandising, cost analysis and control, bookkeeping, personnel, management techniques, customer relations, advertising, and promotion.

A company representative will work with you in the first few days of your business. Thereafter, Primo will give you advice and assistance as you need it. Currently, the chain does not advertise nationally, and it will encourage you to promote your business in your own community.

For further information contact:
Primo, Inc., 21622 N. 14th Ave., Phoenix, AZ 85027, 1-800-528-0297

Roy Rogers Restaurants

Initial license fee: $25,000
Royalties: 4%
Advertising royalties: 5%
Minimum cash required: $175,000
Capital required: $750,000 to $1,000,000
Financing: None
Length of contract: 20 years

In business since: 1968
Franchising since: 1968
Total number of units: 546
Number of company-operated units: 359
Total number of units planned, 1990: 725
Number of company-operated units planned, 1990: 425

Roy Rogers, the Western movie star for whom these fast-food establishments were named, was born Leonard Sly in Cincinnati. Like many entrepreneurs, he started small. In fact, the eventual "King of the Cowboys" began his career in California as a migrant fruit picker in 1929. But by the late 1940s, Roy Rogers, his wife, Dale Evans, his sidekick,

Gabby Hayes, and his horse, Trigger, represented the essence of heroism and goodness in Hollywood's version of the American West. Rogers was also on his way to becoming a multimillionaire.

The Marriott Corporation, which owns this chain, also started small, in 1927, with a nine-seat chili, hot tamale, and root beer stand in Washington, D.C., called The Hot Shoppe. Today, Marriott develops about $1 billion of real estate and purchases more than $1 billion worth of products annually.

You can't start small with Roy Rogers Restaurants, but if you have the necessary finances (including a net worth of at least $500,000, excluding your home), some restaurant experience, and the desire and ability to develop more than one unit, you can become part of a growing and popular chain, which plans further expansion throughout the Northeastern Corridor, from Connecticut to Virginia. Initially specializing in roast beef sandwiches, these fast-food restaurants now offer hamburgers and fried chicken in order to compete with the other big chains.

Roy Rogers Restaurants will guide you through each stage of site selection and restaurant construction. The company will train you or your manager and an assistant manager at its field classroom facilities in Maryland, Pennsylvania, or New Jersey and at a company-operated restaurant. You will pay for lodging and travel expenses. Several weeks before you open your restaurant, the company will work with you to hire your staff. A franchise consultant, assigned to you by Roy Rogers Restaurants, will help with your opening and any problems that arise in your ongoing business. You can get refresher training at almost any time, and the company will offer instruction about new products periodically.

Marriott has a subsidiary that can provide you with equipment and supplies, but you can buy from whomever you choose as long as your purchases meet company specifications.

For further information contact:
Richard T. Parker, Director of Franchise Development, Roy Rogers Restaurants, One Marriott Drive, Washington, D.C. 20058, 301-897-1487

Sonic

Initial license fee: $7,500
Royalties: 1% on first $10,000 of monthly sales; .5% for each additional $10,000
Advertising royalties: 1.5%
Minimum cash required: $30,000

Capital required: $30,000 to $50,000
Financing: The company may finance your equipment purchase.
Length of contract: 15 years

In business since: 1973
Franchising since: 1975
Total number of units: 931
Number of company-operated units: 80
Total number of units planned, 1990: NA
Number of company-operated units planned, 1990: NA

Twenty-five cent hamburgers and ten-cent Cokes have gone the way of automobile tail fins, and most of the cars that pull into Sonic fast food drive-in restaurants are smaller than the ones that brought the car hops out in the 1950s. But in many ways Sonic drive-ins have not changed. Car hops still serve most of the chain's customers, the menu remains simple, and units located in the rural Sun Belt—Texas and Oklahoma—still predominate.

Troy Smith founded the company, originally called "Top Hat," in 1953 when he bought a root beer stand in Shawnee, Oklahoma. The company's management renamed the restaurants in 1958 because Sonic's drive-thru intercom system allowed customers to place their orders "at the speed of sound." With a minimum of twenty drive-thru ordering stations at each unit, Sonic restaurants maintain that quick service. Sticking to basics by providing fast food, take-out style, Sonic still features hamburgers accompanied by fresh onion rings. Unlike most other fast food restaurants, though, it also sells hot dogs—"coneys"—with cheese, chili, and chopped onions.

Present Sonic management purchased the company in a leveraged buyout a few years ago—with TV personality Art Linkletter a major investor—and has begun to make some changes, including opening more restaurants with indoor seating. But management pledges to retain the basic drive-in concept that has made Sonic successful.

Your Sonic drive-in will require at least 20,000 square feet of land, with the restaurant occupying about 1,150 square feet. The company will help you choose a site, give you prototype construction drawings, and will confer with your architect or general contractor on the details of building the unit. All your equipment and supplies must meet Sonic's specifications, but you have the option of buying either from the company or from other vendors, except that you must purchase paper products from one source designated by Sonic. In recent years the company has encouraged its franchisees to form purchasing collectives.

You will pay any travel expenses incidental to the training of your restaurant's manager at Sonic headquarters in Oklahoma City. Additional people may attend this program at "a nominal fee." The course covers equipment use and maintenance, sanitation, food preparation (with hands-on experience), personnel, purchasing, accounting, advertising, and promotion.

Sonic will assist you at your opening and throughout the first few days of your business. A field consultant will provide general advice for your ongoing operations and help you solve specific problems as they come up. The company may also offer seminars and workshops from time to time on various subjects.

You will spend part of your advertising fee on local advertising. The company encourages its franchisees to form advertising cooperatives to spend these funds collectively.

Sonic sells area franchises as well as individual territories. Areas in which Sonic seeks to expand include the states of Alabama, Georgia, Tennessee, Kentucky, South Carolina, and California. It also wants to sell franchises in San Antonio, Waco, and Dallas, Texas; and Kansas City, Missouri.

For further information contact:
Franchise Sales Department, Sonic Industries, Inc., 6800 North Bryant, Oklahoma City, OK 73121-4444, 405-478-0731

Wendy's International, Inc.

Initial license fee: $25,000
Royalties: 4%
Advertising royalties: 4%
Minimum cash required: $627,000
Capital required: $627,000 to $1,300,000
Financing: Available
Length of contract: NA

In business since: 1969
Franchising since: 1971
Total number of units: 3,120
Number of company-operated units: 1,150
Total number of units planned, 1990: NA
Number of company-operated units planned, 1990: NA

The fast-food business slowed a bit in the mid-eighties, and Wendy's, like the other giants of the industry, experienced lagging sales. In an effort to generate more revenue, the company targeted the breakfast trade with a new early-morning menu based on omelets. But the public didn't bite, and the company ended up with egg on its face. To pull out of this bumpy financial period, Wendy's decided to revamp its top management. On his appointment, Wendy's new president, James W. Near, stated: "We don't like being number three. So we have a strategic plan in place, and you'll be hearing from us soon."

Despite its recent worries, Wendy's deals from a position of strength. R. David Thomas, who founded Wendy's Old Fashioned Hamburgers, started with the idea that cooked-to-order hamburgers would stand out amidst the prepackaged and reheated food sold by other chains. Highly publicized taste tests, in which Wendy's has done well, have borne out his strategy. Wendy's was among the first of the fast-food chains to offer a salad bar, baked potatoes, and chicken sandwiches. And at a time when people have grown more cholesterol-conscious, the fact that Wendy's burgers are broiled, not fried, has given the chain a good image among consumers. The company's most famous series of commercials highlighted Wendy's quality by comparing its substantial product to the supposedly skimpy offering of its competitors. The slogan "Where's the beef?" caught the public's fancy and greatly enhanced the public's consciousness of Wendy's as an alternative to other fast-food chains.

Wendy's now considers applicants for individual franchise ownership. The company had previously favored groups intending to buy the rights to entire areas. But opportunities to buy franchises, according to the company, are "limited," and the company forbids absentee ownership. In fact, franchise owners must live within fifty miles of their restaurant.

If you do buy a Wendy's franchise, you will have an experienced corporate staff ready to guide and assist you in developing your restaurant. Staff will help you select the right site and provide you with drawings and specifications for your restaurant. Your management team will receive a thorough grounding in the company's operations at the Wendy's Management Institute. Company representatives will visit your Wendy's periodically to assist you with operational details, and the company's advertising department will supplement your efforts to publicize your business locally while continuing to promote the Wendy's image nationally.

Wendy's also operates a subsidiary called Sisters Chicken and Biscuits. Now numbering about a hundred restaurants, this chain features fried chicken.

For further information contact:

Wendy's International, Inc., P.O. Box 256, Dublin, OH 43017, 614-764-3100

Ice Cream and Yogurt

Baskin-Robbins Ice Cream Company

Initial license fee: None
Royalties: 0.5%
Advertising royalties: 3%
Minimum cash required: $60,000
Capital required: $140,000
Financing: The company offers some bank financing to qualified candidates.
Length of contract: 5 years

In business since: 1945
Franchising since: 1948
Total number of units: 3,225
Number of company-operated units: 68
Total number of units planned, 1990: 3,325
Number of company-operated units planned, 1990: 68

Ever since Alexander the Great concocted chilled wines, people the world over have enjoyed frozen desserts. Everybody loves ice cream: Over 1 billion gallons of ice cream are produced each year in the U.S. alone, and the average person consumes about 15 quarts every year. For years Baskin-Robbins has been satisfying the world's ice cream cravings with flavors from Vanilla, the all-time favorite, to Oregon Blackberry and Mississippi Mudd. Dedicated to the notion "We make people happy," the company has developed 548 ice cream flavors so far.

Franchising almost since its inception, Baskin-Robbins offers franchisees the opportunity to become part of a smooth-running international franchise system. Its tried-and-true methods and its standards of quality, service, and cleanliness are among the best in the industry. By investing in a Baskin-Robbins franchise, you can benefit from years of experience, not to mention exceptional name recognition. "Where do we go from here?" asks Ron Marley, Baskin-Robbins' president. "I think the next broad strategy will be to take advantage of the unique opportunities we have in the over-fifty major markets we serve. Some stores will benefit from serving coffee, tea, and hot chocolate; for others it will not be appropriate. We are, therefore, beginning to develop a series of optional products, which each store owner can consider on the basis of his or her knowledge of the customers to be served." There are still plenty of Baskin-Robbins franchises available across the country, both new locations that the company has researched and planned and existing franchises that owners offer for sale. (Owners may sell their stores at any time to buyers approved by the company.)

You must train for two weeks before opening your store. Instructors teach product handling and preparation, employee recruiting, training, management, and customer relations. Your training will take place at the national training center in Glendale, California, and in the national training stores, five operating retail stores in the Glendale-Burbank area. When you complete your training, your district manager will help you open your store and will remain available to advise you about trouble spots and provide a link between you and the home office.

Baskin-Robbins continually researches products and markets in an effort to keep the company in a position of market leadership. With national and regional publicity and advertising, participation in high-exposure activities such as the Tournament of Roses Parade, and development of promotions and store decor, the company aggressively pursues a place in the forefront of consumer consciousness. As Ron Marley puts it, the company's marketing efforts "are all designed to attract customers—to get them to think of us when they think of ice cream."

The market and product research division studies the viability of new products and keeps watch over existing products to make sure that they satisfy customers' changing tastes. But the key to Baskin-Robbins' marketing success is its franchisees. Carol Kirby, vice president of marketing, calls on "store owners to play a very vital role in evaluating the results of all our marketing programs. There is no single, one, right marketing plant for Baskin-Robbins or any other retailer. . . . It is critical that we understand what works well and what does not. To do this requires objective, systematic evaluation at the store level." The company regularly solicits franchisee opinion through surveys published in *Scoops*, the company magazine.

Division managers meet periodically with you and other franchisees in your area to keep you informed about developments in the Baskin-Robbins system. Management workshops will give you the opportunity to learn about consumer-oriented management systems and to share your experiences with other franchisees. Baskin-Robbins staff will help you develop and implement an annual business plan designed specifically for your needs and potential.

Prospective franchisees must meet rigorous standards before they are granted a Baskin-Robbins license. You can purchase a franchise as an investment, but Baskin-Robbins will want to make sure that you have a qualified manager to operate your store. Before approving you as a franchisee, the company will not only review your financial position and business experience, but will also seek to learn about you on a more personal level through interviews and maybe even a visit to your home and family. While this may make some applicants nervous, it helps the company ensure that all of its franchisees are not only qualified, but well-suited to operate a Baskin-Robbins franchise. Based on years on experience, the company has concluded that the most important characteristic of successful Baskin-Robbins franchisees is that they like people, especially children. Baskin-Robbins also looks for some other vital traits in applicants: an ability to manage people, a long-range outlook and goals, a true desire to succeed in a small retail business, and a willingness to be actively involved in the franchise.

For further information contact:
International Headquarters, Baskin-Robbins Ice Cream Company, 31 Baskin-Robbins Place, Glendale, CA 91201, 818-956-0031

Ben & Jerry's Ice Cream

Initial license fee: $15,000
Royalties: None
Advertising royalties: 4%
Minimum cash required: $80,000
Capital required: $100,000
Financing: None
Length of contract: 10 years

In business since: 1978
Franchising since: 1981
Total number of units: 16
Number of company-operated units: 1
Total number of units planned, 1990: 100
Number of company-operated units planned, 1990: 3

A bright young upstart is competing for a share of America's ice cream dollar and hopes to find enough qualified franchisees for dramatic expansion in all of the country's biggest ice cream markets: the East Coast, from Maine to Florida; Chicago; and Southern California. Based in Vermont (of course), Ben & Jerry's has developed a formula for success: rich, all-natural, old-fashioned ice cream. A relatively small operator, Ben & Jerry's offers progressive entrepreneurs the chance to get in on the ground floor. With thirty-four flavors and some of the best commercially produced ice cream around, a Ben & Jerry's franchise could serve up some delicious profits.

Ben & Jerry's requires all new franchisees to attend the one-week start-up training session in Vermont, which teaches you about customer service, quality and portion control, operations, bookkeeping, and office procedures. For five days preceding the opening of your store, the company's field personnel helps you with store setup and employee hiring and training. The Ben & Jerry's operations manual provides guidelines for continuing store operations. When the company introduces new products, or whenever you request it, company publications and field representatives will provide training updates.

You can only sell Ben & Jerry's products in your store, and the company also specifies all other supplies and equipment. If you like, you may purchase major equipment through the company. A bonus of the Ben & Jerry's franchise contract is that you are not prohibited from operating or having an interest in a similar business either during or after the term of your contract.

With its "new age" image, Ben & Jerry's appeals in particular to the young upscale crowd. A Ben & Jerry's franchise would do well in a college town, tourist area, or any affluent urban or suburban region. You can select your store site for company approval or have Ben & Jerry's choose one for you. In either case, the company will negotiate your lease.

For further information contact:
James Rowe, Ben & Jerry's Ice Cream, Route 100, P.O. Box 240, Waterbury, VT 05676, 802-244-5641

Bressler's 33 Flavors, Inc.

Initial license fee: $10,000
Royalties: 6%
Advertising royalties: 4%
Minimum cash required: $50,000
Capital required: $100,000 to $130,000
Financing: The company will help you obtain third-party financing.
Length of contract: 10 years

In business since: 1963
Franchising since: 1963
Total number of units: 335
Number of company-operated units: 5
Total number of units planned, 1990: 475
Number of company-operated units planned, 1990: 25

One of life's quintessential joys is the ice cream cone: a rich scoop of any flavor ice cream, packed with crunchy nuts or plump fruits, all atop a crisp sugar cone. Bressler's 33 Flavors shops serve up thirty-three flavors of ice cream in cones, soda fountain specialty items, and hand-packed quarts, and also offer frozen yogurt. Bressler's invites you to become part of its plans for nationwide expansion—and to dip into some of the sweetest profits around.

The company will execute a sublease for your approved location and grant you territorial exclusivity for the term of your ten-year contract. To prepare you for ice cream parlor operation, Bressler's conducts an intensive two-week training program. Covering all phases of your new business, the classroom-style program takes place at the company's Training School in Des Plaines, Illinois. Training is free except for your out-of-pocket expenses for your room and board. Once you complete the training program, Bressler's staff will give you eight days of hands-on instruction and assistance in opening your shop. Providing as much assistance as you need, the company will make sure your ice cream parlor gets off to a smooth start.

Company personnel will return for periodic visits to provide ongoing support and counseling. To help you with daily operations, Bressler's provides you with comprehensive manuals. Bressler's conducts quarterly franchise meetings at which franchisees can discuss new developments in the market and the industry with one another and with the corporate staff. You can receive refresher training in ice cream technology and management technique at these meetings. Upon request, Bressler's will also provide refresher training at no charge on any topic, at their training facility or at your shop.

For further information contact:
Howard Marks, Bressler's 33 Flavors, Inc., 999 East Touhy Ave., Suite 333, Des Plaines, IL 60018, 312-298-1100

Gelato Classico Italian Ice Cream

Initial license fee: $25,000
Royalties: None
Advertising royalties: 1% for local, possible additional 2% for national promotion
Minimum cash required: $50,000
Capital required: $100,000 to $150,000
Financing: None
Length of contract: 10 years

In business since: 1976
Franchising since: 1982
Total number of units: 35
Number of company-operated units: 5
Total number of units planned, 1990: 155
Number of company-operated units planned, 1990: 5

Gelato Classico claims that the Emperor Nero created the first Italian ice cream by mixing snow with fruit flavoring in Rome in A.D. 40. But its gelato first saw the light of day in a small shop in San Francisco, which makes it as American as . . . well, as a banana split. If this product follows the traditional American pattern of new things starting in California and then being widely accepted by the rest of the country, it should be well on its way to becoming a national dish. Write-ups in the *San Francisco Chronicle, Los Angeles Times,* and *The New York Times* have helped Gelato Classico on its way.

Gelato franchisees do not have to pioneer new frontiers of taste. Americans already consume upwards of 400 million gallons of ice cream every year. Nor should Gelato's especially dense consistency and texture, which the company likens to taffy, be any problem in gaining customers' acceptance in any regional market. American palates have already been educated to richness in ice cream by the likes of brands such as Haagen Dazs.

You will serve up this confection—made without anything artificial—in relatively small (300 to 1,000 square feet) retail stores. This, the company points out, makes it possible to locate them in high-traffic areas without having to pay excessive rents. The company's plant produces about twenty to twenty-two of its thirty flavors at any given time. In addition to old standards, Gelato Classico makes flavors such as Joseph Saint Almond, Reverse Chocolate Chip, White Chocolate, and Pumpkin. Other treats available include sorbettos, Italian frozen yogurt, and a special ice cream sandwich called a "Yo Yo." The shops also serve coffee and soft drinks.

The design for company stores features chrome and glass, Italian marble, mirrors, high tech lighting, and the predominance of the color green. Serving staff wear simply designed company aprons. The flowers gracing the countertops are reflected on the mirrored walls. Operating an espresso machine is the most complicated technology you will need to master to run one of these units.

The East Coast now offers the best Gelato franchising opportunities in the continental United States. The company also wants to expand in Hawaii, Canada, and the Far East. Franchisees train in California. The franchise fee covers this instruction, but you must pay for your own transportation, food, and lodging. Training includes proper serving etiquette and salesmanship. If needed, the company will supplement your basic training after you've opened.

Gelato Classico will give you blueprints for your shop's design. Site location is your responsibility, but the company will offer guidance. The gelato you sell must come directly from the company, since it's made according to an exclusive secret formula. Equipment will come either from the company or suppliers it authorizes.

For further information contact:
Tom Cassidy, Gelato Classico Italian Ice Cream, 369 Pine St., Suite 90, San Francisco, CA 94104, 415-433-3111

International Dairy Queen, Inc.

Initial license fee: $30,000
Royalties: 4%
Advertising royalties: 3% to 5%
Minimum cash required: $95,000
Capital required: $95,000+
Financing: The company will finance one-half of the initial license fee over 5 years.
Length of contract: No term

In business since: 1940
Franchising since: 1944
Total number of units: 4,805
Number of company-operated units: 7
Total number of units planned, 1990: NA
Number of company-operated units planned, 1990: NA

Dairy Queen, the world's largest dessert franchise, began in 1940 with one store in Joliet, Illinois, selling a soft ice cream product that contained less milk fat than regular ice cream. The ice cream, served with a distinctive curl at the top, came on a cone. The product was a big success, and in 1944 Dairy Queen began to sell franchises, one of the first food companies to do so. The company reorganized into International Dairy Queen in 1962. The current ice cream menu features parfaits, shakes, sundaes, banana splits, and various frozen novelty items, in addition to the cone with the curl that started it all. The Blizzard, an ice cream-and-candy shake introduced in the mid-eighties, has done especially well. One franchisee in Chicago said that the product had boosted his sales by $300 per day.

Also in 1962, some Dairy Queens substantially widened their product mix to include nondessert food. The trend began when a Georgia franchisee added a selection of fast foods to the company's dessert line, thus converting the local Dairy Queen to a restaurant. This Dairy Queen/Brazier store, now one of the forms in which the company sells its franchises, carried items like hot dogs, hamburgers, chili dogs, cheese dogs, fish sandwiches, and french fries. Eventually, even stores that had continued to concentrate on the ice cream trade added some fast-food items. The conversion helped make Dairy Queen a year-round operation, drawing customers even during the winter.

Whether you buy an ice cream-only Dairy Queen or a Dairy Queen/Brazier, you will pay the same fees and require the same amount of land. Your investment in construction and equipment, however, will total at least 50 percent more if you buy a Dairy Queen/Brazier instead of an original Dairy Queen.

Dairy Queen provides guidelines for site selection and the construction of your Dairy Queen store. It will give you plans and specifications for your building and make two on-site inspections during its construction. For an additional fee, Dairy Queen also offers to coordinate construction and equipment installation. The company refers to this service as "optional but highly recommended."

While you're at an advantage if you have had food service experience before buying your Dairy Queen franchise, you don't need it. You will get all the necessary training from the company at its Minneapolis training center. The licensing fee covers instruction for two people; the company charges an additional $550 fee per person for training more of your employees. You pay for traveling expenses related to training. The company's training program includes instruction in product preparation, equipment operation and maintenance, financial management, service etiquette, "suggestive" selling, marketing and merchandising, sanitation procedures, and personnel training.

The company's team of opening experts will oversee the start-up of your business and will offer on-site assistance for your entire first week of operations. Additional help will come from your field representative in the form of frequent consultations on new products, quality/purity evaluation, and employee retraining. National and regional conventions will enable you to compare your experiences with those of other franchisees and also to get a preview of new products and procedures that the company plans to introduce in the coming year.

You must purchase equipment and supplies for your store from the company's list of approved vendors. Dairy Queen's affiliate, DQF, Inc., will sell you equipment for your store and finance your purchase over five years.

For further information contact:

Franchise Sales Department, International Dairy Queen, Inc., 5701 Green Valley Drive, Minneapolis, MN 55437, 612-830-0327

Swensen's

Initial license fee: $25,000
Royalties: 5.5%
Advertising royalties: Up to 3%
Minimum cash required: $150,000
Capital required: $390,000 to $520,000
Financing: None
Length of contract: 20 years

In business since: 1948
Franchising since: 1963
Total number of units: 386
Number of company-operated units: 18
Total number of units planned, 1990: NA
Number of company-operated units planned, 1990: NA

Picture a turn-of-the-century ice cream parlor with marble tabletops, Tiffany-style lamps, old-fashioned ice cream fountains, and hand-etched glass, where customers eat ice cream out of soda glasses, glass goblets, and malt tins. That's Swensen's, where you can order soups, sandwiches, and salads as well as the chain's made-on-the-premises ice cream. You might think that the nostalgia for America's good old days evoked by Swensen's ambience is the key to the chain's success. But Swensen's has also been successful with the same decor in Brazil, Canada, Guam, Hong Kong, Indonesia, Japan, Kuwait, Malaysia, Mexico, New Zealand, Puerto Rico, Saudi Arabia, Singapore, Taiwan, and Thailand. This leaves only one other possibility: the ice cream.

Swensen's doesn't call its training facility "Sundae School" for nothing. Some of the more successful units in the chain may do 60 percent of their business on meals, which helps keep them busy throughout the day instead of just in the afternoon and evening, but it's the ice cream that draws the customers. Earl Swensen first sold his ice cream at Swensen's Ice Cream Factory atop San Francisco's Russian Hill in 1948, in a store that's still dishing it out. Always made fresh from a proprietary recipe, this ice cream comes in various delicious concoctions, topped with real whipped cream.

Your Swensen's, as either an in-line or free-standing store, will occupy about 3,000 square feet. Swensen's will help you secure a site and will provide assistance in negotiating the lease. The store should be in an area where at least 50,000 people live or work within three miles and have a median income level of $22,000. The company will give you preliminary interior design and construction specifications and a list of the equipment you must purchase. You can buy your batch freezer, an especially important piece of equipment, from Swensen's or other authorized sources.

Swensen's helps you find a dairy that can supply you with the company's ice cream mix, which you must use exclusively. It also provides a standardized menu, which you must follow, although you determine prices. You and your manager will receive ten days of training in company operations, and the Swensen's opening crew will come to your restaurant to train your staff just before you open.

If your full-service restaurant does well, and you would like to open additional units, you can choose from several types of operations. In 1986 Swensen's began to offer a smaller modified full-service restaurant both for highly competitive and more sparsely populated areas, requiring a smaller investment than the standard size. In addition to the full-service units, Swensen's has also designed restaurants and kiosks for installation in malls, department stores, and hotels. Some of them just serve ice cream.

For further information contact:
Swensen's Ice Cream Company, 7500 North Dreamy Draw Drive, Suite 200, Phoenix, AZ 85020, 602-955-1130

Tastee-Freez International, Inc.

Initial license fee: $10,000
Royalties: 4.25%
Advertising royalties: 1%
Minimum cash required: $45,000
Capital required: $45,000
Financing: None
Length of contract: NA

In business since: 1950
Franchising since: 1950
Total number of units: 537
Number of company-operated units: None
Total number of units planned, 1990: NA
Number of company-operated units planned, 1990: NA

In the burgeoning franchising field, where a franchisor who has operated for five or more years can speak from "experience," Tastee-Freez International is truly a seasoned veteran. Some of its current franchises have sold ice cream continually for three decades. But this doesn't mean the company is content to sit back and keep doing things the old way. Tastee-Freez management knows that, to keep its franchisees in thirty-eight states and Canada successful, it must constantly innovate to keep up with the competition.

Recently, in fact, competing companies had begun to take away some of Tastee-Freez's business with new and popular products. Tastee-Freez's response: homemade gourmet ice cream and the Freezee. The company that made its reputation with soft-serve ice cream knew it had to cater to changing public tastes. Hence the new, made-on-the-premises gourmet ice cream that has 14 percent butterfat, compared to the 10 percent found in most other brands, for a creamier flavor.

Tastee-Freez sells the equipment to make gourmet ice cream and instructs its franchisees on how to prepare it. Flavors include Oreo Cookie Chip, French Menthe, Coconut Pineapple, and Lemon Chiffon. The gourmet ice cream also comes in four kinds of cakes—including "the Grasshopper" and "Chocolate-Chocolate-Chocolate"—and four kinds of pies. The company supplies an attractive glass case to show off the pies and cakes, which, it says, give bakery birthday cakes a run for their money. Contrary to the fears expressed by some franchisees that the gourmet product might reduce sales of the soft-serve ice cream, the new variety appears to have increased store traffic and sales of soft ice cream.

Tastee-Freez has also tossed its hat into the newest—and highly competitive—ring in the soft ice cream industry with the Freezee, a blend of ice cream, candy, and fruit in a thick concoction that must be eaten with a spoon. Franchisees who want to carry the Freezee can buy from the company the ten-speed "monster blender with a full half-horse-drive motor" needed to make it.

Tastee-Freez's recent revitalization also includes a new restaurant design. The company calls it the "heritage" look, which involves extensive use of roof shingles and a color scheme of red, white, and blue blended with earth tones. Many of the units have wooden tables outside, and the larger ones serve hamburgers and fries as well as ice cream. The company will advise you on all aspects of securing and preparing a good location for your store.

The company charges a nominal fee—in addition to the initial franchise payment—for your training. Tastee-Freez doesn't stop with the basics when it comes to keeping franchisees up to date. For example, when Tastee-Freez introduced its new ice cream, it started a "College of Ice Cream Knowledge," a two-day seminar and workshop covering everything from ice cream history to the workings of the Taylor 121 Batch Freezer required to make the new product.

A company representative will come to your store to guide you through your opening period, and you can consult your regional office on any aspect of your business. Aside from running a wide variety of national advertising, the company will also support your business through promotional activities. In a recent promotion, a Tastee-Freez sweepstakes, it offered as a prize a 1960 Studebaker Lark Convertible.

For further information contact:
Tastee-Freez International, Inc., 8345 Hall Rd., P.O. Box 162, Utica, MI 48087, 313-739-5520

TCBY (The Country's Best Yogurt)

Initial license fee: $20,000
Royalties: 4%
Advertising royalties: 3%
Minimum cash required: $93,000
Capital required: $93,000 to $155,000
Financing: None
Length of contract: 10 years

In business since: 1981
Franchising since: 1982
Total number of units: 281
Number of company-operated units: 18
Total number of units planned, 1990: NA
Number of company-operated units planned, 1990: NA

It wasn't always "The Country's Best Yogurt." Called "This Can't Be Yogurt" until 1985, a suit filed by a competitor with a similar name forced the company to switch its name to the acronym TCBY. But one thing hasn't changed: TCBY was and is the fastest growing chain of yogurt stores in America. It opened its one hundredth store in 1984; ten months later it had two hundred stores. In 1985 the company ranked third in stock appreciation among over-the-counter stocks by *U.S. News & World Report* and first in stock appreciation among restaurant and fast-food stocks by *Nation's Restaurant News*.

Frank D. Hickingbotham, TCBY's founder and president, was repelled by the very thought of yogurt until a few years ago when he tried the frozen variety and got hooked. With only about half the calories and 20 percent of the butterfat of ice cream, yogurt fits the lighter diet many Americans have adopted in recent years. TCBY stores sell the product in a variety of forms: specialty pies, shakes and fruit smoothies, cones—just about every way that people eat ice cream. The company makes more than twenty flavors of yogurt, with four to six available on a given day. To make sure that its frozen yogurt keeps on selling through the cooler months, TCBY also features it in waffle and crepe dishes. Recently, the company added frozen tofu, a lactose- and cholesterol-free food, to its menu.

The company will advise you on site selection and the construction or remodeling of your store. Free-standing TCBY stores and units located in shopping centers occupy 1,000 to 1,600 square feet, with twenty-four to forty-four seats and counters for carry-out as well as a self-service business. Some franchises have begun to add drive-thru service. Shopping mall stores occupy 450 to 650 square feet. Green predominates in the color scheme in all TCBY stores, accentuated by hanging plants and wall graphics featuring flowers. Customers sit in wicker chairs at butcher-block-style tables.

You will train to run your store at the company's Little Rock, Arkansas, headquarters, where you'll learn inventory control, equipment maintenance, operational techniques, quality standards, bookkeeping and accounting, advertising, promotion, and staff training. You pick up the tab for travel, lodging, and meals. A regional manager will come to your store for five days at the time of your opening to help train your staff and provide whatever advice you need to get your operation up and running. Later on, field representatives will visit your store to provide ongoing support, and you can get advice on specific problems through a phone call to TCBY headquarters.

You can buy your supplies from any vendor that sells products that meet TCBY's specifications, or you can buy through the company's extensive program. TCBY's product manufacturing subsidiary, Americana Foods, Inc., recently completed a 36,000-square-foot plant capable of producing enough yogurt products to supply 1,500 stores, and TCBY has an agreement with the Martin-Brower Company, a major food service chain distributor, to make weekly deliveries of yogurt and other items to TCBY stores.

TCBY advertises on radio, television, and in the print media. It also uses direct mail marketing. The company conducts much of its advertising in cooperation with franchisees.

For further information contact:
Don Terry, Vice President, Franchise Development, TCBY, 11300 Rodney Parham, Little Rock, AR 72212, 501-225-0349

Pizza and Italian Fast Food

Domino's Pizza, Inc.

Initial license fee: $1,300 to $3,250 plus $3,000 grand opening deposit for first-time franchisees
Royalties: 5.5% weekly
Advertising royalties: 3% weekly
Minimum cash required: $60,000

Capital required: $60,000 to $135,000
Financing: Certain lenders have agreed to provide financing to qualified franchisees.
Length of contract: 10 years

In business since: 1960
Franchising since: 1967
Total number of units: 2,826
Number of company-operated units: 796
Total number of units planned, 1990: NA
Number of company-operated units planned, 1990: NA

One of the fastest-growing segments of the food service industry, pizza offers something for everyone. This most versatile of foods can satisfy every taste, with variations ranging from thin-crusted New York slices topped with pepperoni to deep-dish Chicago pies with the works, to nouvelle cuisine California creations featuring sun-dried tomatoes and fresh basil. Add to its widespread appeal busy people's growing demand for microwavable, prepared, and take-out food, and you've got a ready-made market for pizza delivery and carry-out. Domino's Pizza, Inc., specializes in pizza-to-go, promising its customers that their orders will always be delivered hot within thirty minutes of their call. The company's proven system, its commitment to freshness, and its national advertising campaign have made it the largest pizza delivery chain in the country. Domino's controls close to 10 percent of the $9 billion pizza business and continues to claim a greater and greater portion of the market.

Domino's will help you select just the right location for your store and will provide guidance in your purchase or lease negotiations. Because any lease for your site must contain certain conditions, Domino's reserves the right to review it before you sign. Once you are ready to develop your site, the company will provide you with equipment, fixtures, furniture, and signs. All food and beverage products, supplies, and materials must meet the company's standards. You can purchase them from Domino's or any other source that can meet the specifications.

Before you open your doors, Domino's requires you to complete its training program at headquarters in Ann Arbor, Michigan, and at an existing store location. The program covers the fundamentals of pizza preparation, bookkeeping, sales, and other topics related to the operation of your franchise. Besides store operations, you will learn franchise development (to prepare you to develop your region), commissary operations (if you run your pizza shop in connection with another store), and management. When you graduate and are ready to open for business, Domino's will develop and implement preopening advertising, promotions, and publicity at no cost to you.

"A big advantage to the Domino's franchise is that you can capitalize on the exposure the company gives you through its high-quality, high-frequency advertising program," says William Morrow, a Domino's owner in Charlottesville, Virginia. In 1985 the company spent $17.8 million on television advertising—part of its ongoing campaign to carve out a larger portion of the market. An employee of Domino's Pizza for five years before becoming a franchisee, Mr. William Morrow notes as well that "the abundance of rapidly improving training materials, the company's orientation to people, and its use of incentive initiatives to encourage development" have been particularly helpful to him as a franchisee. The company's program of ongoing support to franchisees includes operating assistance in hiring and training employees, planning and executing local advertising and promotional programs, inventory control, and administrative, accounting, and general operating procedures.

William Morrow is pleased with his Domino's franchise. "Given the smaller amount of money involved in entering the food franchise business, my rate of return has been very high. Running my own franchise has been a profound learning experience. I would recommend franchising to anyone who is willing to work hard and long hours, who is financially stable, and who can maintain a sense of humor."

For further information contact:
Deborah S. Sargent, Director of Franchise Services, Domino's Pizza, Inc., Prairie House, Domino's Farms, 30 Frank Lloyd Wright Drive, P.O. Box 997, Ann Arbor, MI 48106-0997, 313-668-6055

Mazzio's Pizza

Initial license fee: $20,000
Royalties: 3%
Advertising royalties: 1%
Minimum cash required: $200,000
Capital required: $800,000
Financing: None
Length of contract: 20 years

In business since: 1961
Franchising since: 1968
Total number of units: 134
Number of company-operated units: 45
Total number of units planned, 1990: NA
Number of company-operated units planned, 1990: NA

Approximately one third of all people who have tried at least two types of ethnic food like Italian the best, according to *Nation's Restaurant News*: "Pasta, pizza *et. al.* are the best-known, most tried, most frequently ordered and most likely to-be-ordered again ethnic foods sold in restaurants." Mazzio's Pizza has ridden the tide of popularity, but it has also made some innovations to position itself more profitably in an already competitive market.

Mazzio's' marketing begins with its menu. To the several varieties of pizza—including deep dish—you might expect in any pizza restaurant, and the familiar assortment of sandwiches and salad bar, Mazzio's adds a Mexican touch, including nachos as an appetizer and a taco pizza. Some Mazzio's also serve gelato.

Mazzio's wants to attract affluent people in the eighteen- to thirty-four-year-old range with its restaurant design and decor as well as its food. Mazzio's features red brick restaurants surrounded by shrubbery, with striped awnings, plenty of neon, an art deco look, and limited table service. They also offer video games.

You may choose from several restaurant design formats. The most popular one occupies 3,300 square feet, seats 124, and requires a staff of about forty to fifty. Currently available locations include the Southwest, Southeast, Midwest, and West. The company does not select your site or put up your building, but it does offer advice, and it will evaluate and must approve your location and construction.

You and one other employee—presumably your manager—will train at a Mazzio's restaurant near the franchisor's Tulsa, Oklahoma, headquarters. You must absorb all of your expenses, except tuition. The course lasts fifteen weeks and covers everything involved in running a Mazzio's, including product preparation, customer service, and personnel. A week before your opening, Mazzio's special opening crew will come to your restaurant to train your staff. Company representatives will stay on the premises through your third week of operations to help you get off to a good start. Throughout your term as a Mazzio's franchisee, the company will update your staff's training through field seminars as needed.

The franchisor will show you how to set up a bookkeeping system, and it will help you keep tabs on your finances so that you can maximize your restaurant's profitablity. The company also makes available, as an option, its computer service center. It says that most franchisees pay the "modest cost" to use the center for their record keeping.

Mazzio's does not directly supply food and equipment, but the company does check what you buy from others to make sure it meets its standards.

The franchisor specializes in on-site promotions. A recent program featured punch cards, which restaurants punched every time a patron made a purchase. After a customer had made a minimum dollar amount of purchases from Mazzio's, they became entitled to free merchandise.

The company encourages multiunit ownership by franchisees who have built successful businesses at a single location. Henry Leonard, vice president of Pizza Systems, Inc., which owns several Mazzio's, has enjoyed his experience as part-owner of a multifranchise operation. He especially likes "the autonomy of the situation. Franchisees for the most part are entrepreneurs and want to act independently from a parent company. Without that autonomy, the relationship would be dramatically changed."

Ken's Restaurant Systems, of which Mazzio's is a part, also sells franchises for its Ken's Pizza restaurants and Scooter's Pizza Delivery.

For further information contact:
Bradford J. Williams, Jr., Ken's Restaurant Systems, Inc., 4441 S. 72nd E. Ave., Tulsa, OK 74145, 918-663-8880

Noble Roman's Pizza

Initial license fee: $12,500
Royalties: 5%
Advertising royalties: None
Minimum cash required: $70,000
Capital required: $235,000 to $375,000
Financing: None
Length of contract: 20 years

In business since: 1972
Franchising since: 1973
Total number of units: 127
Number of company-operated units: 55
Total number of units planned, 1990: NA
Number of company-operated units planned, 1990: NA

"So good, so good, I cry," it says on the cover of Noble Roman's menu. But before that, your mouth waters. These cedar-walled restaurants, replete with beams, columns, patterned ceilings, plants, ceiling fans, Tiffany-style lamps, and wooden blinds, feature continuously running silent movies and soft background music and shamelessly start the juices flowing with a "pizza window," through which patrons can watch employees toss the dough for their pizzas and add the enticing toppings before baking.

Noble Roman's pizza comes in four basic varieties: hand-tossed round, pan brio, Sicilian, and monster, which has more of everything. For a special price during the lunch hour, customers can buy individual pizzas and salad from the salad bar. Noble Roman's makes its pizza from fresh, never-frozen, dough and a cheese blend of mozzarella and Muenster. Customers have their choice of eleven toppings: sausage, chunky Italian sausage, mushrooms, green peppers, pepperoni, ground beef, ham, bacon, black olives, anchovies, and onions.

Other menu items include sausage, roast beef, and ham and cheese sandwiches, meatballs and spaghetti, and Italian bread sticks served with a dip. Noble Roman's serves beer and wine as well as the usual soft drinks. These pizzerias also feature take-out service.

Noble Roman's offers its franchisees training at its corporate center in Bloomington, Indiana, and at franchisees' restaurants. The course covers accounting, marketing, real estate, and construction. In addition, the company will train your hourly employees at your restaurant shortly before your grand opening and will supervise the opening and your initial days in business.

Noble Roman's will help you find a good site for your pizza restaurant, and it will provide you with construction floor plans and equipment layout. It will give you specifications for both equipment and supplies, and it will help you find reliable local vendors. You can consult the company about marketing and operational matters at any time, and a Noble Roman's representative will come to your restaurant periodically to inspect the premises.

Your company marketing manual will help you put together any type of advertising campaign you might care to run. It includes a catalog of varied radio and television spots available from Noble Roman's.

For further information contact:
John West, Noble Roman's Pizza, P.O. Box 1089, Bloomington, IN 47401, 812-339-3533

Pizza Inn, Inc.

Initial license fee: $17,500
Royalties: 4%
Advertising royalties: 3%
Minimum cash required: $75,000
Capital required: $75,000
Financing: None
Length of contract: 20 years

In business since: 1961
Franchising since: 1963

Total number of units: 725
Number of company-operated units: 280
Total number of units planned, 1990: NA
Number of company-operated units planned, 1990: NA

Pizza Inn sells its Pan Pizza, this company's version of deep-dish pizza, as well as thin-crusted and Sicilian pizza, hot Italian dishes, and fresh salad in twenty-nine states and seven foreign countries. Recently the company added to the menu Stuffed Pizza and Light Pizza, a dish lower in sodium, cholesterol, and calories than regular pizza, to keep up with changing tastes. The Noon Buffet and the Tuesday Night Special Buffet draw large numbers of customers to every store throughout the chain.

The mid-eighties were not the best of times for Pizza Inn. With 87 percent of its domestic operations in the South, and Texas accounting for about 38 percent of them, unemployment from the decline in the price of oil depressed the company's fast-food sales. Further, in 1985 alone, the number of new pizza establishments in the U.S. increased by 15 percent over the previous year, making for more competition. And eating-out tastes changed with respect to pizza. With the increase in home entertainment—especially due to the sale of VCRs—and greater use of microwave ovens to re-heat take-home food, many people opted for dining at home.

But Pizza Inn altered its strategy to deal with this challenge. Many of the chain's units added home delivery in 1985 and 1986, and the company began to encourage its franchisees to consider opening smaller take-out and delivery-only units, eschewing the larger space and higher rents and land prices required for the addition of booths.

The company stands ready to assist all franchisees in choosing a good site and in building, leasing, or converting a facility for a Pizza Inn operation. Pizza Inn uses two types of building plans: 3,000-square-foot free-standing restaurants and a 2,200-square-foot design more suitable to strip shopping centers. You will get your first chance to make this business your own when you choose the decor. Available styles include Western, Yesteryear, Pueblo, or Oceanside.

Pizza Inn franchisees receive their initial training at the franchisor's headquarters in Dallas. Topics covered range from dough making to cost controls. The packaged employee training program available from the company, called Hourly Operations Training, or HOT, combines video-taped instruction with written materials and quizzes to help you train your employees at convenient hours and at a pace they can handle.

The Pizza Inn field representative, your liaison with the company, confers with you regularly on particular problems and assists you in adapting company operating forms to your accounting system. The forms provide an easy method of reporting on cash, inventory, employee performance ratings, and food consumption rates.

The company requires that you buy your food from an approved list of suppliers. In practice, most franchisees use the company distribution system.

For further information contact:
Paul R. Brown, Vice President, Franchise Development, Pizza Inn, Inc., 2930 Stemmons Freeway, Dallas, TX 75247, 1-800-527-1483

Round Table Pizza

Initial license fee: $20,000
Royalties: 4%
Advertising royalties: 3%
Minimum cash required: $80,000
Capital required: $280,000 to $300,000
Financing: None
Length of contract: 15 years

In business since: 1959
Franchising since: 1962
Total number of units: 481
Number of company-operated units: 10
Total number of units planned, 1990: NA
Number of company-operated units planned, 1990: NA

Round Table, the biggest pizza chain in the West, has used the same recipe for its made-fresh-daily sauce for twenty-five years. And why change, when a 1984 survey by CMO Research, conducted in several California metropolitan areas, found that 54 percent of pizza restaurant customers ages eighteen to forty-nine ranked Round Table's pizza as their favorite? The closest competitor claimed 14 percent of the vote. The whole-milk mozzarella, provolone, and cheddar cheeses, and the fresh—never freeze-dried or frozen—vegetable toppings probably contribute to Round Table's popularity as well.

Round Table Pizza's thirteen different meat, vegetable, fruit, and seafood toppings include pepperoni, salami, Italian sausage, ground beef, pastrami, ham, linguica sausage, mushrooms, black olives, tomatoes, pineapple tidbits, anchovies, and shrimp. Specialty pizzas combine large helpings of these toppings in various combinations, with mini-pizzas also available. In addition, the menu features Camelot Calzones, Pizzatato (baked potato with a pizza filling), several kinds of sandwiches, and a salad bar. Round Table restaurants serve beer and wine in addition to soft drinks.

Round Table will train you at its training center in Pacifica, California. The course lasts four weeks and includes everything from pizza baking to personnel. As part of your training, you will receive hands-on experience in a Round Table restaurant.

Your Round Table Restaurant will probably occupy about 3,000 square feet and feature cushioned booths, wood paneling, and plants. The company helps you choose a site, architects, and contractors, and negotiate the lease. The franchisor maintains the Round Table Supply Company as a nonprofit division to supply equipment to franchisees at factory level prices, but you may buy your supplies from any source, with Round Table's approval.

Round Table's operations consultant will help you line up local suppliers, hire and train your staff, and set up a bookkeeping system. He or she will also assist you with ongoing support after you open for business. The consultant can provide expertise in many areas, including food and labor costs, inventory, and hiring.

The franchisor's marketing department will customize a marketing plan for you, possibly including a direct mail campaign. On a wider scale, Round Table promotes the chain through an extensive radio and television advertising program.

For further information contact:
Franchise Sales, Round Table Franchise Corporation, 655 Montgomery St., San Francisco, CA 94111, 415-392-7500

Sbarro

Initial license fee: $35,000
Royalties: 5%
Advertising royalties: 3%
Minimum cash required: $108,500
Capital required: $217,000 to $550,000
Financing: None
Length of contract: 15 years

In business since: 1977
Franchising since: 1977
Total number of units: 147
Number of company-operated units: 93
Total number of units planned, 1990: 500
Number of company-operated units planned, 1990: 325

Sbarro has created a simple formula for success: Satisfy a trencherman's appetite for Italian food at moderate prices in pleasant cafeteria-style surroundings. Salamis, prosciutto hams, and cheeses hanging from the ceiling evoke an Italian delicatessen motif. Pizza with a variety of toppings is the mainstay of the menu, but Sbarro shops also serve large portions of pasta and other hot and cold Italian entrées, sandwiches and salads, and desserts, like cheesecake made in Brooklyn. Some units sell beer and wine, although these beverages do not generally account for a large share of the revenues. Shopping mall locations predominate in the chain, although Sbarro has recently opened a few center city cafe-type operations. These cafes have a somewhat more upscale ambience and the same moderate prices as the mall locations and they have done well.

Sbarro mall stores range from 1,500 to 3,000 square feet, seat 60 to 120 people, and usually require seven to twenty-six employees, including part-timers. Each restaurant has a manager and two assistant managers, and their hours coincide with the mall's—often twelve hours a day, seven days a week, covering the lunch and dinner periods.

Currently, Sbarro emphasizes multiunit operations for new franchisees. You will sublease your restaurants—probably in-line units in shopping malls—from the company. Sbarro will give you plans for store layout and specifications for construction and equipment. You may purchase supplies and equipment from any approved supplier, although most franchisees buy from Sbarro at a reduced cost. Your license agreement will include a clause requiring you to refurbish the premises when necessary—probably every five years.

You pay the travel expenses incidental to the five-week training program, which you or your manager must complete in Commack, New York. Aside from hands-on experience working in a company restaurant, the training will include background in quality control, personnel management, marketing, and financial management.

A district manager, usually responsible for six to ten restaurants, will assist you in training your employees for three weeks before you open. Thereafter, he or she will be your liaison with Sbarro. Should you need it, you can get refresher training at your regional office or at corporate headquarters in Commack.

You can purchase your supplies from any vendor maintaining Sbarro's level of quality. Most franchisees buy from the same distributor as company restaurants because of the price advantages achieved by volume purchasing. The cheesecake, however, must come from Sbarro's Brooklyn facility.

For further information contact:

Erwin Protter, Sbarro, Inc., 763 Larkfield Rd., Commack, NY 11725, 516-864-0200

Shakey's Pizza Restaurant

Initial license fee: $20,000
Royalties: 4.5%
Advertising royalties: 2%
Minimum cash required: $175,000
Capital required: $175,000 to $212,000
Financing: None
Length of contract: 20 years

In business since: 1954
Franchising since: 1958
Total number of units: 271
Number of company-operated units: 11
Total number of units planned, 1990: NA
Number of company-operated units planned, 1990: NA

Shakey's, although a national franchisor, is most firmly entrenched in California, with 109 franchised and 9 company-owned units in that state alone. Shakey's Pizza Restaurants feature sit-down meals—not just pizza—in a casual family-style atmosphere. The menu in these self-service establishments features chicken, spaghetti and other pastas, and sandwiches. Customers can order beer at most Shakey's and wine at some of the restaurants.

Shakey's strives for an atmosphere of conviviality. Some units in the chain feature live entertainment and movies. The menu reflects a light touch, with dishes like "Idiot's Delight," "Big Ed Special," "Mad Merriment," and "Right-Hander's Special." Printed advisories to customers state: "Pizza is always eaten with the fingers."

While Shakey's sells area franchises involving ten or more restaurants, it also welcomes individual applications. Shakey's will evaluate one restaurant site you have selected without charge, but you will have to pay for further evaluations if the first site is not approved. The company gives you building plans and specifications for your restaurant, and it also provides an interior design and layout. The typical in-line mall or shopping center facility is about 2,800 hundred square feet.

Your manager—and any subsequent manager you may hire—and other key employees will take a two-week training program at Shakey's Parlor Operations Management School in Dallas. Topics studied include purchasing, receiving, storage, sanitation, product preparation, salad bar management, safety, personnel, security, payroll, and marketing. Students work in the training center kitchen as well as in the classroom. You will pay for travel and living accommodations for each of your employees.

The company requires you to purchase certain ingredients from Shakey's or other vendors it has licensed. Such ingredients include Shakey's pizza spice blend, pizza sauce, chicken marinade, Italian sausage mix, beef seasoning blend, dough blend, and chicken breading. Shakey's may make a profit on supplies bought from them, but the profit will be limited to 7 percent.

Your advertising royalty pays for Shakey's national advertising program. In addition, you are also required to spend 2.4 percent of your gross sales on local advertising, which might include television advertising in cooperation with other Shakey's in your area.

For further information contact:
Shakey's Inc., The Courtyard at Las Colinas, 1320 Greenway Drive, Suite 600, P.O. Box 165348, Irving, TX 75016, 214-580-0388

Restaurants

Benihana of Tokyo

Initial license fee: $50,000
Royalties: 5%
Advertising royalties: 0.5%
Minimum cash required: $375,000
Capital required: $1 to 2 million
Financing: The company helps franchisees prepare financial documents for review by lenders.
Length of contract: 15 years

In business since: 1964
Franchising since: 1970
Total number of units: 44
Number of company-operated units: 37
Total number of units planned, 1990: 60
Number of company operated units planned, 1990: 45

An evening at Benihana is more than just eating out. From the authentically detailed Japanese country inn decor, to the communal seating around hibachi tables, to the service provided by kimonoed waitresses, everything about a Benihana steakhouse transports diners to the Far East. But what makes Benihana truly famous is its simple high quality cuisine, dazzlingly prepared by skilled chefs right before patrons' eyes. Tabletop cooking, Benihana's trademark, makes every meal entertaining as well as delicious, and helped make Benihana the country's most popular full-service restaurant in 1985.

Headed by the dynamic and energetic Rocky Aoki, Benihana has grown from one restaurant in New York City to a chain with over $60 million in sales. Aoki has become famous for his love of risk, which leads him to race offshore powerboats and sail hot-air balloons, among other things. His involvement in such activities serves as one of Benihana's more successful marketing ploys. "Every year," says Aoki, "I try to do something new to promote the name of Benihana." The company also pursues a bigger chunk of America's dining dollar via more traditional but equally aggressive advertising and marketing efforts. Its strategy for expansion includes company-owned units in foreign markets as well as franchises and joint ventures in the U.S., focusing in particular on the midwestern states.

You can purchase a Benihana franchise either as an investor or as an owner/operator. Benihana reserves the right to approve your selection of a restaurant, and must approve your building construction or leasehold improvements in writing. Depending on your approach to the management of your restaurant, you and/or your management staff must attend a twelve-week training course at a company-owned restaurant. A full-time Benihana employee will train you in restaurant operations, covering such topics as cost controls, staffing, and sanitation.

Essential to your restaurant's success, your chefs must have qualified as chefs in Japan and completed Benihana's thorough training in hibachi-table cooking. Benihana offers an intensive eight- to twelve-week training course for chefs, conducted at a company-owned restaurant. You are responsible for chefs' wages and living expenses during this period. To further ensure the success of your franchise, Benihana operations personnel will help you train all other new staff, like your waiters and waitresses. You will receive company assistance throughout the pre-opening phase and during restaurant opening, including promotional help from the Benihana public relations staff.

Throughout the life of your franchise, Benihana staff is available for free consultation in all aspects of restaurant operations. Manuals provide guidance in daily operations, and all franchisees receive standard office forms and Benihana recipes. Benihana designates approved sources of equipment and supplies, but will waive the requirement to purchase from these sources if your alternate suppliers meet their approval. Because "to franchise a first-class restaurant like this is not easy," according to Rocky Aoki, the company conducts seminars for restaurant management at its Miami,

Florida headquarters each year. The workshops cover all areas of concern to unit managers, including bookkeeping, inventory control, menu development, salaries, and benefits.

For further information contact:
Michael W. Kata, Director of Licensee Operations, Benihana of Tokyo, P.O. Box 020210, Miami, FL 33102-0210, 305-593-0770

Bob's Big Boy Restaurant System

Initial license fee: $25,000
Royalties: 3%
Advertising royalties: 4%
Minimum cash required: $100,000
Capital required: $897,500 to $1,430,000
Financing: None
Length of contract: 20 years

In business since: 1936
Franchising since: 1954
Total number of units: 800
Number of company-operated units: 200
Total number of units planned, 1990: NA
Number of company-operated units planned, 1990: NA

The baby boom generation has grown up, gotten married, and settled down to raise families. Now, the same population that spurred the growth of fast-food restaurants in the sixties and seventies is dining at family restaurants, and this $20 billion segment of the food industry is preparing for an era of rapid expansion. "We believe strongly in the growth potential of family restaurants. In fact, Marriott Corporation has made a commitment to make Bob's Big Boy a leading name in this restaurant segment," states Richard E. Marriott, executive vice president of Marriott Corporation. Bob's Big Boy is a division of Marriott.

Family restaurants offer waiter/waitress service, a casual atmosphere appropriate for children, and a more extensive menu than fast-food restaurants. But families aren't the only patrons of family restaurants. Everyone from young singles to senior citizens enjoys the quality fare many of these restaurants serve up.

Each Big Boy offers a clean, comfortable setting in which diners can enjoy a basic American menu or a variety of ethnic foods, all moderately priced and attractively presented. Featuring greenhouse additions, oak furniture, and tile floors, the airy contemporary restaurants include salad, fruit, and breakfast bars that draw people for every meal—and for snacks in between. The Big Boy Hamburger and Big Boy Strawberry Pie remain the centerpiece of the Big Boy menu, but individual restaurants offer dishes suited to local and regional tastes as well.

Big Boy owners enjoy the benefits of a partnership with Marriott, the third largest corporation in the food industry. The company provides systems for strategic planning, market research, volume purchasing, distribution, financial controls, and more. Marriott maintains a policy of operating only one company-owned unit for every three franchised units in order to best serve its Big Boy franchisees. If they meet the minimum net worth requirement of $500,000 per restaurant to be developed, franchisees can buy the rights to develop key geographic areas and open one or more locations according to an approved business plan.

The company will help you select the best available site for your restaurant(s) and help your throughout the building process. You (and your restaurant manager, if you will not be managing the franchise yourself) must then complete six weeks of intensive training at corporate headquarters in Washington, D.C., before opening your unit. Classroom and hands-on instruction will orient you to the Big Boy concept, operating standards, systems, and procedures, and such areas as customer service and sanitation. Training crews will help you prepare your employees, and a Big Boy opening team will help you open your new restaurant.

You will be equipped with manuals on various topics, from management philosophy to restaurant inspection. Field personnel will provide you with as much or as little assistance as you desire, and the company will conduct workshops in your restaurant to meet your specific needs. Your marketing support kit, prepared by Marriott's marketing department, will advise you on conducting your own promotional programs as well as equipping you with coupons and print, radio, and television ads.

Big Boy's menu development program tests new and existing products for marketability and advises you on profit-maximizing menus. Other departments offer support in every area, from traffic planning to labor relations, to safety, to human resources development.

While investors with qualified operating managers can, when approved, run Big Boy franchises as absentee owners, Marriott strongly believes that the success of a Big Boy restaurant is closely related to day-to-day, hands-on owner involvement. The company seeks franchisees who are committed to working full-time with their franchises and who have the motivation, management ability, and the financial resources to develop multiple units in their exclusive area over a five-year period.

For further information contact:

Bob's Big Boy Restaurant System, Franchise Division, Marriott Corporation, Marriott Drive, Washington, DC 20058
1-800-638-6707, Ext. 7863

Cucos Restaurantes

Initial license fee: $20,000 to $30,000
Royalties: 4%
Advertising royalties: 2.5%
Minimum cash required: $275,000
Capital required: $300,000 to $500,000
Financing: None
Length of contract: NA

In business since: 1981
Franchising since: 1984
Total number of units: 30
Number of company-operated units: 10
Total number of units planned, 1990: 100
Number of company-operated units planned, 1990: NA

According to the National Restaurant Association, Mexican food represents one of the fastest-growing segments of the food service industry. As Vincent Liuzza, president of Cucos, puts it, "We've just seen the tip of the iceberg as far as Mexican restaurants are concerned." With the dominance in the eating-out market of twenty-five- to forty-year-old consumers, and their interest in finger foods and exotic alcoholic beverages like margaritas, the market for restaurants serving something other than meat and potatoes has expanded rapidly. The Cucos concept is to serve the freshest available made-to-order food to diners in the casual atmosphere of a festive watering hole.

Operating from smaller buildings located in areas of limited population, Cucos specializes in Sonoran cuisine, which differs markedly from chili- and pepper-dominated Tex-Mex cuisine. "We're going for a full rich flavor rather than a spicy 'heat'," explains Vincent Liuzza. "We feel that our menu is acceptable to a lot of people who think they don't like Mexican food." The Cucos menu features appetizers like guacamole, chili con queso, and six types of nachos, and entrées ranging from the house specialty chimichangas to flautas and enchiladas. Many dishes are distiguished by the use of Cucos special sauce, a rich brown sauce, which can be altered to taste at the table. The restaurants attract a lot of bar business, which they encourage by featuring happy hours. Their locations in less populous areas often make Cucos the most prominent eating establishment in town, and their smaller size makes them appear crowded and successful, thereby attracting new patrons.

Cucos specializes in conversions of existing chain restaurants or independent operations, which, in combination with the restaurants' modest 3,800- to 6,000-square-foot size, makes for relatively low start-up costs. Because of its emphasis on conversions, Cucos allows for variations in decor. "We wanted our look to be standardized in 'feel' rather than by actual specifications. Our feeling is upbeat southwestern," says Vincent Liuzza.

The company offers development agreements only to franchisees who agree to open multiple units, with fees set at $30,000 for the first restaurant, $25,000 for the second through sixth restaurants, and $20,000 for any other restaurants you develop. The company's multi-unit conversion strategy has so far limited franchisees to those who wish to convert their existing operations or those with restaurant experience who can demonstrate the ability to manage a multiunit operation.

Each of your Cucos Restaurantes must be operated by a principle operating officer who owns a share in the business and devotes full time to managing it. Prior to your first restaurant opening, at least four of your restaurant management personnel must complete the eleven-week initial training period in order to become certified Cucos managers. The intensive course covers every aspect of Cucos operations. After the first unit, you can conduct management training at your location following company guidelines. Upon completing your training, your managers must complete a two-week certification program at the Cucos training facilities.

Cucos staff will help you in the opening of your unit, providing assistance in everything from construction to advertising. The preopening team will stay at your site throughout the initial operations of your restaurant to provide continuing day-to-day help until you feel fully confident in your abilities. Thereafter, you can count on your "System Confidential Manual" and constant telephone contact with the home office to answer any of your questions. Periodic visits by company staff to inspect your restaurant will help you evaluate your operation.

Since Vincent Liuzza was a Sizzler Steakhouse franchisee long before he founded Cucos, he knows what it's like to be a franchisee and has designed the Cucos franchise program specifically to encourage the entrepreneurial spirit of franchise owners.

For further information contact:

Dennis Staub, Vice President, Franchise Development, Cucos Restaurantes, 3009 25th St., Metairie, LA 70002, 504-835-0306

El Chico Corporation

Initial license fee: $40,000
Royalties: 3%
Advertising royalties: 4%
Minimum cash required: $300,000
Capital required: $750,000 to $1,400,000
Financing: None
Length of contract: 15 years

In business since: 1940
Franchising since: 1960
Total number of units: 106
Number of company-operated units: 81
Total number of units planned, 1990: 165
Number of company-operated units planned, 1990: 115

El Chico, a chain of middle-priced family-style Tex-Mex dinner restaurants in the South and Southwest, can brag that 60 percent of its customers eat at an El Chico three times a month, a number more often associated with fast-food restaurants. Customer loyalty had wavered in the late seventies and early eighties, when the chain passed from the hands of the Cuellar family, which had founded it, to ownership by Campbell Taggart, the huge baked goods company and subsidiary of Anheuser-Busch. Campbell Taggart tried to run El Chico using management with experience in other businesses. Efforts to improve profits by cutting costs led to a decline in service, and the situation did not improve until the Cuellar family bought it back.

Today, the Cuellars concentrate on slow and cautious expansion within the same geographical areas El Chico has always served, with an emphasis on service and quality food. Management realizes that with over thirty regional and national chains featuring Mexican food, whatever El Chico does, it had better do it right. Noticing how business had declined as many El Chico restaurants were allowed to age, the company has recently emphasized remodeling as a merchandising technique. "El Chico's new look is a lot brighter, a lot more open, and has really got a better feel than the old El Chico design," says Gilbert Cuellar, Jr., the chain's president. "Many of the old units didn't even have windows—that's how dark and dreary they were."

The menu in these casual restaurants, where liquor accounts for only 16 percent of revenues, features traditional Mexican dishes. Offerings include fajitas, nachos, tacos, enchiladas, burritos, flautas, and chimichangas. El Chico also serves a limited American menu.

You will build your El Chico restaurant in a densely populated suburban area on or near a major road. Your unit will probably occupy about 5,300 square feet, with seating for approximately one hundred ninety. You will select three possible locations for your restaurant, and the company will inspect them. If none proves satisfactory, you may submit more choices. The company will give you drawings and specifications for your establishment, but you will build the restaurant. Your premises must follow the company's general guidelines for the appearance of an El Chico restaurant, but you can choose many of the decorating details. In order to prevent El Chico units from aging as they had in the past, the company stipulates that it may require you to remodel your restaurant, at your expense, every five years to reflect any change in the El Chico image as expressed by the franchisor.

You may designate two of your managerial-level employees—including yourself if you serve as general manager—to receive the company's training at one of its Dallas restaurants. This training will last ten weeks, unless the trainees' experience allows completion of the course in a shorter time and covers everything involved in running an El Chico restaurant.

The company performs an additional service for franchisees with respect to training. It will give your designated trainees a management aptitude test to see if the individuals you intend to hire have managerial talent. El Chico insists that a competent and dedicated manager run your restaurant, and to ensure that person's loyalty to your enterprise, it requires that the manager either own 10 percent of the business or at least participate in a profit-sharing plan.

The El Chico training team will come to your restaurant for the ten days before you open your doors for business, helping to train your staff and prepare the premises for your first customers. El Chico personnel will also travel to your restaurant to train employees hired after you open for business, but the company charges a fee of seventy-five dollars per day for that service plus the travel and lodging expenses of the trainer.

El Charrito, a company owned by Campbell Taggart, has a supply contract with El Chico. If you buy supplies through that company, El Charrito will ship recipe ingredients, prepared foods, and avocados directly to you but will bill El Chico. You will pay El Chico, which adds 2 percent to cover administrative services. If you prefer to buy supplies elsewhere, El Chico will help you find local suppliers.

You must spend 3 percent of your gross sales on advertising and promotion. If there are other El Chico franchisees nearby, that sum will go for cooperative advertising.

For further information contact:
Robert P. Flack, El Chico Corporation, 12200 Stemmons Freeway, Suite 100, Dallas, TX 75234, 214-241-5500

International House of Pancakes

Initial license fee: $50,000
Royalties: 4.5%
Advertising royalties: 3%
Minimum cash required: $50,000
Capital required: $50,000 to $600,000
Financing: Available for conversions
Length of contract: NA

In business since: 1958
Franchising since: 1958
Total number of units: 450
Number of company-operated units: 115
Total number of units planned, 1990: NA
Number of company-operated units planned, 1990: NA

For over twenty-seven years, International House of Pancakes has made it a little easier for Americans to get up in the morning. The company has recently directed its advertising toward increasing its name recognition among the early risers who already find it easy to remember McDonalds and Burger King later in the day. In an effort to expand its market, IHOP has implemented an aggressive campaign to let diners know that they can find great lunches and dinners right where they're used to eating delicious breakfasts. So, while continuing to turn out the pancakes, strawberry waffles, and omelets, the House of Pancakes has been gradually filling its menus with lunch and dinner food: hamburgers, London broil, Italian specialties, salads, and seafood. IHOP has extensively promoted its new culinary approach with ad lines like: "The only dinners in town that stack up to our pancakes."

International House of Pancakes has recently encountered stiff competition for its breakfast clientele, but its twofold marketing strategy has helped the company to maintain a strong market position. The big fast-food franchises have in the past several years tried to take a bite out of the company's share of the breakfast trade. And pancakes have traditionally finished behind eggs, sausage, and bacon as the favorite main course of Americans who eat out for breakfast: 44 percent prefer eggs, 31 percent prefer bacon and sausage, and 16 percent prefer pancakes. But by combining promotional activity aimed at increasing demand for pancakes with its pursuit of the wider lunch and dinner market, IHOP remains one of the best-known names in food—and continues to grow.

There are three ways you can become part of International House of Pancakes. You can purchase a company-owned restaurant, in which case your franchise fee ($50,000 initital license fee plus value of building and land) may range as high as about $600,000, depending on the location of the operation. Alternately, you may become an investor for $50,000 and find a site and build your unit to House of Pancakes' specifications. Or else you can convert another restaurant to an International House of Pancakes franchise, remodeling to company specifications. The fee for conversion is also $50,000.

International House of Pancakes will train you at the House of Pancakes nearest you. The course lasts six weeks and covers use of equipment, purchasing, floor management, sanitation, advertising, and insurance. Management seminars, given at least once a year, will supplement introductory instruction.

An International House of Pancakes field representative will visit your operation periodically. He or she will supervise and help you in the running of your business. You can get specific advice at any time from the home office about any problems that arise.

For further information contact:
Anna Ulvan, International House of Pancakes, Inc., 6837 Lankershim Blvd., North Hollywood, CA 91605, 818-982-2620

K-Bob's, Inc.

Initial license fee: $25,000
Royalties: 3%
Advertising royalties: 1% plus 1% required local spending
Minimum cash required: $125,000
Capital required: $200,000 to $350,000
Financing: None
Length of contract: 20 years

In business since: 1966
Franchising since: 1968
Total number of units: 101
Number of company-operated units: 3
Total number of units planned, 1990: 230
Number of company-operated units planned, 1990: 30

In recent years many fast-food and budget restaurants have added salad bars to accommodate the new American taste for light, low-fat food. K-Bob's had a salad bar in its first restaurant, opened in Clovis,

New Mexico, in 1966, making the company something of a pioneer. K-Bob's features steak-and-potatoes and sit-down dining with full table service. Its restaurants in Texas, New Mexico, Colorado, Kansas, and Oklahoma reflect the tastes of the Southwest. In an informal atmosphere, K-Bob's serves Mexican favorites such as tacos, guacamole, fajitas, and nachos, in addition to several varieties of steak, hamburgers, fried chicken, kabob, and a number of seafood entrées, including catfish.

Typically, K-Bob's occupies a 5,500-square-foot free-standing or shopping center unit. The company will help you select a site and will give you preliminary drawings and scale architectural blueprints for your restaurant. K-Bob's will also consult with your architect or contractor during construction and order equipment and furniture for your facility. Its equipment company will sell you what you need at cost-plus-10-percent and you can order supplies from a list of approved vendors.

K-Bob's trains your manager for six weeks at its Dallas headquarters, with transportation and lodging the only extra expense for you. The training program covers food preparation, staff training, equipment use, sanitation, merchandising, inventory control, customer service, management, accounting, record keeping, cash control, and profit-and-loss analysis.

K-Bob's four-person grand opening team will prime your business for a fast start, spending two weeks on the premises seeing to it that everything is in place and functioning as it should. The franchisor will also provide advertising and promotional materials to introduce your restaurant to your community. In addition to your 1 percent royalty for national advertising, you will also be spending 1 percent of your gross revenues on local advertising, possibly through cooperative programs with other franchisees.

K-Bob's pledges that you will get all the problem-solving, troubleshooting assistance you need as a franchisee. The company will update your training free of charge when it adds new products to the menu and will also train any new managerial employees you hire.

For further information contact:

Andrew Gunkler, Vice President of Development, K-Bob's, Inc., 5757 Alpha Rd., Suite 716, Dallas, TX 75240, 214-392-1881

Po Folks, Inc.

Initial license fee: $37,000
Royalties: 4%
Advertising royalties: 3.5%
Minimum cash required: $100,000
Capital required: $650,000 to $900,000
Financing: None
Length of contract: 20 years

In business since: 1975
Franchising since: 1975
Total number of units: 167
Number of company-operated units: 56
Total number of units planned, 1990: NA
Number of company-operated units planned, 1990: NA

While the name of this chain of table-service restaurants evokes a down-home, friendly atmosphere, it does not reflect the profitability of its franchises. Nor does the company treat its franchisees like poor folks. Po Folks is committed to the idea of franchising. Both a franchisor and a major franchisee of the Wendy's chain of fast-food hamburger restaurants with exclusive rights to the Baltimore and Saint Louis areas, Po Folks has recently modified its own franchise policy, and this might mean good news for you. The company, which had focused on the sale of whole territories to corporate franchisees, now stresses the individual owner-operator. Po Folks has upgraded its training and support programs in order to more effectively integrate single-unit operators into the growing company.

Recent changes in the decor of Po Folks units have given them more of a homey look. The menu adds to the country ambience both by the selection of dishes it offers and by its design and humorous text. Seafood dinners, for instance, come with "yore choice of two vegetables, hush puppies an' some good sauce." Greens and "po-taters" complement a variety of chicken and beef dishes. Customers can wash it all down with soft drinks ("belly washers") served in mason jars. If they don't want a whole dinner, they can always have a "samwich." The entire staff wears a uniform of blue jeans.

Po Folks seeks franchisees with some restaurant experience. If you fit the bill, it will train you at either its Nashville corporate offices or at a regional location. In either case, you will absorb the cost of your travel and lodging. Training covers employee management, food preparation and delivery, bookkeeping, public relations, advertising, restaurant maintenance, guest relations, ordering supplies, and sanitation.

Po Folks will help you find the right site for your restaurant and will give you plans for the building design and interior layout, but you must build your restaurant. Before you open, a team of helpers from the company will come to your restaurant to train your hourly staff in all facets of Po Folks operations. The Po Folks opening team will also remain for a few days after you open for business to make sure all the kinks get ironed out. The company offers ongoing motivational training for your employees and special instruction on new products through on-premises classes, slides, video tapes, and audio cassettes.

A typical Po Folks is a free-standing unit of about 5,500 square feet, which seats 180 to 200 patrons. It employs 100 to 120 hourly workers and 4 to 6 managers working two shifts. The company does not maintain a central distribution system for food supplies, so you will purchase your supplies from a list of company-approved sources.

Po Folks, which has previously concentrated its operations in the South, wants to expand to other parts of the country, including the entire states of Connecticut, Massachusetts, Minnesota, and New York.

For further information contact:
John A. Scott, Vice President, Franchising, Po Folks, Inc., 435 Metroplex Drive, Nashville, TN 37211, 615-366-0914

Rax Restaurants, Inc.

Initial license fee: $25,000
Royalties: 4%
Advertising royalties: 4%
Minimum cash required: $100,000
Capital required: $500,000
Financing: None
Length of contract: 20 years

In business since: 1978
Franchising since: 1978
Total number of units: 486
Number of company-operated units: 153
Total number of units planned, 1990: 921
Number of company-operated units planned, 1990: 200

Rax began as a chain of roast beef restaurants called Jax. Since then, management has adapted its restaurant concept to changing tastes and demographics and developed a new menu and look that has made Rax popular with the "middle market" of the fast-food industry—customers in the twenty-five to forty-nine-year-old age bracket. Rax customers also include many retired people. In 1984 and 1985 a *Restaurants and*

Institutions poll rated Rax the most popular fast-food, varied-menu restaurant in America.

The Rax menu features a variety of sandwiches, including roast beef, ham, chicken, and turkey. Customers may also order baked potatoes with a variety of toppings, and several kinds of soup. Rax's salad bar offers fifty varieties of fruits and vegetables, and the restaurants also serve a smaller version of Rax sandwiches for children. The company has added several items to its menu that fit in with the growing demand for foods low in fat and salt. In addition to a salad bar, Rax Restaurants feature low-fat roast beef and turkey and plain baked potatoes served with margarine, all of which meet standards for good nutrition set by the American Heart Association.

Custom-built Rax Restaurants contain a solarium. Buff-colored stucco on the side and rear walls, decorative tile, and plum-colored awnings distinguish restaurant exteriors, while ceiling fans, upholstered or rattan chairs, and butcher-block tables create attractive interiors. The 118-seat, usually free-standing restaurants provide parking for twenty-five to fifty-five cars.

Rax seeks experienced food service people to buy its franchises. If you meet the company's requirements, it will assist you with site selection, looking at several of your choices in order to find one acceptable to both you and Rax. You can also consult Rax on negotiating land costs or rental and lease terms. Rax requires that you equip your restaurant with items from approved dealers, and in some cases it will specify the machine models that you must purchase. Similarly, you will buy supplies only from company-approved vendors.

Rax will train your management-level employees in a five-week course, for which you will pay only travel-related expenses and employee salaries. The first two weeks of training consist of classroom work in supervisory skills, cost controls, quality assurance, sanitation, equipment maintenance, and other subjects, and takes place at one of three regional training centers: Columbus, Ohio; Orlando, Florida; or Saint Louis, Missouri. Trainees receive three weeks of on-the-job experience at a Rax unit near the location of their new restaurants. Several days before your opening, the company's training instructors will come to your restaurant to train your other employees and will remain for your first two days of operations.

The Rax franchise area supervisor will take care of any problems that arise in your ongoing business and will offer you advice on subjects like cost control and updating your business plan. Should you need it, your supervisor can arrange for supplementary training at your premises. In any case, the supervisor will visit your restaurant four times a year.

Rax promotes itself through regional television and radio advertising, local newspaper advertisements, and direct mail marketing.

For further information contact:
William Dolan, Rax Restaurants, Inc., 1266 Dublin Rd., Columbus, OH 43215, 614-486-3669

Village Inn Pancake House Restaurants

Initial license fee: $25,000
Royalties: 5%
Advertising royalties: None
Minimum cash required: $80,000
Capital required: $80,000
Financing: The company sometimes offers a variety of financing.
Length of contract: 15 years

In business since: 1958
Franchising since: 1961
Total number of units: 266
Number of company-operated units: 132
Total number of units planned, 1990: 390
Number of company-operated units planned, 1990: 216

Village Inn family restaurants aim to please with ambience and service as much as with moderate-priced food. Carpeted dining rooms, with their acoustical sound controls, allow for a relaxed dining experience not always possible in family restaurants. When customers order coffee, the waiter or waitress leaves a coffee pot on the table for refills. The menu, which includes all three meals, is so big it requires an index. Aside from pancakes cooked with batter made fresh each morning, the fare includes steak, shrimp, salads, soups, stews, Italian specialties, hamburgers, and desserts.

The company sells single-unit franchises for communities of 30,000 to 60,000. Larger populations require the purchase of an area franchise. Village Inn will help you select a location for your restaurant and will provide you with plans and specifications for your unit, which will seat at least 160 people. Should you wish the company to provide extensive architectural, engineering, and construction consulting services, it will do so for an additional $7,500. But even if you do not require such services, the company still inspects your building's progress and must give its final approval to all construction.

Your general manager and kitchen manager will receive their training at the company's headquarters in Denver, Colorado. The program lasts five to seven weeks and covers restaurant management, service, maintenance, accounting, and quality control. If you wish, Village Inn will help you hire your managers. A Village Inn field staff will train your hourly employees a week before you open and will remain at your restaurant during your first week of business to make sure everything runs smoothly. Regional training meetings update key employees on company products and techniques during the year, and field trainers can come to your unit, at your expense, to work with particular individuals who need new or additional training.

Vicorp, Village Inn's parent company, has an equipment division, but you do not have to purchase from it. Similarly, you do not have to buy food from any particular company, but what you do purchase must always meet company specifications.

The company has a marketing staff that will prepare advertising and promotional materials for you at your request. Any other marketing materials you use must first receive company approval.

For further information contact:
James T. Orr, Vicorp Restaurants, Inc., P.O. Box 16601, Denver, CO 80216, 303-296-2121, Ext. 204

Sandwiches

All American Hero

Initial license fee: $25,000
Royalties: 5%
Advertising royalties: 1% to 3%
Minimum cash required: $140,000
Capital required: $140,000
Financing: None
Length of contract: 10 years

In business since: 1980
Franchising since: 1980
Total number of units: 84
Number of company-operated units: 4
Total number of units planned, 1990: 252
Number of company-operated units planned, 1990: 12

For lunchtime diners, the sandwich is a perennial favorite—each year, over 500 million sandwiches (not including hamburgers) are sold by delis and sandwich shops. An All American Hero franchise in a location with lots of lunchtime traffic can give you a taste of the same success many other independent business people have already enjoyed. All American Hero shops serve up a wide variety of hot and cold submarine sandwiches, specializing in Philadelphia-style steak sandwiches. French fries, onion rings, and soft drinks round out the menu, and a special breakfast menu caters to the morning crowd. The company's standards of quality and service have proven a formula for success.

All American Hero prepares its franchisees for sandwich shop operation with two weeks of training at its Fort Lauderdale, Florida, headquarters. You will learn food preparation, sandwich making, grill operation, bookkeeping, cost control, and personnel management. All American Hero selects and leases your location and subleases it to you, eliminating one of the more confusing aspects of opening a business. Once you sign the sublease, you work with a contractor to develop the site according to the company's specifications, assisted by a company representative who advises you during construction and helps you purchase equipment and opening inventory.

Your company representative also oversees your shop opening to make sure everything runs smoothly, and provides training and supervision on site until you feel confident in taking all the responsibilities of a restaurant manager, from food pricing to menu planning. During the term of your franchise contract, All American Hero gives refresher courses in sandwich shop operations, which you can attend whenever you feel the need. The training also provides updates on new techniques, products, and menu developments. Your only expense for refresher training is the cost of your travel and hotel.

As an All American Hero franchisee, you will receive ongoing operational guidance, assistance in your promotional efforts, and strategic planning advice. In exchange for the support of the home office, you are required to maintain the company's image of quality by maintaining its standards. You may purchase the necessary equipment and supplies from any supplier as long as they meet the companies specifications. Steak must be bought from company-approved sources. Throughout the term of your ten-year contract, and for one year afterward in certain locations, you are not permitted to have an interest in a similar business.

For further information contact:
Joseph Piazza, Franchise Director, All American Hero, 2200 West Commercial Blvd., Suite 100, Ft. Lauderdale, FL 33309, 305-486-7000

Arby's, Inc.

Initial license fee: $20,000 to $32,000
Royalties: 3%
Advertising royalties: 4.2%
Minimum cash required: $100,000

Capital required: $235,000 to $304,500
Financing: The company offers guidance in obtaining financing.
Length of contract: 20 years

In business since: 1964
Franchising since: 1965
Total number of units: 1,500
Number of company-operated units: 200
Total number of units planned, 1990: NA
Number of company-operated units planned, 1990: NA

Take some fresh lean roast beef, thinly slice it onto a toasted roll, maybe top it off with a tomato slice, some lettuce, and a little horseradish, and you've got the quintessential sandwich. Put some french fries and a Jamocha Shake on the side, and you've got Arby's. No other name in the fast-food business is as closely associated with roast beef as Arby's. Consistently ranked among the world's top ten fast-food franchises, Arby's sells about one third of all the roast beef sandwiches consumed in American restaurants. Its system-wide sales approach $1 billion annually.

Arby's restaurants worldwide offer a variety of roast beef and other sandwiches, home fried and french fried potatoes, a salad bar, soft drinks, and Arby's exclusive Jamocha Shake, a thick coffee-chocolate milkshake. The company's menu-development staff has recently been developing additions to the menu in response to the dining public's changing tastes and in preparation for Arby's further expansion into new geographic regions.

Reflecting their satisfaction with the Arby's franchise system, a great number of the company's franchisees are multiunit owners. Arby's encourages multiunit ownership by offering second and subsequent restaurants at reduced license rates. You can still find openings in prime markets for multiunit operation as well as single unit, and you can develop either free-standing, storefront, or mall locations. With the company's national advertising program behind you, developing one or more Arby's units will be a lot easier than trying to break into the roast beef sandwich industry as an independent.

Arby's reserves the right to approve your proposed site and provides counseling and written guidelines to make your search for the right location easier. All restaurants conform to the company's easily recognizable energy-efficient building design. Following the company's specifications, franchisees purchase equipment and supplies from approved sources: food service equipment, furniture, signs, employee uniforms, etc. You can purchase food and other supplies at significant savings through ARCORP, Inc., a nonprofit franchisee-purchasing cooperative operated jointly by Arby's and its franchisees. ARCORP members pay a one-time initiation fee of $100 plus quarterly dues of $60 per licensed restaurant.

Of your 4.2 percent advertising royalty, 1.2 percent goes toward national network advertising and the development of marketing materials. The other 3 percent contributes to local advertising programs. Owners control the application of their advertising contributions through an elected board of directors and a marketing advisory council.

"We take pride in and emphasize the importance of Arby's training programs," states John Ofsharick of Arby's Training Department. "We have put together a group of management training programs that emphasize our commitment to quality products, quality service, and quality management." New licensee training takes place over four weeks at the company's Atlanta, Georgia, headquarters. Designed to develop your management, technical, and business skills to their fullest, the program covers everything from risk management to customer service, and from employee recruitment to equipment maintenance. After completing the classroom portion of your training, you will get hands-on experience at one of the company-operated stores. You and all of your management personnel must complete the training at least three weeks before your restaurant opens, when a field service representative steps in to provide full pre- and postopening assistance.

Each month at corporate headquarters and in major cities across the country, Arby's conducts training and development seminars for restaurant owners and their employees because "just hiring good employees is not enough. We must help them grow and make them an integral part of the Arby system," according to John Ofsharick. You and any of your staff can participate in these seminars at no charge other than your out-of-pocket expenses for travel and lodging. The Specialized Operations Seminar covers the nuts and bolts of restaurant operation and serves as a good refresher for franchisees several years out of initial training. Impact Supervision Skills sharpens your supervisory and employee relations skill, while New-Age Thinking gives management personnel a better understanding of motivation, goal setting, and other human dynamics issues. Models for Management explores topics of managerial style and effectiveness. Offered monthly for two to four days, "these programs offer a unique opportunity to hone operational and personal skills that will benefit the individual and the Arby's system," says John Ofsharick.

For further information contact:

Jim Squire, Jack Harris, Arby's, Inc., 3495 Piedmont Rd., NE, Ten Piedmont Center, Suite 700, Atlanta, GA 30305-1796, 404-262-2729, Ext. 416 or 428

International Blimpie Corporation

Initial license fee: $15,000
Royalties: 6%
Advertising royalties: 3%
Minimum cash required: $50,000
Capital required: $70,000 to $110,000
Financing: None
Length of contract: 20 years

In business since: 1964
Franchising since: 1977
Total number of units: 240
Number of company-operated units: 1
Total number of units planned, 1990: NA
Number of company-operated units planned, 1990: NA

"I was looking for a growing franchise with a great product," says Thomas Gallagher, a Blimpie franchisee in Levittown, New York. The product turned out to be a sandwich. Whether you call an amply filled sandwich on Italian bread a submarine, sub, torpedo, hoagie, wedge, grinder, poor boy, or hero, Blimpie specializes in it. It calls its version, which comes with lettuce, tomatoes, onions, and a special sauce, "America's Best-Dressed Sandwich." *Esquire's* cooking critic called the company's Blimpie Best, a combination of ham, salami, prosciuttini, cappicola, and cheese, the best fast food he had ever eaten. He gave it his top rating: four crumpled paper napkins.

The Blimpie menu, which has seen few changes since the first store opened in Hoboken, New Jersey, features other cold sandwiches and a few varieties of hot sandwiches. Store personnel use a slicer and a scale to insure that each sandwich contains a standard amount of food. The restaurants also serve soup, chili, salads, soft drinks, tea and coffee, and breakfast. Desserts include cookies, cakes, and pastries.

Blimpie is the largest franchised chain of sandwich shops in the country. The food served in this franchise requires no cooking, only some heating in the microwave oven for the hot sandwiches, chili, and soup. This means low overhead and relative simplicity compared to other food operations.

Sandwich shops, although the smallest segment of the franchised fast-food industry, are growing faster than any other kind of fast-food business. Their sales have increased by over 200 percent in the past decade. Blimpie, formerly thought of as a New York operation, now has locations in many areas of the country, from Atlanta, Georgia, to Boise, Idaho. At the moment, its expansion plans center on New York, New Jersey, Connecticut, Georgia, Tennessee, and Florida.

The company prefers to sell its franchises to people who have already demonstrated managerial proficiency in other businesses or professions. It trains its franchisees in New York or Atlanta, where they are taught advertising, marketing, and statistical controls. "The company insists you have at least two weeks of in-store training," notes Thomas Gallagher. But he adds, "You may train for as long as you feel it is needed." Franchisees can receive advanced training from time to time if needed.

Constructing the free-standing or in-line building that usually houses a Blimpie, according to the company, is relatively simple. The company will negotiate the lease for your business—typically a store of about 1,200 square feet that seats fifty—and then sublease the premises to you. The company will help you plan a successful grand opening, and it will provide you with a list of approved vendors of supply and equipment. It will also give you a set of business forms that will help you maintain control over cash flow. A Blimpie representative will visit your store periodically to give you advanced management training.

The Blimpie formula is "No Cooking + Limited Menu = Success." Thomas Gallagher, who says that the value of his franchise "has tripled in eight years," couldn't agree more.

For further information contact:
Stephen Sloane, Astor Restaurant Group, Inc., 740 Broadway, New York, NY 10003, 212-673-5900

Subway Sandwiches and Salads

Initial license fee: $7,500
Royalties: 8%
Advertising royalties: 2.5%
Minimum cash required: $15,000
Capital required: $30,000 to $80,000
Financing: Equipment leasing program available
Length of contract: 20 years

In business since: 1965
Franchising since: 1975
Total number of units: 800
Number of company-operated units: 11
Total number of units planned, 1990: 2,045
Number of company-operated units planned, 1990: 25

"I love the business and the people," says Cathy Bauer, who owns a Subway shop in West Lafayette, Indiana. "After ten years of teaching school and four years of laboratory research, I have finally found a field that gives me satisfaction and enjoyment that more than offsets all the hours of hard work."

Subway has nothing to do with underground transportation, except that one of its founders comes from Brooklyn. And Doctor's Associates, Subway's parent company, has nothing to do with medicine. A seventeen-year-old premed student and a nuclear physicist started the company in Connecticut with one store. When that store did not do well, they took the least obvious course of action: They opened a second store, and then business began to take off.

All of this may sound like an improbable start for the second-fastest-growing fast-food company in America. But through trial and error, the student, Fred DeLuca, and his partner, Peter Buck, developed a simple operation that has brought satisfaction and enjoyment to many of the company's franchisees. In fact, current franchisees continue to purchase about half of all new Subway franchises sold. New Subway shops open at the rate of about two per day.

A Subway sandwich shop, depending on its sales volume, may require as few as two employees to run it. The menu is simple and requires no cooking. Stores sell ten varieties of sandwiches and several salads, which use the same ingredients as the sandwiches. The company also encourages franchisees to experiment with sandwiches that have local appeal. For the past two years, many franchisees have baked their own Italian bread on the premises with an easy-to-use oven obtained through the franchisor.

Subway Sandwiches and Salads will advise you on lease negotiations for your store. Although some franchisees locate in free-standing stores, most open in storefronts or strip shopping centers. The stores occupy 300 to 800 square feet and seat as many as twenty-five people. A distinctive mural featuring photographs of the store's overstuffed sandwiches and scenes from the history of New York City's subway system highlight each unit's decor.

You don't need previous food service experience to own one of these shops. About 80 percent of current franchisees had never worked in the industry before opening their Subway. The company will train you for two weeks in all aspects of its operation at its headquarters in Milford, Connecticut. Classroom study accounts for half of the instruction; hands-on experience in a Subway Sandwiches and Salads shop makes up the other half. You pay for all training-related expenses except for tuition. A field representative will then spend a week with you while you open your business and will be on call whenever you need assistance in your ongoing operation. You can always reach the company via a toll-free number.

The company points out that because of its national contracts, it can save you considerable sums of money if you purchase equipment through Subway. You can, however, buy from any vendor acceptable to Subway. You will purchase your supplies locally, through a distributor approved by the company.

Subway Sandwiches and Salads franchisees control the spending of their advertising funds through an elected council. The company does not place national advertising.

For further information contact:
Richard Pilchen, Subway Sandwiches and Salads, 25 High St., Milford, CT 06460, 1-800-243-9741

Specialty Foods

Frontier Fruit & Nut Company

Initial license fee: $15,000
Royalties: 6%
Advertising royalties: None
Minimum cash required: $23,000
Capital required: $35,000 to $120,000
Financing: None
Length of contract: Coincides with length of lease

In business since: 1977
Franchising since: 1978
Total number of units: 196
Number of company-operated units: 89
Total number of units planned, 1990: NA
Number of company-operated units planned, 1990: NA

Picture your kiosk or in-line fruit and nut store in a regional shopping mall. The decor of your 144- to 200-square-foot establishment relies heavily on wood paneling. Bins of colorful dried fruits, nuts, combination mixtures, candies, and cookies fill its glass cases. Small open wooden baskets, leaning out at an angle from countertops, temptingly display fruits and nuts for maximum customer appeal. Other items like teas and flour are packed in clear plastic containers and tied with bright yellow, pink, or white ribbons—perfect for gift giving.

Frontier stores try to project an image of old-fashioned natural goodness. The company maintains that image by selling only "natural" products that do not contain artificial ingredients. And while the company will not insist that you buy your stock—about $10,000 worth of inventory at any given time—from its supply subsidiary, it will closely examine products from any other vendor you might choose to patronize.

When you buy a franchise, Frontier will do a site survey at its expense to make sure you have the right mall location for your store, given the demographics of the area. It will negotiate the lease for you, and in some locations it will lease the space itself and sublease it to you on terms similar to those in the original lease. If you must build, the company will give you design and construction plans for the store, charging a small fee for the drawings. It will also help you plan your initial inventory.

Frontier trains its franchisees at company headquarters in Norton, Ohio. Your licensing fee covers your tuition, but you will have to pay for transportation, food, and lodging. Your training will consist of three days of classroom work on all aspects of Frontier operations—including merchandising, sales, accounting, and promotion—and a day and a half of hands-on experience at a working store.

Frontier will help you set up your bookkeeping system, with which you must generate periodic reports for the franchisor, including a weekly sales report. A company representative will attend your grand opening, and Frontier will advise you on dealing with any specific problems that might come up after you begin operations.

For further information contact:
Alex E. Marksz, Frontier Fruit & Nut Company, 3823 Wadsworth Rd., Norton, OH 44203, 216-825-7835

Hickory Farms of Ohio, Inc.

Initial license fee: $20,000
Royalties: 6%
Advertising royalties: 6%
Minimum cash required: $215,000
Capital required: $215,000 to $327,000
Financing: Available for purchasing company-owned stores
Length of contract: Coincides with term of store lease

In business since: 1959
Franchising since: 1960
Total number of units: 550
Number of company-operated units: 300
Total number of units planned, 1990: NA
Number of company-operated units planned, 1990: NA

Specialty food shops, which have been around a long time, have experienced an especially robust market for their products in the past decade or so. Americans have developed more sophisticated palates. They drink wine with dinner more often than they used to, with more concern for the kind of wine they serve. And with that wine they eat a wider range of food than before. They have, for example, grown choosy about cheese. Where Americans' cheese tastes once ended with cheddar, American, and Swiss, growing numbers now enjoy Brie, Camembert, and a host of others with hard-to-pronounce and even harder-to-spell names.

Hickory Farms, since 1980 a subsidiary of the General Host Corporation, has responded to the shift in tastes with an assortment of specialty food items particularly good for giftgiving. Nuts, preserves, crackers, candies, and their famous Beef Stick Summer Sausage, in addition to the cheeses, constitute its stock and trade. Hickory Farms takes a twofold approach to merchandising. While catering to sophisticated tastes, it also taps the appeal of old-fashioned, wholesome country goodness. The design motif in these stores is cracker-barrel modern— country baskets and barrels with the latest in retail store fixtures. The ambience radiates warmth and friendliness, and the company encourages its franchisees and their staff to reflect that spirit in their dealings with customers.

Generally, the company will tell you which sites—usually in enclosed shopping malls—it has developed and can make available to you, although it will evaluate any site you may already have in mind. You will equip your store with fixtures bought from suppliers of your choosing, but you must follow the company's guidelines and obtain its approval. While you will probably want to stock the company's specialty food items, since Hickoy Farms' advertising has made them popular with the public, you are not obligated to purchase any particular item. You may sell any food product appropriate to this type of store, but the company must approve your choices and your sources of supply.

Hickory Farms will train you at its headquarters in Maumee, Ohio. There you will receive a week of instruction on store operations, sales techniques, merchandising, and personnel administration. The company will pay for transportation and lodging, with meals your only responsibility. The company will have a representative at your business for the week before you open and will arrange any supplementary training you might need after you open for business. You must run nine weeks of local advertising coinciding with your opening. The company counts this toward the 4 percent of your sales each year that you must spend on local advertising.

Hickory Farms products lend themselves well to Christmas gift giving. The company captures the Christmas market with attractively arranged gift boxes containing assortments of its products. Franchisees sell the gift boxes through their full-time stores and through satellite stores, small kiosks set up in malls just for the Christmas shopping season. These temporary kiosks—in the future the company may sell some permanent mall kiosks—are available as franchises requiring a smaller total investment than a full-size store.

For further information contact:

Richard A. Steinbock, Vice President, Franchise Operations, Hickory Farms of Ohio, Inc., P.O. Box 219, Maume, OH 43537, 419-893-7611

The Peanut Shack

Initial license fee: $5,000 to $20,000
Royalties: 5%
Advertising royalties: 1%; not to exceed $1,500/year
Minimum cash required: $60,000
Capital required: $20,000 to $130,000
Financing: None
Length of contract: 5 years

In business since: 1975
Franchising since: 1975
Total number of units: 196
Number of company-operated units: 39
Total number of units planned, 1990: 316
Number of company-operated units planned, 1990: 59

If you buy this franchise, you will make peanuts only in the literal sense of the word. According to the latest figures available from the Department of Agriculture (1981), the average American consumes 6.1 pounds of shelled peanuts per year. That grew .6 pounds from the previous year. So one of The Peanut Shack's shopping mall outlets for fresh-cooked nuts and homemade candies, most of which franchisees prepare on the premises, could represent a substantial opportunity for you.

Your license fee will vary according to the amount of work The Peanut Shack has to do to set up your store, which the company usually builds itself. If, like some franchisees, you build your own store, you will pay a lesser fee, although The Peanut Shack would still have to approve all the details of construction.

Your training will begin at a company-operated store chosen by The Peanut Shack. You will spend three days there with a company field representative, receiving exposure to The Peanut Shack way of doing business. About a week before your store opens, the company will have its representative on your premises to give you intensive training in cooking the products, machine operation, accounting, personnel, merchandising, and inventory control. Your manager, if you have one, will receive training similar to yours, and your other employees will also receive instruction in their duties. The field representative will help you stock your Peanut Shack and will remain with you for several days after you begin your operation to make sure everything goes smoothly.

You can expect company management to contact you every week for the first three months of your business. After that, the franchisor will hold periodic conferences at its Winston-Salem, North Carolina, headquarters on subjects like sales techniques, performance standards, advertising, and merchandising. If you choose to attend, you will bear your own travel expenses.

You do not have to buy supplies or equipment from The Peanut Shack, although it does sell these items (at a profit). The company does not keep a list of other approved suppliers, so they approve alternate vendors on a case-by-case basis.

Specialty Retail Concepts, Inc., owns The Peanut Shack. It also franchises several other operations, including Coffee, Tea & Thee, retail stores that carry coffee beans, bulk teas, spices, coffee grinders, and teapots, and The Cookie Store, which sells ice cream and frozen yogurt, as well as cookies.

For further information contact:
Ed Williams, The Peanut Shack, P.O. Drawer 11025, Winston-Salem, NC 27116, 919-761-1961

Steakhouses

Bonanza Restaurants

Initial license fee: $30,000
Royalties: 4.8%
Advertising royalties: 2% plus $1,150/year
Minimum cash required: $90,000
Capital required: $250,000 to $1,000,000
Financing: None
Length of contract: NA

In business since: 1962
Franchising since: NA
Total number of units: 551
Number of company-operated units: NA

Total number of units planned, 1990: NA
Number of company-operated units planned, 1990: NA

"Our chain is perfectly positioned to meet the needs of today's customers. Bonanza product/service mix matches the key industry trends that our competitors are now scrambling to satisfy," according to Jeff Rogers, president of USACafes, Bonanza's parent company. Among these key industry trends are the simultaneous increases in the frequency with which Americans dine out and in their preference for lighter, more nutritional foods. Originally established as a chain of steakhouses, Bonanza repositioned itself in 1980 to target the growing market for budget-priced full-menu family restaurants. "The cornerstone of our philosophy is offering nutritious meals priced at a genuine value to the consumer," explains Jeff Rogers. At the core of Bonanza's strategy are its line service system and the Freshtastiks® Food Bar.

In order to offer customers its steaks, seafood, and chicken entrées at low prices, Bonanza utilizes a "limited service" system in its restaurants. This service-line setup, similar to a cafeteria or counter operation, greatly reduces labor costs and improves efficiency while providing customers personalized service. The restaurant operator passes labor savings on to customers through lower prices on meals, and diners save even more because the line service system eliminates the need for tipping.

To complement the foods offered on the serving line, Bonanza offers the Freshtastiks® Food Bar. The first chain to introduce all-you-can-eat salad bars back in 1975, Bonanza has had plenty of practice in managing this restaurant feature, which is popular with customers but can be costly for operators. In 1980 the company developed the Freshtastiks® concept, which expands the traditional salad bar to include deli salads, fruits, cheese, breads, and desserts.

Freshtastiks® has helped Bonanza Restaurants attract a younger, more affluent clientele than it did as a steakhouse chain, and "our emphasis on broiling and selective introduction of healthy new products is an excellent complement to what many consider to be the best salad bar in the industry," says Jeff Rogers. By aggressively pursuing a wider spectrum of customers, the chain outpaced the industry in traffic growth in 1984—with sales of nearly $400 million. And Bonanza has plans for rapid franchise expansion.

Whether you're interested in a new free-standing restaurant, a shopping mall location, or conversion of an existing facility, Bonanza can help you design your site to achieve the maximum return on your investment. Once you select a site, Bonanza will prepare a detailed market study upon which it will base its approval of your choice. The company will provide you with plans and specifications for both new locations and conversions and lists of approved equipment, products, and suppliers from whom you can secure bids.

The company conducts in-depth training for new franchisees and their managers at its headquarters in Dallas, Texas. A combination of classroom and in-store instruction teaches you and your managers the skills and procedures essential to the efficient operation of your restaurant—even if you have no restaurant experience. And prior to your grand opening, a member of Bonanza's franchise services staff will help ensure that every detail is attended to. The average Bonanza opens its doors for business 120 days after groundbreaking.

Bonanza franchise-relations managers will consult with you regularly to provide advice on operations, merchandising, and controls, to help you solve any individual problems you might have, and to keep you informed on company-sponsored programs. An operations manager will periodically analyze your restaurant's food quality, efficiency, and profitability, and the operations department can let you know how your performance compares to that of other Bonanza franchises. Your Bonanza operations and procedures manual will cover every aspect of restaurant operations, and other company publications will update you on Bonananza products, restaurant industry trends, and management technique.

To help you build traffic and volume at your Bonanza, the company's marketing department will help you develop strategies for the most effective use of your advertising dollars. You must spend 2 percent of your gross on local advertising, in addition to which you can join the National Creative Group (NCG), a nonprofit organization of Bonanza franchisees that conducts market research and develops national advertising programs and other promotional items to benefit its members. Each member makes an annual contribution of $1,150 to NCG, which is matched with an equal contribution from Bonanza. In return, you receive advertising materials free or at reduced cost.

For further information contact:

Bonanza Restaurants, USACafes, 8080 North Central Expressway, Suite 500, Box 65, Dallas, TX 75206-1666, 214-891-8400

The Ground Round, Inc.

Initial license fee: $30,000
Royalties: 3%
Advertising royalties: 2%
Minimum cash required: $30,000
Capital required: $250,000
Financing: None
Length of contract: 20 years

In business since: 1969
Franchising since: 1970
Total number of units: 207
Number of company-operated units: 167
Total number of units planned, 1990: 347
Number of company-operated units planned, 1990: NA

Do you have your heart set on opening a restaurant in the Northeast or Midwest that will cater to shoppers and business people having lunch—in a shopping center or similar high-traffic area? How about a nice family dinner place that also attracts senior citizens? Or would you rather run a livelier establishment targeted at the late-evening young adult trade? According to Ground Round, open one of its establishments and you get all three under the same roof for one price.

Ground Round's management feels it has the all-purpose restaurant for the densely populated—a market of at least 50,000—average-income area. On the one hand, Ground Rounds give out free popcorn, stage weekly visits from personalities like Bingo the Clown, and cater children's birthday parties. On the other hand, franchisees must get an all-alcohol license. The Ground Round strategy is to keep the food flowing to the table even during hours when many restaurants concentrate on serving drinks.

The menu at Ground Round, redesigned in 1986 to feature charbroiling, features steak, hamburger, chicken, and seafood entrées, like shrimp and swordfish with Cajun sauce, at reasonable prices. Mexican and Italian dishes, and sandwiches and salads fill out the menu. All-you-can-eat family days may feature selections like buffalo wings or a fish fry. For those wishing to avoid alcohol, there are "Imposters," nonalcoholic drinks such as the "Sourpuss" and the "Unbloody Mary." Ground Round offers distinctive desserts that include New York-style cheesecake (topped with hot fudge, if you wish) and Mexican Apple Delight: "Some apple crisp wrapped in a flour tortilla, deep fried, and topped with powdered sugar and whipped cream."

The design of these 215-seat restaurants forms part of their appeal. Ground Round's design and construction department will give you guidelines so that you may achieve the effect that the company has found most appealing. Track lighting, hanging plants, prints, and ceiling canopies all play a part in creating the right atmosphere. But although Ground Round must approve the franchisee's decorating plans, the owner has a certain amount of leeway to put his or her imprint on the restaurant's look.

You or your manager will undergo 120 hours of training in all aspects of the business at one of Ground Round's fifteen regional training centers. An eight-member team from corporate headquarters will train your staff at your restaurant for two or three weeks. You pay for the lodging and food for these corporate trainers. Once in business, you may want to take advantage of Ground Round's advanced training. Currently, the company offers twenty 1- to 3-day seminars.

You purchase your food from approved local vendors or from the same source that stocks the company's own restaurants. Some of the products that you sell are pre-prepared by the company.

Ground Round promotes the company image through national advertising. It also provides you with ideas and material for local campaigns and point-of-sale promotions. You may draw on the company's library of TV, radio, and newspaper ads to supplement your own marketing efforts. And the company has timetested employee incentive programs.

Robert Bonin, a Ground Round franchisee in Shrewsbury, Massachusetts, enjoys being part of the company. He gave Ground Round high grades, and says, "The company has given me strong support. Excellent communications and the availability of the franchising department have been particularly helpful."

For further information contact:
Lynn E. Reichel, The Ground Round, Inc., 541 Main St., South Weymouth, MA 02190-1898, 617-331-7005

Ponderosa Steakhouses

Initial license fee: $15,000
Royalties: 4%
Advertising royalties: Variable
Minimum cash required: $125,000
Capital required: $125,000
Financing: Available through the company's financing subsidiary
Length of contract: 20 years

In business since: 1965
Franchising since: 1966
Total number of units: 630

Number of company-operated units: 430
Total number of units planned, 1990: NA
Number of company-operated units planned, 1990: NA

From one steakhouse in Kokomo, Indiana, Ponderosa has grown into an international chain, with units in twenty-five states, primarily in the Northeast and Midwest, and in Puerto Rico, Canada, and the United Kingdom. In 1985 it served 142 million meals. It prepares steak eleven ways, features four chicken dishes, and also offers seafood and pork entrées. Customers can have just a sandwich or a complete dinner, which comes with the chain's popular salad bar. For dessert, diners can custom design their own sundae, buffet-style. Many Ponderosa restaurants also serve breakfast.

Patrons order their food in a modified self-service style, in which they order at a counter and wait for waitresses to bring their meals to them at their table. There is no tipping. The carpeted restaurants seat about two hundred, and parking outside the stucco and glass units accommodates at least eighty cars.

One of Ponderosa's advertising slogans is "You're the Boss." While aimed at the restaurant's customers, it also applies to franchisees. Ponderosa suggests that the boss be on the premises of his or her restaurant whenever possible. The company does not want entirely absentee ownership, preferring that even the manager have some equity in the business.

Once Ponderosa accepts your application for a franchise—opportunities for new franchises are currently greatest in the Sunbelt—it will give you guidelines for choosing a site and erecting a building, including standard building plans. While not required to buy equipment for your restaurant from the franchisor, you must get it from an approved source. Because of the complexity of the equipment, the company does require you to come to its headquarters to confer with management regarding equipment before you begin construction of your unit. If you do buy your equipment from the franchisor, it will supervise its installation. You can buy food from any supplier approved by the company, although it recommends you use its subsidiary, ESI Meats, Inc., as your source, since this will enable you to reduce your costs and consolidate and simplify delivery.

Franchisees must go to Dayton, Ohio, for their four-week management training program. The course covers all aspects of steakhouse management, and franchisees get a chance to work in a restaurant as well as to receive classroom instruction. The company offers additional training seminars and other types of brushup and advanced instruction throughout the year.

The Ponderosa licensing field consultant and a special new-unit-opening team will come to your business to help train your staff before your opening. The consultant will help you coordinate your opening activities, and he or she will be your first source of advice once you open your doors for business.

For further information contact:
Ponderosa, Inc., Licensing Sales Department, P.O. Box 578, Dayton, OH 45401, 1-800-543-9670; in Ohio: 513-890-6400

Sizzler Restaurants International, Inc.

Initial license fee: $30,000
Royalties: 4.5%
Advertising royalties: 3.5%
Minimum cash required: $200,000
Capital required: $750,000
Financing: None
Length of contract: NA

In business since: 1957
Franchising since: 1961
Total number of units: 472
Number of company-operated units: 144
Total number of units planned, 1990: NA
Number of company-operated units planned, 1990: NA

The sizzle coming from these restaurants sells more than just steak. Sizzler stresses its "fresher and lighter menu" that includes seafood and salad as well as red meat. A tablet-shaped menu board displays the coming attractions as you enter the restaurant (it includes a special Senior Citizen's Menu). Gourmet Steak and Lobster is the most expensive dish on the menu, and other mouth-watering temptations include Broiled Halibut, Steak and Snow Crab, Giant Fried Shrimp, Super Sirloin Steak, Pacific Red Snapper, and Fried Scallops. Diners eat these tempting entrées with salad in a "casual" atmosphere designed to capture the middle-priced trade: patrons ages eighteen to fifty-four, from households with incomes over $20,000, who want something more than fast food but not quite fancy restaurant fare.

Sizzler restaurants have come a long way over the years. In the beginning, in Culver City, California, there was sawdust on the floor, and patrons ate at picnic tables. By 1967 there were 160 Sizzlers in more than twenty states. Collins Foods International bought the company that year and upgraded the Sizzler image, making the units look more like regular restaurants. The company has kept up with the times, adding fresh fruit and salad bars; Sizzlers also serve wine.

Sizzler's style of service is a cross between cafeteria and fast-food self-service and waiter/waitress service of patrons seated in a white tablecloth dining room. An order taker greets patrons as they enter the establishment. Diners order and pay the cashier, then pick out a table. A waitress brings their food. Customers can choose from a wide selection at the fruit and salad bar while they wait for their cooked-to-order food to arrive.

Business is burgeoning, so this chain must be doing something right. Prudential-Bache rated Sizzler stock *"the single best-performing stock in our universe"* in 1985. The investment house reported: "Under Tom Gregory [company CEO], Sizzler has effectively divorced itself from the highly cyclical budget steakhouse market by extensively remodeling its units and implementing major menu changes that reduced the company's red-meat-dependency and boosted its average check about 50 percent over four or five years. In so doing, sales per store have moved from barely $700,000 to about $1,100,000, margins have more than doubled, and earnings have more than quadrupled. . . ." And Freimark Blair & Co. reports: "Sizzler is in the right place at the right time in the restaurant industry."

If that whets your appetite, you should first be aware that franchises are currently unavailable in the West, south Florida, the Chicago area, and much of the mid-Atlantic seaboard, including the New York City metropolitan area. If you have another location in mind, Sizzler will guide you in its development. The company will evaluate and appraise the site for you before giving you the go-ahead to build. Once you receive your license, you will get architectural plans from central headquarters. It's your responsiblity to adapt those plans to suit both local laws and the nature of your site.

The company will require you—and your unit operating managers if you plan to open more than one restaurant—to take a total of fourteen weeks of training without any reimbursement for expenses. You will spend thirteen of those weeks in a training restaurant, and the last week at Sizzler headquarters in Los Angeles. The company prefers that you complete the training at least a month before your opening.

You will equip your restaurant from a company-approved list of suppliers. As opening day approaches, Sizzler will maintain full support. "We will be there to help," the company assures its franchisees. And that begins with advice on advertising and public relations for your grand opening. The company's support is not only continuous but also constantly updated. It revises its training materials, including films, handbooks, and manuals quarterly.

Sizzler insists on quality. In fact, it calls part of its training program *OPERATION PRIDE* (PROVIDE A REALLY INCREDIBLE DINING EXPERIENCE). Its operations support group will periodically visit your restaurant to make sure that you are operating at your very best. Retraining is available to help you refine your operations.

For further information contact:
William R. Hobson, Director of License Development, Sizzler Restaurants International, Inc., 5400 Alla Rd., Los Angeles, CA 90066, 213-827-2300

Western Sizzlin Steak House

Initial license fee: $15,000
Royalties: 2%
Advertising royalties: None
Minimum cash required: $125,000
Capital required: $425,000 to $800,000
Financing: None
Length of contract: 20 years

In business since: 1962
Franchising since: 1966
Total number of units: 582
Number of company-operated units: 3
Total number of units planned, 1990: NA
Number of company-operated units planned, 1990: NA

Nick Pascarella, president of Western Sizzlin Steak House, opened the first of these budget family-style restaurants in Augusta, Georgia. Western restaurants, located throughout the country but concentrated in the Southeast, combine cafeteria-style service with plush decor: red upholstered banquettes, red patterned rugs, and simulated exposed ceiling beams. In 1984 and 1985 a *Restaurants and Institutions Magazine* survey declared Western the most popular steakhouse in America.

It shouldn't take customers long to decide what to order when they enter your Western Sizzlin Steak House restaurant. Once they choose the cut and how they want their steak prepared, and whether they want baked or french fried potatoes, they've exercised most of their options on the simple menu. Salad and vegetables accompany the dinners, and customers can also order beverages and desserts. Western ensures that its franchisees serve fresh meat by having them buy their meat locally instead of shipping precut and frozen steaks.

The company requires that you purchase its building plans and specifications for your Western Sizzlin Steak House and stick to them. The typical facility occupies a plot of about 50,000 square feet, with the building occupying approximately 6,000 square feet. Your restaurant will seat 250 to 275 people and provide parking spaces for 90 to 100 cars.

You do not need experience running a restaurant to buy this business. You, your butchers, and your cooks will train at Western's headquarters in Augusta, Georgia, for six days. The curriculum will cover all aspects of running a Western Sizzlin Steak House. A restaurant-opening team will then train your hourly employees and help prepare your restaurant for its grand opening. You will pay a separate fee for this service.

You can purchase most of your supplies and equipment from your choice of vendors, as long as their products meet company specifications. However, Western requires you to buy its special seasoning and marinade from it.

You decide whether or not—and how much—you will advertise, although the company will advise you on advertising and other marketing procedures. If you decide to advertise, however, Western requires that you submit all advertisements for its approval.

For further information contact:
Western Sizzlin Steak House, 1537 Walton Way, Augusta, GA 30904, 1-800-241-7652

Western Steer Family Steakhouse

Initial license fee: $20,000
Royalties: 4%
Advertising royalties: 2%
Minimum cash required: $200,000
Capital required: $200,000 to $300,000
Financing: None
Length of contract: 20 years

In business since: 1975
Franchising since: 1975
Total number of units: 191
Number of company-operated units: 25
Total number of units planned, 1990: NA
Number of company-operated units planned, 1990: NA

These free-standing budget restaurants, concentrated in the South, feature a limited menu with twenty-two items and a forty-two-item salad bar. Main dishes include steak in a variety of cuts, chicken, and shrimp. Franchisees may also offer their customers two of nine company-approved regional dishes. Recently Western Steer added the hot vegetable bar to its menu.

Western Steer favors urban locations, preferably near shopping centers and malls, with a substantial representation of people in the middle to upper income brackets. The lot should be at least 52,500 square feet. The company will help you evaluate possible sites for your restaurant and will provide building plans, specifications, and equipment layout. Company representatives will inspect your unit as you build it.

Western Steer will train your key personnel at one of its own restaurants in Hickory, North Carolina, and at its headquarters in Claremont, North Carolina. Your manager (of whom Western Steer must approve) and assistant manager will each receive thirty-six days of classroom and hands-on training, and your meat cutter will train for ten days. You will pay for their salaries, living, and travel expenses during that time.

Several days before you open for business, a grand opening team will come to your restaurant to train your other employees. The operations supervisor, who heads the training crew, will stay an additional week to help you get your enterprise off to a good start. Thereafter, if conditions warrant, the company will send a representative to help you deal with specific problems. In addition, a Western Steer quality-assurance representative will visit your restaurant every six weeks to make sure that it operates just the way it should.

You may purchase the furniture and equipment for your restaurant from the vendor of your choice, although Western Steer has two affiliates, Denver Equipment Company and Howard Furniture Company, that sell these items. The company has an agreement with Wes-Mar Food Service Distributors, which supplies company-owned restaurants and many franchisees, although the only products you must buy from them are Western Steer seasoning salt and marinade.

Although your franchise contract calls for an advertising royalty of 2 percent, the company does not currently collect it. Instead, franchisees spend these funds on company-approved advertising.

Western Steer has recently focused on multiunit franchises. If your interests lie elsewhere, you should ask about the availability of individual franchises.

For further information contact:

Western Steer-Mom 'n' Pop's, Inc., P.O. Box 399, Ham House Drive, Claremont, NC 28610, 704-459-7626

Tacos and Mexican Fast Food

Del Taco, Inc.

Initial license fee: $20,000
Royalties: 5%
Advertising royalties: 5%
Minimum cash required: $150,000
Capital required: $150,000 to $450,000, depending on which type of facility you buy
Financing: None, but Franchise Finance Corporation of America has a special package for qualified Del Taco franchisees.
Length of contract: 20 years

In business since: 1965
Franchising since: 1981
Total number of units: 160
Number of company-operated units: 134
Total number of units planned, 1990: NA
Number of company-operated units planned, 1990: NA

With the large number of establishments serving Mexican food increasing every day, how does a company distinguish itself from the competition? In both big and little ways. Del Taco, whose operations were described in a recent edition of *Restaurant Business* as "a unique approach to the quick-service format," does it with a combination of a varied menu and an adaptable physical setting—adaptable to local markets and local real estate and construction costs.

The target age group for Del Taco restaurants are the eighteen- to thirty-four-year-olds. The company tries to span the teenage-young-adult-family trade gap with offerings that include dinner platters as well as the standard quick-food burritos, nachos, and tacos. The restaurants themselves are designed both for efficiency and relaxed dining. Service counters resembling those in most fast-food places combine with table areas to suggest a cafe atmosphere. Photographs of some of the dishes above the serving counter make the customer's mouth water. And building exteriors have a touch of Spanish California with their awnings and red tile roofing, and usually feature drive-thru service.

The company constantly adapts its units to profit from new opportunities. A recent example of this are the "Express" units in shopping malls, which resemble the serving counters of Del Taco restaurants without the table area.

Del Taco's two-decade corporate history has been complex but dynamic. In 1977 the then Del Taco, Inc., of California joined with the giant W.R. Grace & Co. to form Del Taco Corporation, with Grace providing the resources for national expansion. In 1983, to franchise the restaurants outside California, the licensing company of Creative Food 'N' Fun was setup. That company merged with Taco Villa, Inc., in 1985. Under the present setup, Creative Food 'N' Fun also licenses units of Applebee's, a drinking and eating establishment. You don't have to have restaurant experience to be a Del Taco franchisee, but if you don't, the company suggests you should be prepared to hire an operations manager. In any event, your management staff will be trained in the operation of your franchise in a six-week course given by the company.

You will pick out your own site and develop it, subject to the company's approval. The company will have a representative at your site to guide you through the start-up process and your first week of operation. You will order your supplies from a list of vendors approved by Del Taco.

Once in business, you can expect continued guidance from the company in dealing with all phases of your business. A Del Taco franchise consultant will periodically drop in for direct discussion of any problems, as well as to make sure that your operation is up to company standards.

For further information contact:
Director, Franchise Sales, Taco Villa Creative Food 'N' Fun Company, 1801 Royal Lane, Suite 902, Dallas, TX 75229, 214-556-0955

Taco Bell Corporation

Initial license fee: $35,000
Royalties: 5.5%
Advertising royalties: 4.5%
Minimum cash required: $100,000
Capital required: $200,000
Financing: None, but the company will recommend several approved financial institutions.
Length of contract: 20 years

In business since: 1962
Franchising since: 1964
Total number of units: 2,200
Number of company-operated units: 1,150
Total number of units planned, 1990: NA
Number of company-operated units planned, 1990: NA

Taco Bell franchisee Craig Fenneman knew why he wanted to open his own business. He wanted the freedom to operate a restaurant for himself, not for somebody else. But wanting to be his own boss was "tempered by a need to be part of a consistent company image." He settled on a franchise as the way to combine freedom, maximum independence, and solid identification with a nationally known name. The result? He's been "very happy with the business."

Twenty years ago, the chances of such a business flourishing outside California and the Southwest would have been a lot dimmer than they are today. But now Mexican food is in. Tacos, enchiladas, and burritos are as ubiquitous as chow mein, egg rolls, and wonton soup. Americans are more willing to try different ethnic foods. And among ethnic foods, Mexican is one of the most popular choices.

While many urban professionals enjoy frozen margaritas and quesadillas in the latest high-priced establishments, the vast majority of Americans are likely to get their Mexican food less expensively and more informally. The more than two thousand Taco Bells, fast-food Mexican restaurants, are thus well positioned to cash in on the shift in culinary taste.

If you've got the finances to open a Taco Bell franchise, the only other thing you'll really need is the willingness to work hard. Operating this business is not especially complicated, and the company will familiarize you with all aspects of their operation at the training restaurant or training center closest to you. Instruction is free, but you pick up the tab for travel and lodging.

You will have some leeway in the choice of a specific site and the development of your unit, but all decisions and plans must meet Taco Bell standards. Your choice of vendors for supplies and equipment must similarly have company approval.

The company's operations and marketing specialist will be at your side for the week before and during your grand opening. From time to time, as you proceed with the development of your business, you will have to take refresher training, because the company continually introduces new products and equipment. But that shouldn't be much of a burden, since the additions being made to your menu will increase your profits.

While the ratio between company-operated franchises and total number of franchises doesn't guarantee anything, it is interesting to see that Taco Bell runs about as many restaurants as it franchises. That does seem to indicate *its* own belief in its business. For Indianapolis franchisee Craig Fenneman, buying into Taco Bell has meant "a reasonable rate of return with good growth potential." Has his franchise been a good investment? In a word, "Yes."

For further information contact:
Michael J. Collins, Taco Bell Corp., 16808 Armstrong Ave., Irvine, CA 92714, 714-863-4595

Taco John's International

Initial license fee: $16,500
Royalties: 4%
Advertising royalties: 2%
Minimum cash required: $21,000
Capital required: $70,000 to $500,000
Financing: None
Length of contract: 20 years

In business since: 1969
Franchising since: 1969
Total number of units: 400
Number of company-operated units: 5
Total number of units planned, 1990: 620
Number of company-operated units planned, 1990: None

John Turner opened the prototype of this chain of Mexican fast-food restaurants in Cheyenne, Wyoming, and called it the Taco House. Jim Woodson and Harold Holmes, the current president and secretary/treasurer of the company, later bought the franchising rights and gave the chain its present name. The first Taco John's, walk-up plywood stands measuring 12 by 30 feet, have given way to 1,400- to 1,600-square-foot units with drive-thru service and seating for thirty to fifty customers.

The menu—mandatory in all its restaurants—features standard Mexican food: several varieties of tacos and burritos, tostadas, enchiladas, nachos, and chili. Customers can also order a taco burger. Taco John's does business in thirty-two states and Canada. At present, the company has targeted the Southeast and the Pacific Northwest for expansion.

The site you choose for your Taco John's, and your building or remodeling plans, must receive company approval. Taco John's will advise you at all stages of this process, and for a fee the company will also do some of the actual work involved in preparing your building for business. You and your manager will take a fifteen-day training course at "Taco Tech," the company's training facility in Cheyenne. You pay for all travel, lodging, and meal expenses incurred. The training, both classroom and hands-on, covers everything involved in running your business, from taco production to cost control. Managers and other employees who join your business after you open can attend the company's periodic regional seminars.

About five days before you open, the company will send a representative to your restaurant to train your crew and help you with last-minute tasks. Ongoing support comes from your franchise services representative, who works with thirty to forty restaurants. The representative will advise you in various areas of your business, including inventory, cash control, food and labor costs, marketing, and customer service, and will help make sure that you run your restaurant according to company guidelines. You can get in touch with your representative at any time through the company's Wats line.

Taco John's will give you a list of approved equipment suppliers and independent food distributors. These distributors carry the company's proprietary items, and they will call you weekly to take your order.

Each year the company will send you eight packages of material, such as banners and posters, for in-store promotions. Your advertising fund money pays for cooperative advertisements with other franchisees in your region, and Taco John's also does national advertising. Gary L. Anderson, who owns several Taco John's in South Dakota, feels that the image built by the company over the years has been vital to his success. He says "the public has a very good perceived value" when they think of Taco John's

For further information contact:
Paul C. Wolbert, Taco John's International, 808 W. 20th St., Cheyenne, WY 82001, 307-635-0101

Taco Time International, Inc.

Initial license fee: $15,000
Royalties: 5%
Advertising royalties: 0.5%
Minimum cash required: $110,000
Capital required: $110,000 to $175,000
Financing: The company will help you put together a loan package. Currently, the Money Store Investment Corp. has a special loan package for Taco Time franchisees.
Length of contract: 15 years

In business since: 1959
Franchising since: 1961
Total number of units: 234
Number of company-operated units: 17
Total number of units planned, 1990: NA
Number of company-operated units planned, 1990: NA

Taco Time serves Mexican fast food: several varieties of tacos and burritos as well as nachos, enchiladas, tostados, refritos, and guacamole. Desserts include cherry and berry empañadas. The company features some of the most attractive Mexican fast-food restaurants in the business. The interior decor of these establishments includes arched windows, tile, Spanish stucco, and wall hangings. Franchisees building new units have their choice of including a solarium or a wood beam trellis atrium. The free-standing restaurants, which occupy a minimum of at least 1,600 square feet, also have drive-thru windows. If you locate your unit in a shopping mall, you will build a smaller in-line unit.

The company will help you select the site for your restaurant and advises you during the lease negotiation. It will also work with you to design an attractive and profitable unit. The several restaurant plans and interior decor packages available will allow you to build a restaurant that reflects your personal taste within the confines of the company's standard "look."

You will train to run your Taco Time restaurant at the company's headquarters in Eugene, Oregon. In the three-week classroom and hands-on program, you will study maintenance, safety and security, sanitation, payroll, marketing, scheduling, and interviewing and hiring. A grand opening team will assist you with the last minute preparations at your restaurant, and the company will offer ongoing supervision and field support in operations and marketing.

Taco Time will also help you find local suppliers of equipment and fixtures and will permit you to buy from anyone if they approve the items first. You may buy your food supplies either from local food distributors suggested by the company or from company-approved vendors you have located yourself.

The present advertising fee may rise to as much as 4 percent in the future. Currently, the Taco Time Marketing Council, controlled by franchisee representatives, allocates advertising funds.

For further information contact:

Jim Thomas, Vice President, Franchise Sales, Taco Time International, Inc., P.O. Box 2056, Eugene, OR 97402, 1-800-547-8907

12. The Health and Beauty Industry

Contents

Fitness and Weight Control

Diet Center, Inc.

Initial license fee: $12,000 to $24,000
Royalties: The continuing license fee is based on dieter participation.
Advertising royalties: Included in continuing license fee
Minimum cash required: $12,000
Capital required: $22,000 to $39,000
Financing: None
Length of contract: 10 years

In business since: 1972
Franchising since: 1972
Total number of units: 2,090
Number of company-operated units: None
Total number of units planned, 1990: 2,570
Number of company-operated units planned, 1990: None

In the United States 37 percent of the population is on a diet at any given time. And sometimes it seems as though the other 63 percent have either just gotten off a diet or are planning to start one—tomorrow. Every year hundreds of books appear in the bookstores promising to reveal the secret to quick and painless weight loss. Dieters' support groups, weight-loss resorts, television exercise programs, "lite" foods, and all the miraculous pills and powders that cram druggists' shelves cater to people's dreams of beauty without sacrifice. A seemingly limitless demand for such products supports a multibillion dollar industry, and the market is far from saturated. If you have a desire to help overweight people regain and maintain their health—and to make a healthy profit while doing so—Diet Center, Inc., offers a solid franchise opportunity.

Since its inception in 1972, Diet Center has grown to become the number-one weight-control program in North America. Based on the recognition that dieters need plenty of support to stick with it, the Diet Center Weight-Control Program consists of daily counseling and weekly classes for clients. The five-phase program, designed for nutritional soundness, includes the use of various vitamins, foods, and other nutritional products generally sold under the Diet Center brand name. Clients receive assistance in designing a personalized weight-control program, sticking with it, and modifying their behavior so they won't gain back the weight they've lost.

After she successfully completed the Diet Center Weight-Control Program, Kay Bradford of Vienna, Virginia, decided to purchase her own Diet Center. "The franchisor seemed to be honest and fair in all respects," she notes, recalling her initial investigation of the business opportunity. "My husband, who's my partner, is a CPA, so that answered a lot of questions about running a business, and the franchisor answered all of my questions about the particulars of the actual diet and the Diet Center franchise program."

Like all new franchisees, Kay Bradford received a full week of training at Diet Center's counselor training school in Rexburg, Idaho. Your initial franchise fee will cover training for one person in the operation of your Diet Center. The seminar provides instruction on nutrition, counseling, administration, and the five-phase weight-control program. For the first three months after your training, the company will pay all of your telephone expenses for long-distance calls to the home office, where company staff is always ready to answer any questions you might have.

As a Diet Center owner, you will have "plenty of freedom," according to Kay Bradford. The company requires that you open your Diet Center within 120 days after the execution of your license agreement, and you are responsible for selecting a suitable site and facility for the operation of your business. "You can rely on the franchisor to help you, and the training and phone calls are very helpful. For the most part, the company is in tune with us," says Kay Bradford. "But you are your own boss, and you can make or break your business. The money potential is whatever you want to put into it." If you enjoy taking responsibility and making business decisions, you will enjoy the independence that a Diet Center franchise offers.

Diet Center does, however, provide the full battery of support services. You can return to the counselor training school at any time to participate in the regular training sessions, or attend continuing education courses that the company conducts throughout the year at regional counselor training seminars. Held annually, the international Diet Center conventions offer further updates on nutrition, marketing, and business management, which Kay Bradford finds "most useful." The company charges fees for the seminars and conventions, and you must pay for your own travel and lodging.

To keep you current on industry and company developments, Diet Center publishes the *AdVantage* magazine, the *Diet Center* newsletter, and the *Franchisee Forum* newsletter. The company makes available Diet Center-brand vitamins, food, and nutritional products for use at your Diet Center, as well as offering stationery and office forms designed specifically for Diet Center owners. You can purchase products approved for use in the program from the company or any other approved sources.

Kay Bradford can recommend the Diet Center franchise because "our investment has more than doubled, and we are making an income to support ourselves and our family. I love what I am doing. It's a good opportunity to have fun, to receive satisfaction from the type of work we are doing, and to make money. And we've got name recognition, the company's national advertising program, and the franchisor's support services."

For further information contact:
Franchise Department, Diet Center, Inc., 220 South 2nd West, Rexburg, ID 83440, 208-356-9381

Jazzercise, Inc.

Initial license fee: $500
Royalties: 25%
Advertising royalties: None
Minimum cash required: $500
Capital required: $2,000
Financing: None
Length of contract: 5 years

In business since: 1976
Franchising since: 1983
Total number of units: 3,275
Number of company-operated units: None
Total number of units planned, 1990: 7,500
Number of company-operated units planned, 1990: None

Contrary to what some people may think, Jane Fonda did not invent aerobic exercise. In fact, the contemporary emphasis on exercise that promotes cardiovascular efficiency got its biggest boost from a best-selling book in the 1960s that described the aerobic conditioning program of the Canadian Air Force. But the healthy sales of Fonda's exercise videotapes do reflect and reinforce the popularity of workouts.

Judi Sheppard Missett has also appeared in several home fitness videos and made a name for herself. But even more familiar than her name is the name of the company she started, Jazzercise, which boasts more than four hundred thousand students worldwide in its dance fitness classes.

Franchisees hold Jazzercise classes in community centers, Y's, churches—wherever they can rent centrally located, relatively inexpensive but large spaces by the hour. The basic equipment consists of a record player. Only people in good shape can run this hands- , arms- , shoulders- , legs- , torso- , and feet-on business, learning current dance exercise routines and teaching them. You and your employees must also be enthusiastic and supportive, with the ability to motivate other people.

The company wants only instructors in good shape. It requires you to submit with your franchise application a 5 by 7-inch full-body photo of yourself in leotard and tights. And that's not the last test you will have to pass. The four-day regional training workshop required of new franchisees—for which you will absorb travel expenses—also tests your knowledge of physiology (based on nontechnical written material sent to you before you begin training) and your ability to do and teach typical Jazzercise routines. In fact, it is an audition.

You must acquire a certificate in cardiopulmonary resuscitation (CPR) before attending the workshop. About a month before the workshop, the company will send you a training packet, which includes a videotape containing dance routines, six records with routine sheets, and a physiology manual. The company suggests that you prepare for the workshop by attending Jazzercise classes to get a feel for its system.

The company evaluates you during the first two days of the workshop. If you pass, you will complete the seminar, receiving further instruction in teaching and business skills. Should you not pass, Jazzercise will tell you why, and you can apply again in the future. You will also receive a refund of the cost of the materials in the workshop packet.

As franchises go, this one has very low start-up costs, and the expenses don't increase much once you begin conducting classes at your own location. You will, of course, need a record player, as well as a TV and a VCR. You will use the video equipment to study the tapes you receive from headquarters every two months. Each tape—accompanied by written instructions—contains twenty-five to thirty new routines and currently costs about eighty dollars. You have to purchase the tape, and you must confine your teaching to official Jazzercise routines.

Jazzercise gets a lot of publicity, which should pay off in increased enrollments for your classes. Judi Sheppard Missett's guest column on exercise appears in prominent magazines, and the company enagages in joint promotions with firms like J.C. Penney and Revlon.

For further information contact:

Jan Kinney, Jazzercise, Inc., 2808 Roosevelt St., Carlsbad, CA 92008, 619-434-2101

Nutri/System

Initial license fee: $49,500
Royalties: 7%
Advertising royalties: None
Minimum cash required: $10,000
Capital required: $10,000 to $75,000
Financing: None
Length of contract: NA

In business since: 1971
Franchising since: 1972
Total number of units: 683
Number of company-operated units: 133
Total number of units planned, 1990: NA
Number of company-operated units planned, 1990: NA

In the mid-eighties, Nutri/System, which offers professional help to clients who wish to lose weight, became aware of the need to trim some fat from its own middle. It cut loose an operation in Germany that had not worked out, and a new management team sold the corporate jet. The new management refocused the company's efforts on providing quality weight-reduction counseling and assistance both through its own centers and those of its franchisees. It assumed that with more than half of all adult Americans overweight, a tightly run business that helped people deal with this problem could do as well as it had in previous years.

Nutri/System's weight-reduction program, a multifaceted approach involving professional supervision, personalized diets, behavior education, and mild exercise, never includes injections, drugs, or any fad treatments.

Weight counselors employed by franchisees use a computer program to analyze clients' life-style, including age, physical activity, eating habits, etc., to come up with a weight-loss goal and the length of time it should take to reach that goal. The company guarantees, in writing, that clients will reach their goal. Otherwise they will have full use of the company's services until they reach their goal.

Some states require Nutri/System centers to have doctors on staff. But even where not required, the staff consults clients' personal physicians in working out a diet plan. At the heart of the program, of course, is the Nutri/System diet. Clients find it easy to follow—and the company and its franchisees have another source of profits—in the sales of the exclusive line of Nu System Cuisine, available nowhere else. These frozen, freeze-dried, and canned foods are balanced not only for calorie content, but also for carefully controlled levels of saturated fat, cholesterol, and salt.

Your staff will have the skill to devise special diets for clients with particular problems, such as diabetes or hypertension. Weight-loss counselors supplement all diets with suggestions for an exercise program, and some centers have exercise facilities on the premises. Centers also offer classes that help clients change the habits that lead to weight gain. The center encourages clients to continue coming to the center for advice and monitoring for a year after they have achieved their goal, just to make sure they don't backslide.

If you would like to open one of the company's centers as your own business, Nutri/System will train you for a week in its methods at its home office in suburban Philadelphia. The company will teach you how to handle your medical staff, as well as other specifics of the weight-loss business. It will help you choose a site for your unit and advise you on its construction. And it will provide all the diagnostic and therapeutic equipment you will need.

In addition, Nutri/System provides its franchisees with an accounting system, business forms, and manuals detailing the daily operation of the weight-loss center. The company also supplies radio and television tapes and newspaper ads, as well as promotional items for any kind of local campaign you care to run.

For further information contact:
Nutri/System, 3901 Commerce Ave., CS 925, Willow Grove, PA 19090, 215-784-5600

Physicians Weight Loss Centers

Initial license fee: $18,500
Royalties: 10%
Advertising royalties: 2%
Minimum cash required: $45,000
Capital required: $45,000 to $50,000
Financing: None
Length of contract: 5 years

In business since: 1979
Franchising since: 1980
Total number of units: 195
Number of company-operated units: 20
Total number of units planned, 1990: 600
Number of company-operated units planned, 1990: 50

The weight-loss industry currently weighs in at $10 billion a year in the U.S.. American men average about ten pounds more than they did a decade ago; women, about five pounds more. According to this company, there are over 30 million overweight adults in the United States, most of them obese.

With its medically supervised diet, behavior modification program, and aggressive marketing, the management of Physicians Weight Loss Centers sees their company as well placed to take advantage of this large market. The key is medical supervision. All centers have a staff physician and a registered or licensed practical nurse, as well as weight reduction counselors, two examination rooms, two counseling rooms, and a laboratory.

To ensure that patients can fit the center's activities into their work schedules, these weight-loss centers remain open from 9:00 A.M. to 7:30 P.M. The staff puts patients on the "Futra-Loss Diet," a strict regimen, which the company guarantees will enable them to shed three to seven pounds a week. Physicians Weight Loss Centers says this diet stimulates the patient's body to burn off excess fat. The company produces the supplementary vitamins and minerals required on this diet, and it sells them to the patients as part of the plan. To bolster their efforts to lose weight and keep it off, patients also receive behavior modification counseling from center employees.

When patients have achieved their dietary goal, they graduate to a weight-maintenance plan. This provides Physicians Weight Loss Centers and its franchisees with an additional opportunity to profit by selling the various drinks, shakes, soups, and puddings produced under the company name, in addition to the vitamins and minerals.

Some company franchisees are doctors or nurses, but a medical background is not necessary. When you purchase your franchise you will receive new owner's training at the franchisor's suburban Akron, Ohio, headquarters, where you will have to pick up your own expenses. The week's course will cover the diet program, behavior guidance, marketing and enrolling, as well as the financial and operational systems used at these weight-reduction centers.

The company offers extensive supplementary training. Any members of your staff can receive thorough training in center operations at one of the company's monthly five-day general training seminars in Akron. Physicians Weight Loss Centers also gives semiannual motivational sales seminars, special seminars for managerial-level employees, and a four-day college-level course covering advanced sales techniques. It also has a special set of weekly lesson plans and learning exercises for your behavioral guidance counselors.

Physicians Weight Loss Centers prides itself on the continuous assistance it gives franchisees every step of the way, from site selection and layout through help in securing the services of a physician and nurse. The franchisor also conducts frequent consultations to monitor the operational and financial progress of your business.

Should local doctors raise any questions about patients and treatment at your center, you can refer them to the company's national medical director. You can also tap the expertise of the franchisor's Corporate Legal Counsel for problems or questions involving legal matters.

Advertising is a company strong point. Physicians Weight Loss Centers has an in-house ad agency that can create customized materials for any kind of media campaign you wish to run.

For further information contact:

Marty Uranker, Physicians Weight Loss Centers of America, Inc., 30 Springside Drive, Akron, OH 44313, 216-666-7952

Victory International, Inc.

Initial license fee: $25,000
Royalties: $350/month or 7% of gross sales, whichever is greater
Advertising royalties: 3%
Minimum cash required: $65,000
Capital required: $45,000 to $62,000
Financing: Negotiable
Length of contract: 5 years

In business since: 1969
Franchising since: 1982
Total number of units: 202
Number of company-operated units: None
Total number of units planned, 1990: 600
Number of company-operated units planned, 1990: None

About twenty years ago, Victoria Morton decided to do something about her cellulite, and in the process she created a successful business. She developed a mineral solution that, when applied to elastic bandages and used as a body wrap, gets rid of cellulite. Over a million wraps later, no client has ever had a bad reaction to the treatment. The company she founded is so confident in the treatment's efficacy that it guarantees a minimum six-inch loss (four inches for men) after the first wrap, and no return of the lost cellulite as long as the client does not gain weight.

Although clients spend only about seventy minutes in the wrap, a visit to a Suddenly Slender center usually lasts about two hours, much of it taken up by dressing and undressing, body measuring, and filling out forms. Clients can move around while undergoing treatment, during which the toxic fluid responsible for creating cellulite passes through their pores and collects in the plastic boots they wear for this purpose. The company encourages customers to come for a treatment once or twice a week until they have reached their goal. After that, it recommends three or four visits a year for maintenance.

Victory International markets its service to both men and women. In fact, one client is a professional football player. Body builders have used the process for better definition; women have used it to tighten skin loosened by pregnancy. Minor weight loss may accompany the treatments, but that is not the goal, which is the removal of toxic fluids from the body.

The company will work with you to open your Suddenly Slender center. It will assist you in selecting a site, negotiating a lease, and constructing a facility to house your business. It will also show you how to order supplies, and it will introduce you to vendors who sell the products you will need. The only item you must buy from Victory International is the mineral solution (on which a patent is pending) used for the wrap. The company will include furniture and equipment in your franchise package.

Victory International will train up to three people as part of your franchise agreement. You will take an intense three-week training course in Denver, and the instructors will expect you to have first mastered printed material that you received before arriving. The program covers business topics like sales, personnel, and management, as well as the procedures you will use in treating clients and in training your staff.

The company holds quarterly seminars in Denver to provide advanced training to franchisees. Topics include any specifically requested by franchisees, as well as body shaping, skin care products, nutrition, public relations, and promotion. The company encourages franchisees to call whenever they have any questions about their business.

The company requires you to spend $2,000 on advertising during your first four months in business. Thereafter your 3 percent advertising fee goes toward local advertising, and the company will reimburse half of what you spend.

For further information contact:

Victoria Morton, Victory International, Inc., 1231 S. Parker Rd., Suite 105, Denver, CO 80231, 303-753-6337

Hair Care

Command Performance

Initial license fee: $21,500
Royalties: 6%
Advertising royalties: None
Minimum cash required: $35,000
Capital required: $35,000
Financing: The company offers some financial assistance to qualified franchisees.
Length of contract: 15 years

In business since: 1976
Franchising since: 1976
Total number of units: 352
Number of company-operated units: 10
Total number of units planned, 1990: 605
Number of company-operated units planned, 1990: 25

Command Performance salons provide salon hair care in an attractive, modern environment. Men, women, and children can receive sophisticated hairstyling and related services like manicures at any of the Command Performance salons across the country. With high-tech decor, the latest styling techniques, and a high-quality product line, the franchised salons attract an upscale clientele. Additionally, recent market studies show that 75 percent of those surveyed knew the company's name. Its high-end image in the marketplace can mean high-end profits for the right franchisee.

The company follows an aggressive and focused advertising and marketing policy, a vital ingredient of which are its criteria for salon location. When you decide to become a Command Performance franchisee, the company will select a location for you that it feels enhances the Command Performance name, and it will negotiate the lease for you. The company will also help you review contractor bids for the construction or renovation of your salon and guide you in meeting the company's design specifications for your facility. "All of the company's advice and assistance was quite helpful," says Wayne Miller, a Command Performance franchisee in Shawnee Mission, Kansas. "The company shared its experience with me, and I didn't have to learn everything by trial and error."

Wayne Miller believes that Command Performance, almost exclusively a franchisee-operated system, is "still the only franchisor to bring modern, effective management practices to an industry that was strictly a cottage industry and had never made use of such procedures before." As a new franchisee, you will learn the company's approach to salon management in a comprehensive thirty-hour course conducted at a national (Wilmington, Massachusetts) or regional training center. Among other things, this training covers employee selection, management, advertising, inventory control, bookkeeping, and operations control. Even if you have no previous business experience, learning the Command Performance system will be relatively easy, since your business will be an all-cash, no-receivables, little-inventory operation.

About a month before your grand opening, Command Performance will help you make decisions regarding your public relations, advertising, and promotion campaigns. The company will supply you with an opening equipment and supplies package and will help you recruit and interview your staff. Once you've opened your salon, the company will provide "considerable support in the area of staff training and development," according to Wayne Miller. "The home office keeps us informed via weekly news bulletins and occasional phone calls, and the institute for ongoing education is very helpful."

Command Performance's program of ongoing education includes the Hair Art Institute, conducted regionally and nationally. Through a series of workshops, seminars, and audio-visual programs, the Institute furnishes managers and stylists with training in hair care and related topics. The company recommends that franchisees attend frequent refresher training sessions on the exclusive eight-step customer service system. Despite the availability of ongoing training and the accessibility of the corporate staff for consultation, Wayne Miller feels that Command Performance franchisees should be able to manage their businesses on their own without relying on the company for daily guidance. "Be prepared to be involved in an enterprise that occupies your mind and requires your attention almost constantly, including weekends," he advises. But he's happy to put in the extra hours because "our return has been better than if we had invested the same amount in securities."

For further information contact:
Carl M. Youngman, Chairman, Command Performance, 335 Middlesex Ave., Wilmington, MA 01887, 617-658-6586

CutCo Industries, Inc.

Initial license fee: $18,000
Royalties: 6%
Advertising royalties: None

Minimum cash required: $50,000
Capital required: $72,000 to $155,000
Financing: Available
Length of contract: 15 years

In business since: 1955
Franchising since: 1967
Total number of units: 612
Number of company-operated units: 52
Total number of units planned, 1990: 1,000
Number of company-operated units planned, 1990: 100

In the old days—that is, 1955—men got their hair cut in barber shops and women went to beauty parlors. And never the twain did meet. Then Lillian and Karl Stanley put their $10,000 life savings into a beauty parlor in Jericho, Long Island, New York. "I'm only ten minutes from the shop," Lillian Stanley remembers thinking at the time, "and I can be home when the children come home from school." But the instant success of the store kept her busier than she had anticipated. Before long, that shop became the basis for the Cut & Curl chain, and the profits poured in.

Meanwhile, Lillian Stanley's children thrived. In fact, her son, Richard, is now the president of the $110 million CutCo Industries, the hair-care empire into which that little shop eventually grew. The Cutco empire is divided into two franchised parts. HairCrafters—to which the remaining Cut & Curl operations were converted—is usually located in shopping centers. The stores concentrate on inexpensive family haircuts—and have done about 100 million to date. Great Expectations Precision Haircutters caters to the fashion-conscious, but its prices are also low. Both chains are decidedly unisex, a policy the company claims to have pioneered.

HairCrafters was ranked number one among hair-care franchisors by *Entrepreneur*, while Great Expectations was rated number three in recent surveys. These establishments, which, according to CutCo's president, "have put the last nail in the coffin of barbershops," do not require appointments. Their hexagon-shaped styling booths are designed for an open and airy atmosphere, as well as for privacy. One operation in Phoenix offers the ultimate in convenience for the harried worker with unusual hours: all-night service.

The full-service salons offer what the company would like to think of as a social experience. "We are dealing more with feelings than just the service of haircutting," Stanley says. The background music is upbeat, and one successful slogan the company has employed is "Talk to me."

Whatever else Cutco franchisees may be—and they have included dentists, bankers, and financial analysts—they are usually not professional hairstylists. Cutco doesn't market the franchise as one requiring your technical expertise and full-time presence on the floor. Potential franchisees are encouraged to think big. The company will stress to you that most of their franchisees have ended up buying more than one franchise. Those who have been aboard for more than a decade, according to CutCo, typically own more than eight franchises.

The company helps its franchisees pick a location and set up their business. In fact, if you wish, they will choose the site and build on it for you. Cutco trains you at your store. The instruction covers employee selection and training, advertising and merchandising, marketing, bookkeeping, inventory control, pricing, and accounting. Your stylists receive updated training—the latest in "slide cutting" and "scrunch drying," for example—at your location at least once a year. Company representatives visit each shop about three times a year. Occasionally that representative is Richard Stanley himself.

While you do not have to buy supplies and equipment from the company, Cutco does make them available. One of the added advantages of the franchise is your ability to sell at retail the company's own brand of hair-care products.

For further information contact:
Don vonLiebermann, CutCo Industries, Inc., P.O. Box 265, Jericho, NY 11753, 516-334-8400

Fantastic Sam's, The Original Family Haircutters

Initial license fee: $25,000
Royalties: $136.50/week
Advertising royalties: National (NAF): $63.18/week; regional (RAF): $104.50/week
Minimum cash required: $55,000
Capital required: $55,000 to $67,000
Financing: None
Length of contract: 10 years

In business since: 1974
Franchising since: 1976
Total number of units: 1,064
Number of company-operated units: 3
Total number of units planned, 1990: 3,507
Number of company-operated units planned, 1990: 7

You say you don't know the first thing about haircutting? You can't tell the difference between a body wave and a blow drier? You've heard how profitable the haircare business can be, but you don't know how to tap into this $15 billion market? Not to worry. Ninety-seven percent of current Fantastic Sam's franchise owners had no previous knowledge of or experience in the hair-care profession. They are business people, not beauty operators. Many even choose to run their Fantastic Sam's shops as absentee owners. But whether they're accountants, former schoolteachers, or retired airplane pilots, hundreds of entrepreneurs have become successful salon operators by following the Fantastic Sam's system—and their individual successes added up to more than $60 million in system-wide sales in 1985.

The Fantastic Sam's idea is to offer "one-stop shopping for the entire family's haircutting needs," according to George Carnall, the company's president. Before Fantastic Sam's got into the business, "nobody did children's hair. So we started the 'family haircutter' concept," he explains. Individuals or entire families can have their hair styled by haircutters identified by company nicknames like "Sparkie" and "Rocky," which are printed above the cutters' stations. The company requires cutters to use these nicknames rather than their own in order to build customer loyalty to Fantastic Sam's instead of individual haircutters. Though as an owner you don't need a cosmetology or barber's license, your staff of haircutters must be fully licensed and trained in the Fantastic Sam's patented haircutting technique.

When customers enter your store, you or your staff will immediately greet them, offering the adults complimentary coffee and the children games, bubble gum, and balloons. While they wait for their own haircuts, or for their parents to be styled, children can play with coloring books and puzzles, or watch cartoons on TV. Fantastic Sam's' special attention to children has given the system a unique position in a market that is virtually recession-proof: People continue to get haircuts regardless of the state of the economy. Fantastic Sam's is both the largest and fastest-growing family hair-care franchisor in the world.

Art Littell, a Fantastic Sam's salon owner in Wichita, Kansas, decided to purchase his franchise after careful research. "I checked ten or twelve Fantastic Sam's owners after reading an article in a magazine," he recalls. "Then I called Sam Ross, the company's founder, and he explained the Fantastic Sam's franchise to my wife and me. After speaking with Sam, my wife and I went to several shops around the Midwest and spoke with the owners." Upon becoming Fantastic Sam's franchisees, the Littells spent a week in owners' training, which they call "invaluable."

All new Fantastic Sam's owners must complete the franchise owners' training class, which consists of one week of intensive training in every detail of Fantastic Sam's store operations. At Fantastic Sam's headquarters in Memphis, Tennessee, or at one of the training centers located throughout the U.S. and Canada, you will learn about the franchise sytem, advertising (the company spends millions each year on national advertising and direct mail campaigns), accounting, management, employee relations, and hair-care products and services. The Littells were impressed with the thoroughness of the training they received and feel that it "left nothing to chance. We were given a system to follow, and it has done a wonderful job for us."

In addition to the required owners' training, the company makes available a managers' training class and a haircutters' class for your staff, and marketing and advertising classes for you and/or your management. In a one-week session, the managers' training class covers daily operations of Fantastic Sam's stores. The haircutters' class offers technical training in every aspect of hair-care products and services. Unlike other training, the haircutters' class takes place at your location. All training is free of charge.

The Fantastic Sam's business development department will keep in touch with you throughout your initial twelve-week opening period and will help you recruit and hire staff. Thereafter, the business development department and your regional subfranchisor will maintain regular communications with you to ensure everything runs smoothly. And of course, if you ever have any questions, the company is always available to help out by telephone.

At no expense to you, Fantastic Sam's provides continuing technical training to the employees at your store. This on-site haircutter training is conducted at least twice a year. You or your staff can return at any time to your regional training center for refresher training in any of the monthly classes. Attorneys, accountants, marketing representatives, and business development experts make presentations at these sessions, sharing with you their expertise in a variety of topics related to the successful operation of your business.

Fantastic Sam's conducts annual regional seminars in each of the three geographical regions (eastern, central, western) of the U.S. to provide owners, managers, and haircutters with continuing education. The company's annual national convention, which the company calls a "family reunion," takes place in a different city every year, rotating among regions. Various franchise owners' committees and special franchise owners' classes provide franchisees with the opportunity to work closely with Fantastic Sam's staff and other franchisees to improve the system and increase profits. The Littells attend "several management seminars a year where we meet with other owners and company managers. The seminars are very good, and we learn every time. The guest speakers at the seminars really help."

Monthly newsletters and the president's quarterly report will help keep you up to date on developments in the company and the industry, and the company's ongoing efforts to improve your operating manuals ensure that your operation stays on the cutting edge of hair-care technology. All in all, according to the Littells, "our franchise is a good investment, which completely repaid itself in less than three years. A well-managed franchise like Fantastic Sam's gives you tracks to follow and keeps you from making a lot of mistakes."

For further information contact:

Sam M. Ross, Chairman of the Board, S.M.R. Enterprises, Inc., P.O. Box 18845, Memphis, TN 38181-0845, 901-363-8624

First Choice Haircutters

Initial license fee: $15,000
Royalties: 10%
Advertising royalties: 1%
Minimum cash required: $35,000
Capital required: $60,000
Financing: Some
Length of contract: 10 years

In business since: 1980
Franchising since: 1981
Total number of units: 166
Number of company-operated units: 82
Total number of units planned, 1990: 829
Number of company-operated units planned, 1990: 115

Hair. Twenty years ago they wrote a musical about it. But some barbers then were going out of business due to people's growing reluctance to part with it. Not anymore. Now the average person in this country spends almost $100 a year on haircuts. That's a $15 billion-a-year industry.

And those haircuts are not what they used to be. Even barber shops catering primarily to men have begun to resemble beauty salons. The prices in those shops also bear a resemblance to salon prices. "Styling" has brought with it a revolution in how Americans approach haircuts.

The founders of First Choice looked at this phenomenon and came up with an interesting idea that would combine the best of recent developments with an economical service that could take care of the whole family's hair-care needs under one roof: an à la carte, no-frills hair salon. It includes free parking at every location, and no appointment is necessary—just like old times. And it's all topped off with a written money-back guarantee that if you don't like your haircut, you can get a refund or a free recut within one week.

A First Choice franchise is ideal for somebody who already has some managerial or business experience, since the overwhelming number of the company's franchisees do not lay a hand on anybody's head: They hire experienced professionals to do the cutting. Although the company is Canadian and seeks to expand in Quebec and the Maritime Provinces, it is also expanding the number of franchises it has in the United States, especially in the East and the Midwest.

This franchise is a cash business with almost no inventory. The company claims the business is recession-proof, in part because the demand for its services is based on hair's special characteristics. After all, in how many businesses do you get to deal with a market that, as Cheryl Kostopoulos, First Choice's director of franchising puts it, "regenerates itself"?

If you decide to invest in a First Choice franchise, the company will help you select the right site for your store. Then you learn the ropes at two weeks of training at the company school in Toronto. A First Choice training officer will also train your staff for ten to thirteen days at your place of business. Direct assistance from the company extends to five days beyond your grand opening, and a week's refresher course in Toronto will be available to you after that if you feel you need it. Three-day franchise seminars, offered periodically, also provide brushup training and franchisor updates.

Ed Furman, who recently open his First Choice franchise in Lansdale, Pennsylvania, was pleased with his training, especially the class size of two or three people. He says that his relationship with the franchisor so far has been "excellent, First Choice is very responsive to our needs and questions."

For further information contact:
George Kostopoulos, First Choice Haircutters, 6535 Millcreek Drive, Unit 64, Mississauga, Ontario Canada, L5N 2M2, 1-800-387-8335

Great Clips, Inc.

Initial license fee: $12,500
Royalties: 6%
Advertising royalties: 5%
Minimum cash required: $74,000
Capital required: $74,000
Financing: None
Length of contract: 10 years

In business since: 1982
Franchising since: 1983
Total number of units: 123
Number of company-operated units: 7
Total number of units planned, 1990: 520
Number of company-operated units planned, 1990: 20

To indicate its confidence in its operations, Great Clips will send you income statements from all its company-owned stores. You will also get the names, addresses, and home and business phone numbers of all its franchisees so you can check company claims for yourself.

Great Clips' business is providing no-frills haircuts at a low price. The customer pays only for specific services rendered. For example, Great Clips advertisements suggest that customers shampoo their hair the day they come in for a haircut to avoid the cost of having Great Clips do it for them. Great Clips guarantees the customer a good haircut—and without an appointment. If not satisfied, the customer can have it recut for free or get a refund. With the shop's stylists kept constantly busy cutting hair, profits come from high volume.

The nationally franchised haircutting shop has reached just the right point in franchising development, according to Great Clips. No longer a new and high risk—undertaking, but not too old and overdeveloped, it could offer a good investment opportunity to somebody who wants to open a business. Great Clips sees great opportunities for carving out a big niche in the $15-billion-a-year hair-care business. Its projections for growth attests to its optimism.

As franchises go, Great Clips has low start-up costs. The company says that most stores achieve profitability inside of four months.

The stores, often located in shopping centers, have a distinctive look, which comes mainly from the colorful canvas sails serving as partitions to create private hairstyling areas. The red and white stripes on the blouses of Great Clips hairstylists adds another splash of color.

One of the key advantages to operating a Great Clips franchise, the company stresses, is the minimal amount of time you have to spend on the business, even during the opening period. You can even retain your present job while you get under way. Assuming you hire a manager to run things, the business should not demand more than a few hours a week of your time.

Great Clips will train you in your area. Instruction will cover selecting a site and negotiating a lease, and the basics of advertising, financing, and shop operation. You will purchase your supplies from a list of vendors approved by Great Clips.

Your stylists will get a free four-day training course in the Great Clips method of haircutting, although, of course, you have to pay their salary while they study. After passing a test on what they've learned, stylists receive the company's "Certificate of Competency." They cannot work in your shop without it. Any stylists you hire after your business has started will receive the same training, but at a cost of seventy-five dollars to you for each one trained.

The Great Clips grand opening promotion, part of your franchise package, includes special coupons with money-off offers on permanents and haircuts. Direct mail advertising, also part of the company's promotional strategy to draw customers to your new store, should also help your fledgling business get off to a good start.

For further information contact:
Raymond L. Barton, Great Clips, Inc., 3601 West 77th St., Suite 145, Minneapolis, MN 55435, 612-893-9088

The Hair Performers

Initial license fee: $15,000
Royalties: 6%
Advertising royalties: 4%
Minimum cash required: $15,000
Capital required: $50,000 to $125,000
Financing: The company directs financial assistance.
Length of contract: 10 years

In business since: 1967
Franchising since: 1977
Total number of units: 234
Number of company-operated units: 7
Total number of units planned, 1990: 675
Number of company-operated units planned, 1990: 7

The mother of John Amico, The Hair Performers' founder and president, was an artist; his father, an architect. The son started out to become an architect, but eventually saw his true calling in hairstyling. After running his own salon for a few years, he decided that he had something special to offer other prospective salon owners, and he began to franchise his operation.

Amico got the idea for the Progressional System of haircutting, his exclusive approach to styling, from his early training in art and architecture. "Hairstyling involves the same type of line, design, balance, and rhythm that you find in architecture and art," he says. With his system, qualified cutters can "design and style by using degrees of angles and elevations. We can create any style by adding volume and taking away weight."

His system has generated The Hair Performers' success. The full-service family hair-care salons also sell cosmetics, skin-care services, suntanning beds, a variety of beauty products, and the services of nail technicians.

Early on, notes Amico, he recognized the difference between cutting hair and running a franchise system. After spending some time working with McDonald's, he put his observations about the franchise business to work in creating his own franchise concept. "A good franchise takes the inherent problems of the industry and constructs a system around them," Amico says of his thinking about the business. "A bad franchise ignores the inherent problems, constructs a hamburger franchise, and applies it to the hair industry. If you don't allow appointments and don't allow the clients to choose their stylist, you are going against the industry. Stylists develop a doctor/patient-type relation with their clients, so this should be kept intact in a franchise system."

The company stresses the stylist-client relationship in its guidelines for giving service. "Designers," as the store's stylists are called, don't simply chat idly with the customers. Instead, the designer explains what happens at each stage of the customer's haircut, educating the customer about new styles. Customers appreciate the extensive attention. Cosmetics sales and services are also personalized. A Hair Performers employee applies the makeup to one side of the client's face, then the client does the other side under the supervision and comment of the professional.

The Hair Performers looks for potential franchisees with extra ambition and drive. You do not have to be a hairstylist. In fact, company franchisees have included doctors and corporate executives. Absentee ownership is fine; indeed, the company encourages multiunit operations because, as Amico puts it, "it really takes little more to develop several units than it does to develop one." The Hair Performers assists investor-franchisees by setting up service companies to operate their units.

Franchisees must take an introductory training course at The Hair Performers headquarters in Chicago. You pay for travel and lodging in Chicago. The course covers all aspects of salon management, sales, personnel hiring, advertising, and promotions. The company sends several people to help you set up your business and train your employees, including personnel from its advertising, operations, and technical training departments. The Hair Performers will see to it that your stylists train thoroughly in the company's system. Semiannual refresher training at corporate headquarters is mandatory.

You select the site for your store with the company's guidance. Store design stresses durability as well as comfort and aesthetics, since it must handle as many as 1,000 clients a week. The Hair Performers assists you in all aspects of advertising, including placing want ads to staff your business. You may buy your supplies and equipment from whomever you wish, with company approval of the vendor.

For further information contact:
William H. Patton, The Hair Performers, 7327 W. 90th St., Bridgeview, IL 60455, 1-800-323-8309

Optical and Hearing Aids

American Vision Centers, Inc.

Initial license fee: $10,000
Royalties: 8.5%
Advertising royalties: 6%
Minimum cash required: $60,000
Capital required: $170,000 to $200,000
Financing: The company maintains a relationship with several banks, but loan approval by the bank is based on the individual franchisee's qualifications.
Length of contract: 10 years

In business since: 1977
Franchising since: 1977
Total number of units: 67
Number of company-operated units: 24
Total number of units planned, 1990: 140
Number of company-operated units planned,1990: NA

As long as people have less than perfect vision, there will be a market for eyeglasses. Just think of all the people you know who wear glasses or contact lenses, and imagine how much each of them has to spend each year just to be able to see things clearly. A lot of them spend their eye-care dollars at American Vision Centers, Inc.

A national network of full-service eye-care centers, American Vision offers eye exams, soft, hard, and extended-wear contact lenses, designer eyeglasses, bifocals, and tinted lenses. In many cases, centers can complete orders in one hour, and the company's purchasing power allows franchises to offer attractive discounts.

A good portion of American Vision franchises are conversions: independent opticians who decided to convert their shops to American Vision franchises to benefit from the company's advertising, name recognition, and corporate clout. Conversions, obviously, bypass the site selection process, need little, if any, shop setup, and require a much lower investment than new store start-ups. But franchisees starting from scratch can get advice on store layout and equipment purchasing from American Vision, which in turn subleases the sites to its franchisees. Franchisees have the freedom to purchase inventory, supplies, and equipment from any source they choose.

Before you open you American Vision Center, you must train at the nearest operating location. Your training covers sales, administration, systems, and technical areas. When you complete the training, a regional supervisor will join you at your store for a week to help you in all phases of opening.

Throughout the course of your contract, corporate staff and regional supervisors will visit your store on a regular basis. These visits serve as quality-control checks, troubleshooting sessions, and training updates. The company makes every effort to address any issue of concern to you through a combination of on-site consultation, telephone contacts, and franchise newsletters. In addition, American Vision implements various advertising, marketing, and promotional strategies for the benefit of all franchisees.

For further information contact:

Marvin Convissar, Vice President, American Vision Centers, Inc., 138-49 78th Ave., Flushing, NY 11367, 1-800-221-2395; in New York State: 1-800-442-0440

Dahlberg Electronics, Inc./Miracle Ear Centers

Initial license fee: $12,500
Royalties: $33 per instrument
Advertising royalties: None
Minimum cash required: $25,000
Capital required: $5,000 to $50,000
Financing: None
Length of contract: 20 years

In business since: 1948
Franchising since: 1984
Total number of units: 214
Number of company-operated units: 14
Total number of units planned, 1990: 800
Number of company-operated units planned, 1990: 25

When you stop to think that the first baby boomers—who grew up with hula hoops and poodle skirts—have already celebrated their fortieth birthdays, you realize that America is aging. By 2011, the first baby boomers will join the ranks of people age sixty-five and over, a segment of the population that has already started to grow rapidly. The population in the sixty-five-plus age group increased nearly 130 percent between 1950 and 1984, and they now make up over 12 percent of the population. By 2030, more than 20 percent of Americans will be sixty-five or older. While the hard of hearing can be found in any age group the overwhelming majority of hearing aid users are those who have suffered hearing loss as the result of the aging process. The demand for hearing aids can only increase as the country continues to grow older.

Dahlberg Electronics manufactures hearing instruments and franchises retail outlets for its products. One of the longest-established companies in the business, Dahlberg decided to join the franchising revolution in 1984 when it recognized its potential for expansion. The company believed it can best meet the nation's growing need for hearing instruments through independently operated distribution centers, known as Miracle Ear Centers.

If you are a trained audiologist (or otherwise involved in the hearing aid business), you can convert your operation to a Miracle Ear Center. For much less than the start-up cost of a new outlet, you will gain the advantage of association with a national company: name recognition, research and development, operational support, and more. Dahlberg will work with you to help you install display systems and do any other work that might be required for your office to conform to the company's standards. These changes can be made gradually if your budget is limited.

If you are new to hearing instrument sales, Dahlberg will require you to meet construction and design standards in your new store. You will also attend training on location or at the company's home office in Golden Valley, Minnesota. This training is free of charge, though you will be responsible for your out-of-pocket expenses. You will learn basic audiology and instrument fitting, as well as operations. The license-preparation class will help you obtain the licenses necessary for legal operation of an audiology office and hearing aid store.

The company provides a full range of preopening assistance in such areas as advertising, hiring, and additional technical help. Upon request during your contract, you and/or your employees can receive refresher training in any aspect of Miracle Ear Center operation. The company's fully qualified staff will provide ongoing support in advertising and marketing and will help you develop business plans, and relocate when you are ready to expand your business.

For further information contact:
Norman L. Blemaster, Executive Vice President, Dahlberg Electronics, Inc./ Miracle Ear Centers, 7731 Country Club Drive, Golden Valley, MN 55427, 1-800-328-0626

NuVision, Inc.

Initial license fee: $8,000
Royalties: 8.5%
Advertising royalties: 7%
Minimum cash required: $25,000
Capital required: $8,000 to $100,000
Financing: Information available on request
Length of contract: 10 years

In business since: 1950
Franchising since: 1983
Total number of units: 113
Number of company-operated units: 77
Total number of units planned, 1990: NA
Number of company-operated units planned, 1990: NA

Don't think of this business as medically related. True, NuVision and all other eyeglass centers have optometrists on the premises to give eye exams and grind lenses. And, of course, they fill prescriptions for eyeglasses from ophthalmologists. But it's a more interesting and lucrative enterprise than just that.

When you buy a NuVision franchise you tap into a fashion industry. People care a great deal about how they look. They don't just want to see better, they want to be better seen. The excitement in this field comes from the contact lenses, designer sunglasses, and the wide variety of frames—some very expensive—that hold the eyeglass lenses. You won't just turn out glasses as a NuVision franchisee. Rather, you will own and operate a business dedicated to selling products that make people look good.

You needn't worry if you lack knowledge about this field. NuVision will show you the ropes. The franchisor will work with you on site selection and development, and you will need the company's go-ahead before you build or remodel. Your training will take place at corporate headquarters in Flint, Michigan, with transportation, lodging, and meals your responsibility. That training will cover all procedures needed to operate a NuVision franchise, including advertising, product buying and handling, personnel management, and record keeping. You will also receive a copy of the company's confidential operations manual.

Every business involves lots of paperwork. Eyeglass centers, with their varied and specialized inventory and customer invoicing, have as much as any, maybe more than most. NuVision recognizes this and takes special steps to help you prepare all the business forms you will need to operate your franchise.

The company will have representatives on the premises to help you clear the opening day hurdles. You can also request follow-up visits. Should you need brushing up afterwards, you can take advantage of the franchisor's refresher training courses, offered monthly either at your location or, for more in-depth training, company headquarters. Aside from general management techniques, this advanced instruction covers subjects like cost control and sales training. NuVision also pledges to keep you on top of the changing technical aspects of the optical industry.

NuVision's full-service laboratory will provide you with all the products you need to operate your franchise, including those for resale. Your purchases must be made from that lab or from other suppliers approved by the franchisor.

For further information contact:
David J. Mace, NuVision, Inc., P.O. Box 2600, 2284 South Ballenger, Flint, MI 48501, 313-767-0900

Pearle Vision Center, Inc.

Initial license fee: $20,000
Royalties: 8.5%
Advertising royalties: 8%
Minimum cash required: $25,000
Capital required: $25,000 to $35,000
Financing: Company will finance 90% of start-up over 10 years.
Length of contract: 10 years

In business since: 1962
Franchising since: 1980
Total number of units: 1,130
Number of company-operated units: 450
Total number of units planned, 1990: NA
Number of company-operated units planned, 1990: NA

Pearle has experienced several corporate mergers and restructurings since Dr. Stanley Pearle started it in 1962. For a while, in the early

1980s, G.D. Searle & Co. owned Pearle. Currently, it is a subsidiary of Grand Metropolitan, a British firm.

Besides prescription eyeglasses, the stores sell contact lenses, sunglasses, and a variety of other optical products and accessories. Customers can have their eyes checked and then shop for fashionable eyewear—all under one roof. Pearle sells franchises only to licensed opticians, optometrists, or ophthalmologists with previous experience in the retail optical business. Since some states have restrictive laws governing the employment of optometrists or ophthalmologists on the premises of a business such as Pearle's, potential franchisees should consult a lawyer about such an operation in their state. If state law prevents you from offering one-stop eye care, the company will still consider selling you a franchise, and it will adjust the royalty and other fees to make them commensurate with your reduced level of business.

Pearle offers you two methods of developing your store. Either you can choose a site and direct construction yourself, with advisory services available from the franchisor on a fee-for-service basis, or you can pay Pearle $15,000 to evaluate and lease a site, plan the store, hire a contractor, and supervise construction for you.

The Pearle franchisee training program involves three days of instruction at the company's Dallas headquarters or, if possible, at a site nearer your location. During training you will study sales, material and labor cost controls, frame selection, marketing and merchandising, legal problems, employee benefits, quality standards, lab operating procedures, accounting, and business management. You will have to pay a tuition of $1,000 for this instruction in addition to absorbing the cost of transportation and lodging.

The company also charges for supplementary training for you and your employees, but your franchise package includes a $1,000 credit toward this training during your first year of operation. Optional training programs cover new employee orientation, sales, contact lenses, management development, fitting of multifocals, measuring pupillary distance, and machine maintenance. Some courses are conducted by correspondence, some held at your business, and others require a trip to Dallas, which involves additional expenses for travel.

Pearle requires that you kick off your business by spending $15,000 on advertising. The company will match your spending and will finance your $15,000 expense for four years at 3 percent above Citibank's prime rate, adjustable each quarter.

Pearle operates two company divisions from which you can purchase supplies. Its Pearle Laboratories sell prescription lenses, eyeglass frames, and various lab services, while Morgan Laboratories produces hard contact lenses. Both make a profit on their sales to franchisees. You can buy from any other company-approved supplier, but 10 to 15 percent of the frames approved by the company are imported fashion models available only from the franchisor. Buying through the company offers you the convenience of having one source for your varied inventory. Pearle carries frames from fifty different companies, in 350 styles and more than 1,400 colors and sizes.

Each Pearle Vision Center offers customers a "Great Eyeglass Guarantee." Every Pearle store will repair or replace, at no charge, any broken or defective eyeglasses bought from any store in the chain for up to one year from the purchase date. The guarantee will draw many customers to your store, according to the company, but the cost for participating in the required program will be minimal.

For further information contact:
Franchise Sales Department, Pearle Vision Center, Inc., 2534 Royal Lane Drive, Dallas, TX 75229, 214-241-3381

13. *The Home Construction, Improvement, and Maintenance Industry*

Contents

Miscellaneous Services

Dial One International, Inc.
Dynamark Security Centers, Inc.
Lawn Doctor
Mr. Build International
RainSoft Water Conditioning Company
Spring-Green Lawn Care Corporation

Construction and Home Improvement

California Closet Company, Inc.

Initial license fee: $25,000
Royalties: 6%
Advertising royalties: 6%
Minimum cash required: $60,000
Capital required: $60,000 to $95,000
Financing: The company offers assistance in obtaining financing.
Length of contract: 10 years

In business since: 1978
Franchising since: 1982
Total number of units: 74
Number of company-operated units: 3
Total number of units planned, 1990: 245
Number of company-operated units planned, 1990: 20

Ever notice how no one ever seems to have enough places to put all the things they own? How most closets are a jumbled attempt to fit too much into too little space? Few people today have the time or energy to spend rearranging their closet, but—especially in urban apartments notoriously short on closet space—an organized closet can banish the frustration of never being able to find anything, replacing it with the satisfaction of having a place for everything and everything in its place.

A pioneer in the growing home services industry that taps America's need for more organized personal time and space, California Closet Company specializes in redesigning the use of existing space in closets, garages, and offices. Instead of building or buying new cabinets or closets or throwing away beloved possessions that won't seem to fit anywhere, California Closet Company offers a different solution to the clutter question: trained consultants who analyze available space and discuss clients' need, and then design entire systems to increase storage capacity by dramatic proportions. As the era of stay-at-home wives draws to a close and as people become increasingly concerned with maximizing both their work and leisure time, home services companies like California Closet Company look forward to a period of rapid growth.

As a California Closet franchisee, you will receive two weeks of comprehensive training in closet design, manufacturing, sales, advertising, and management. Training takes place at the company's Woodland Hills, California, headquarters at no expense to you except for travel and lodging. From site selection to state and local licensing requirements, the company will give you complete preopening support. The company must approve your site and the interior design of your store and will help you with equipment purchases. You will also receive a California Closet printing package.

High-quality materials and construction, and design responsive to your clients' needs, are essential to the success of your business, so California Closet sets high standards in each area, which you are contractually obliged to meet. The company will maintain close telephone contact with you and will visit your location whenever necessary to make sure you receive the support you need to operate profitably. Regional meetings, held quarterly, will keep you advised in matters of management, marketing, and manufacturing, and will address various regional topics and problems. The annual national convention brings all franchisees together with corporate staff to review the past and prepare for the future.

A California Closet franchise should do particularly well in urban, upscale areas, or in any region where people tend to hire help rather than do it themselves. If you have a flair for design and an enjoyment of light carpentry, a California Closet franchise could net you a tidy sum.

For further information contact:
Neil Balter, President, California Closet Company, Inc., 6409 Independence Ave., Woodland Hills, CA 91367, 818-888-5888

CHEM–CLEAN Restoration Centers

Initial license fee: $4,500 to $24,000
Royalties: None
Advertising royalties: None
Minimum cash required: $4,500
Capital required: $4,500 to $40,000
Financing: Limited financing available.
Length of contract: 10 years

In business since: 1966
Franchising since: 1968
Total number of units: 52
Number of company-operated units: None
Total number of units planned, 1990: 100
Number of company-operated units planned, 1990: None

Each year, more and more people recognize the appeal of antique furniture—not just of Chippendale and French Provincial pieces, but also of less exotic turn-of-the-century and Depression-era American items.

As the antiques market booms, the demand for restoration and refinishing services explodes. Most people think refinishing that favorite dining room set might be fun—if it weren't for the stripping. An entire industry has arisen to satisfy these almost-do-it-yourselfers: furniture stripping. CHEM–CLEAN is the only patented paint-removing system on the market today. The company's unique equipment and techniques allow trained professionals to strip off old paint and varnish in an astonishingly short period of time, without harming the wood beneath. The company sells franchisees its equipment and solvent, and helps them start their own CHEM–CLEAN shops.

Though it is not required, CHEM–CLEAN recommends that you train with them before you open for business. At the company-certified training center in California, you will receive all the training you need to become a professional furniture refinisher. The course usually takes a minimum of one week and covers all pertinent skills, but the company will adapt the program to meet your level of proficiency.

With the assistance of CHEM–CLEAN, you can purchase or lease your site. The company will also assist you in conforming to local code requirements for your facility. You must purchase the solvent you use from CHEM–CLEAN, but you may obtain all other supplies from any source you choose.

As part of the franchise agreement, CHEM–CLEAN will provide you with advertising packages and will maintain weekly communication with you to make sure things are running smoothly. CHEM–CLEAN franchisees have established a support network among themselves, from which you can obtain any further assistance you might need. And once a year the company holds its national convention, during which you can hear about current trends in furniture refinishing as well as developments within the company.

For further information contact:
Mel O'Donnell, CHEM–CLEAN Furniture Restoration, Restoration Systems Co., Rural Route 2, Box 285, Freeport, ME 04032, 207-865-9007

Decorating Den Systems Inc.

Initial license fee: $15,500
Royalties: 11%
Advertising royalties: 2%
Minimum cash required: $18,500
Capital required: $20,000
Financing: Van and equipment lease available
Length of contract: 10 years

In business since: 1969
Franchising since: 1970
Total number of units: 485
Number of company-operated units: None
Total number of units planned, 1990: 5,000
Number of company-operated units planned, 1990: None

"Without a game plan to follow, I don't know if I could have succeeded as I have. But with a proven program it was so simple," remarks Cynthia Patton-Key, a Decorating Den Systems franchisee in Roanoke, Texas. "On a scale of one to ten, the Decorating Den staff and fellow decorators would have to get a healthy nine and three quarters for all the help and support they have given me over the years. It is in large part due to this support that I am as successful as I am."

Decorating Den is a national firm that franchises interior decorators. These decorators operate out of the unique "color vans" that have become the trademark of the Decorating Den System. Filled with three thousand samples of upholstery, draperies, rugs, carpets, and wallcoverings, the color vans contain everything you need to work with your clients in their homes. As a decorator, you travel to customers' locations to discuss their needs, plan decorating schemes, and show them samples from which to choose.

Your van is your Decorating Den office, and with no need to lease or purchase a location, your start-up and overhead costs are minimal. You don't have to maintain an inventory, either, because you only order materials when you need them. Decorating Den has proven to be popular with customers not only because of the in-home service, but because there is no expense to them for the design consultation. All they pay for are the products they purchase.

Decorating Den has developed a system dedicated to the support of its franchisees. "They gave me step-by-step instructions on what needed to be done, when, and how, to get off to a healthy start," says Cynthia Patton-Key. Decorating Den will provide you with one week of intensive training in its classrooms in Indianapolis, Indiana, or Dallas, Texas. The required courses cover design techniques and principles, business operations, and promotion of your business. And, according to Cynthia Patton-Key, "there was one week of bookkeeping classes that picked up where the other initial training left off. They explained invoicing, filing, and setting up your systems." Training plus market research meant that "the groundwork was already laid when I opened my franchise." An experienced decorator/manager will provide personal assistance as you start to build from this foundation.

Central to the Decorating Den system are the weekly meetings of local decorators. Held in a city no more than two hours from your home, these meetings provide ongoing training as well as "decorating information, sales techniques, and emotional support" that Cynthia Patton-Key has found very useful. "The group meetings are great for immediate needs," she says. "The decorators can help each other in every way and keep the 'family' closeness so special to the Decorating Den system. Without these meetings the Decorating Den franchise just wouldn't be the same. They are inspiring."

Decorating Den provides intensive support and personal assistance in marketing, operations, and customer service by telephone. You can take advantage of this management guidance whenever you feel you need it, no matter how frequently that might be. "I feel that the lines of communication between me and the company are open most of the time and that I can discuss whatever whenever," comments Cynthia Patton-Key. Decorating Den conducts periodic seminars, conventions, and intermediate and advanced schools. There are twelve intermediate and advanced courses available, held monthly in cities throughout the country. You can attend these classes to sharpen your product knowledge, your management skills, or your sales and marketing techniques, among other things.

There are some nominal materials fees involved in the training programs, but your only significant investment as a Decorating Den franchisee will be the franchise fee itself and your color van. Cynthia Patton-Key notes, "Obviously, if you didn't go into franchising you wouldn't have to pay the fees, but you would probably waste at least that much money 'testing the water' before you could get your business off the ground. Your advertising costs alone could take all your profits, but because of the franchisor's advertising program, my advertising expenses are brought down to an affordable figure." And you can save elsewhere as a Decorating Den owner, because franchisees get discounts from approved suppliers, thanks to the company's purchasing power.

"Before owning my own business, I had little self-confidence or direction. Decorating Den helped me start and build a business and be proud of myself. I know it probably sounds too good to be true, but I am truly happy with my choice of a Decorating Den franchise," concludes Cynthia Patton-Key.

For further information contact:

Jim Bugg, Decorating Den Systems Inc., 4630 Montgomery Ave., Bethesda, MD 20814, 301-652-6393

Four Seasons Greenhouses

Initial license fee: $30,000
Royalties: 2.5%
Advertising royalties: None
Minimum cash required: $25,000
Capital required: $50,000 to $200,000
Financing: Available from C.I.T. Credit Corporation
Length of contract: 10 years

In business since: 1975
franchising since: 1985
Total number of units: 165
Number of company-operated units: 4
Total number of units planned, 1990: 1,000
Number of company-operated units planned, 1990: NA

Four Seasons sees big profit potential in the trends reflected in certain U.S. housing statistics, and many entrepreneurs apparently agree, because in its first year of franchising, the company sold 160 units. With more than 40 million homes over twenty-five years old in the U.S., a fertile market exists for the remodeling business. In 1985 alone, Americans added 1.5 million rooms, 3.6 million kitchens, and 4.1 million bathrooms to their homes. About two thirds of Four Seasons' business comes from people improving their homes, and the remainder comes from commercial clients and new home construction.

Professionally installed glass enclosures, the main product you will sell as a franchised dealer, include atriums and solarium-type room additions. The company points out that people are sensitive about work done on their homes, and they will go out of their way to find a "name" company to do the work. However, few big names exist in the remodeling business. Since Four Seasons builds name recognition through extensive advertising, owning one of its franchises gives you an advantage over your competition.

Opportunities to sell glass enclosures to commercial customers are expanding as businesses design their premises for a more light and airy look. Some of the big fast-food chains that have added these structures to their restaurants include Arby's, Burger King, McDonald's, and Taco Bell.

You will sell your product from a showroom located on an easily accessible road, preferably near other businesses that sell home building, renovating, and decorating products, such as lumber yards, appliance stores, and carpeting businesses. You will not rely on walk-in trade in this field, so you don't have to pay high shopping center rents for the

1,500 to 3,000 square feet you will need. In fact, you can convert an old factory building or free-standing house to a Four Seasons center.

In your showroom you will display ten models of the company's prefabricated greenhouses. Skilled subcontractors will do most of your installations, usually working on a fixed-fee basis. The company will put you in touch with subcontractors in your area. You will need a general manager and sales manager, if you don't plan to fill those roles yourself, and a construction manager with at least five years of construction experience. Your construction manager will work directly with the subcontractors.

The company trains franchisees at its Farmingdale, New York, home office for two weeks. Classroom instruction there covers business management, selling, product knowledge, accounting, and marketing. Then franchisees receive a week of hands-on training at their showrooms, just before their grand opening.

Advertising is a strong point with Four Seasons. The company commits 7.5 percent of its total revenue to advertising, with 5 percent going directly to you and your fellow franchisees for local campaigns. In effect, it runs a cooperative advertising program in which the company's contribution is 100 percent instead of the more typical 50 percent. The remainder of the advertising budget goes for company advertisements in publications like *House Beautiful, House and Garden, Better Homes and Gardens, Home, New Shelter, Metropolitan Home,* and *Popular Science.* The company will also send you the names of anyone from your area who responds to one of its national magazine advertisements so that you can follow up and possibly make a sale.

You do not have to confine your business to the sale of glass enclosures. Four Seasons franchisees often sell related products, such as doors, windows, skylights, ceramic tiles, hot tubs, and spas.

Your protected franchise territory will include about two hundred and fifty thousand people, although for a lesser fee you can buy a minifranchise in a rural area, at a smaller investment, that encompasses a population of about seventy-five thousand.

For further information contact:

Ed Treixeira, Four Seasons Greenhouses, 5005 Vets Highway, Holbrook, NY 11741, 516-737-4000

Lindal Cedar Homes, Inc.

Initial license fee: None
Royalties: None
Advertising royalties: None

Minimum cash required: $5,000
Capital required: $15,000 to $20,000
Financing: The company will help finance a model home at a commercial location after you're "firmly established" in business for at least 18 months.
Length of contract: 1 year

In business since: 1945
Franchising since: 1962
Total number of units: 178
Number of company-operated units: 4
Total number of units planned, 1990: 550
Number of company-operated units planned, 1990: 5

The Indians of the Pacific Northwest called western red cedar "the tree of life." Many American homeowners call this popular building material—both for log-style and contemporary homes—warm and attractive. Lindal Cedar Homes has the best of both styles. It had designed and manufactured contemporary style homes for several decades when in 1983 it bought the Justus Company, a producer of log homes in the Pacific Northwest. Today Lindal leads the industry as the largest manufacturer of cedar homes in the world.

The company markets both lines of homes—Lindal and Justus—to an upscale audience. Lindal makes all its houses of kiln-dried wood for excellent fit. It uses one- or two-inch vertical cedar siding, with attractive interior finishing and heavy insulation. The houses' post-and-beam construction means that dividing walls are not load bearing, making possible a wide variety of interior designs. Justus homes, built with horizontal log construction, feature four-inch-thick timbers that provide natural thermal insulation. Customers can mix and match floor plans with roof styles. The company assembles materials for these build-it-yourself homes and numbers the parts at its manufacturing plants in Vancouver and Seattle.

As a new Lindal dealer you must put down a $5,000 deposit against the purchase of a model home for yourself, unless you already own a Lindal home, from which you will sell the company's product. Once you have etablished your business, Lindal will finance your purchase of another house, which you will build at a commercial site. Initially, the company pays you a commission of 15 percent on the houses you sell. Your commission increases to 20 percent once you sell $100,000 (at wholesale prices) worth of houses in a given year.

Training takes place at a four-day seminar in Seattle. You pay a $300 fee and your travel and lodging expenses. Topics covered include pricing, sales, financing, construction, advertising, and public relations. You will also tour the Seattle factory and inspect a display of the company's homes. Lindal requires you to attend regional training seminars twice a year, and a company representative will call on you monthly at your place of business.

Marketing, a company strong point, begins with the printed materials in your franchise package. The Lindal/Justus plan books, which prospective customers purchase from the company, feature lavish color photographs of house exteriors and interiors, and have sold millions of copies. The company spares no expense to make these books strong marketing tools—the most recent one cost about $350,000 to produce.

Many plan books sell through Lindal's extensive national advertising. The company's ads appear in *Better Homes & Gardens, House Beautiful, Home,* and *Country Living*. It pinpoints the professional builders' market through specialized periodicals like *Engineers* and *Architectural Digest.*

Franchised dealers benefit directly, as well as indirectly, from these ads. When people from your area order a plan book through an ad, they get a personalized letter with it, which includes your name and address as the company's local distributor. You will also receive a list of the names of those who have purchased plan books on mailing labels so that you may market directly to them yourself. Lindal also joins its franchisees in cooperative advertising.

The company sells commercial distributorships and subdivision distributorships in addition to the standard franchise.

For further information contact:
Lindal Cedar Homes, Inc., Box 24426, Seattle, WA 98124, 206-725-0900

New England Log Homes

Initial license fee: $7,500
Royalties: $3,000 per year
Advertising royalties: None
Minimum cash required: $50,000
Capital required: $150,000
Financing: None
Length of contract: 5 years

In business since: 1969
Franchising since: 1970
Total number of units: 87
Number of company-operated units: 1
Total number of units planned, 1990: 155
Number of company-operated units planned, 1990: 5

Had Abraham Lincoln been born in one of the log houses young families put up today, his political backers might not have made such a big deal about it. While inexpensive, there's nothing humble about these houses. Indeed, they have all the comforts of . . . well, of home.

Perhaps you've seen the advertisements New England Log Homes dealerships place in magazines like *The Atlantic, Sunset, House Beautiful, Bride's, Family Circle,* and *The Mother Earth News.* They emphasize the units' ease of construction and stylishness. The cut-to-fit logs make on-site cutting unnecessary, and precut gable ends support the roof. Purchasers can choose from over forty basic models, ranging from 300 to 3,000 square feet, with various design options for each. The logs are guaranteed fumigated and in compliance with the specifications of the three national code agencies. And the company guarantees its weather-tight sealing system. The company can keep down the price of shipping because the logs come from one of its regional plants, located in Great Barrington, Massachusetts; Lawrenceville, Virginia; Houston, Missouri; and Marysville, California.

Franchised dealers would not want to exaggerate the ease with which a person can successfully construct one of these buildings. The logs weigh between 125 and 150 pounds each, and the customer must lift them by a crane to build a second story. And flooring, plumbing, and heating are not included in the deal. Nevertheless, handy customers can build the shell of the building themselves in three to six weeks, saving about a third of the cost of having the shell built for them.

When New England Log Homes (NELHI) started up its business, do-it-yourselfers loomed larger in their trade than they do now. In recent years there's been a trend toward turnkey units—already built and ready-to-live-in—as the popularity of this kind of house has brought more people into the market who want the building put up for them.

What can that mean for you, the NELHI franchisee? Possibly more profits, if you have the ambition to work for them. NELHI points out that the increasing emphasis on turnkey buildings could provide a fine opportunity for you to start an affiliate contracting business, wrapping up the purchase and construction of a log home in one simple package for your customers. And your customer base will extend beyond home buyers. Sporting goods stores, restaurants, ski resort lodges, antiques shops, and churches also occupy NELHI buildings. And these clients will almost certainly want a contractor to build the structure.

As a NELHI dealer you get an initial discount on your model log home, which you locate at a site selected by you but approved by the company. If you choose to make it your home as well as your office, you not only save money on your living expenses, but also get a tax advantage in the bargain—not to mention the sales advantage of showing prospective buyers that you practice what you preach.

The company wants to make sure you are thoroughly familiar with their Total Building System so you can offer technical advice to your customers. It will teach it to you during the training you will undergo at company headquarters in Hamden, Connecticut. You pay for travel, room, and board related to the training. In addition to technical knowledge, you will also get a grounding in sales techniques. Your regional sales manager will be on site to help you start your business. The company also provides an annual regional refresher training session, which you must attend.

NELHI dealer support includes lists of people in your region who have sent inquiries to the company in response to its extensive national advertising. You may purchase miniature models of log homes to use at home shows, and the company will pay part of the rental for space at these shows. You can distribute NELHI's promotional color photographs of finished homes to potential customers, and there is also a cooperative advertising plan.

For further information contact:
Franchise Director, New England Log Homes, 2301 State St., P.O. Box 5427, Hamden, CT 06518, 1-800-243-3551

Stained Glass Overlay, Inc.

Initial license fee: $34,000
Royalties: 5%
Advertising royalties: 2%
Minimum cash required: $45,000
Capital required: $45,000 to $66,000
Financing: None
Length of contract: 5 years

In business since: 1974
Franchising since: 1981
Total number of units: 260
Number of company-operated units: None
Total number of units planned, 1990: NA
Number of company-operated units planned, 1990: NA

Traditional interior design has made a comeback in recent years. Tired of the slick—and often impersonal—decorative elements that dominated residential and commercial design in the sixties and seventies, many people have begun mixing the old with the new. Refinished antique furniture, American folk crafts, and stained glass have grown in popularity among those interested in creating attractive, comfortable home and business environments. Stained Glass Overlay will put you in the business of selling and installing simulated stained glass in both residences and businesses. As part of your franchise, you will also receive the right to distribute the company's, oak, mahogany, and beveled glass doors.

Your exclusive Stained Glass Overlay territory will cover an area with a population of about two hundred thousand. You are not required to have a store or a showroom. The company will offer advice on setting up shop, but how you do it is entirely up to you.

The franchisor pays for the airfare to its training site in Costa Mesa, California, for you and one other person, but you pay for lodging and living expenses during the six-day course. Training covers color coordination and all details of fabricating and installing stained glass. As part of your instruction, you will make sample products and put together custom installations. The training will also include material on bookkeeping, marketing, and sales.

You can expect to receive periodic technical updates and managerial assistance via phone contact with the franchisor—daily if necessary. However, Stained Glass Overlay reserves the right to charge by the hour for more extensive posttraining assistance if management feels that such requests for consultation are "excessive." On the other hand, the company notes that since it began franchising, only one franchisee has needed this type of refresher training. Semiannual regional meetings and annual national meetings provide additional opportunities for advanced training.

Your franchise package contains everything you need to get started in the stained glass business. Stained Glass Overlay sells supplies to franchisees at a profit, although you can buy your supplies elsewhere after getting company approval for your source. The franchisor states, however, that it is currently the only major supplier of the material you need.

You must do a minimum level of business to retain your franchise. At the time of this writing, the company requires a gross sales revenue of $50,000 in your first thirty-six months in business and $30,000/year gross sales revenue thereafter.

The company advises that the Midwest and the East offer the best opportunities for its franchisees.

For further information contact:

Jim Fitzpatrick, Stained Glass Overlay, Inc., 151 Kalmus Drive, J-4, Costa Mesa, CA 92626, 1-800-654-7666; in California: 1-800-367-8542

Laundry and Dry Cleaning

Dryclean-U.S.A.

Initial license fee: None
Royalties: $250/month
Advertising royalties: $300/month
Minimum cash required: $35,000
Capital required: $35,000 to $70,000
Financing: Some financing available for equipment
Length of contract: NA

In business since: 1977
Franchising since: 1977
Total number of units: 145
Number of company-operated units: 51
Total number of units planned, 1990: NA
Number of company-operated units planned, 1990: NA

When you drop off your shirts, blouses, and suits for cleaning, you patronize one of the biggest retail businesses in America. The 25,000 dry cleaning stores in this country employ about two hundred thousand people. The machines these services use to dry-clean your clothes only look forbidding and complicated. In fact, they operate much like your household washing machine, except that they use a solvent instead of soap and water. And pressing is simply ironing on a larger scale.

All this suggests that you don't need special mechanical skills or knowledge to succeed in the dry cleaning business. That's the point that Dryclean-U.S.A. representatives will make when you discuss the purchase of a franchise with them. They will also emphasize the crucial choice of location in establishing a profitable dry cleaning business. The single most important thing from the customer's point of view—aside from good service and competitive prices—is convenience. In a "drop-off" business, the store must be near other places that customers frequent, like supermarkets. Dryclean-U.S.A.'s site selection research, conducted by a full-time expert staff with years of experience, offers franchisees a distinct advantage over going it alone.

In addition to helping you choose a location and negotiate a lease, Dryclean-U.S.A. will teach you the dry cleaning business at a regional training center. You and your manager will get a thorough grounding in processing, spotting, pressing, packaging, quality control, customer service, public relations, and employee training. The company will gear the training, a mix of classroom work and hands-on experience in a store, to your needs and abilities, although most people gain proficiency in about six weeks.

You and your manager will get further training at your store before it opens, and the company will arrange for the delivery of your equipment, which it will install and test to make sure it operates smoothly. The company will provide ongoing instruction in new equipment and processes.

You will find Dryclean-U.S.A.'s expertise in promotional activities particularly valuable to you in your new business, since your customer's dry cleaning needs change with the season. You will need to bring your various services—cleaning down comforters before winter comes, for example—to your customer's attention as each season approaches. Throughout the year the franchisor will give you advice on advertising and makes available a special grand opening advertising package at a nominal charge.

Currently available locations include Arizona, California, Florida, and Texas.

For further information contact:
Dryclean-U.S.A., 9200 South Dadeland Blvd., Penthouse 25, Miami, FL 33156, 305-667-3488

Duds 'n Suds Corporation

Initial license fee: $27,500
Royalties: $450/month
Advertising royalties: 2%
Minimum cash required: $50,000
Capital required: $160,000 to $210,000
Financing: limited
Length of contract: 10 years

In business since: 1983
Franchising since: 1984
Total number of units: 34
Number of company-operated units: 8
Total number of units planned, 1990: 675
Number of company-operated units planned, 1990: 175

Remember the dingy old laundromat in your neighborhood? The one with the narrow corridors between lines of washers and dryers? Remember being bored to death while you waited for your wash to be done? Forget it. These days, a "night out" could mean going to the laundromat. Put your wash in the machine; then turn to the large-screen TV, play a video game, or shoot some pool. Then hoist a long cool one at the bar. You might even meet somebody interesting. And, you would never even leave the laundromat while doing any of this.

Phil Akin, who has developed just such a business, was a young man with an interesting idea just a few years ago. The offspring of parents in the coin laundry business, Akin earned money while a student at the University of Iowa by installing machines in frat and sorority houses. Then he opened his own laundromat—strictly conventional—in a nearby town. When a store became available in a shopping center in Ames (the location of the University) he rented it for still another laundromat, even though it had more space than he thought he needed.

What Phil Akin did with that space was the beginning of something big for him—and maybe for you. Knowing that his operation needed to draw large numbers of young single people who rented apartments, he turned the store into a place that would attract them. He grouped the machines in small bunches on islands, with chairs nearby. "The one thing that is important to a Duds 'n Suds store is that open, spacious look," says Akin. A typical Duds 'n Suds is decorated with ceramic tile, carpeting, and oak and brass fixtures. He also added entertainment and refreshments: soft drinks and munchies as well as draft beer.

Phil Akin's ideas were more than just clever and novel: They also cut costs and increased business. Grouping his machines in bunches reduced energy consumption. Changing the image of the laundromat experience brought in the customers, the eighteen- to thirty-five-year-olds, many of them professionals who rent apartments. Machine usage tells the tale. In a typical laundromat, machines are used about five times a day; this chain's machines go through the cycle twelve times in a day.

The company is actively seeking new franchisees, especially in Canada. If you're one of its future licensees, the company will select your store site, negotiate your lease, and hand you building plans. Stores do best in areas where at least 20 percent of the population consists of professionals, ages eighteen to thirty-five. Although you are free to buy equipment and supplies from whomever you like, the company states that most franchisees buy through it, taking advantage of volume discounts. Training will last a week at Ames, Iowa (you pay for transportation, food and lodging), and will cover management, bookkeeping, inventory, advertising, maintenance, and laundry procedures.

Company representatives will not only attend your grand opening, they will also help set up the advertising that will get you off with a big splash. Should you encounter any problems once you're under way, retraining will be available. The regional company meetings, held quarterly, will give you an opportunity to critique the operations of your peers as well as get valuable feedback from them about your own store. Company personnel will visit you at least three times a year, both to assist you and to inspect your operations.

Duds 'n Suds is flexible. Whatever works—within reason—to draw in customers at your location is fine with the company. That could be slot machines in Las Vegas or tanning beds in the Midwest ("Beach While You Bleach" is how Phil Akin describes this lure).

Franchises haven't encountered any problems in obtaining licenses to sell beer. Stores sell the brew to laundry customers only. Should you meet any resistance in getting a local license, a special Duds 'n Suds videotape will help you explain the inclusion of beer in your operation. So far, it's worked every time.

For further information contact:
Bob Schutz, Duds 'n Suds, P.O. Box B, Welch Station, Ames, IA 50010, 515-292-4626

Martin Franchise, Inc.

Initial license fee: $16,000
Royalties: $1,500/year
Advertising royalties: None
Minimum cash required: $50,000
Capital required: $127,000 to $216,000
Financing: The company will help you find sources of financing.
Length of contract: 3 years

In business since: 1949
Franchising since: 1949
Total number of units: 1,100
Number of company-operated units: None
Total number of units planned, 1990: NA
Number of company-operated units planned, 1990: NA

Before the late 1940s, this business could not have existed. The biggest selling point of Martinizing dry cleaning stores is that garments, cleaned on premises, can be be ready in as little as an hour. But until the late forties, highly flammable solvents, the only ones available for dry cleaning, could not be used in densely populated areas. Typically, dry cleaners sent out for processing clothes dropped off at their local stores, and customers could not get them back for as much as ten days. A substance called perchloroethylene changed that, making possible this very successful business.

Martin, the largest dry cleaning franchisor, stresses the importance of store image in the $2.2-billion-a-year dry cleaning business. Most small independent stores, the company says, look dingy and unappealing to the consumer, creating a golden opportunity for Martin stores, with their bright, airy appearance. The company adds that, with the increasing use of natural fabrics and the rise in the number of two-career families, the demand for dry cleaning services will go up sharply. Martin's quick processing, offering consumers convenience, puts its franchisees in a good position to take advantage of this increase in business. (Some Martin franchises add to their profits by supplementing dry cleaning with shirt laundering and alterations.)

Just as Martin offers consumers convenience, it offers franchisees efficiency. The company, through much experience, has developed a store layout based on a design it calls "Work Flow." Martin systematizes the entire dry cleaning process, from the moment the customer brings in garments to the final delivery of those cleaned garments into the customer's hands, reducing all unnecessary movement. This not only speeds the cleaning process, it reduces the cost. The company says it supplies state-of-the-art dry cleaning equipment, and you can consult the company's experts via a hot line on any problems related to the machines.

You do not need experience in the dry cleaning business to become a franchisee. But you—or at least your manager—will have to take a four- to five-week training program given either at company headquarters in Cincinnati or at a regional training center. The program consists of two weeks devoted to classroom work and two to three weeks of in-store experience. Management subjects covered include staffing and personnel management, advertising, marketing, and accounting. Technical skills covered include marking-in and tagging, spotting and cleaning, finishing, assembly, and packing.

The company provides guidance to its franchisees at every stage of the start-up process, beginning with site selection. Through its computer data base, the company will prepare for you a grand opening promotion specifically targeted to the potential customers in your area.

For further information contact:

Carole Bartley Johnson, Manager, Franchise Sales, Martin Franchises, Inc., 2005 Ross Ave., Cincinnati, OH 45212, 513-351-6211

Maid Services

Maid Brigade

Initial license fee: $7,900
Royalties: 7%
Advertising royalties: 2%
Minimum cash required: $14,000
Capital required: $14,000
Financing: None
Length of contract: 5 years

In business since: 1982
Franchising since: 1982
Total number of units: 133
Number of company-operated units: None
Total number of units planned, 1990: 265
Number of company-operated units planned, 1990: None

Recent changes in the American economy have provided fertile ground for the growth of services like housecleaning. Neither adult in the increasing number of two-income families really has the time to clean house. And with their increased income, why should they have to perform this task when they can easily pay others to do it? In addition, young professional singles who work long hours and make good salaries can also afford to pay someone else to clean their home.

Maid Brigade franchisees take advantage of this growing market by providing speedy, efficient housecleaning service through a system of four-person cleaning teams. Each team cleans several homes a day, carrying cleaning equipment and supplies (except for floor wax, which clients supply) with them from house to house in company cars. Maid Brigade owner-operators keep numbered keys to their customers' homes in their office, unless customers prefer to leave a key for the cleaning team in a concealed place. Customers pay simply by leaving cash or a check on their kitchen table.

The franchise package from Maid Brigade includes uniforms, equipment—featuring two commercial duty vacuum cleaners—and supplies for your first team of maids. You also receive 15,000 advertising mailers and pamphlets, stationery supplies, route logs, customer record forms, and decals for your first company car. In addition, you can bond your employees through Maid Brigade.

Your week of training in the Maid Brigade system will take place either in Atlanta or Toronto. Your license fee covers this instruction, but you pay for travel and lodging. The training will include field experience with a Maid Brigade team as it cleans customers' homes. Classroom work will cover all aspects of personnel, including interviewing, evaluation, and training. Administrative topics include payroll, scheduling, dealing with complaints, insurance and bonding, vehicles, key control, and the company's optional scheduling computer software. You also learn about marketing, with units on advertising, promotional mailings, the competition, and pricing.

Maid Brigade offers a special fleet-leasing plan to its franchisees through the Gelco vehicle leasing company. The plan requires no down payment and offers discount rates. Through it you can lease a white Chevrolet Cavalier station wagon with special options added for Maid Brigade.

To assist you with your local promotional campaign, Maid Brigade supplies you, where available, computer-generated market research based on the demographics of your area.

Maid Brigade has no requirements about your place of business—you can even work out of your home—nor does it require you to buy any products from the company.

For further information contact:
Don Hay, Maid Brigade, 850 Indian Trail, P.O. Box 1901, Lilburn, GA 30247, 404-564-2400

Merry Maids, Inc.

Initial license fee: $17,500
Royalties: 7%
Advertising royalties: None
Minimum cash required: $17,500
Capital required: $10,000 to $15,000
Financing: None
Length of contract: 5 years

In business since: 1980
Franchising since: 1980
Total number of units: 325
Number of company-operated units: 1
Total number of units planned, 1990: 1,000
Number of company-operated units planned, 1990: 1

Merry Maids, the largest franchisor of home-cleaning services, sells a systematic cleaning service in which two-person teams do the work. It also includes in its franchise package exclusive computer software that provides franchisees with an entire management system.

The convenience of Merry Maids' turnkey operation appealed to Paul and Evy Hatjistilianos, who own a Merry Maid franchise in Roxbury, Massachusetts. They chose to go with this franchisor rather than operate their own independent business because, as they put it, they wanted "to put the company's system to use immediately and start earning a profit rather than spending time reinventing the wheel."

The franchise fee covers a package of equipment, supplies, and the company's cleaning products—enough to equip two 2-member cleaning teams. Merry Maids manufactures and/or distributes over 250 home-cleaning products, which franchisees receive within two days after placing an order over the company's twenty-four-hour toll-free line.

Merry Maids trains its franchisees in its system at the home office in Omaha, Nebraska. The five-day course, taught by instructors experienced in running a franchise, covers hiring, training, marketing, selling, cleaning, and scheduling. Maria Surnovsky, who operates three Merry Maids franchises in California, found the training "very thorough and extensive."

The company provides guidelines on site selection, lease arrangements, and furnishing a Merry Maids office. You can consult company personnel on the problems of your ongoing business—they were "as close as the phone," say the Hatjistilianoses—but just as important is the support franchisees receive from their fellow Merry Maids operators. As a Merry Maids franchisee, you will get help from regional coordinators, who also are franchisees, and you can take advantage of the company's buddy system, in which established franchisees keep their eyes on new Merry Maids businesses and lend a helping hand to nearby units when they need it.

There are three regional meetings a year and a national convention in Omaha, where company franchisees can exchange hints, share experiences, and receive further assistance from Merry Maids professionals. The company also uses newsletters, videotape presentations, and special field workshops to extend help during the year. The Hatjistilianoses, while grateful for company help, also say they "appreciate the independence we have and do not wish for the home office to take a more active role in our business."

"Merry Maids is good old mid-America in the 1950s," according to Maria Surnovsky. It goes back to a time "when word of honor and handshakes meant a lot. Merry Maids is also the most organized and professionally run company I have ever been associated with," she continues. "I came out of large corporations and it's a breath of fresh air to be associated with a company like Merry Maids."

For further information contact:
Dale Peterson, Executive Vice President, Merry Maids, Inc., 11117 Mill Valley Rd., Omaha, NE 68154, 1-800-345-5535

Molly Maid, Inc.

Initial license fee: $12,900
Royalties: 8%
Advertising royalties: 2%
Minimum cash required: $4,000
Capital required: $4,000
Financing: Available up to $5,500
Length of contract: 10 years

In business since: 1984
Franchising since: 1984
Total number of units: 226
Number of company-operated units: 1
Total number of units planned, 1990: 1,000
Number of company-operated units planned, 1990: 75

This business' time has clearly come. With the United States now largely a nation of two-income families, people have fewer hours to devote to housecleaning. In some families, the wife has the double burden of both bringing in an income and doing the housework. Other families split cleaning chores between husband and wife. Still others, especially professionals with good incomes, hire a maid. People in that last category, and single professionals, provide a potentially huge market for franchised maid services.

As Frank Flack, president of Molly Maid, Inc., puts it: "Our customers are not prepared to engage day maids on a direct basis, as was common with their mothers. They don't have time to find them, provide transportation and meals, supervise their work, and find substitutes when they don't show."

The franchise connection is especially important for household services. The maid often works while people are away. They need to be able to trust the person they hire—difficult to do unless they find somebody with ironclad recommendations. A franchised name suggests stability and reliability.

Enter Molly Maid—and possibly you. Molly Maid bought the rights to use the name of a Canadian company that has operated a similar business since 1980. The Molly Maid system rests on two premises: Two people, working systematically, can quickly and efficiently clean a home, and clients will use a service that removes doubt and risk from the hiring of a maid.

Molly Maid franchisees outfit their maids in English-type standard maid's uniforms and give them a company car (with pink-and-blue company logo on the side) to drive to work. The maids bring equipment and supplies to clients' houses. Clients supply only wax if they wish their floors waxed. The maids work through the house systematically, vacuuming, dusting, and cleaning and sanitizing the kitchen and bathroom. The client also gets peace of mind, with a warranted service and bonded and insured maids.

Franchisees offer several inducements to persuade maids to give up some of their independence to work for the company. Benefits include paid hospitalization and vacations and use of the company car overnight (for the head maid of the team).

The company helps franchisees get off to a good start with a five-day training program at its headquarters in Ann Arbor, Michigan, which covers marketing, accounting, the training and hiring of employees, and the Molly Maid systematic cleaning method. The company also helps you to actually open your business.

Gerri Immel owns a franchise in Augusta, Georgia. She expressed satisfaction with the company's initial help: "Molly Maid helped me with insurance, bookkeeping, organizing in general. They supplied me with eight years of experience. I feel that the strongest points of their training was the one-on-one contact with existing Molly Maid franchises and Molly Maid workers."

Molly Maid maintains a toll-free number to provide franchisee support when needed. A company representative visits you at least two or three times a year, and you also have the opportunity to get support and exchange ideas with other franchisees at annual regional meetings.

A Molly Maid franchise requires little start-up capital, no office space (you operate out of your home), and offers a considerable degree of independence. As Gerri Immel says: "I have all the freedom in the world. If I need help, they are there. If I don't need help, they leave me alone."

For further information contact:

Frank Flack, President, Molly Maid, Inc., 707 Wolverine Tower Building, 3001 S. State St., Ann Arbor, MI 48104, 313-996-1555

The Maids International, Inc.

Initial license fee: $7,500 to $11,500
Royalties: 5% to 7%
Advertising royalties: 2%
Minimum cash required: $30,000

Capital required: $30,000 to $100,000
Financing: Available for multiple offices
Length of contract: 5 years

In business since: 1979
Franchising since: 1981
Total number of units: 161
Number of company-operated units: None
Total number of units planned, 1990: 500
Number of company-operated units planned, 1990: None

The Maids doesn't just say it wants your business to grow, it gives you the financial incentive to increase your sales volume. In an unusual policy for a franchisor, The Maids will reduce your royalty payments when you pass certain set levels of sales.

The Maids, founded and still directed by prominent commercial cleaning and maintenance services experts, offers its franchisees a total of 175 years of experience. Before they began to sell franchises, the company's founders did professional time-and-motion studies to develop its four-person-team housecleaning system. You will receive the benefits of their specialized knowledge from the day you become a franchisee.

"Among the ranks of The Maids franchisees you'll find both active and retired corporate executives, lawyers, scientists, teachers, and engineers," says company head, Daniel J. Bishop. "Most of them are also investors who buy two or three territories, as opposed to mom-and-pop operators who have one fast food store." In fact, about 70 percent of The Maids franchisees own more than one unit.

The company believes in thoroughly preparing its franchisees for their new careers. A three-week counseling period precedes your formal training at the company's Omaha, Nebraska, headquarters. In Omaha, you and your management staff learn personnel, marketing, promotion, pricing, bookkeeping, and computer operation from The Maids' professional corporate trainers. In addition, you receive videotapes that will help you train your crews, plus instructional tapes on how to handle special projects like carpet, upholstery, oven, and floor cleaning. Further counseling during the three weeks following your training prepares you to open your business. An 800 number provides you with easy access to help at any time.

Dave Meiers, a franchisee in Greenbay, Wisconsin, is enthusiastic about The Maids training program. "We send our managers back for training once a year," he says. Not only do they receive refresher training, "they also get their batteries recharged." The Maids' ninety-two-piece supply and equipment package will allow you to put two cleaning teams in the field right away. You have the option of buying supply refills from the company or purchasing them elsewhere. The Maids' vehicle-leasing program also wraps up all your transportation needs in one package. You can lease vans from a dealership in Omaha and have them delivered to you through an affiliated dealer in your community. The cars come with the company logo and your phone number already painted on the side.

The Maids' computerized management system will permit you to spend more time managing and less time keeping records. You can lease or purchase your IBM or compatible computer at a special price, and it comes with customized software that will handle customer and personnel records, scheduling, income and tax reports, and payroll.

The Maids franchise also features one of the most comprehensive insurance packages in the industry. If you choose to purchase it, it will cover liability, crime, property damage, and advice from the insurer on loss-control procedures.

The Maids encourages you to do extensive local advertising through its cooperative advertising program. An advertising agency will place your yellow pages display, and The Maids will supply you with promotional items. The company also provides material for you to use in all advertising media, including a recorded jingle for radio spots.

For further information contact:
The Maids International, 5015 Underwood Ave., Omaha, NE 68132, 1-800- THE-MAID

Miscellaneous Services

Dial One International, Inc.

Initial license fee: $6,500
Royalties: $400 to $2,000/year
Advertising royalties: $300 to $800/year
Minimum cash required: $10,000
Capital required: $6,000 to $20,000
Financing: Available in some areas
Length of contract: 4 years

In business since: 1982
Franchising since: 1982
Total number of units: 833
Number of company-operated units: None
Total number of units planned, 1990: 6,000
Number of company-operated units planned, 1990: None

Your roof leaks, the lights in the basement flicker, the porcelain in your bathtub is cracked, the neighbor's kid hit a baseball through your window, or your air conditioning is on the fritz. All this is not likely to occur all at once, but each is common in the life of a homeowner. If you had one of these problems, would you be able to find a repair person in whose skill and honesty you had absolute confidence? How long would it take you to find help?

Most homeowners know one or two people they can rely on for basic repairs and services. But few people would know where to get a *good* gardener, exterminator, locksmith, tile and ceramic person, carpet cleaner, *and* furnace repair person. Even asking your friends for recommendations has its limits.

Everyone knows what it's like to hire somebody to perform one of these services simply by picking a name out of the yellow pages. You could end up with a stiff bill for shoddy work. So it would be good to know of a company that could put you in contact with and guarantee the skill and honesty of a wide variety of businesses engaged in property and personal services. And an independent business person (or contractor) who sells one or more of those services would find the use of that company's name and reputation even more valuable.

Dial One has just the people homeowners need for quality home services. Upholsterers, chimney cleaners, plasterers—you name it, Dial One can direct you to it. As the company puts it: "Everything from your roof to your rose garden."

The homeowner can find a Dial One franchisee in one of two ways. He or she can call information or look in the phone book under "Dial One." Or a franchisee may get a referral from another member of the Dial One family. As a franchisee you will have a directory of Dial One people available in your region in trades other than your own. Dial One franchisees generate a lot of business for one another through the referral system.

The company is careful about who it accepts as franchisees. Its reputation for reliability is, after all, its main selling point. You can therefore anticipate a thorough examination of your business' reputation—with other businesses as well as with your customers.

Your training as a Dial One franchisee involves participation in the company's Certified Manager Program, a forty-hour course covering money management, customer satisfaction, leadership skills, advertising, marketing, and equity building. You can draw on the company's expertise and experience as you convert your service or contracting business to a Dial One franchise, and Dial One will offer you supplemental instruction if you need it. Subjects typically included in this postopening training include the legal aspects of your business, tax issues, and business development.

The company places no restrictions on your sources of supplies. But you must display the Dial One logo prominently. That shouldn't be a problem. It's the reason you bought a franchise in the first place.

For further information contact:
John Hartfield, Dial One International, Inc., 4100 Long Beach Blvd., Long Beach, CA 90807, 213-595-7075

Dynamark Security Centers, Inc.

Initial license fee: $12,000
Royalties: 1% to 4%, depending on volume of business
Advertising royalties: 1%
Minimum cash required: $18,000
Capital required: $31,000
Financing: Up to 50%
Length of contract: 3 years

In business since: 1977
Franchising since: 1984
Total number of units: 172
Number of company-operated units: None
Total number of units planned, 1990: 400
Number of company-operated units planned, 1990: None

There is a reason Dynamark has made *Inc.*'s list of the top 500 fastest-growing companies in America. This well-managed franchisor of home security systems is in a field that grows with every new headline about the rising crime rate. It wasn't more than a few years ago that fewer than 2 percent of the homes in this country were protected by a security system. Now that figure has passed 10 percent. You need only turn on the news to understand what motivates that increase: fear of crime. One of every five homes in this country will be affected by a crime this year.

Awareness of the increasing crime rate has motivated some Dynamark franchisees to get into the security business. Richard B. Tom, now a Dynamark franchisee, recalls when he first got the idea. "I was an agent with Nationwide Insurance and we had a number of claims in a year's time for burglaries," he says. "I began to see that an alarm stopped those claims. I checked into the industry. I also read a lot of crime reports, and there was a recession going on in 1981. Crime was at its peak, so it made sense to get into the alarm business."

Dynamark's answer to the threat of crime—the product that Richard Tom now sells—is a system of electronics designed to detect danger in the house and alert the family. The network of sensors and digital controls sounds a warning if it detects fire, or intruders. The company cites a startling statistic gleaned from a report by the National Commission on Fire Prevention and Control, which argues for the inclusion of fire protection as an integral part of the home security system: The average American will see the fire department pull up to their house in response to a legitimate alarm at least once in their lifetime.

Dynamark markets two basic security systems. The smaller, less expensive one is geared mainly for apartments. The other is designed to protect a house, with sensors for ten windows. The electronics for these systems come from outside suppliers but are exclusively Dynamark's and are made to their specifications.

An additional service that franchisees market is called Dynawatch. Dynawatch provides twenty-four monitoring of customers' residences by tying their security systems into a telecommunications network. Then, if the system should detect an intruder or fire, it alerts a central monitoring station, where the person on duty summons the police or fire department. The client may also call for help in a medical emergency by pushing a button. In that case, the on-duty person follows the instructions for summoning help that the customer gave when he or she contracted for the service.

If you decide to become a Dynamark franchisee, you will train for six days at the company's training center in Charlottesville, Virginia, and for another week to ten days at your site, which will most likely be an office. The company believes strongly in reinforcing what it has taught you, especially in the light of your first experiences with the business. So after three months as a franchisee, you will return to Charlottesville for three more days of training.

You can receive aditional training at optional monthly classes at the training center. Every three months, the company conducts workshops around the country. Franchisees are never more than three hours' drive away from a workshop. Phil Stone, whose franchise is in Bridgeport, Connecticut, says "these workshops are so valuable that I will never miss one."

Phil Stone continues: "The security industry is no simple business. Most people don't accomplish in a lifetime what we've been able to do in just two years!" He describes his feelings about his relationship with the franchisor: "I'm very happy with our franchise arrangement. I'm also happily married. The success of each, I feel, is determined by the attitudes and integrity of those involved."

For further information contact:
Dennis Puleo, Dynamark Security Centers, Inc., P.O. Box 2068, Hagerstown, MD 21742-2068, 1-800-342-4243

Lawn Doctor

Initial license fee: $26,500
Royalties: None
Advertising royalties: 5% to 10%
Minimum cash required: $26,500
Capital required: $31,500
Financing: The company will help you put together a loan package.
Length of contract: 20 years

In business since: 1967
Franchising since: 1969
Total number of units: 301
Number of company-operated units: 1
Total number of units planned, 1990: 554
Number of company-operated units planned, 1990: 4

Picture a million acres of crabgrass and dandelion—enough to break a suburbanite's heart. Lawn Doctor cares for that amount of territory, and the lawns under its treatment no longer have such problems. Lawn Doctor franchisees have a curbside manner that has made the company number one in America in franchised automated lawn care.

"It was one of the least costly ways to get into my own business and get good training," says Robert Dekraft of his experience as a Lawn Doctor franchisee. He started his business in Fairfax, Virginia, because he "could see the growth potential for the future in the lawn-care industry," He adds: "I have applied myself diligently for sixteen years, and the rewards have been gratifying."

A Lawn Doctor franchise involves no inventory or real estate, so you can focus your attention on attracting customers and giving them good service. That service consists of seeding, weeding, feeding, and spraying lawns with liquid and granular chemicals using Lawn Doctor's Turf Tamer, a patented machine that looks something like a lawn mower. With Turf Tamer, you can cover a 12-foot-wide area with one pass and distribute four separate materials simultaneously over at least 1,000 square feet per minute—all evenly and accurately with only an hour of training. The self-propelled machine also saves you a lot of huffing and puffing.

You will get the training you need at the company's training center in East Windsor, New Jersey. In two weeks you will learn all aspects of the Lawn Doctor system, including sales, equipment maintenance, and agronomy. According to Robert Dekraft, the company has a "good training and retraining staff." Periodic local and regional seminars will enable you to get additional training after you start your business. In addition, to help you through your crucial first year of operations, the company will assign you one of its field representatives, who will keep in close touch with you, offering advice and guidance in your new endeavor.

Your franchise package includes hand tools and accessories, the right to lease a Turf Tamer, truck layouts and modifications, a bookkeeping system, and advertising and promotional support. You must lease Lawn Doctor's patented equipment—mainly the Turf Tamer—from them. You can buy or lease all other products and supplies from other companies.

For further information contact:
F.I. Reid, National Franchise Sales Director, Lawn Doctor, 142 Highway 34, Matawan, NJ 07747, 1-800-631-5660

Mr. Build International

Initial license fee: $6,000 to $12,900
Royalties: Average $90/week, with increases based on the Consumer Price Index
Advertising royalties: Approximately $70/week, with increases based on the Consumer Price Index
Minimum cash required: $20,000
Capital required: $15,000 to $35,000
Financing: None
Length of contract: 5 years

In business since: 1981
Franchising since: 1981
Total number of units: 450
Number of company-operated units: None
Total number of units planned, 1990: 1,700
Number of company-operated units planned, 1990: None

The management of Mr. Build, a conversion franchise for those engaged in the repair, maintenance, and remodeling of residential and commercial property, believes that today's skilled construction professionals must forge ties to a larger organization if they are to succeed. According to Mr. Build, consumers in the $100 billion property services market prefer to hire professionals who are part of a firm with an established reputation and a recognized name.

Mr. Build is an umbrella group offering the strength that comes with numbers to a myriad of tradespeople. Each entrepreneur in the organization makes referrals for other members. Professionals affiliated with Mr. Build include specialists in air-conditioning, cabinetry, deck installation, gardening, glass repair and services, insulation, janitorial services, locksmithing, masonry, plumbing, roofing, termite control, window and door installation, and many other services.

Franchisees, in the words of Mr. Build consultant Orla Coakley, "must be capable of making the transition from thinking like good tradespeople to planning and acting like good business people." The company's training program, given at its headquarters in Windsor, Connecticut, will help you make that transition. Topics covered include sales presentations, lead generation, business management, advertising and image development, staffing, and time management.

Mr. Build administers its franchising program through regional offices. Regional personnel will run refresher and updating seminars and training courses for you and your personnel, and you may consult them about any problems you come across in your business. They will also provide you with a list of company-approved suppliers.

When the need exists, regional offices will run special programs to assist franchisees. One such program, developed in Mr. Build's New England regional office, helped franchisees cope with the shortage of skilled workers during the 1986 building boom. The office set up a job bank, with advertisements in major newspapers and an 800 number to attract qualified tradespeople. The regional office passed on the names of applicants to franchisees, enabling them to fill many positions.

Mr. Build also sells master licenses to franchisees who take responsibility for developing operations in entire regions. Areas currently available for master licenses include the Midwest, Arkansas, Oklahoma, West Virginia, Kentucky, Tennessee, the Dakotas, Minnesota, Wisconsin, and Louisiana.

For further information contact:
Mr. Build International, Inc., One Univac Lane, Suite 402, Windsor, CT 06095, 203-285-0766

RainSoft Water Conditioning Company

Initial license fee: None
Royalties: $4,000 to $7,000/year
Advertising royalties: None
Minimum cash required: $10,000
Capital required: $20,000 to $50,000
Financing: some financing available
Length of contract: 5 years

In business since: 1953
Franchising since: 1963
Total number of units: 220
Number of company-operated units: None
Total number of units planned, 1990: 300
Number of company operated units planned, 1990: NA

RainSoft runs substantial national advertising for its water purification and softening systems, but it accomplishes some of its most important marketing through the news columns of your daily newspaper and the evening news on television. The company hopes consumers learn from the news that the water they drink is far from pure and, depending on where they live, possibly even harmful. RainSoft advertisements remind people who haven't been paying attention to this disturbing news that the water in some communities contains solvents, hydrocarbons, phosphates, nitrates, pesticides, detergents, metals, cyanide, phenols, and even radioactive material.

Even when it does not contain pollutants, most community systems supply hard water, often clogging toilet valves, forming scum on porcelain, leaving deposits on pots and pans, damaging washing machines and requiring you to use excessive amounts of soap to get your laundry clean, and harming water heaters. The company's equipment treats hardness while it purifies water.

RainSoft, the third largest water treatment company in America, has installed water treatment equipment at Michigan State University, the TWA flight kitchen in St. Louis, the Chicago Medical School, and the Dow Chemical company in Midland, Michigan, as well as in homes.

If you decide to become a franchised RainSoft dealer, the company will train you in all aspects of the business at its headquarters in Elk Grove, Illinois. You'll learn how to sell RainSoft systems to homeowners and commercial establishments. The company will also teach you the fundamentals of water treatment and how to install its equipment, which ranges from under-the-sink units to custom built systems that can serve an entire village. You can receive additional training through refresher courses given regionally eight times a year.

RainSoft will teach you an effective, dramatic sales method: how to do a simple drinking water analysis in your customers' homes. Seeing the sediment and other impurities in that water will capture your customers' attention. They may also be surprised by the price differential between bottled and treated water. The heavy, bulky bottles of water, whether delivered to the door or lugged home by the consumer, can cost as much as 20 to 25 times more than RainSoft conditioned water.

RainSoft promotes recognition of its brand-name through extensive advertising in national magazines like *Reader's Digest, Prevention, Newsweek, People Magazine, TV Guide,* and *Better Homes & Gardens.* The company's advertisements have also run on TV programs like *The Price is Right, Let's Make A Deal,* and *Hollywood Squares.* In addition, RainSoft sponsors the Mrs. America contest, and the winner appears in company advertisements and at promotional events.

RainSoft requires that you, as a dealer, use and sell only its equipment. However, the location of your business is entirely up to you.

For further information contact:
Dave Cole, RainSoft Water Conditioning Company, 2080 Lunt Ave., Elk Grove, IL 60007, 312-437-9400

Spring-Green Lawn Care Corporation

Initial license fee: $13,500
Royalties: 7%
Advertising royalties: 2%
Minimum cash required: $10,000
Capital required: $30,000 to $35,000
Financing: The company leases equipment and will offer financing for the purchase of additional franchises.
Length of contract: 10 years

In business since: 1977
Franchising since: 1977
Total number of units: 118
Number of company-operated units: 3
Total number of units planned, 1990: 278
Number of company-operated units planned, 1990: 3

Families with incomes over $22,500 own about 20 million of America's 52 million backyards and front lawns. They can afford to spend on home maintenance, so prospects for the sale of home lawn-care services look good. Currently, no more than about three million homeowners use such a service, but the increase in the number of two-income families has put leisure time at a premium. Growing consumer concern about the chemicals needed to treat lawns also encourages people to hire a professional who knows how to handle weed killers and fertilizers. And most homeowners know that beautiful and healthy trees and shrubs can add to the value of a house. All these factors kept the industry growing without a hitch during the recession of the early 1980s, and it topped $2.1 billion in sales by 1984.

Spring-Green thoroughly prepares you to open and operate your business, which you can run from your home. Robert O'Brien, a

Spring-Green franchisee in Morrisville, Pennsylvania, says: "They provided an excellent business plan format with which I easily obtained a business loan from a bank." The company's franchise package contains everything you need to begin treating lawns: a supply of chemicals, a Chevrolet heavy-duty pickup truck, a 300-gallon lawn-spray unit with hose and reel, and a rotary spreader. With this equipment, you can service twenty to thirty lawns a day.

You also receive the benefit of the company's technical expertise in this field. Spring-Green's founder and president, Bill Fischer, has a degree in horticulture. While you don't need that kind of background, the company's intensive training will teach you about lawn problems and make you competent to deal with them. By the time you arrive at company headquarters in Plainfield, Illinois, for your week of formal instruction, you will have spent a week with a pretraining home-study program. The instruction in Plainfield alternates classroom sessions with hands-on training at Spring-Green's local franchise. You pay only for your airfare to and from Plainfield. Once you return to your region, a company field representative will come to help out with your grand opening.

During your term as a franchisee, "The company provides many training seminars, where new ideas are provided for both franchise owners and employees. This constant use of new ideas and methods keeps us on top of the industry," notes Robert O'Brien. The topics of these seminars range from technical updates to business management, financial planning, marketing, and other such subjects. Robert O'Brien observes that franchisees can buy supplies "at a very economical price by using the purchasing clout of all the franchises," although you can buy from any vendor whose products meet Spring-Green's specifications. The company will send a field representative to your location to assist in your ongoing operation.

Spring-Green's accounting system minimizes the amout of time you have to spend on your books. Every week you will receive computer-generated reports on your sales performance and other important items. The company has special computer programs designed to handle the financial data of large franchises.

The company will set up a customized direct marketing program in your area and route responses to the mailing to you for follow-up.

For further information contact:

James C. Gurke, Director, Franchise Marketing, Spring-Green Lawn Care Corporation, P.O. Box 908, Naperville, IL 60566, 1-800-435-4051

14. The General Maintenance Industry

Contents

Acoustic Ceiling Cleaning

Clentech/Acoustic Clean

Initial license fee: $10,000
Royalties: 3% to 4%
Advertising royalties: 1%
Minimum cash required: $10,000
Capital required: $19,700 to $29,000
Financing: The company will counsel prospective franchisees on sources of financing.
Length of contract: 10 years

In business since: 1976
Franchising since: 1984
Total number of units: 300
Number of company-operated units: None
Total number of units planned, 1990: NA
Number of company-operated units planned, 1990: NA

Nearly every office building in the country has acoustic tile ceilings. An estimated 15 billion square feet of the tiles cover ceilings in the United States, and every square foot is continually soiled by smoke, dust, and air-handling systems. Have you ever wondered who keeps those countless acres of tiled ceiling clean? It's done by entrepreneurs like Richard Steht, a Clentech/Acoustic Clean franchisee from Naperville, Illinois, who says, "I'm a natural for this business." According to Richard Steht, if you have "management ability, definite financial plans and goals, and the support of your family," you can use Clentech/Acoustic Clean's state-of-the-art methods to make a tidy profit: Businesses everywhere always need reliable maintenance services.

Clentech will not allow anyone to purchase its cleaning solutions or application equipment unless that person has first been trained by them. This ensures that only qualified franchisees will handle the chemicals, virtually eliminating the chance of dangerous and costly errors on shoddy work. Only Clentech franchisees have access to the company's special formulas and techniques, giving them an edge over many of their competitors. And because the company sells only one franchise per 200,000 to 300,000 population, Clentech operators have a large pool of prospective clients. The state-of-the-art cleaning process restores customers' ceilings more effectively than a paint job and at a quarter of the cost of tile replacement.

Clentech's mandatory training program for new owners covers all the basics of acoustic tile-ceiling cleaning: solution selection, tile and soil identification, cleaning procedures, marketing, advertising, and introductory business management. Franchisees are given a $450 travel allowance to attend the training session at the home office in Minneapolis, Minnesota. Richard Steht suggests that, in addition to the instruction provided by Clentech, you "get help on what the company doesn't provide for you. If you don't have management and supervisory experience, you should take college or home-study courses in those areas to be sure you're really prepared to run your own business."

You can operate your Clentech franchise as a primary business or as a sideline to any other business you might have, and you can work from any location—even your home—because you service clients at their own locations. The company will help you get started by sending out press releases in your area and by being available for phone consultations. You will receive updates on techniques, products, and the industry through the Clentech newsletter, and you can attend the annual national Clentech/Acoustic Clean convention for insight into the problems and successes experienced by other franchisees.

Richard Steht has found that the Clentech/Acoustic Clean franchise system has helped him succeed where his previous independent efforts did not: "Not only does the home office answer all my questions when I call, they also give me sales leads, they research and test new methods, and the ship chemicals and supplies on the day I order them. This is all very important. I think Clentech/Acoustic Clean is great!"

For further information contact:
Gordon Hamilton, President, and Wayne B. King, Operations Manager, Clentech/Acoustic Clean, 2901 Wayzata Blvd., Minneapolis, MN 55405, 1-800-328-4650

Coustic-Glo International, Inc.

Initial license fee: $8,750 to $25,000, depending on territory
Royalties: 5%
Advertising royalties: 1%
Minimum cash required: $8,750
Capital required: $10,000 to $28,000
Financing: None
Length of contract: 10 years

In business since: 1977
Franchising since: 1980
Total number of units: 143
Number of company-operated units: None
Total number of units planned, 1990: 305
Number of company-operated units planned, 1990: None

Bruce Weldon, a Coustic-Glo franchise owner in Saint Louis Park, Minnesota, is enjoying "all the pleasures of owning my own business." So is Ray Kleman of Chillicothe, Ohio, who says his Coustic-Glo business has allowed him to break into "a market that had not yet been tapped." And Jeff Newby of Studio City, California, says his Coustic-Glo franchise is "growing into a big money-maker. We are developing a solid base of clients with repeat business."

The Coustic-Glo system is a safe, low-cost, effective means of cleaning suspended or sprayed-on acoustic ceilings, which can be provided to businesses and institutions without interfering with their normal schedules. The simple spray-on Coustic-Glo process not only cleans ceilings but improves acoustics, luminescence, and fire retardancy. Approved by the USDA, the FDA, and OSHA as safe and nontoxic, and praised by satisfied customers nationwide, Coustic-Glo's patented products form the basis of what Bruce Weldon calls a "unique service business with enormous income potential. The initial entry fee is low, and the business does not require large sums of money tied up in inventory."

While you maintain your clients' overhead assets, your overhead costs will remain low because you can operate your business from any site, even your home. Your franchise fee covers the cost of a comprehensive start-up package, which includes your equipment, supplies, and the Coustic-Glo products. And you will receive thorough training in how to run your business profitably. "We received three days of very sound training," recalls Jeff Newby. "In addition, our crew was trained by the company. The application training was excellent, and the sales and marketing training was good, although it was probably more useful to franchise owners in smaller markets than ours."

During initial training, Coustic-Glo emphasizes business plan development and will help you set goals and strategies based on its proven marketing and management techniques. And to make sure you get off to a running start, the company will provide you with ad materials and advice on purchasing advertising space and will issue press releases in your area. "A company representative spent three days at my location," says Ray Kleman. "This initial on-the-job training covered all phases of my business and was very useful."

The company's technical advisors and field representatives will pay frequent visits to consult with you and keep you informed about newly developed Coustic-Glo products. Bruce Weldon has found that "the traveling troubleshooter is very helpful, and of course the company is only a phone call away with a toll-free number." Coustic-Glo will help you get in touch with local branches of national clients so you can follow up on those accounts. Its numerous publications will update you on topics of interest, and its national advertising programs will inform potential customers about the services you offer.

"Every seven months there is a sales seminar, and the last one in Las Vegas was very exciting," Jeff Newby relates. Covering sales, applications, and new products, the semiannual seminars supplement the refresher training available at Coustic-Glo's headquarters in Minneapolis, Minnesota. In both initial and ongoing training and support programs, the importance of sales takes center stage. Marketing will be the backbone of your Coustic-Glo business, and Jeff Newby recommends that, "if you can't sell, hire someone who can."

But if you sell your services well, according to Jeff Newby, a Coustic-Glo franchise can prove to be "an excellent investment. We were billing work within one week of training, and we will bill three times our initial investment in the first year alone. The profit ratio is exceptionally high throughout the system, and there are several franchisees who are getting very rich." Ray Kleman agrees: "I have done well and feel my opportunity to grow is very good, because I have been prepared to work hard and follow the system." And Bruce Weldon notes, "My business has been successful because of the great relationship I have with the company. I appreciate their knowledge and support, but I'm glad I have the freedom to operate and control my own business."

For further information contact:
Scott Smith, Coustic-Glo International, Inc., 7111 Ohms Lane, Minneapolis, MN 55435, 612-835-1338

Carpet and Upholstery Cleaning

Chem-Dry Carpet Cleaning

Initial license fee: $9,900
Royalties: $103/month
Minimum cash required: 4,900
Capital required: $9,900
Financing: The company finances, at zero interest, the balance of the license fee after a $4,900 down payment. The balance is amortized for thirty months.
Length of contract: 5 years

In business since: 1977
Franchising since: 1977

Total number of units: 759
Number of company-operated units: None
Total number of units planned, 1990: 1,750
Number of company-operated units planned, 1990: None

Gary Sollee of Anaheim Hills, California, decided to buy a Chem-Dry Carpet Cleaning franchise after speaking with friends who operated their own successful Chem-Dry Service, and he's glad he did. "Chem-Dry is the most innovative franchisor in the U.S.," he says. "The main office gives me almost complete freedom in the management of my business, which is how I like it. And the returns on my investment have been phenomenal."

In 1977, Harris Research, Inc., developed and patented the Chem-Dry process, a unique "carbonated" carpet-cleaning system. Chem-Dry uses a nontoxic effervescent cleaning solution to lift dirt out of carpets without leaving behind dirt-attracting residue, or overwetting the carpet. This method, available only to Chem-Dry franchisees, has proved highly successful, and the company continues to improve the process. Franchisees can purchase carpet protectors that retard soiling, fungicides that prevent mold, and a citrus deodorizer, as well as recently developed drapery and upholstery cleaning formulas.

To provide you with a protected market area in which to grow, Harris Research sells only one Chem-Dry franchise per 60,000 population. Though the company has sold out some of its franchise regions, most market areas are still wide open, and the company seeks to expand in all areas of the U.S. and internationally. Within your territory, you are free to work full- or part-time, to set your own prices, and to develop your market at your own pace: Harris Research sets no quotas.

Your initial fee is virtually the only initial investment you need make because it covers a complete equipment package and enough cleaning solution to yield about twenty-five hundred dollars in gross receipts. The advertising package also included in the fee supplies you with everything you need to promote your business: a taped radio advertisement, brochures, discount certificates, slicks for print ads, letterheads, business cards, vehicle signs, uniforms, and other items that will help you establish a recognized name in your territory.

Conducted at the Harris Research headquarters in Cameron Park, California, or by videotape if you prefer, initial training occurs in two phases. First you will learn how to use the Chem-Dry system and maintain your equipment. According to Gary Sollee, "The Chem-Dry cleaning system is very simple and can be learned quickly." Phase two of your training consists of instruction in sales and marketing, employee training, management procedures, and basic accounting. Once you have completed the course in bookkeeping, the company will give you a complete bookkeeping set and a training manual, which has been time-tested to improve your operational efficiency.

Equipped with your advertising materials, bookkeeping set, and three VHS training tapes, as well as the Chem-Dry equipment and chemicals, your only further expense in opening for business will be a vehicle if you do not already have one and any miscellaneous licenses or telephone costs. The equipment fits easily into a small station wagon, so many franchisees use the family car until their profits warrant the purchase of a van exclusively for their Chem-Dry operations.

A monthly newsletter will keep you updated on new ideas and products and will let you know what's going on with other franchisees nationwide. In addition, you will receive new advertising materials developed by the Harris Research marketing department. The company conducts refresher training monthly or whenever you feel you need it, and by special request corporate staff will come to your location to update you or your employees. The annual convention keeps franchisees in touch with one another and corporate officers. And the main office is always available to answer your questions by phone or by mail.

You must use Chem-Dry products, available exclusively from Harris Research, in your business. your orders for supplies will be turned around quickly—usually within twenty-four hours—and your line of credit with the company allows you to pay for supplies on a thirty-day net basis.

As a Chem-Dry owner, you are truly an independent business in complete control of your franchise. The flat monthly fee means that the more you make, the more you can keep. Chem-Dry's elimination of the percentage-of-gross monthly payment not only allows you to keep a greater share of your profits, but it also answers one of the only complaints many franchisees (of other companies) make: As you become more independent and require less support from the franchisor, it only makes sense that you should have to pay a smaller percentage of your gross. But while the company's costs in maintaining you as a franchisee decrease, your payments to it increase—because your revenues increase. Harris Research has decided that, in the case of its own operations, the percentage-of-gross practice would be unfair. With a Chem-Dry Carpet Cleaning franchise, you truly have your own business. As Gary Sollee puts it, "Other franchises may bleed you dry. But if you have a positive attitude and are willing to work your tail off, Chem-Dry can make you wealthy."

For further information contact:
Steven M. Oldfield, Executive Vice President of Sales, Harris Research, Inc., 3330 Cameron Park Drive, Suite 700, Cameron Park, CA 95682, 1-800-841-6583

Coit Drapery and Carpet Cleaners

Initial license fee: $7,500 to $150,000, depending on population
Royalties: 5% to 7%
Advertising royalties: $55/month plus 10%
Minimum cash required: $35,000
Financing: None
Length of contract: 10 years

In business since: 1950
Franchising since: 1962
Total number of units: 54
Number of company-operated units: 8
Total number of units planned, 1990: 75
Number of company-operated units planned, 1990: 8

Coit Drapery and Carpet Cleaners is one of the largest on-site carpet, drapery, and upholstery cleaning services in the world, and the company plans to keep on growing. Its strategy for expansion is twofold: Coit continues to add new franchises in new locations worldwide while simultaneously adding new cleaning services to its product line.

Coit provides you with the tools you need to operate a successful carpet and upholstery cleaning business, and the leaves the rest up to you—if you want it that way. Why pay the franchise fees instead of striking out on your own? For two reasons, according to Coit franchisee Richard Routley of Costa Mesa, California: name recognition and training. "I have been a Coit franchisee for over twenty years and have built a service business with sales in excess of $2 million per year," he says. "It would have been very difficult to succeed to the extent I have without franchising."

As a Coit franchisee, you may operate from any location and use any equipment and supplies that meet the company's high standards. Coit will train you in all phases of operation for four weeks. Conducted at a Coit franchise near your location, training covers the technical, administrative, and marketing aspects of your business. Following your training session, a company staff member will come to your site to assist with plant and office layout, additional technical questions not covered in earlier instruction, and your kickoff advertising campaign. The company representative will work with you for three weeks after your grand opening.

Coit will continue its support program with constant updates, evaluations, and training for yourself and your staff. Both at corporate headquarters in Burlingame, California, and at local sessions, your employees will receive the instruction they need to become truly professional carpet and upholstery cleaners. The company maintains monthly contact with you to make sure business is going well and coordinates a cooperative advertising program for franchisees on a regional basis. Regional meetings, held quarterly at locations chosen by franchisees, and national franchise conventions keep you up to date on technical and business methodologies.

Richard Routley finds owning a Coit franchise "very rewarding. I have recommended the program to many people who now run successful franchises. The rewards aren't just financial—my success gives me a sense of worth."

For further information contact:
Dennis R. Duarte, Franchise Director, Coit Drapery and Carpet Cleaners, 897 Hinckley Rd., Burlingame, CA 94010, 415-342-6023, Ext. 224

Duraclean International, Inc.

Initial license fee: $13,900 to $26,800
Royalties: None
Advertising royalties: None
Minimum cash required: $5,900
Capital required: $5,900 to $9,800
Financing: Available on the lower priced dealerships
Length of contract: NA

In business since: 1930
Franchising since: 1930
Total number of units: 1,000
Number of company-operated units: None
Total number of units planned, 1990: NA
Number of company-operated units planned, 1990: NA

A Duraclean franchise is about as close as you can come to starting on a shoestring, but the potential income is substantial, especially if you get to the point where you're hiring other people to work for you. You can, however, run a Duraclean franchise in your spare time. According to the company, gross profits are in the 50 to 70 percent range on jobs that run from an average $120 for cleaning in somebody's home to thousands of dollars for your services at a commercial establishment such as a hotel.

Although you will clean carpets as your major activity in this business, cleaning upholstered furniture and drapes are other important sources of income. The potential market for these services, the company notes, is expanding rapidly. That's especially true in the case of upholstered furniture, where sales of cleaning services have risen 30 percent in the past four years.

Duraclean has been refining its products for over half a century. The company claims that the cleaning solutions you will be using are much better than the competition's because of a "foam absorption method," which gets the dirt out rather than temporarily pushing it deeper in where it can't be seen. Several national magazines have given the process favorable reviews, including *Parents*, which said: "The Duraclean process is one of the best."

Starting this business is relatively inexpensive, and you can do it in your spare time and with absolutely no previous experience. In fact, according to Duraclean, you do not even have to take the training offered by the school and can instead get started simply by reading their instruction manual and working for a while with a nearby cooperating dealer.

However, there is good incentive to take the training at the Duraclean school. The company will pay for your transportation, room, and meals. What's more, they encourage your spouse to come. Your spouse will have to pay for his or her transportation, but food and lodging will be paid for by Duraclean.

At the Chicago training center, you will get a thorough grounding in all aspects of the Duraclean system. You will learn, for example, about the properties of all major fabrics used in home decorating, how to remove spots and stains and, of course, how to operate the equipment you will be using on the job. The company will also teach you how to find customers, a vital activity in this kind of business. The course also covers routine business practices such as management and bookkeeping.

The tools of your trade, which are part of the franchising package, resemble the vacuum cleaner you use at home. The company provides a good starting supply of the chemicals and concentrates you will use with these machines. If you opt for their "Standard Plus" dealership, Duraclean's package will also contain products that will enable you to do water damage restoration and carpet repair. Still higher priced dealerships offer more elaborate equipment that can be mounted in a van.

Make no mistake about it; you have to hustle in this business. Cooperative arrangements with carpet and furniture dealers should get you referrals, and once your business is well established, you can expect about 50 percent of your sales to be to repeat customers, according to the company. But you will also have to make good use of the phone book and the telephone. Wherever you're located, there are likely to be businesses with carpeting in high traffic areas that could use your services—restaurants, motels, and offices, for example. It's up to you to go out and bring in their business. The company points out that since most other cleaners don't do furniture and drapes, you already have an edge over the competition in snaring this business.

Your dealership package will contain several promotional aids, including copies of articles in prestigious magazines praising the company's products, material to help you put together a yellow pages ad, and information about the best ways of promoting your service in the local media. Duraclean provides further market assistance with ads in national magazines like *House Beautiful* and *Interior Design*.

Duraclean says that its reputation for quality will enable you to charge about 42 percent more for your services than the competition (they give you a pricing guide to help you set your prices). They also say that the jobs you will be able to do using your initial shipment of supplies will enable you to earn back the cash you put down to start your business.

For further information contact:
Paul B. Tarman, Jr., Franchise Sales Director, Duraclean International, Inc., 2151 Waukegan Rd., Deerfield, IL 60015, 312-945-2000

Langenwalter Carpet Dyeing

Initial license fee: $15,000
Royalties: None
Advertising royalties: $100/month
Minimum cash required: $15,000
Capital required: $20,000
Financing: None
Length of contract: 3 years

In business since: 1972
Franchising since: 1981
Total number of units: 152
Number of company-operated units: None
Total number of units planned, 1990: 790
Number of company-operated units planned, 1990: None

A simple one-person operation requiring minimal inventory, you can run a Langenwalter Carpet Dyeing service from your home—even as a part-time operation. And yet this business is definitely high tech, using an exclusive hot liquid dye formula with a special cleaning solution.

Company founder Roy Langenwalter, once an aerospace chemist and engineer, opened a small chemical manufacturing business when he grew tired of working for others and not making enough money. While doing work for maintenance firms and carpet cleaning companies, he developed the formulas that form the basis of Langenwalter Carpet Dyeing.

Langenwalter Carpet Dyeing claims that 75 percent of the carpeting replaced by homeowners and businesses is in good physical shape and would look like new if dyed and cleaned. Until recently, consumers and business people took a chance having their carpets dyed, since dyes provided uneven results. But its process, according to the company, solves that problem, making it possible for franchisees both to clean and dye carpets and upholstery at a given location—all in one afternoon. The operation involves shampooing and coloring the carpet with a floor scrubber, then using a steam extractor to rinse, deodorize, and sanitize.

Langenwalter will pay for your transportion to Anaheim, California, for your training, which will take five days. The company also picks up the tab for your lodging. The comprehensive training covers equipment, color blending, dyeing, cleaning, fabric testing, patching and repairing, stain removal, chemicals, advertising and promotion, sales, and estimating. The company also offers refresher training at its headquarters, and Langenwalter will customize the course if you need to brush up on a particular aspect of the operation. You can consult the company on any problems that come up by calling Langenwalter's toll-free line during business hours.

The comprehensive Langenwalter franchise package includes everything from the equipment and chemicals you will need to start up your business to marketing aids like brochures, flyers, and signs. The package even includes a baseball cap with a company logo imprinted on it. You can buy the company's exclusive dye only from Langenwalter, but you can purchase all other supplies and equipment from the vendor of your choice.

For especially ambitious entrepreneurs, Langenwalter also sells area franchises. These cover a territory with a population of at least 3 million and can usually support at least sixty franchisees.

For further information contact:

Roy Langenwalter, Langenwalter Carpet Dyeing, 4410 East La Palma, Anaheim, CA 92807, 1-800-422-4370

Rainbow International Carpet Dyeing and Cleaning Company

Initial license fee: $15,000
Royalties: 7%
Advertising royalties: None
Minimum cash required: $10,000
Capital required: $10,000 to $13,000
Financing: Some financing available
Length of contract: 20 years

In business since: 1981
Franchising since: 1981
Total number of units: 975
Number of company-operated units: 2
Total number of units planned, 1990: 2,000
Number of company-operated units planned, 1990: None

If you would like to join a company that focuses on dynamic growth, consider a Rainbow franchise. Among the top franchising organizations in its line, this company is the youngest and the biggest. Ultimately, its plans call for the formation of a conglomerate called "Synergistic International," with capitalization of over $400 million.

Rainbow refurbishes expensive household and commercial carpeting at a cost considerably cheaper than replacing the carpets. The company emphasizes convenience in its service, since franchisees can use its chemicals and procedures to dye, tint, and colorize carpets on location, without inconveniencing customers for more than the few hours it takes to get the job done.

As a franchisee, you will train at the company's headquarters in Waco, Texas, where you will study the fibers, construction, and chemistry of carpeting. Instruction emphasizes management and motivational skills as well as the particular techniques and materials involved in cleaning carpets. Seminars and telephone contact with experts at the company via its toll-free lines (open sixteen hours a day) provide further training and support once you open for business. The company also provides training tapes. At its home office, Rainbow runs week-long training updates to keep you abreast of everything happening in your industry.

Rainbow manufactures its own equipment, chemicals, and dyes. However, you may buy from other sources if Rainbow approves them.

For further information contact:

Don Dwyer, Rainbow International Carpet Dyeing and Cleaning Co., P.O. Box 3146, Waco, TX 76707, 1-800-433-3322; in Texas: 1-800-792-3266

Stanley Steemer International, Inc.

Initial license fee: $33,847 to $200,000
Royalties: 6% (10% in parts of Ohio and California)
Advertising royalties: The company requires that you spend 10% of your gross sales on advertising.
Minimum cash required: $10,000
Capital required: $20,000 to $50,000
Financing: The company will finance 25% to 50% of your initial license fee and has a lease plan for vehicles.
Length of contract: 20 years

In business since: 1947
Franchising since: 1972
Total number of units: 253
Number of company-operated units: 20
Total number of units planned, 1990: 413
Number of company-operated units planned, 1990: NA

According to *Consumer's Research Magazine*, carpet manufacturers suggest steam cleaning when they indicate a preference for a cleaning method. Stanley Steemer is one of the biggest firms in the business of steam cleaning carpets and upholstery. In 1985 the company, which has grown steadily at a healthy rate, increased its sales 45 percent over the previous year.

The machinery used in performing this service remains largely in the franchisee's truck. Franchisees use the truck's engine as a generator to produce the steam they need to clean, and they bring only the cleaning nozzle and hose into the customer's home. Franchisees do not have to use customers' electricity and hot water for the operation, and customers do not have to worry about a service person lugging big pieces of equipment through their house. In addition to cleaning, Stanley Steemer franchises also offer Scotchgarding service and Lysol deodorizing, and sell the company's own brand of professional spot remover.

According to Phil Dean, a franchisee in Maryland Heights, Missouri, Stanley Steemer offers a combination of expertise and an effective product in the context of a franchising relationship that permits plenty of freedom. The company is "franchise-oriented," he says. "Stanley Steemer owns just enough branches to understand the needs of the franchisee."

The license fee varies, depending on the population of your exclusive territory, competition in the area, and the amount of advertising Stanley Steemer runs locally. The company does not specify any particular location or building type for your operation, but you must use its equipment and purchase supplies from designated sources.

You will train to run your franchise at Stanley Steemer headquarters in Dublin, Ohio. The five-day program, for which you must pay expenses other than tuition, covers marketing, accounting, customer relations, sales, public relations, and operation and maintenance of equipment, and gives you hands-on experience cleaning carpets. Once in business, you can call the company's toll-free number for any advice or help you might need, including on-site assistance from a field representative.

The company holds twelve regional meetings annually, aimed especially at your employees. These meetings provide an overview of the business and offer refresher training. At the annual convention, you have an opportunity to get an update on new cleaning techniques and marketing methods.

At your option, you can lease or purchase the company's computer system, which has 250 customized programs to handle everything from invoicing to inventory control. You can also participate in the company's new telemarketing program. Barbara Haydock, manager of the telemarketing division, says of this sales technique: "It is the most intrusive of all advertising, taking your message into your prospect's consciousness. For the business person who needs to reach out and touch a large number of people who are individually going to produce a relatively small ticket, it is the most economical and sensible way to *sell.*

Finally, Stanley Steemer expresses its commitment to quality service—and its faith in its cleaning techniques—in its customer guarantee: "We'll rub a white towel over your just-cleaned carpet. If any dirt shows, we'll stay and reclean it at no extra charge."

For further information contact:
Philip Green, Vice President and Director of Marketing,
Stanley Steemer International, Inc., 5500 Stanley Steemer Parkway, Dublin, OH 43017, 614-764-2007

Steamatic

Initial license fee: $10,000 to $50,000
Royalties: 5% to 10%
Advertising royalties: 5%
Minimum cash required: $10,000
Capital required: $15,000 to $50,000
Financing: The company may finance all or part of the initial fee.
Length of contract: 5 years

In business since: 1948
Franchising since: 1967
Total number of units: 202
Number of company-operated units: 12
Total number of units planned, 1990: NA
Number of company-operated units planned, 1990: NA

The Steamatic business is one of the less complex to get into. Your initial license fee will include everything you need to get started—except a van. You can operate your business out of any location, providing you have a telephone answering machine. And you can begin your operation within a month of signing your franchise agreement.

The Steamatic franchise fee covers the equipment and supply package you need to begin cleaning carpets, furniture, drapes, and vehicles for businesses and individuals, including a portable carpet and furniture cleaning machine and a portable furniture and drapery dry cleaning unit. You also receive from the company a three-month supply of cleaning chemicals, stationery and business forms, and advertising materials. The franchise fee is $28,000 for a territory with 100,000 or more people, $23,000 for one with between 50,000 and 100,000 people, $18,000 for 25,000 to 50,000 people, and $10,000 for a population of fewer than 25,000.

The continuing license fee also varies. You pay 10 percent the first year, 8 percent the second, and then successively 1 percent less per year until you reach 5 percent for the fifth and subsequent years.

Your training and equipment enables you to do general cleaning jobs and restoration work following fires and flooding. On occasion, the company may step in if a big accident or natural disaster in your exclusive franchise territory creates a restoration job you can't handle. If that happens, Steamatic will pay you a referral fee. Conversely, should the company solicit such business in your territory for you, you will pay a referral fee to the company.

Steamatic training takes place at its headquarters in Grand Prairie, Texas, and at training centers in Dallas and Fort Worth. Topics studied include fire and water restoration; carpet, furniture, and drapery cleaning; air duct cleaning; wood restoration; and deodorizing. Steamatic also instructs you in equipment use and marketing. You pay for transportation and living expenses incidental to your training.

As part of its ongoing support, Steamatic will consult with you by phone on any problems that arise and will provide field assistance if the company's management deems it necessary. The company will also show you how to set up an accounting system, and it will analyze your budget and finances at your request. A company representative will confer with you in person at least once a year.

You buy your own advertising, including your listing in the yellow pages. The company will supply television and radio commercial tapes, but *you* pay a fee to use them. You may also be required to participate in a cooperative advertising program.

Should you wish to expand your business, the company has a leasing program for additional cleaning machines.

For further information contact:
Steamatic, Inc., 1601 109th St., Grand Prairie, TX 75050, 214-647-1244

Janitorial and General Maintenance

Jani-King International, Inc.

Initial license fee: $8,500
Royalties: 10%
Advertising royalties: Up to 0.5%
Minimum cash required: $13,500
Capital required: $11,000 to $11,500
Financing: Minimum of $3,000 down payment required; remainder financed over a negotiable period as determined by each regional office
Length of contract: 10 years

In business since: 1969
Franchising since: 1974
Total number of units: 825
Number of company-operated units: None
Total number of units planned, 1990: 5,000
Number of company-operated units planned, 1990: None

"I'm probably one of the few persons that can honestly say, 'I've scrubbed toilets from Atlanta to Los Angeles'"—honestly and proudly, according to James Cavanaugh, president and founder of Jani-King. And it has made him wealthy.

Ranked the second most profitable franchise in America by *Venture*, number seven among the top twenty-five low-investment franchises and ninth among the twenty-five fastest-growing franchises by *Entrepreneur*, Jani-King stresses to potential franchisees that Jani-King operators function as business people, not janitors. At the same time, however, the company notes gladly that, according to the U.S. Department of Labor, janitors, and not computer or finance personnel, will constitute the fastest-growing job category between now and 1995.

In fact, most Jani-King franchisees have had some janitorial experience—although previous occupations have ranged from sweeping floors to teaching college students—and, at least at the beginning, the business tends to be a hands-on-the-mop operation. That can be an advantage, since you will clean most banks and office buildings—the main market for these services—between 6 P.M. and 9 P.M., enabling you to keep your present job while you supplement your income at night, and without having to hire a big staff. Once established, you may choose to spend most of your time managing others, although the company assumes that, even then, you will periodically check your employees' work.

By franchising this business, rather than having a huge, centralized organization responsible for all cleaning jobs, the company maintains a contract turnover rate half the industry's average. Each franchisee, working to build a strong business, either does the work directly or supervises others with care, and satisfied Jani-King customers have no reason to look elsewhere for janitorial service.

The company guarantees $1,000 a month worth of business. Major corporations like Hertz, General Motors, IBM, Avis, Frito-Lay, Boeing, Bank of America, and Xerox have used the service. Contracts can range from about $100 a month to the substantial sums that cleaning the Xerox Tower in Dallas brings in.

Franchisees receive a week of training at a regional company office. You pay for your travel expenses. Training covers cleaning techniques like dusting, disinfecting, vacuuming, stripping and waxing floors, and washing windows. You will also learn business techniques, such as bookkeeping, marketing, and personnel management. The company provides refresher training through regional seminars, self-study materials, and videotapes. You can call the company's toll-free help number for assistance with everyday problems.

The company must approve your office layout and decor. New franchisees receive, as part of the franchise package, basic equipment and enough cleaning supplies to last a few months, with refills available through the company at a discount. The equipment supplied does not include expensive machines, such as wax buffers, which you will have to supply yourself.

Jani-King's regional office will drum up most of your business and also do your invoicing. It charges you a finder's fee for that business and deducts the fee from clients' payments before handing them over to you.

For further information contact:

Jim Meeker, Jani-King International, Inc., 4950 Keller Spring, Suite 190, Dallas, TX 75248, 214-991-0900

ServiceMaster

Initial license fee: $5,450 to $11,500
Royalties: 4% to 10%
Advertising royalties: None
Minimum cash required: $5,350
Capital required: $10,700 to $19,800
Financing: The company finances one half the cost of the total franchise package.
Length of contract: NA

In business since: 1948
Franchising since: 1952
Total number of units: 3,250
Number of company-operated units: None
Total number of units planned, 1990: NA
Number of company-operated units planned, 1990: NA

ServiceMaster franchisees provide carpet and upholstery cleaning, postaccident and disaster cleaning, and general contract cleaning to homes, businesses, and institutions. The company's business statistics reflect its excellent standing in the cleaning industry: *Fortune* rated it the number-one service company in America. The company passed the $1 billion mark in revenues in 1985; and *Forbes* declared it first in return-on-equity among all industrial service companies. Yet, at the same time, it is one of the less expensive businesses to buy—and one for which you need no previous experience—and *Entrepreneur* ranked it number-one among low-investment franchises.

The company sells three different franchises. The basic franchise involves cleaning carpets and upholstery in businesses and homes. Most franchisees begin this business working alone. The second franchise concentrates on cleaning up, restoring, and deodorizing after fires, floods, explosions, and other accidents and disasters. The third type of franchise targets institutions, offering them regular cleaning services.

ServiceMaster offers a three-tiered training program. You will first receive a package of home-study manuals and audio-visual aids that explain and illustrate methods of running and building your business. At the company's headquarters in Downers Grove, Illinois, company experts will then teach you the basics of sales, operational procedures, and business management, and one of the company's local distributors will give you on-the-job training that includes an introduction to making sales calls.

When you're ready to begin your own ServiceMaster business, a company representative will spend two days in your hometown showing you how to set up a simple bookkeeping system and develop a marketing strategy. The company's field manager will keep close tabs on you during your first year, monitoring your progress and arranging for training in any areas in which you need additional work. And the company continually runs seminars, workshops, and conferences to update you on new methods and materials that you can use in your business.

Your franchise package includes everything you need to start your business, including stationery, initial chemical supplies, and even a company blazer. You must buy refills of the proprietary cleaning chemicals that you use in your business from your local ServiceMaster distributor.

ServiceMaster sponsors cooperative advertising for its franchisees. It will also provide you with prepared advertisements for your own advertising in the print and electronic media and will assist you in placing your yellow pages advertisements.

For further information contact:
ServiceMaster Residential and Commercial Corporation, 2300 Warrenville Rd., Downers Grove, IL 60515, 1-800-852-1212

Servpro Industries, Inc.

Initial license fee: $17,800
Royalties: 7% to 10%
Advertising royalties: 0% to 3%
Minimum cash required: $13,000
Capital required: $15,000 to $20,000
Financing: The company will finance up to 50% of your investment.
Length of contract: 5 years

In business since: 1967
Franchising since: 1967
Total number of units: 600
Number of company-operated units: None
Total number of units planned, 1990: 800
Number of company-operated units planned, 1990: None

Servpro aims to offer customers one-stop shopping for most of their house-cleaning needs, so its franchise licenses authorize Servpro operators to sell a wide range of services—carpet, furniture, and drapery cleaning; fire and flood restoration; janitorial and maid services; acoustic ceiling cleaning; deodorization; and carpet dyeing—using the company's name. Franchisees purchase supplies and equipment from Servpro, unless the company has specifically authorized another vendor.

Kathy Stone, a Richardson, Texas, franchisee for the past nine years, remembers how she decided on a Servpro franchise. She wanted to get into the cleaning business, but didn't want to get bogged down in technical details. "We have known others who have done it on their own," she says. "A great deal of their time and effort is spent in researching chemicals, literature, etc. Servpro provides most of this and leaves us free to do what we do best."

Through extensive training, Servpro will prepare you to perform and supervise a variety of cleaning services. Your classroom instruction will involve ten days of work at the company's national training center in Rancho Cordova, California. The course covers office procedures and filing systems, telephone sales, invoicing, accounting, cash flow, employee recruiting and training, advertising, and public relations.

Back home, you will work with a nearby established Servpro franchisee for two weeks—during which you will draw a salary—and will receive an on-the-job introduction to the Servpro system. A company representative will then spend two days helping you set up your Servpro business, accompanying you on your first sales calls. The representative will make sure that your facilities reflect Servpro standards, but the company does not require franchisees to rent any particular type of store or office. That representative will also assist you as your franchise grows, helping you with advice on specific problems that may arise. For Kathy Stone, access to such advice was "critical," especially once she got started.

Kathy Stone finds the company's ongoing training, offered at various meetings throughout the year, a great help. "Management and financial information are particularly helpful after you have been in business awhile. Sales and motivation training are also provided," she notes. The company sponsors four franchisee meetings a year in local areas, two regional conferences, and an eight-day national convention at a resort area. Servpro will refund 10 percent of your royalties each year as a "convention allowance" if all your payments to the company have been timely.

For further information contact:
Richard Isaacson, Servpro Industries, Inc., 11357 Pyrites Way, Rancho Cordova, CA 95670-0050, 1-800-624-6550

15. The Printing and Photographic Industry

Contents

Quick Printing and Photographic Services

American Speedy Printing Company, Inc.

Initial license fee: $37,500
Royalties: 5%
Advertising royalties: 2%
Minimum cash required: $30,000
Capital required: $90,000 to $100,000
Financing: It can be arranged to meet the individual needs of qualified applicants. Equipment is financed on a lease or a loan basis.
Length of contract: 20 years

In business since: 1977
Franchising since: 1977
Number of company-operated units: None
Total number of units planned, 1990: 2,000
Number of company-operated units planned, 1990: None

"Success is preparation meeting opportunity," according to Vern Buchanan, the founder, president, and chief executive officer of American Speedy Printing Centers, Inc. There are plenty of opportunities in the quick-printing business, which is entering an era of increasingly sophisticated technology. No longer just offset and photocopying, quick-printing shops now offer a broader range of services, from thermography to computerized phototypesetting. These smaller businesses claim a larger slice of the $24 billion printing industry pie each year. The opportunity is there, and American Speedy can help you prepare for success.

American Speedy grossed an estimated $55 to $60 million in 1985 and is one of the nation's three largest quick printers. The aggressive young company recently initiated Operation 2000, an ambitious plan to open 2,000 enters by 1990—and possibly go international. American Speedy is committed to the success of its franchised units, developed through a decentralized organization that does not include any company-operated stores. The company's marketing strategy is to promote its franchises as full-service "real" printers: more accessible than large commercial printers, yet prepared to meet all printing needs.

American Speedy is a franchise for owner-operators. The company feels that franchisees active in the day-to-day operation of their units can best realize the potential of a quick-printing business. As Vern Buchanan puts it, "We have franchise owners from all walks of life with different strengths and weaknesses, so it is difficult to identify the single most important ingredient [of the success of a quick-printing shop]. However, I would identify that the most common ingredient is hard work and a desire to succeed." Based on this philosophy, American Speedy provides complete support services to its franchisees to help their efforts pay off, and encourages successful owners to open multiple units.

American Speedy will work with you to find the best possible location for your printing center. You will then attend the two-week national training class, which prepares new owners in management, technical, and marketing operations, including accounting, credit collections, job pricing, and computer operation. When you graduate, American Speedy will refund to you your costs of attending the program at corporate headquarters in Birmingham, Michigan. The company will also help arrange a third week of on-the-job training at an existing center.

Prior to opening, operations staff help you review your preopening checklist and answer your questions regarding the layout of your center, leasehold improvements, signs, equipment, yellow page advertising, and any other topics that may need clarification. American Speedy has contracts with all of the major equipment suppliers, so you can take advantage of special dealer rates on equipment (which American Speedy will order for you), although you are under no obligation to do so. When equipment arrives at your shop, a company technical representative will install it.

A franchise consultant will spend a week with you to help you open your printing center, assisting you in every area from advertising to administration. The consultant will help you make sales calls to get your business off to a running start. American Speedy feels that the first ninety days of your operation are crucial to your business, and so they will do everything possible to ensure that your opening goes smoothly. The company provides funds for your cash drawer on opening day, your opening inventory and supplies, and offers financial incentives to encourage aggressive marketing. The home office will contact you each week for the first three months you are in operation to offer whatever support you need and will initiate a direct mail campaign to the businesses in your area.

As an American Speedy owner, you receive discounts on equipment and supplies, a quarterly advertising planner, regular newsletters, and the benefit of the company's research and marketing efforts. You can call the toll-free hot line at any time for assistance, and an American Speedy field consultant will make quarterly visits to offer support and advice. The company trains managers and production personnel for its franchisees and conducts seminars, meetings, and annual conventions to meet your continuing need for up-to-date information. Advertising co-ops in concentrated market areas can save you money by pooling your funds with other local franchisees' advertising monies and applying the combined resources toward purchasing advertising media.

For further information contact:
Robert S. Phillips, American Speedy Printing Centers, Inc., 32100 Telegraph Rd., Suite 110, Birmingham, MI 48010, 1-800-521-4002

Insty-Prints, Inc.

Initial license fee: $28,500
Royalties: 4.5%
Advertising royalties: 2%
Minimum cash required: $30,000
Capital required: $30,000
Financing: Available
Length of contract: 15 years

In business since: 1965
Franchising since: 1967
Total number of units: 330
Number of company-operated units: 4
Total number of units planned, 1990: NA
Number of company-operated units planned, 1990: NA

Think of all the printed forms you see in one day. At work, there are letterheads and business cards, standard business forms and special forms for specialized business needs. Depending upon where you work, you might also encounter stacks of resumes. And when you get home, there's the wedding invitation that came in the mail and the thank-you card from a friend for the condolence card you sent.

Print circumscribes modern life, much of it the kind of printing that small shops do in a short period of time. Did it ever occur to you that somebody makes a good living doing all that work? And that you could be that somebody? The quick-print industry has enough business to supply a good living to thousands of people. According to Insty-Prints, only about 25 percent of quick-printing work is currently being done by franchise shops. That, as the company sees it, leaves a lot of business that can be lured away from the independents by the brand-name recognition that can be built by national advertising and the purchasing clout that can be created by buying in volume.

Insty-Prints wants you to know that you can easily enter this field if you have the necessary finances. You do not need to know printing. Someone else can manage your store—or stores —someone whom the company will help you find and train if you wish. It only takes two to run an Insty-Prints store, and your franchise package includes free training for both.

If you do run things yourself, you may be delighted to know that this franchise keeps normal business hours. So you can have your cake and eat it too—at a normal dinner hour, with your family. Husband-and-wife teams, in fact, operate many Insty-Prints shops. One such family was formed when an Insty-Prints franchisee married one of his customers and brought her into the business. And it is interesting to note that women independently operate 35 percent of all stores in the chain.

The franchisor will supervise your site selection and building or remodeling work. A clean, efficient look is part of the company image, and your store has to reflect this. To make sure that it does, Insty-Prints will help you set up a layout that facilitates efficient work traffic.

You will learn good business management in your four weeks of training at Insty-Prints' Minneapolis headquarters as well as the nuts and bolts of running the machines you will use in your shop. A week of on-site training at your printing center will lead up to your opening day. After opening, you can get help via the company WATS line at any time.

Although you can ultimately run your store through a manager, the company insists that for the first few weeks you get your hands dirty and run it yourself. Insty-Prints wants you to get a feel for the way your business works. It wants you to know what you're doing, even if you finally pay somebody else to do it for you.

Of your initial investment, $43,000 goes toward an equipment package and $5,000 goes for inventory. After that, you can choose your own sources for supplies, although the company emphasizes that you can reduce your costs by buying through it.

The initial investment you make for an Insty-Prints franchise and the royalties you pay fall at the low end in the quick-printing industry. To further tempt you, the company offers a "5-pak" area development agreement with which you can secure the right to open as many as four additional stores in the future, at a franchise fee of $11,750 per store.

For further information contact:

Clifford E. Cochrane, Jr., Insty-Prints, Inc., 1215 Marshall St. NE, Minneapolis, MN 55413, 1-800-228-6714

Kwik-Kopy Corporation

Initial license fee: $41,500
Royalties: 4% to 8%
Advertising royalties: 2%
Minimum cash required: $46,500
Capital required: $78,200
Financing: The company will finance all but $10,000 of the franchise fee at simple interest over 120 months; equipment can be leased for 96 months.
Length of contract: NA

In business since: 1967
Franchising since: 1967
Total number of units: 972
Number of company-operated units: None
Total number of units planned, 1990: NA
Number of company-operated units planned, 1990: NA

"I guess that for every good idea you have," Bud Hadfield, Kwik-Kopy's founder, once said, "you have nineteen bum ones. Well, I had my nineteen bum ones first." Today, almost a thousand Kwik-Kopy stores in the United Kingdom, Canada, Israel, Australia, and South Africa, as well as the U.S., owe their existence to idea number twenty: that the direct image camera and the small offset press would revolutionize the small printing shop. Bud Hadfield's idea made Kwik-Kopy the largest retailer of instant-printing services in the world.

You don't need knowledge of or experience in the printing industry to buy a Kwik-Kopy franchise. The company doesn't care if you don't know what a printing press looks like. You can easily hire an operator to run your machines. Company franchisees have come from teaching, accounting, engineering, and business management, among other professions and careers.

Kwik-Kopy will do a market analysis of prospective sites and help you secure a good lease. Sometimes it leases the store and subleases to the franchisee. The company provides you with a detailed layout, which has proved effective in facilitating a smooth work flow.

Kwik-Kopy franchisee training involves three weeks of your time at the attractive company campus in Cypress, Texas. The franchisor will send you videotapes and printed material to study before you go to Texas. At Kwik-Kopy headquarters, your training will focus on store management and marketing, not the technical side of the business. The company uses audio-visual materials to teach you some aspects of the business, while role-playing helps you prepare for potential business situations in a realistic atmosphere.

A company representative will visit you several times during the period that extends from a week before you open your store through your first few months of business. The company's special opening promotion will also help. It includes materials for a direct mail advertising. You may purchase supplies through Kwik-Kopy, or you can get them from other sources approved by the company.

Kwik-Kopy runs a special quarterly direct mail program for its franchisees. The company also has a library of cassette, videotape, and printed materials that can help you in your business. And the franchisor provides every franchisee with free disability insurance during their first year of operations.

Kwik-Kopy constantly innovates, making sure that its franchisees use only the latest technology and procedures, including, at this writing, digitized typesetting and four-color presses.

At your request, Kwik-Kopy will give you a written analysis of how your business is doing, and you can call one of its eight toll-free WATS lines for help with a specific problem at any time. In many of the company's offices you will find this sign on the wall: "The most important phone call we get is from a franchise owner with a problem. The second most important phone call is from a prospective franchise owner." Call them on it.

For further information contact:
Marketing Department, Kwik-Kopy Corporation, Kwik-Kopy Village, One Kwik-Kopy Lane, P.O. Box 777, Cypress, TX 77429-0777, 713-373-3535

Minuteman Press

Initial license fee: $22,500
Royalties: 6%
Advertising royalties: None
Minimum cash required: $22,500
Capital required: $22,500 to $32,500
Financing: The company will help you apply for loans; equipment financing is available through 3M Minnesco.
Length of contract: NA

In business since: 1973
Franchising since: 1975
Total number of units: 524
Number of company-operated units: None
Total number of units planned, 1990: NA
Number of company-operated units planned, 1990: NA

In 1973 Minuteman Press saw a void in the printing industry: There were very few printers serving individuals who needed printing services that fell somewhere between the the kind of work done with the office copier and the kind that had to go to a general printer. By filling that void, Minuteman Press has built a thriving enterprise. A Minuteman print center can turn out black-and-white and color quick-print literature for small and big businesses. Franchisees use AM International's 1250 Multigraphic presses and the 3M MR-412 Camera Plate System. This may sound a little esoteric, but according to Minuteman, these machines are some of the best in the business. Among franchised quick-print shops, only Minuteman Press stores use this equipment.

According to the company, Minuteman Press can be an excellent family business because its operation requires no previous experience or specialized education. Minuteman Press has tried to come up with a profile of its typical franchisee, but hasn't managed yet. "We've tried to analyze them," says Roy Titus, company president, "but we've never been able to find the formula of what background makes a good franchise owner. We have lawyers, accountants, housewives, former corporate executives—our people come from almost every background."

Minuteman Press covers your transportation and lodging expenses for its two-week franchisee training course in Farmingdale, New York. There you will study accounting, bookkeeping, computerized pricing, customer relations, advertising, management techniques, and the operation of the machines with which you will produce brochures, booklets, and annual reports once you're in business.

The franchisor will help you find a location for your shop and will provide you with a pretested layout that will both attract customers and facilitate an efficient work flow. The company will supervise the installation of your equipment, and a Minuteman representative will help you hire and train your personnel. Minuteman will start you off in business with a supply of stationery and sample yellow pages and newspaper advertisements. The company will also offer you low prices on your purchases of supplies through MMP Supply Company, Minuteman's nonprofit supply service. You can, however, buy from any company-approved supplier.

Minuteman suggests that you might want to open more stores once you have established a profitable operation in your first. "No one's going to be a millionaire overnight," comments company president, Roy Titus. "It's a good, solid business, with a good profit margin. But you have to work at it."

For further information contact:
Minuteman Press, 1640 New Highway, Farmingdale, NY 11735,
1-800-645-9840; in New York: 516-249-1370

One-Hour Moto Photo

Initial license fee: $35,000
Royalties: 6%
Advertising royalties: 0.5%
Minimum cash required: $37,000
Capital required: $150,000 to $250,000
Financing: 25% of the fee down and the remainder over 66 months at prime plus 2%
Length of contract: NA

In business since: 1981
Franchising since: 1982
Total number of units: 160
Number of company-operated units: 3
Total number of units planned, 1990: NA
Number of company-operated units planned, 1990: NA

The development of the U.S. film-processing industry bodes well for Moto Photo. The industry's sales have increased annually for the past twenty years, and it currently does $3.5 billion a year in business. Over a quarter of that already goes to laboratories that produce prints virtually while you wait, and analysts think the almost-instant processing segment of the business will increase. Moto Photo is the largest franchisor in this field.

Moto Photo has received smash reviews in the business and trade press. *The National OTC Stock Journal* wrote: "The very nature of Moto Photo's operations suggests a long and healthy life in the photo-processing industry." According to *Photo Weekly*, "Moto Photo has never been a play-it-by-ear operation. It was carefully conceived, every detail planned, and all of it executed with great skill and intelligence." And *Processing Week* points approvingly to the company's "top-notch advertising program, including TV and radio commercials. Their new Moto Master system is the ultimate in computerized quality control."

About 90 percent of the company's franchisees have no background in photofinishing. They have been homemakers, government employees, accountants, and retail store managers. A few who already owned a photofinishing operation decided to convert to Moto Photo because of the franchisor's advertising program and the discounts available through its volume purchasing of paper, film, and supplies.

The company assists franchisees with site selection, store design, construction, and equipment installation. Since both the industry and the franchisor are relatively young, franchisees have a wider latitude in choosing locations than they would in a more mature business, such as fast-food franchising with a major company.

Training at Moto Photo corporate headquarters in Dayton, Ohio, lasts four weeks. Your franchise package includes a $1,000 rebate to cover traveling expenses for your instruction. As part of its store-opening assistance, a Moto Photo representative will work at your side during your first week in business. Thereafter a company representative will visit your store monthly to give you any technical assistance you might need. The company customizes an advertising and marketing plan for each franchise and requires that you spend 6 percent of your gross sales on local advertising and contribute 5.5 percent for co-op ads.

For further information contact:
Paul Pieschel, Vice President, Franchise Sales, Moto Photo, Inc., 4444 Lake Center Drive, Dayton, OH 45426, 513-854-MOTO

Postal Instant Press

Initial license fee: $40,000
Royalties: 6% to 8%
Advertising royalties: 1%
Minimum cash required: $32,500
Capital required: $58,500
Financing: The company will finance $32,500 of the license fee at lower-than-market interest; equipment can be leased.
Length of contract: 10 years

In business since: 1965
Franchising since: 1968
Total number of units: 1,072
Number of company-operated units: 5
Total number of units planned, 1990: NA
Number of company-operated units planned, 1990: NA

Buying a PIP franchise will make you part of the biggest chain of printing shops in the world. The quick-printing industry has grown every year in the past few years, and this franchisor has grown with it. Less than twenty PIP franchises have failed since 1968. Vern Gates, who owns four PIP shops in Honolulu, Hawaii, will testify to his own prosperity as a franchisee: "We have made good money. We were started on the right foot and have shown good growth in sales *every* year for the past sixteen years. Our profits have gained almost every year."

The customers who come into your PIP shop will find themselves in a clean, efficiently laid-out establishment with a prominent red, white, blue, and gray color scheme. While they sit and sip a cup of coffee, you can run off anywhere from 10 to 10,000 business cards, letterheads, envelopes, resumes, brochures, or catalogs on your A.B. Dick Press, with plates made using negatives from your Itek camera.

Virtually all PIP franchisees came to the business without previous experience in printing. PIP's training program, which teaches franchisees about sales, profit-and-loss statements, customer relations, and management, in addition to the technical side of the business, makes up for any lack of experience. According to Vern Gates, the training is "excellent."

The company will help you pick a good site for your store, and it will give you a floor plan designed to promote efficiency from the day you open for business. PIP will supervise the installation of your equipment, and a field representative will actually work in your store for the first week, getting you accustomed to your equipment and showing you how to serve customers. During your third week in business, you will get further assistance, this time from a marketing expert, who will help you with point-of-sale merchandising. After that, you can call PIP's toll-free number for advice at any time, and in regional seminars, you and your employees will periodically receive further instruction in marketing, finance, and new printing technology. Vern Gates especially appreciated the company's preopening support when, as he puts it, "the supervisors helped train our personnel and checked to be sure we knew what we were doing."

When you examine PIP's national marketing policies, you may come to think of the company's advertising royalty as a bargain. The company's advertising agency is BBDO/West, and you will have direct access to the agency for advice on running local advertising campaigns simply by dialing one of the special 800 numbers set aside for the exclusive use of PIP franchisees. PIP's national commercials appear during some of the most widely watched programs on television, including the "Tonight Show," ABC's "Monday Night Football," and "Nightline."

PIP runs extensive direct mail campaigns, mailing more than 15 million brochures annually. It also supplies its franchisees with calendars and other point-of-sale promotional pieces.

Your franchise package includes an opening inventory of supplies. You can purchase refills through PIP at substantial discounts.

For further information contact:

Postal Instant Press, 8201 Beverly Blvd., Los Angeles, CA 90048, 1-800-421-4634; in California: 1-800-638-8441

Print Shack International, Inc.

Initial license fee: $34,500
Royalties: 5%
Advertising royalties: 5%
Minimum cash required: $50,000
Capital required: $50,000
Financing: Available for up to 80% of your start-up cost
Length of contract: NA

In business since: 1982
Franchising since: 1983
Total number of units: 71
Number of company-operated units: None
Total number of units planned, 1990: NA
Number of company-operated units planned, 1990: NA

Douglas Varrieur, founder and president of Print Shack International, gained a lot of marketing experience during the seven years he spent at Radio Shack before striking out on his own. Today he puts that expertise to use in Print Shack's ambitious marketing program.

Print Shack's young management team manifests its aggressive attitude in its innovative approach to the business. Among other chains in its industry, only Print Shack features imprinted specialty promotional items as well as printing in its product mix. Such items include ashtrays, key tags, glasses, pens and pencils, coffee mugs, T-shirts, caps, and other items with slogans or company names printed on them. Through the Print Shack system, franchisees can offer their customers over fifty thousand different items from about eighteen hundred sources. In effect, notes the company, franchisees get two franchises for the price of one.

When you become a franchisee, Print Shack will select your site, preferably one with a heavy traffic flow and high visibility. Your store, for which Print Shack will negotiate the lease, will probably occupy a 1,000- to 1,300-square-foot unit. The franchisor will also provide you with an efficient layout and design and give you a list of suggested furnishings with specifications. Your store will have a beige and brown showroom with corkboard displays, 18-foot mirrored wall shelves holding samples of specialty advertising products, a self-service copier, a worktable, and chairs for your customers.

To make sure that your production runs as smoothly as your showroom, Print Shop will give you three weeks of classroom and in-store instruction at its training center, covering everything you need to know about sales, accounting, and equipment operation. After that, a company representative will spend a week at your shop, preparing you and it for the start of your business. You can get after-opening help via the franchisee toll-free hot line, and Print Shack will call you weekly to see how you're doing. The company will also give you the home phone number of the company representative assigned to you, just in case a problem should come up at an odd hour.

Print Shack sends all its franchisees a monthly marketing package containing flyers and other promotional items. The marketing department will also work with you to customize a promotional program that meets your specific needs. Other assistance you can expect from Print Shack includes advice on pricing and discounts on supplies through the franchisor's national vendor contracts.

Just as Print Shack offers you two franchise product lines for the price of one, it also offers you two franchises for one license fee. You can open a second Print Shack within your exclusive territory without having to pay an additional fee. Print Shack also sells master franchises, through which you can buy exclusive rights to an entire region.

For further information contact:
Christopher Menchen, Print Shack, 500 N. Westshore Blvd., Suite 610, Tampa, FL 33609-1924, 1-800-237-5167

Quik Print

Initial license fee: $10,000
Royalties: 5%
Advertising royalties: None
Minimum cash required: $72,500
Capital required: $72,500
Financing: Available
Length of contract: NA

In business since: 1963
Franchising since: 1966
Total number of units: 185
Number of company-operated units: 60
Total number of units planned, 1990: NA
Number of company-operated units planned, 1990: NA

Quik Print franchisees require no background in the printing field and need no technical expertise. In fact, Quik Print likens its presses to office machines—even though they turn out everything from forms, letterheads, and envelopes to bulletins, catalogs, and price sheets. Store owners create plates for their presses with a "push-button" camera, use a paper drill no more complicated than a drill press, work with an easy-to-use paper cutter, and fold paper with a machine that works with the turn of a screw—all this in a store that occupies 800 square feet.

Finding the location for your Quik Print franchise is also easy. Quik Print will select the site for your business (a downtown or suburban area with a dense population) in consultation with you, and it will examine the lease, give you a floor plan, check the building codes, arrange utility service, and put you in touch with suppliers.

Your franchise package will also include all the cabinetry, office and printing equipment, supplies, and inventory you need to start your business. While you can buy your supplies from whomever you wish (as long as they meet Quik Print's standards), the company will offer you the opportunity to take advantage of its national contracts.

Quik Print franchisees train for four weeks at company headquarters in Wichita, Kansas, where the company picks up all expenses, including your round-trip flight to and from Wichita. There you will study bookkeeping, personnel, marketing, and advertising.

Two weeks before you open your Quik Print business, a company representative will come to your store and train you in the operation of your equipment. After you start your business, Quik Print will monitor you through daily reports and generate periodic analyses from them that will give you an overview of your ongoing performance. Your bookkeeping, done according to Quik Print's system, which you will implement using the daily work ledger, invoices, and statement forms the company provides, should take no more than twenty minutes of your time each day. To minimize your financial burdens during the start-up period, Quik Print will not collect a royalty the first ninety days you are in business.

Quik Print will set up and conduct a direct mail campaign during the first few weeks of your business without any additional expense to you, and it will give you the mailing list to use in the future. In addition, the company will give you advice on how to customize an advertising campaign to your market and will also provide advertising copy at your request.

For further information contact:

Jim Pirtle, Vice President, Franchise Operations, Quik Print, 3445 North Web Rd., Wichita, KS 67226, 316-681-2229

Sir Speedy, Inc.

Initial license fee: $17,500
Royalties: 4% the first year; 6% thereafter, reduced on a sliding scale as you pass preselected sales volumes
Advertising royalties: 2%
Minimum cash required: $86,000
Capital required: $86,000
Financing: Equipment can be leased at below-market rates; the franchisor also assists with applications for SBA loans.
Length of contract: 20 years

In business since: 1968
Franchising since: 1968
Total number of units: 600
Number of company-operated units: None
Total number of units planned, 1990: NA
Number of company-operated units planned, 1990: NA

In the mid-seventies, Sir Speedy's printing presses almost came to a final stop when the original company filed a Chapter XI proceeding. But Kampgrounds of America, an experienced franchisor, came to the rescue. KOA bought the floundering firm and set it on a straight course for expansion in the $800 million franchised printing industry. KOA continues to provide the guidance that has made Sir Speedy successful in the eighties. KOA's affiliate, Canyon Capital, Inc., also plays a role in Sir Speedy operations, supplying printing equipment (at a profit) to Sir Speedy franchisees.

Your Sir Speedy printing store will have the capacity to turn out a variety of material, including credit forms, catalog sheets, employment applications, legal briefs, purchase orders, maps and charts, form letters, menus, contracts, and scratch pads.

Sir Speedy chooses the right spot for your quick-print store—typically occupying 1,000 to 1,500 square feet—and helps with the lease negotiations. Your franchise package contains all the supplies you need to begin your business, from a roller desensitizer to box wax, which you can reorder from the company or other approved sources. You can get discounts of up to 40 percent off retail prices by ordering through Sir Speedy.

The company pays for the training of two people, including their transportation and lodging (but not including food), at its training center in Laguna Hills, California. The two-week course consists of units on equipment operation, business management, marketing, and sales. You can also send additional people to the company school in California, but you will pay for all expenses incidental to their training, except tuition.

Sir Speedy also offers "graduate training." At your option, you can spend an additional week learning the company's system at one of the Sir Speedy stores. This will give you hands-on experience in counter sales, pricing, and paper recognition.

A company representative will help you hire your employees in the two-week period before you open, and he or she will assist you in establishing a work routine that will keep your shop functioning smoothly. You can call the company expediter toll free to discuss any problems that arise once you begin operations.

For further information contact:
Sir Speedy Printing Centers, 23131 Verdugo Drive, Laguna Hills, CA 92654-0740, 1-800-854-3321

16. The Real Estate Industry

Contents

Property Inspection

HouseMaster of America

Initial license fee: $17,000 to $35,000
Royalties: 6%
Advertising royalties: 4%
Minimum cash required: $27,000
Capital required: $22,000 to $34,000
Financing: The Company will advise on best sources of assistance.
Length of contract: 10 years

In business since: 1971
Franchising since: 1979
Total number of units: 72
Number of company-operated units: None
Total number of units planned, 1990: 150
Number of company-operated units planned, 1990: None

Marge Rodell needed a change. "I was working for a large corporation, and I wanted to start my own business—something I was directly responsible for," she says. The business she decided on? A HouseMaster of America franchise in New Fairfield, Connecticut. This house inspection service caters to the needs of home buyers who want to know ahead of time if there are flaws in what will easily be the biggest purchase they will ever make. Currently, the company seeks franchisees who want to own a branch in the Midwest, Northwest, and Canada. The initial fee varies with the number of owner-occupied homes in the area.

The company points out that franchisees have not yet oversaturated this field. HouseMaster management feels confident that house inspection is just coming into its own. If you buy this franchise, you will operate a cash business, which simplifies accounts receivable; and you will conduct business over the phone rather than in a walk-in office, so site selection is not critical. You will even work reasonable hours: Home inspections must take place during daylight hours.

What exactly will your staff of engineers check for during a house inspection? Each inspection checks the central heating and cooling system of a house; its interior plumbing and electrical systems; the structural soundness of the siding and roof and whether water leaks through the roof; the structural soundness of the basement, walls, floors, and ceiling; and the large kitchen appliances. Some franchisees also offer other services, like inspection for termites and wood borers, evaluation of well and septic systems, checking of docks and bulkheads, and swimming pool inspections.

HouseMaster sells insurance to both home inspectors and clients. To their franchisees, HouseMaster sells pay-as-you-go errors-and-omissions insurance. As a local franchisee, you can sell to client home buyers an optional one-year warranty on the roof and structural and mechanical elements of the house.

HouseMaster pays for all your training-related expenses. You will spend a week at their Bound Brook, New Jersey, headquarters for technical instruction in the classroom and field and then a day in an active office for operations training. Then you spend two days in the field for sales training.

The training schedule allows you to spend extra time on anything you feel you need to concentrate on. Marge Rodell appreciates that she "was able to spend any amount of time I needed to at the home office." And she also remembers the help she received after her formal training. She says the yearly operational meeting "is very informative," as are "the updates on the technical and operations part of the business." "Most important" she notes, HouseMaster personnel "were always available by phone."

Marge Rodell cautions all potential franchisees that they "must be totally dedicated to making their business work because that can get one through the first couple of years when the work is high and the profits are low." But she doesn't mind the hard work. In fact, she says, "I love it!"

For further information contact:

Robert J. Hardy, HouseMaster of America, Inc., 421 W. Union Ave., Bound Brook, NJ 08805, 1-800-526-3939

Paul W. Davis Systems, Inc.

Initial license fee: $25,000 to $45,000
Royalties: 2.5%
Advertising royalties: None
Minimum cash required: $50,000
Capital required: $50,000
Financing: The company will finance over half of the franchise fee.
Length of contract: 5 years

In business since: 1966
Franchising since: 1970
Total number of units: 115
Number of company-operated units: None

Total number of units planned, 1990: 409
Number of company-operated units planned, 1990: None

Insurance costs may be one of the few exceptions to the rule that whatever goes up must come down. Litigation and the economy continue to push up costs for insurers, who pass these costs along to a population more inclined—and often required—to purchase insurance than in any in recent memory. Paul W. Davis Systems, Inc., founded in response to these developments in the insurance industry, provides a valuable service to both property insurers and property owners. Paul W. Davis franchisees make property damage estimates for every major insurance company in the country. Franchisees inspect damaged property insured by their clients and make recommendations designed to allow insurers to make equitable but not excessive payments to property owners for their claims. And for property owners, Paul W. Davis provides property restoration management services to help them repair damage in the most cost-efficient manner possible.

When you buy a Paul W. Davis franchise, the company will grant you exclusive rights to a territory with a population of 80,000 or more people. Within your region you can operate your business from any location you choose. The company will train you at its headquarters in Jacksonville, Florida, for three weeks, at no cost to you other than the expense of your meals. Once you complete your training, you will be proficient in the Paul W. Davis computer system—the foundation of your business. Paul W. Davis has developed and refined its computer system over years of work in the field. You will use the technology to provide accurate property damage estimates to insurers and the design restoration programs for property owners.

A Paul W. Davis professional will come to your location during your opening period to help you in all phases of your start-up. Once your franchise is fully operational, you can keep in touch with the home office via the company's toll-free hot line. The company will provide ongoing support in the form of promotion programs directed at insurance companies and will recommend sources for supplies. You have the freedom to purchase your supplies from any source you choose. Both at the home office in Florida and at franchise locations, Paul W. Davis will conduct refresher training whenever its computer system technology changes. Because Paul W. Davis operated no company-owned units, its resources are completely dedicated to the success of its franchisees.

For further information contact:
Paul W. Davis Systems Marketing, Inc., 1900 The Exchange, Suite 655, Atlanta, GA 30339, 1-800-722-3939

Sales

Earl Keim Realty

Initial license fee: $8,500
Royalties: 5%
Advertising royalties: 1%
Minimum cash required: $8,500
Capital required: $10,000 to $25,000
Financing: Available
Length of contract: 5 years

In business since: 1958
Franchising since: 1968
Total number of units: 92
Number of company-operated units: None
Total number of units planned, 1990: 162
Number of company-operated units planned, 1990: 12

In almost thirty years, Earl Keim Realty has sold over one hundred thousand homes, with a market value of $5.5 billion. Earl Keim Realty is a subsidiary of The Keim Group, Ltd., a holding company that in turn is a subsidiary of Central Holding Company, a Michigan organization created to run banks.

Earl Keim Realty trains its franchisees, whether they're just starting their businesses or converting them from independent brokerages, at the company's headquarters in Southfield, Michigan. The training stresses how to manage a real estate brokerage and the intricacies of real estate financing. Franchisees can also take quarterly refresher courses.

The services offered by Keim's various subsidiaries play an important role in its franchisee's businesses; an integral part of your initial training will be instruction in how you can use these services. Through one of these subsidiaries, Guardian Financial Services Company, Earl Keim agents can help clients secure mortgages with favorable terms. From this company, by computer, Earl Keim's 2,000 agents get up-to-the minute interest rates. The Earl Keim Relocation Services Division gives Keim agents even more clout, numbering among its clients the Equitable and Merrill Lynch relocation companies.

Also on the Keim corporate tree is the Guardian Home Warranty Corporation, which will make your life as an Earl Keim franchisee easier since, as *Newsweek* wrote, ". . . warranted houses sell 50 percent faster . . . and at better prices than nonwarranted houses." The company's marketing group gives you an extra edge as well. This in-house agency is active in promoting the Keim image, making it easier for you to convert "For Sale" signs into "Keim Sold Mine" placards.

Still more subsidiaries serve the Earl Keim broker. The Resort Realty Division markets resort property. Its inventory includes some of the most desirable resorts in the country. And the Earl Keim real estate school is a reliable source of trained personnel for help in running your brokerage.

The company assists its franchisees in all aspects of getting their businesses going, from site selection to opening. You'll get the help you'll need, but you'll also have the freedom to set up and operate your office according to your own management ideas.

Earl Keim's current expansion plans focus on Michigan (its home state) and Florida.

For further information contact:
William McMullen, Earl Keim Realty, 1740 West Big Beaver, Suite 200, Tory, MI 48084, 313-649-0200

Gallery of Homes, Inc.

Initial license fee: $7,000
Royalties: 4%
Advertising royalties: 2%
Minimum cash required: $2,000
Capital required: $2,000 to $100,000, depending on whether you already have a real estate brokerage firm
Financing: May be available for part of the fee
Length of contract: 3 years

In business since: 1950
Franchising since: 1950
Total number of units: 500
Number of company-operated units: None
Total number of units planned, 1990: NA
Number of company-operated units planned, 1990: NA

If real estate is your game, you may need help to compete with the major players. With all the financial muscle flexed recently, you could get muscled right out of business. One way to get an edge on the competition is to build your marketing power and your ability to offer a variety of services to your customers by joining a national network of realtors such as Gallery of Homes.

The clout behind Gallery comes from its parent institution, the $8.6 billion Empire of America federal savings bank in Buffalo, New York. The Empire "empire" also includes Empire of America Relocations Services, Inc., a corporate relocation company, and the Empire of America Realty Credit Corporation.

Gallery welcomes first-time brokers, but most of its franchisees have converted their independent brokerages to a Gallery operation. Some franchisees operate as many as eighteen separate brokerages. Franchisees can tap the resources of a powerful national network to supply relocation services and loans of all kinds to their customers as well as to sell their houses or find them new ones. Types of financing available include construction and equity loans, purchase money, and wraparound mortgages.

Gallery franchisees also benefit from a substantial national advertising campaign. In 1986, the company's advertising appeared in *Money, Time, Newsweek,* "Cable Network News," and the three major radio networks. The print ads featured the slogan: "We'll find someone who loves your home," while the TV promotion stressed the idea of finding "the right fit" for customers.

As a Gallery franchisee, you must display the company logo and have a street-level office. You have to install an attractive window display, with real estate photographs the key element. You will choose the site for your office, subject to Gallery's approval.

Outside real estate consultants under contract to Gallery run the three-day seminar required of new franchisees, although Gallery staff members usually deliver some of the lectures. The company pays for your hotel accommodations and lunches at the seminar, which is usually given at the company's office in Orlando, Florida. Optional training programs cover subjects such as sales management, increasing personal effectiveness, and the employee relocation service.

All franchisees join the Gallery of Homes Regional Council in their regions. They use half of Gallery's national advertising funds to promote the company in a coordinated regional advertising campaign.

For further information contact:
Gallery of Homes, Inc., P.O. Box 2900, Orlando, FL 32802-9990, 1-800-241-8320

Help-U-Sell, Inc.

Initial license fee: $275/1,000 inhabitants in your franchise area; minimum price of $4,500
Royalties: 7%
Advertising royalties: 7%
Minimum cash required: $25,000
Capital required: $25,000 to $60,000

Financing: Minimum of $2,500 down
Length of contract: 5 years

In business since: 1976
Franchising since: 1978
Total number of units: 6,500
Number of company-operated units: None
Total number of units planned, 1990: NA
Number of company-operated units planned, 1990: NA

"I probably would have given up without them," says Dale Strack, this real estate counseling company's franchisee in Cherry Hill, New Jersey. His one complaint: They "have grown slower than perhaps they could have because they constantly develop the business and test ideas *before* giving them out." But even with its growth carefully controlled, Help-U-Sell has expanded rapidly. *Inc.* ranked it number 340 among the 500 fastest-growing private companies.

A little unusual in its field, Help-U-Sell acknowledges that "traditional" real estate agents do not always look kindly on it. Help-U-Sell offers an à la carte real estate service. The company bases its concept on the idea that what most real estate agents dislike about their job is pounding the pavements and working the phones, canvasing for listings, and conducting open houses. It also assumes that most people would prefer to show their homes themselves when putting them up for sale if they could have professional help with advertising, financial details, and advice when needed.

Here's how the system works. Most sellers pay a flat fee to the franchisee, who helps them sell their house. You, as a franchisee, supply the seller with For Sale signs, place newspaper ads for the property, help the buyer arrange financing for the purchase, assist with escrow/settlement, and generally advise the seller on all aspects of the transaction, including closing costs. The seller shows the house without your assistance, although for an additional fee you will do it for them and add a multiple-listing service.

You charge a flat fee, cheaper than the typical 6 or 7 percent real estate agent's commission. That, according to the company, permits the seller to bring the price of the house down or grant some other concession to a buyer, thus making the house more salable. Word gets around about this kind of service in a community. That, combined with Help-U-Sell advertising, has both buyers and sellers coming to you, rather than you hustling to find them, according to the franchisor.

You, or one of your associates—the company thinks you should have two or three—need a real estate license to buy one of these franchises. If you are not a broker converting an already existing business, you should at least have a knowledge of real estate in your area. The size of the area covered by your franchise, the company estimates, will probably have a population of about thirty thousand, although it does vary.

If you decide to make this business your own, you will travel to Mission Viejo, California, at your own expense, for five days of the company's training for new franchisees. There you will learn Help-U-Sell's exclusive marketing system. Dale Strack was "taught by a successful franchisee who was very able in conveying the knowledge." Later you can also take a refresher course, which is given at least four times a year. It "is excellent and especially useful for new employees—or employees who have been promoted," notes Wayne Colvin, whose franchise is in Manteca, California. Otherwise, you can ask for assistance at any time through the company's toll-free line.

While the company will advise you on choosing a site for your office, you make the final decision. Help-U-Sell says that it has never turned down a franchisee's choice of location. Wayne Colvin feels that providing advice without compulsion is the essential spirit of Help-U-Sell. "The company offers excellent guidelines for running your business," Wayne Colvin says, "but leaves you to make the final decisions on your own." And he adds, "I have made a lot of money."

For further information contact:
Don Taylor, Help-U-Sell, Inc., 110 W. 300 South, Suite 101, Salt Lake City, UT 84101, 1-800-345-1990

Homeowners Concept, Inc.

Initial license fee: $7,500
Royalties: NA
Advertising royalties: NA
Minimum cash required: $22,000
Capital required: $22,000
Financing: None
Length of contract: NA

In business since: 1982
Franchising since: 1985
Total number of units: 21
Number of company-operated units: None
Total number of units planned, 1990: NA
Number of company-operated units planned, 1990: NA

"When I decided to start my own business," says Jeff Knab, a former mortgage loan officer and president of Homeowners Concept, "I thought for a while about whether or not there was a better way to help people sell their homes. I realized that homeowners could do the best job of selling their homes if they were given a hand in the advertising and financing areas." Knab didn't originate this concept, but he has instituted an ambitious plan to make this kind of service available through franchised brokers in every city.

Brokers spend their time most profitably by acquiring new listings and serving large numbers of clients—not by showing houses to potential buyers or sitting around at open houses. Homeowners Concept saves its brokers time and their customers money by having its brokers simply list the house for sale and provide advice to their clients, who actually do the selling. The seller, by using a consultant rather than a full-service broker, saves on the fee. Instead of the 6 or 7 percent standard broker's fee, Homeowners Concept charges $200 for an exclusive listing and $1,800 at the closing.

As part of the package, the Homeowners client receives a "For Sale—Call Owner" sign from the company. He or she also receives phone service through the company's magazine, *For Sale—Call Owner*, which advertises the house for sale. The company informs potential buyers who call them of the available house. It also examines the income and expenses of potential buyers (prequalifies them for a loan), helps them get a loan, and takes care of the purchase contract paperwork. Finally, Homeowners Concept accompanies the seller to the closing.

The company claims that this approach is effective in both a buyer's *and* a seller's market. In a buyer's market, people selling their homes can use the money they save on broker's fees to present a better deal to a buyer. In a seller's market, the Homeowner's approach attracts sellers because they can save substantial sums of money—$10,000 to $20,000, according to Joseph Citarella, a Stamford, Connecticut, franchisee.

Dealing with a young company makes it unnecessary to go through layers of bureacracy to get information or action. At the moment, Jeff Knab, the company's president, trains each new franchisee himself at the franchisee's office. The company includes in the franchise package some of the initial supplies you will need, including cassette training tapes for your sales consultants.

"We are service people," remarks Jeff Knab. "We're for the educated home buyer or seller who wants to save some money. The idea may not be for everybody, and we know that. But it is great for the many who can benefit from it." Among those many are the Homeowners Concept franchisees, ambitious entrepreneurs who want their incomes to grow with the company.

For further information contact:
Jeffrey C. Knabb, President, Homeowners Concept, 7051 Colerain Ave., Cincinnati, OH 45239, 513-923-4050

RE/MAX

Initial license fee: $7,500 to $17,500
Royalties: $60/month
Advertising royalties: $50/month
Minimum cash required: $5,000
Capital required: $10,000 to $20,000
Financing: None
Length of contract: 5 to 20 years

In business since: 1973
Franchising since: 1976
Total number of units: 783
Number of company-operated units: None
Total number of units planned, 1990: 2,600
Number of company-operated units planned, 1990: None

RE/MAX's red, white, and blue hot air balloons embody its corporate slogan: "Above the crowd." The slogan could just as well apply to some of the company's impressive vital statistics. RE/MAX has grown every month since its founding. Currently, the company expands at an annual rate of 40 percent and doubles in size every 2.5 years. RE/MAX sales associates—its agents—average twenty-three transactions a year, better than three times the national average, and earn almost six times the income of the typical real estate agent. In 1986 *Forbes* ranked RE/MAX third in sales volume among real estate firms in the U.S. Yet there's more to RE/MAX than numbers.

Real estate brokers must learn a different way of doing business if they wish to convert to a RE/MAX franchise. In a typical brokerage, real estate agents give half their 5 to 7 percent commission to the broker. Agents who excel thus pay a good deal of money for the privilege of working out of their broker's office. The broker, on the other hand, must devote a great deal of time to the less proficient agents, educating and motivating them to bring in more business. The broker also has to deal with a high turnover rate, especially among the better agents who look for greener pastures.

In the RE/MAX system, you, the broker, run the brokerage more like a cooperative, presiding over and managing it. Agents keep 100 percent of their commissions, sharing common office expenses—rent, administrative salaries, secretaries, phones, etc.—on an equal basis. They also share the cost of advertising. Their only additional expense as part of this group arrangement is the management fee they pay to you.

For an agent who does not do too well, the management fee and shared expense of office space would loom large, like a big rent that had to be paid each month. But to the better agents who hustle and close a healthy number of sales, their fixed expenses under the system amount to a much smaller percentage of their income at the end of the year than paying a broker half of everything they make. In other words, this is a system in which the best can thrive. You will make a fair profit from each agent, rather than depending on half of the commissions of just a few good ones, and you will have a predictable income. You also spend much of your time as a RE/MAX broker recruiting the best agents, instead of retraining mediocre performers in the basics of the profession.

Franchisee Betty D. Hegner, president of RE/MAX of Northern Illinois, Inc., suggests that you think about the implications of the RE/MAX arrangement before you leap at this opportunity: "Will your ego suffer if your salespeople outdistance you?" she asks. "In many companies the owner or manager is the top producer and makes all the decisions. The role of the manager in a 100 percent company is that of leader, advisor, motivator, and organizer. Are you ready to share decision making and planning with your salespeople?" And she adds: "Are you prepared to give up your share of your salespeople's commissions?"

The RE/MAX system also affects the kind of office you will have. To make the system work, you may have to spend a little more to attract the best agents. This will probably mean providing at least semiprivate offices for each agent.

RE/MAX will give you five intense days of training in its system at its Denver, Colorado, headquarters. You pay for your travel expenses. Ongoing assistance and refresher training is available through audio and video cassettes, and you can obtain additional in-person training both in Denver and at your location. You can also consult company professionals on specific problems.

In addition to real estate, many RE/MAX franchisees sell corporate relocation and asset management services as well as insurance.

For further information contact:

Darryl Jesperson, Vice President, RE/MAX, P.O. Box 3907, Englewood, CO 80155, 1-800-525-7452

State Wide Real Estate Services, Inc.

Initial license fee: $9,500
Royalties: 5%
Advertising royalties: 3%
Minimum cash required: $20,000
Capital required: $20,000 to $30,000
Financing: The company may finance the franchise fee.
Length of contract: 5 years

In business since: 1944
Franchising since: 1944
Total number of units: 110
Number of company-operated units: NA
Total number of units planned, 1990: 500
Number of company-operated units planned, 1990: NA

In 1944 Hugh A Harris, State Wide's founder, had the idea of uniting several Michigan real estate brokers in a cooperative under one name to share the expense of supplies and advertising and achieve greater name recognition for each brokerage. Eventually the cooperative spread beyond Michigan and evolved into a conversion franchise, in which brokers who already had an active business could trade some of their independence for the benefits of operating as part of a larger organization.

Andy Sakmar, a Rochester, Michigan, State Wide franchisee, says State Wide has "expanded our business and increased our marketing area." He has found the company's educational program of special value, particularly "the 'Success Series,' which is a week-long course we find very helpful to our new as well as our seasoned agents." The company requires new franchisees to take an orientation course. State Wide's ongoing courses, offered at regional locations, continue franchisee's education in the field and keep them up-to-date on the latest developments. Some courses require the payment of a nominal fee. Franchisees can also borrow books and audio and video cassettes on various topics in real estate from the company library.

State Wide's computerized multilisting system enables you to sell your clients' properties in out-of-town markets. It also permits you to locate properties that might not otherwise be accessible to buyers. If you have a potential buyer for a property on the list, you can either refer that person to the listing office, earning a 25 percent referral fee (probably the highest in the industry), or show the client the property yourself, sharing the commission with the listed broker.

The company emphasizes the cooperative aspect of its organization in every way possible. It encourages franchisees to send in ideas they've used to improve their business, so that other brokers in the network might benefit. You can exchange ideas and experiences with other franchisees at quarterly meetings. These meetings also give franchisees the opportunity to tell the company's management what they think about the company's performance. In fact, these meetings give franchisees a chance to change the way the company does business, since franchisees determine State Wide policies by majority vote.

State Wide likes to think of itself as your back office. It maintains a staff of certified public accountants, investment counselors, and advertising and marketing specialists, as well as real estate experts, to answer your questions over the company's toll-free line reserved exclusively for brokers.

Other features of the State Wide network include regional brochures issued at least three times a year, in which you can reach markets in your region but beyond your local area, company preparation of camera-ready advertising copy to use in promoting your firm, and a home warranty protection program that makes it easier for you to sell houses.

For further information contact:
Richard J. Langley, Vice President, State Wide Real Estate, Box 297, 1801 7th Ave. North, Escanaba, MI 49829, 906-786-8392

17. The Retailing Industry

Contents

Specialty Retailing

Annie's Book Stop
Docktor Pet Centers
Flowerama of America, Inc.
Petland

Video

Adventureland Video, Inc.
National Video, Inc.
Network Video
Sounds Easy International, Inc.
Video Biz
Video Update, Inc.

Clothing and Footwear

The Athlete's Foot

Initial license fee: $7,500
Royalties: 3%
Advertising royalties: 0.5%
Minimum cash required: $50,000 plus a line of credit
Capital required: $125,000 to $150,000
Financing: The company assists prospective franchisees in negotiating with banks for financing.
Length of contract: 10 years

In business since: 1972
Franchising since: 1973
Total number of units: 469
Number of company-operated units: 102
Total number of units planned, 1990: 615
Number of company-operated units planned, 1990: 150

No longer just a fad, the fitness craze is a way of life. Whether through running, aerobics, racquetball, weight training, or another of the myriad exercises popular today, millions of Americans spend countless hours each week pursuing the body beautiful. An increasing demand for well-engineered exercise clothing, combined with a desire to look good while wearing it, feeds the booming sports fashion industry.

In 1985 Americans spent nearly $2 billion on 77.4 million pairs of athletic shoes. And sneakers aren't just for playing sports anymore. "People realized they were real comfortable to walk around in," says Steve Kessler, an Athlete's Foot franchisee in New York City. "They've become like Levi's—casual apparel." Confirming the notion of sports gear as fashion, one of Steve Kessler's stores attracts a celebrity clientele that includes Diana Ross, Mary Tyler Moore, and Dustin Hoffman.

The Athlete's Foot, while tapping the market for fun "active wear," emphasizes the scientific side of fitness. Committed to offering only the best in athletic footwear, The Athlete's Foot operates a "wear test" center in Naperville, Illinois. Working with manufacturers, the company researches sports shoes and tests other products that might be offered for sale by Athlete's Foot franchisees. Manufacturers can use the results to improve their designs, and Athlete's Foot franchisees can make their purchasing decisions based on the technical data they receive from the center.

As a new franchisee, you will learn the particulars of athletic footwear retailing at The Athlete's Foot headquarters in Atlanta, Georgia.

Your training will cover all areas of retailing, including merchandising, cash flow analysis, buying, advertising, and the nuts and bolts of store operation. Instruction geared to helping you understand the design and use of different sports shoes and an introduction to The Athlete's Foot footwear clinics are significant parts of the program. Prior to your opening, the company will help you purchase store fixtures and supplies and work with sportswear suppliers to place your initial inventory orders.

Once your store is set up, The Athlete's Foot will assist you with your grand opening and will maintain close contact with you during the early stages of business operation. As you take control of your new store, you will be given as much freedom as you desire and as much support as you need. The Athlete's Foot franchising philosophy is that a successful franchise system must be based on constant communication between franchisor and franchisee. The home office keeps an open-door policy and publishes monthly newsletters to keep store owners informed. To further enhance franchisees' understanding of the athletic footwear market and retailing techniques, the company is developing training and informational videotapes.

The Athlete's Foot will help you select the right location for your store and requires that your site be approved. You can obtain supplies and equipment directly from the company at cost or from any other source you choose. The only restriction the company places on you during the term of your contract with them is that you do not operate a similar or competing business within your protected Athlete's Foot territory.

For further information contact:
Paul Modzelewski, The Athlete's Foot, 3735 Atlanta Industrial Parkway, Atlanta, GA 3033l, 404-696-3400,

Athletic Attic Marketing, Inc.

Initial license fee: $7,500
Royalties: 3%
Advertising royalties: 0.5%
Minimum cash required: $25,000
Capital required: $90,000 to $180,000
Financing: The company offers assistance.
Length of contract: NA

In business since: 1972
Franchising since: 1973
Total number of units: 200

Number of company-operated units: None
Total number of units planned, 1990: NA
Number of company-operated units planned, 1990: NA

It's hard to believe that as late as the early 1960s, only about one of every four Americans exercised regularly. Today well over half (about 60 percent at last count) consistently engage in some kind of exercise. It's getting to the point where some communities really ought to have traffic signals on the sidewalks in the early morning and evening hours to prevent jogger-pedestrian accidents.

Not surprisingly, retailers have discovered gold in all this huffing and puffing. T-shirts and Keds are out; designer tank tops and fancy footwear are in. When buying sneakers, for example, consumers now look for the right kind of support for the particular physical activity in which they're engaged. They also want to look good, since health clubs and jogging paths have become hot spots for making new social and business contacts. In ever-greater numbers they buy their sports apparel at specialty sports apparel shops.

Athletic Attic was formed as the physical fitness boom swung into high gear. Its founders, Jimmy Carnes and Marty Liquori, knew their field thoroughly. Jimmy Carnes spent twelve years coaching the track team at the University of Florida. He was chosen head coach for the 1980 United States Olympic track and field team and is now president of the Athletics Congress, which is the governing body of track and field in this country. Villanova's Marty Liquori was one of America's greatest milers, author of two books on running, and a TV commentator on ABC's "Wide World of Sports." Marty Liquori's name and image, of course, are exploitable assets for this franchisor and its franchisees.

Athletic Attic's brightly lit stores are located in shopping malls and strips. Store racks display athletic pants, shorts, jackets, and tops. The rear wall is filled with sneakers of all kinds. The company-designed Athletic Lady is a fashion-centered store it recently added to the chain to cash in on the tremendously increasing interest in physical fitness shown by women in recent years.

Should you decide to become part of the Athletic Attic family, the company will help you at every stage of your business—from choosing a site to running a successful store. For example, Athletic Attic prides itself on its strong ongoing relationship with mall developers that puts it in an excellent position to guide you to a good location for your store. The franchisor will also offer advice at all stages of store construction and remodeling. And although Athletic Attic does not offer direct financing, it will help you apply for loans and show you how to set up accounts with suppliers.

You will train for your career as an Athletic Attic franchisee at company headquarters in Gainesville, Florida. While the cost of your training is included in your initial fee, living and traveling expenses for your week's training are your responsibility. The training will cover every aspect of store management, including hands-on experience in an actual store setting. At the end of your training period, you will receive the company's operations manual, a guide to the everyday details of running your store.

An Athletic Attic field representative will help you with preopening preparations and the actual launching of your business. You will probably need advice, since you will determine the variety and size of your inventory. Postopening support includes a steady stream of publications from central headquarters that keep you up-to-date on company policies, outline new ways of increasing your managerial effectiveness, and inform you of special opportunities to acquire merchandise at low prices. The franchisor's servicing department will also be available to discuss any particular problems you may have as they arise.

A special feature of the Athletic Attic national publicity program—from which your store will gain greater name recognition—is the National Track Club. This company-sponsored club enters top athletes at world-class events, thus helping to keep the company's name before the kind of sports fans who are likely to be sports equipment purchasers as well as spectators.

Many Athletic Attic proprietors have found the experience of opening and operating their Athletic Attic franchise rewarding enough to want to do it again. In fact, more than ninety company stores are owned by multistore operators.

For further information contact:

Wayne Lindsey, Director, Franchise Sales/Leasing, Athletic Attic Marketing, Inc., P.O. Box 14503, Gainesville, FL 32604, 904-377-5289

Gingiss International, Inc.

Initial license fee: $15,000
Royalties: 6% first 2 years; then 10%
Advertising royalties: 3%
Minimum cash required: $60,000
Capital required: $120,000 to $160,000
Financing: Available
Length of contract: 10 years

In business since: 1936
Franchising since: 1968
Total number of units: 228
Number of company-operated units: 23
Total number of units planned, 1990: 303
Number of company-operated units planned, 1990: 25

With the final vanquishing of 1960s informality, wedding parties have returned to the formal wear favored by previous generations. Gingiss, the largest retailers and renters of men's formal wear in the country, with sales about 500 percent higher than their nearest competitors, has benefited greatly from this change in tastes.

Seemingly impervious to economic hard times, this business even did well in the recession of 1982, when tuxedo rental volume rose by 8 percent. And sales of tuxedos in the Gingiss Chicago flagship store rose 46 percent. The company, founded during the depression, began its period of greatest expansion in 1968, just when inflation began to shake the economy.

Weddings provide the bulk—75 percent— but not all of Gingiss' business. Prom goers are also going formal again—"On prom night, she should love your body, not your mind," a recent Gingiss advertisement stated boldly. And executives buy or rent tuxedos for an increasing number of social functions.

Politicians and luminaries from the world of sports and entertainment account for some of the company's 600,000 yearly customers. Gingiss franchisees could see the likes of Robert Altman, Muhammad Ali, Liberace, Ed McMahon, Bob Hope, Danny Thomas, Hank Aaron, Bruce Jenner, Conrad Hilton, or William "the Refrigerator" Perry come through their doors.

Gingiss franchisees fit no particular profile. In fact, they include former executives of Gingiss who felt they knew a good thing when they saw it. Multistore owners run more than a third of the company's franchised operations. One of them, the Pacer family, operates seven Atlanta stores, with several more in the planning stages. This husband, wife, sister, brother-in-law, children, grandma and grandpa team shares the work of running its mini-empire.

In a Gingiss franchise, the franchisor makes many of the decisions, at least initially. For example, the company will choose your location after careful research. That may even mean lining up a spot in a shopping center still under construction. The company takes responsibility for design and construction. Gingiss will give you a ready-to-go retail store, a turnkey operation stocked with about two hundred sixty suits.

To learn how to run this operation, you will spend one week in a company store in Chicago getting some hands-on experience. Another week of classroom instruction supplements that, covering topics like merchandising, sales promotion, finance, hiring, personnel training, and advertising. A company representative will also spend the days before and after your opening at your store. Thereafter, your store will get frequent visits from your regional advisor.

Gingiss has the preeminent name in the formal wear business, and they mean to keep it. The company "road tests" new models of formal wear before authorizing them for your stock. That could mean dry-cleaning tuxedos twenty times in a row to make sure they can stand the stress of repeated wear and cleaning.

The company also keeps up its good name by keeping it constantly before the public. Advertising plays a big part in the Gingiss operation. Since the bride usually makes the decisions about even the formal wear for men at her wedding, company advertisements appear in *Modern Bride* and *Brides*, as well as in *Cosmopolitan, Seventeen, Woman's Day, Glamour* and *Mademoiselle*. The company also runs advertisements in *Ebony* and *Essence*. In 1986 the company ran a five-network, thirty-four week radio campaign. Currently, Gingiss seeks to expand in all areas of the country, as well as in Toronto and Quebec.

For further information contact:
John Heiser, Gingiss International, Inc., 180 North LaSalle St., Chicago, IL 60601, 1-800-621-7125

*Just * Pants*

Initial license fee: None
Royalties: 5%
Advertising royalties: 3%
Minimum cash required: $65,000
Capital required: $125,000 to $201,500
Financing: None
Length of contract: The full term of the lease

In business since: 1969
Franchising since: 1969
Total number of units: 116
Number of company-operated units: None
Total number of units planned, 1990: 175
Number of company-operated units planned, 1990: None

Just * Pants isn't just pants. Two Chicago brothers, experienced in the men's clothing business, began the company when they decided to open stores in high-traffic areas, specializing in casual pants for young men. They tailored their stores to their customers' tastes: contemporary decor, rock music, and a young sales staff to attract teenagers turned off by the stuffiness of department stores. Just * Pants displayed major brands, such as Lee and Levi's, and it stocked a wide range of styles and sizes.

But times, tastes, and styles changed, and so did the stores. The company added jackets, shirts, sweaters, and vests to the merchandise mix. And Just * Pants began to sell designer jeans to women. While name-brand clothing still predominated, the company also sold its own private-label merchandise in every store.

Franchisees have the choice of developing their own shopping mall store sites or having Just * Pants do it and subleasing their store from the company. Unlike many other companies that lease a store and then sublease to franchisees, Just * Pants does not charge extra for this service.

New franchisees take a training course at the company's headquarters in Chicago, where they study all areas of store operations and merchandising. But even more important is the guidance and expertise you get from the company's field supervisor, who comes to your store the week you open and returns at least every three months to spend more time at your side. The visits will help you focus on developing your marketing plan, and you can expect help and advice on all aspects of your merchandise mix, inventory levels, and advertising. The company representative will also confer with you on your operating and merchandising budgets, sales, and profits.

Just * Pants helps you tailor your ad campaigns to the demographics of your particular market, and the company also provides co-op advertising opportunities. Just * Pants is experienced in runnning sales promotions with flair. It will keep your store and the company's name in the public eye through activities like on-site remote radio broadcasts, athletic team tie-ins, and rock concerts.

For further information contact:

Harvey Olsher, Director of Real Estate and Franchise Development,
Just * Pants, 201 North Wells St., Suite 1530, Chicago, IL 60606, 312-346-5020

Computers and Software

Computerland Corporation

Initial license fee: $15,000 to $75,000
Royalties: 7%
Advertising royalties: 1%
Minimum cash required: $40,000
Capital required: $200,000 to $450,000
Financing: The company will help franchisees obtain third-party financing.
Length of contract: 10 years

In business since: 1976
Franchising since: 1977
Total number of units: 852
Number of company- operated units: 1
Total number of units planned, 1990: NA
Number of company-operated units planned, 1990: NA

In just a few short years, the way people work, play, and learn has been transformed by the advent of the personal computer. And it will never be the same again: While the years of spectacular growth may be past, demand for personal computers and related products will no doubt remain solid, because for many, computers have become an integral part of life. And within the increasingly competitive arena of smaller businesses, they are a fact of life that cannot be ignored. Computerland, born with the personal computer industry, has since grown and matured with the industry. And as the industry continues to change, Computerland will adapt to the changes. Most of its recent growth has been in international markets, and the company has been exploring the possibilities of offering nonretail sales and service franchises.

The Computerland philosophy involves offering a full range of services to the personal computer consumer. William H. Millard, chairman of the board, founded the company as a "way to bridge the gap between the manufacturers of a new 'personal technology' and the public for whom it was intended. Computerland is a 'bridge' consisting of services such as consultation, training, technical support, and after-sale support." Computerland customers can give hardware and software a test run in the store and make their selections from a wide range of high-quality brands (including the company's own). Specializing in personal computers, Computerland franchisees have in-depth knowledge of the products they sell and can serve business people, families, professionals, and educators alike. That means Computerland not only sells computers, it also offers training and technical support to its customers.

Owning a Computerland franchise is truly a give-and-take arrangement. You will provide after-sales assistance to your customers and receive technical and operating advice from the home office. And you will play an active role in the company's product-approval decisions and in determining how the franchise system should operate. According to William Millard, "franchisees are instrumental in virtually every major decision concerning which products we carry, how we define our market, what will work at the store level, and the kinds of central support Computerland should devote its resources to." You will receive the benefits of the company's national advertising campaign in the print and television media, and Computerland will use its marketing expertise to assist you with your own local and regional advertising.

The company operates a centralized purchasing service from which you can order inventory electronically. Acquisition and distribution facilities on four continents offer a full line of over three hundred items and more than three hundred manufacturers from which you can choose your store's stock. Because of Computerland's purchasing power and its policy of selling to franchisees at cost, you will be able to obtain inventory at significant savings. You are not required to buy through Computerland, but you must carry only approved products in your store. In return for the benefits of working within an established, recognized system, Computerland requires that you meet its operating standards and work to maintain the company's image.

Key to that image is store location and appearance. Computerland will help you select your location and negotiate a lease. As you prepare for store opening, the company will help you design the interior, select furnishings, and install equipment, all of which must meet stringent criteria. And most important, Computerland will advise you on signs and graphics that best display the system's logo, which is recognized nationwide.

You must complete an intensive four-week training program in management and operations, which covers everything from accounting and sales to merchandising and customer service. If you like, the company will also train you and your staff in advanced professional sales techniques. This training takes place at corporate headquarters in Hayward, California. In addition, you can receive refresher training at various locations throughout the country, to sharpen your public relations, financial, and retailing skills.

For further information contact:

Diane Douglas, Computerland Corporation, 30985 Santana, Hayward, CA 94544, 415-475-3449

Entré Computer Centers

Initial license fee: $40,000
Royalties: 8%
Advertising royalties: 1%
Minimum cash required: $90,000
Capital required: $280,000 to $950,000
Financing: None
Length of contract: 10 years

In business since: 1981
Franchising since: 1982
Total number of units: 256
Number of company-operated units: 15
Total number of units planned, 1990: NA
Number of company-operated units planned, 1990: NA

"We are at the dawn of the era of the smart machine—an 'Information Age' that will change forever the way an entire nation works, plays, travels and even thinks." The words of *Newsweek* suggest the lucrative business opportunities that can be exploited by the computer industry. According to *Business Week,* the industry is merchandising its product by "trying a variety of selling outlets. Thus far, none has proved as effective as computer specialty stores."

The mid-eighties, however, were difficult years for many computer retailers. The sale of home computers plummeted, and computer store owners discovered that selling computers to businesses would require more than just displaying the machines and waiting for customers to buy them. Entré Computer Centers survived the shakeout by emphasizing what the company calls its "consultive" approach. This franchisor, which targets professionals, small businesses, and the management of the Fortune 2000 corporations, prides itself on studying its clients' computing needs and acting as "problem solvers" in a professional, comfortable atmosphere.

The very layout of the stores themselves is designed to build confidence in the company as a user-friendly purveyor of computer equipment and software. Private demonstration areas ensure that purchasers will not feel foolish when trying out a machine for the first time. A special training room can be set up, or, when necessary, the main selling area can be converted into classroom space for training clients in a nonthreatening manner on equipment that many of them initially view as forbidding.

Entré's current identity took shape in mid-1986. Steven B. Heller and James J. Edgette, the entrepreneurs who started the company and guided it through the heady days when the industry changed by the week and fortunes were made and lost within a year, left the company. Their "hard-hitting, entrepreneurial style provided the right kind of leadership for a bold young company," says Michael Myers, Entré's director. But they recognized Entré's need for a shift to more traditional management.

The company also seeks solid managerial skills in its franchisees. Potential dealers don't need a technical background. In fact, the franchisor puts more of an emphasis on sales and marketing experience and savvy. So if you want to join the largest publicly held franchisor of retail computer centers, you should have some business experience.

If you do qualify, the company will train you at its headquarters in Vienna, Virginia. The training will last five weeks, with travel expenses, room, and board your responsibility. Aside from your instruction in standard business practices, support personnel will give you technical training and sales reps will thoroughly familiarize you with the products you will sell.

Entré will guide you through every stage of your start-up—from site selection to grand opening. The company's district support manager, your liaison with the company after you're in business, will coordinate that assistance. A distinctive part of Entre's postopening support is its continual reinforcing and updating of what you've learned. As David Brandenburg, a Dallas, Texas, franchisee, puts it: "Training programs are ongoing, extensive programs, not just refresher sessions."

Company professionals test all hardware and software you will sell—including IBM—thus assuring you that you will carry only reliable, high-quality products. You can only sell products approved by Entré, but you don't have to purchase through the franchisor. Entré emphasizes, however, that you will probably want to take advantage of the company's volume-purchasing clout.

For further information contact:
Ed Arrington, Entré Computer Centers, Inc., 1951 Kidwell Drive, Vienna, VA 22180, 703-556-0800

MicroAge Computer Stores, Inc.

Initial license fee: $30,000
Royalties: 6%
Advertising royalties: 1%
Minimum cash required: $150,000
Capital required: $300,000 to $550,000
Financing: The company helps franchisees apply for bank loans.
Length of contract: 10 years

In business since: 1976
Franchising since: 1980
Total number of units: 167
Number of company-operated units: 4
Total number of units planned, 1990: NA
Number of company-operated units planned, 1990: NA

By the standards of the personal computer industry, 1976, the year MicroAge Computer stores started, was close to the beginning of time. It predates the beginning of Apple Computers by two years. Demonstrating astute management, this now large chain of retail stores also survives many computer stores that failed in the great shakeout of the mid-eighties.

MicroAge management believes that computer businesses that survived the mid-decade winnowing out remain good investments because they've proven their mettle in a tough business environment. And they see bright prospects for selling personal computers in the future. According to the U.S. government, for about 50 million white-collar professionals, the ratio of personal computers to desks is still less than one to ten. Add to that the obsolescence of many computers bought in earlier years, the growing prevalence of personal computer networking, and continuing innovations in technology, such as speech recognition, and you have the makings of a healthy market.

Jeff McKeever, president, and Alan Hald, chairman of the board, founded the company and still head its present management. They give MicroAge leadership with solid business roots. Jeff McKeever served as vice president of First Interstate Bank of Arizona. Alan Hald, a Harvard MBA, was named one of the industry's top executives by *Computer Retail News.*

MicroAge would like its franchisees to have a strong business background. If you want to run a MicroAge computer store, you should be able to manage people, and you should have a knack for sales, a good grounding in the basics of accounting, and preferably some experience with personal computers.

When you become a franchisee, MicroAge will help you select a location for your store and negotiate the lease. The company will give you a modular fixture and decor package with which to lay out your facility and will train you, before your opening, in accounting, sales, cash flow, and computer hardware and software. Of the minimum four weeks of training you will undergo, one week will cover management, including vertical marketing, the key to business computer sales.

Your MicroAge zone manager will serve as your direct connection to the company once you start your business. He or she will help you recruit and train your staff and will advise you on advertising, finance, and distribution. The company's management, viewing the sale of complete computer systems designed to meet client companies' needs as vital to MicroAge's business, maintains a special staff to assist you with marketing in this area.

The company prepares you to anticipate and provide for your customers' changing needs by constantly updating your knowledge of the industry. MicroAge personnel will conduct seminars in your store and courses at regional stores and company headquarters. You will take some of this training in your store via the MicroAge satellite network.

As a MicroAge franchisee, you can exercise some independence in selecting stock for your business. The company handles major brands of personal computers like Apple, IBM, AT&T, and Compaq, but you do not have to follow the the central office's suggestions about inventory. You may sell any computer products, and you can get them from any source the company approves. You can also sell MicroAge's private-label products.

For further information contact:
James L. Courtney, MicroAge Computer Stores, Inc., 2308 S. 55th St., Tempe, AZ 85282-1824, 602-968-3168

Software Galeria, Inc.

Initial license fee: $30,000
Royalties: Currently 6%, but expected to be reduced to 4.5%
Advertising royalties: Now 1.5%, but projected to drop to 0.5%
Minimum cash required: $125,000
Capital required: $225,000 to $275,000
Financing: Business plan and consultation to help you obtain financing
Length of contract: 10 years

In business since: 1982
Franchising since: 1983
Total number of units: 59
Number of company-operated units: 1
Total number of units planned, 1990: 500
Number of company-operated units planned, 1990: 1

A few years ago the personal computer business looked like it would continue to grow without a pause. Exaggerated predictions painted a future in which every home would have one of these machines next to its television set. Secure in the knowledge that most businesses would have to computerize—a pretty accurate prediction—computer stores opened almost overnight to get a piece of the action. After all, businesses would have to buy their computers somewhere.

Then came the shakeout. The sale of home computers slowed, and IBM and one or two other maufacturers dominated the business hardware scene at the expense of smaller manufacturers. Many computer retailers, unable to anticipate the computer-buying patterns of businesses, saw their sales drop.

Software Galeria played its cards more carefully right from the beginning. The chain built its business on computer software—the programs that enable people to use computers to do their work. Specialization enabled the company to carve out a niche in its industry. Today Software Galeria is established in the twenty major metropolitan areas of the United States as well as in Canada, Australia, the United Kingdom, Japan, France, Germany, and Italy.

But nobody was immune from the business shocks set off by the maturing personal computer industry. And in the mid-eighties Software Galeria, too, saw the need to make some changes in its operations. Potential franchisees who wrote for information received a note among the brochures. It stated: "Since May of 1985, most Galeria stores have added computers and accessories to their product mix. This requires an additional inventory investment [now accounted for in the updated figures] and while carrying hardware is recommended, it is not required. The decision is left to the franchisee."

The marketing strategy represented by the addition of hardware zeroed in on an increasing and well-defined business need: complete systems of hardware and software dedicated to doing specific jobs. As Software Galeria vice president Jerome Murray told *Computer & Software News*: "Survival in this industry requires selling complete systems to customers with specific needs. In order to sell vertical markets aggressively, you have to sell an entire system."

Software Galeria stores successfully apply this strategy in the fields of accounting and real estate, and in CAD/CAM: computer-aided design/computer-aided manufacturing. Manufacturers in this growing field use computers for virtually every stage of the manufacturing process—from initial design to actual fabrication of finished pieces.

And that's where you will come in if you decide that this is the franchise for you. Naturally, in a field in which customers need to lean heavily on the advice and expertise of the vendor, Software Galeria will insist that you know what you're doing. Toward that end, the company will require you, as a new franchisee, and your top staff to undergo a minimum of six days of intensive training at central headquarters and at the company store in Sunnyvale, California (you pay for lodging and travel expenses). Training will include Software

Galeria's managing, financing, marketing, and merchandising methods, and the basics of promotion and advertising.

In addition, Software Galeria will thoroughly introduce you to the products you will sell. That includes names like AT&T, NCR, Epson, and Olivetti, as well as hundreds of computer programs that have been evaluated by the company as capable of doing the job for your customers. You may carry as many as 1,500 software titles as well as related books and magazines. This will enable you to confidently demonstrate equipment and software for customers as well as to offer on-site training.

The company will help you select the site for your store, design the layout, coordinate your initial advertising campaign with the company's national advertising, and introduce you to the benefits of cooperative advertising with your suppliers. Software Galeria will supply you with brochures and catalogs with your name printed on them. The franchisor will also equip you with a point-of-sale accounting system, which you are required to use.

Once in business, you can expect phone assistance through an 800 number. The company realizes that in a field like this, you have to keep up to date. Software Galeria will keep you current on all you need to know about this constantly changing industry. Its new product evaluations should prove especially useful in updating you on the 5,000 available software titles.

For further information contact:
Jean-Davis Blair, Software Galeria, Inc., 1201 San Luis Obispo, Hayward, CA 94544, 415-487-8300

Hardware and General Merchandise

Ben Franklin Stores, Inc.

Initial license fee: None, but initial training costs $1,390
Royalties: $125/month
Advertising royalties: None
Minimum cash required: $80,000
Capital required: $200,000 to $300,000
Financing: The company will help franchisees obtain bank financing.
Length of contract: 5 years

In business since: 1925
Franchising since: 1946
Total number of units: 1,537

Number of company-operated units: None
Total number of units planned, 1990: 1,937
Number of company-operated units planned, 1990: None

Ben Franklin's parent company, Household Merchandising, Inc., a leading general merchandising company, achieves sales of $5 billion annually. Ben Franklin stores offer a wide selection of merchandise, including housewares, toys, health and beauty aids, tools, clothing, and crafts. The growing size of its primary customer group, thirty-five- to forty-four-year-olds, and the increasing number of working women (who need to find a variety of items in one store) lead Ben Franklin, one of the nation's oldest franchisors, to expect that general merchandising will account for a greater and greater share of the household goods market.

The company's expansion plans call for the addition of 100 stores per year. A full-service franchise system, Ben Franklin recruits experienced retailers eager to get into business for themselves. Al Rhode, who owns three stores in southeastern Wisconsin, typifies the Ben Franklin franchisee: "For fifteen years I worked for a large national retailer, moving from one store to another. With each promotion the pay got better, so I tolerated the long hours and the politics. But finally the frustrations got to me, so I quit. After a long, thoughtful search I found Ben Franklin. Ben Franklin allows a franchise owner like me to make my own decisions and take charge of my own destiny".

Preferring to call itself an "association" rather that a franchise system and its owners "associates" rather than franchisees, Ben Franklin charges no initial license fee and a royalty of only $125 a month. The company does, however, profit from sales of merchandise to associates. Store owners benefit from a training and support system as comprehensive as any in franchising. Starting with an initial training and continuing with support in every area of store operations throughout the term of your agreement, Ben Franklin makes every effort to help ensure your success.

The fee for initial training covers one week of classroom instruction, two weeks of on-the-job training, and the expense of meals, lodging, and textbooks. You must cover the cost of your travel to and from the Rosemont, Illinois, training center. Successful Ben Franklin store owners and company management specialists will train you in daily operational techniques and strategic marketing. You will learn about customer service, advertising, financial management, payroll, hiring, supervising employees, and store layout. For six weeks prior to your store opening, a store-opening manager supervises fixture and merchandise installation and helps you train your new employees.

Once your store opens, your retail field manager will visit and call you regularly to provide merchandising, promotion, systems, procedures, personnel-training, and business-planning support. Regional merchandise specialists will assist you with product assortment planning and new and seasonal merchandising decisions. National and regional merchandise shows let you preview and discuss merchandise with other Ben Franklin store owners and company personnel. You can also take advantage of business seminars and workshops to sharpen your skills in areas of finance, accounting, insurance, merchandising, and human resources management. Ben Franklin charges small fees for participation in these workshops.

Ben Franklin purchases merchandise for all its stores. Associates order stock via an electronic service, which transmits their orders directly to the company's computers. The merchandise is then shipped from strategically located distribution centers. The system minimizes ordering time, maximizes inventory turnover, and improves cash flow and profits. You are not required to purchase through Ben Franklin, but in most cases associates will save time, money, and aggravation by tapping into this system.

As a Ben Franklin associate, you have access to two merchandising tools unique to Ben Franklin: the planogram service and the STAR program. The planogram service provides store owners with photographs and floor plans of suggested layouts for their permanent departments. Updated annually, planograms utilize the latest merchandising technology to optimize floor space, reduce inventory requirements, increase impulse buying, and improve sales. The STAR (Strategic Targeted Analysis and Repositioning) program applies sophisticated market research techniques to your region in order to analyze its demographics and your competition. You can use the results of this research to tailor your Ben Franklin store specifically to your community. The company employs Operation STAR not only for new store openings, but also for major remodelings. STAR-designed stores enjoy a greater consumer loyalty, more impulse buying, and higher sales, among other benefits.

Other services offered by Ben Franklin include: standardized merchandise identification tickets to expedite reordering; preprinted price labels to cut down on time spent stocking shelves; item activity reports, which track fast- and slow-moving sellers; a retail accounting service; and a comprehensive insurance program at competitive group rates. Associates also receive cooperative discounts on certain inventory purchases made through Ben Franklin. Finally, the company prepares a complete advertising and promotional program featuring a weekly printed ad service, advertising circulars, radio scripts, and in-store display and theme materials.

For further information contact:

Central region:

Don Erickson and Steven St. Peter, Ben Franklin Stores, Inc., 1700 South Wolf Rd., Des Plaines, IL 60018, 312-298-8800

Eastern region:

Don Enright, Ben Franklin Stores, Inc., 230 North 4th St., Seymour, IN 47274, 812-522-9400

Western region:

Pete Brown and Gary Crane, Ben Franklin Stores, Inc., 3030 South Atlantic Blvd., Los Angeles, CA 90040, 213-268-9371

Coast to Coast Stores, Inc.

Initial license fee: $3,000
Royalties: $50/month
Advertising royalties: None
Minimum cash required $100,000
Capital required: $200,000 to $700,000
Financing: The company will help you to obtain bank financing.
Length of contract: 5 years

In business since: 1928
Franchising since: 1928
Total number of units: 1,058
Number of company-operated units: None
Total number of units planned, 1990: 1,250
Number of company-operated units planned, 1990: None

Coast to Coast stores stock an assortment of hard-line merchandise, including home, lawn, farm, and garden equipment as well as sporting goods and automotive parts. Tailored to meet local market needs, each store offers a slightly different assortment of goods. The company is looking for franchisees throughout the U.S. who enjoy serving people and who have some retail experience or the aptitude to pick up retailing principles quickly.

When you become a Coast to Coast franchisee, the company will perform a market analysis in your region to select the right location for your store. At no expense to you, Coast to Coast will negotiate the lease and then sub-lease the site to you. Next, the company will train you at its Minneapolis, Minnesota, headquarters. The Coast to Coast training program, developed over sixty years of experience, is designed to give you the skills basic to successful hardware store operation. You will learn how to allocate space and construct displays, order merchandise by computer and control inventory, and handle employee relations and customer service. Following the four-day program, you will spend a day at one of the company's division offices for systems orientation.

While they were preparing to open their Coast to Coast store in Gig Harbor, Washington, Del and Margaret Garber's district manager "spent a lot of time with us—it was very helpful." Your district manager serves as your retail consultant during the term of your contract, keeping you informed on current issues. The Garbers receive "regular visits and input from our district manager. Our district managers have been quite good, and communication with the company has been open and valuable over the years. Coast to Coast will give you as much support as possible—all you need do is ask."

Coast to Coast researches and selects merchandise, which franchisees order via the franchise's computer ordering system. Based on market analysis of your area, the company will help you choose from over eight thousand items so that your store inventory perfectly matches the needs of your customers. Because of the improvement in inventory turnover that will result from the right product mix and because of the savings that you will experience through the company's purchasing power, the system will allow you to maximize your store's profitability. "The structure is there for you to follow," note the Garbers, "but after all, your store is your own business. You must know your own market and flavor your store to suit it."

Held regionally for you and your key employees, the Coast to Coast annual meeting features new-product seminars. The company believes, however, that its opening training programs are truly comprehensive and should prove sufficient for the lifetime of your association with the Coast to Coast chain. The years have shown that, for most franchisees, this is true. "Your store should succeed if you follow the Coast to Coast programs," say the Garbers, "but you have to realize that you make or break your business. It's really up to you."

For further information contact:

Doug Bailey, Coast to Coast Stores, Inc., One Cherry Center, 501 South Cherry St., Denver, CO 80222, 303-377-8400

Home Furnishings

Bathtique International, Ltd.

Initial license fee: $25,000
Royalties: 5%
Advertising Royalties: None
Minimum cash required: $25,000
Capital required: $90,000 to $100,000
Financing: The company does not offer direct financing, but it will help you present your financial proposal to lenders.
Length of contract: 10 years

In business since: 1969
Franchising since: 1969
Total number of units: 92
Number of company-operated units: 36
Total number of units planned, 1990: 149
Number of company-operated units planned, 1990: 50

As the baby boom generation matures, the prime home-buying population of thirty-five- to forty-four-year-olds grows at a rate of 15 percent annually. More than a million people a year become new home owners, spurring the rapid expansion of the home-decorating industry. According to franchising experts, home products and services franchises will remain one of the hottest areas in franchising for years to come. As a retailer of decorative bath accessories and related gift items, Bathtique is one such franchise opportunity.

Specialty retail shops get most of their business from walk-in customers, so as the old adage goes, the three keys to their success are location, location, and location. Accordingly, Bathtique has strict guidelines concerning franchisees' store locations. Enclosed malls or street locations with heavy foot traffic offer prime locations for Bathtique shops, and the company will work with you to select the best possible site from among those available and to negotiate a favorable lease.

Once you've found a location for your store, Bathtique will train you for five days at its Rochester, New York, headquarters. At no cost to you other than the expenses of travel and lodging, the classroom and in-store program covers all pertinent aspects of retailing and provides an introduction to the Bathtique franchise system. The company will then assist you in preparing to open your store. From store design and display to planning stock, buying merchandise, and advertising your grand opening, a Bathtique representative will help you in every area.

Aside from assistance with your grand opening promotion, Bathtique leaves marketing and advertising up to you. Unlike large retailers like department stores, which rely on advertising and their capability to offer a broad selection of merchandise to draw customers, as a speciality retailer you will make most of your profits from customers who buy on impulse. Advertising will play only a small role in your business, so Bathtique does not charge advertising royalties or conduct national marketing campaigns, believing that your local advertising efforts will be more effective.

Bathtique does, however, offer other ongoing support to its franchisees in the form of merchandising, buying, and inventory-control services. Quarterly refresher training, in which you can participate at your discretion, can sharpen your retailing skills. And standardized office forms, an operations manual, and the assistance of your Bathtique representative will make your job as a store owner easier—and more profitable.

For further information contact:
Don Seipel, President and CEO, Bathtique International, Ltd., Carnegie Place, 247 Goodman St. N., Rochester, NY 14607, 716-442-9190

Deck the Walls

Initial license fee: $27,500
Royalties: 6%
Advertising royalties: Liable for 2%, but currently not collected
Minimum cash required: $45,000
Capital required: $150,000 to $200,000
Financing: Up to 75% of total investment
Length of contract: 10 years

In business since: 1979
Franchising since: 1979
Total number of units: 190
Number of company-operated units: 31
Total number of units planned, 1990: 400
Number of company-operated units planned, 1990: NA

Americans like to hang things on their walls, and in recent years they've broadened their choice of style and subject matter for these home decorations. Gone are the days when a painting or print on your neighbor's wall was predictable—Currier and Ives, a Norman Rockwell, or a simple landscape. Now people hang everything from abstractions to photographs to posters advertising long past museum exhibits.

Why are Americans now willing to part with their hard-earned cash for wall decorations that might not have made it past the front door in times past? The three biggest reasons are: more education, constant exposure to art of all kinds through the media, and a desire for the status that can be gained by showing off good taste. Even advertising, with its emphasis on graphics, acts as an educator of the senses, making us tolerant of a whole range of images. And there is the increasing tendency to view what we display as making a statement about ourselves. In an age that values self-expression, any business that can appeal to such feelings taps something powerful.

The management of Deck the Walls spotted the profit potential in this social trend. The company, whose product mix includes 300 types of frame moldings as well as posters and prints featuring 1,100 different images, is a division of Wicks 'N' Sticks, a corporation whose candle stores sell gracious living through home decoration.

You can get into this timely business through the Deck the Walls franchisee training program, conducted at corporate headquarters in Houston, Texas. Subjects covered in the course of instruction include custom framing techniques, merchandising, selling, purchasing, inventory control, bookkeeping, promotion, and employee management. Hands-on experience at a corporate store will give you a taste of the "real thing" before you ever open the doors of your own store for business.

Deck the Walls will research and select the site for your store as well as negotiate the lease and supervise construction or remodeling. The company will also give you an approved list of vendors, from whom you will be able to buy at advantageous prices.

Don't worry about choosing all those pictures for your initial inventory. The company helps you choose your initial stock. It also helps you train your employees. And it will stick with you to lend its expertise right through your first weeks of operation. Deck the Walls offers periodic retraining and publishes monthly merchandising guides to update your "education." Regional franchise directors are also available for consultation on a regular basis.

According to John G. Tipple, who runs a Deck the Walls unit in a shopping mall in Austin, Texas, a franchise from this company "requires close follow-up and hard work." But he likes the mix of company support with the freedom to run his own store and make many of his own decisions. And, Tipple says: "It has been an excellent investment."

For further information contact:

Houghton B. Hutcheson, Deck the Walls, 7915 FM 1960W, Suite 300, Houston, TX 77070, 713-890-5900

Lewis of London

Initial license fee: $40,000
Royalties: 5% to 10% on the wholesale price of merchandise
Advertising royalties: $2,500/year
Minimum cash required: $150,000
Capital required: $200,000
Financing: None
Length of contract: 10 years

In business since: 1950
Franchising since: 1977
Total number of units: 21
Number of company-operated units: 5
Total number of units planned, 1990: 46
Number of company-operated units planned, 1990: 12

"Products aimed at the juvenile market have been selling like hotcakes since 1980," *Business Week* reported not long ago. The market generated by the new baby boom has provided a big lift to this industry. During the 1970s, about 3.15 million babies were born each year, but that figure has increased to more than 3.5 million per year during the 1980s. Even more significant, the percentage of first births has risen from 25 percent in the seventies to about 40 percent now. Parents usually must purchase cribs, high chairs, and other baby furniture for these children, since there are fewer hand-me-downs for them.

Lewis of London has ridden the crest of this phenomenon with a unique approach. Not every children's store carries $1,500 gold-plated cribs. But while Lewis of London caters to luxurious tastes, it more often serves the typical upscale customer. The majority of cribs sold, for example, run closer to $600, where the average department store crib costs about $150. The middle class, rather than the wealthy, constitute the bulk of Lewis' clientele. The two-income family, Lewis' primary market, can afford to act on the conviction that "a room full of run-of-the-mill furniture is no place for a one-of-a-kind baby," as a Lewis of London catalog puts it.

The typical Lewis of London store occupies about 3,000 square feet. "Our stores have a boutique atmosphere, which is achieved by complete room settings," explains Gordon Schurmer, part-owner of the company. "Our floor displays do not consist of a hundred cribs lined up in a row. Instead, we have twelve to fifteen room settings so that the customer can see a complete room with the furniture, soft goods—even wall-hangings and coordinated accessories."

Why should you sign on with Lewis of London rather than start your own upscale baby furniture business? Because of volume buying power and easier credit approval. "Franchising," as Gordon Schurmer puts it, "makes things easier for everyone. For someone to go out and open a baby store now and try to find a line, get suppliers, get credit, would be a lot more difficult than opening one of our franchises, which is basically a turnkey operation." Patsy Jacobs, who owns a Lewis of London store in Highland Park, Illinois, especially appreciates the advantages of the turnkey setup. She has "freedom of operation, and the business is my own."

If you buy a Lewis of London franchise, you will have to locate in a region with a population of more than 800,000, with an average family income of at least $25,000. Lewis of London will evaluate your choice, and if it meets its standards, it will help you negotiate the lease.

At one of its company-owned stores and at its headquarters in Hauppauge, New York, Lewis of London will train you to run your business. The intensive instruction will cover sales techniques, product awareness, bookkeeping, and management. You will also receive a week of on-premises help just before you open your store. Through additional training at the company's annual meetings, you will learn about new products and advertising material. Lewis of London will also be available for consultation—in person if necessary—at any time during the term of your contract. The company "answers all questions," says Patsy Jacobs, and company personnel have even "flown in to give assistance."

Lewis of London stores distinguish themselves from most retailers of children's accessories by carrying high-quality items like beechwood dressing tables, huge plush giraffes, children's designer clothing, Italian high chairs, and Japanese strollers with optional sunroofs. And Lewis of London never holds a sale.

For further information contact:
Joel Rallo, Lewis of London, 25 Power Drive, Hauppauge, NY 11788, 516-582-8300

Scandia Down Corporation

Initial license fee: $25,000
Royalties: 5%
Advertising royalties: 3%
Minimum cash required: $60,000
Capital required: $150,000
Financing: The company will help you apply for a loan.
Length of contract: 10 years

In business since: 1980
Franchising since: 1980
Total number of units: 100
Number of company-operated units: None
Total number of units planned, 1990: 270
Number of company-operated units planned, 1990: None

Scandia Down's mall and storefront shops present inviting displays of brass and designer beds topped with elegant Italian, Swiss, French, German, and domestic bed linens puffed up with soft down. The company gets its down from Canada, Poland, and China, as well as Scandinavia, and has it specially processed in an independent plant in Seattle. Scandia sells only upscale merchandise, much of it exclusive to its shops. Customers can also buy custom-sewn and designed ensemble sets, shams, and dust ruffles.

Scandia leans heavily on research by firms like Yankelovich Skelly and White in formulating its marketing strategy. It takes the same care when choosing a location for your store. Scandia reviews your lease, but you and your lawyer must negotiate the final terms. The franchisor will then assist you in designing your shop's interior. The Scandia store look—track-lit, with a cozy feeling—is an important part of the company's image.

You do not need previous retail experience to run a Scandia shop. The company fills any gap in your background with a two-week training course in Kent, Washington, covering products, sales, advertising, accounting, personnel, inventory control, purchasing, and merchandising. You pay only for travel, lodging, and meals. Later on, you can get refresher training if you need it.

Scandia Down's field operations representative spends at least five days at your store during your grand opening period, helping you start your business. Although you can carry some linens and accessories not in the usual company inventory, you must buy most of your stock from Scandia, which is the only source for the bulk of the merchandise carried by Scandia Down stores.

Scandia advertises in national magazines like *Architectural Digest*, *House Beautiful*, and *Sunset*. It also produces two full-color catalogs each year. You will receive copies of the catalogs to hand out in your shop and use in your direct mail campaigns. And Scandia will forward to you any requests for information that customers in your exclusive territory send directly to the company.

For further information contact:
Tom Hansen, Director of Franchise Development, Scandia Down Corporation, P.O. Box 88819, Seattle, WA 98188, 206-251-5050

Spring Crest

Initial license fee: $10,000
Royalties: 3%
Advertising royalties: 2%
Minimum cash required: $20,000
Capital required: $49,000
Financing: None
Length of contract: 10 years

In business since: 1955
Franchising since: 1968
Total number of units: 275
Number of company-operated units: None
Total number of units planned, 1990: 401
Number of company-operated units planned, 1990: 1

Ankie Meppelink didn't have to research this company before she bought her franchise. She had previously managed a Spring Crest store and purchased her business "knowing full well what the franchise was all about."

What it's all about is perfect pleats. Spring Crest has built a large franchise business by successfully marketing special spring steel pleaters, which keep drapes from bunching and gathering. Spring Crest stores also sell the company's wood drapery poles, made of cherrywood, bamboo, oak, and mahogany. Spring Crest backs all its products with a ten-year warranty.

Spring Crest will help you locate a good site for your store, and the franchise agreement will take effect only after both you and the company agree to the location. Although the company will advise you on the design and layout of your place of business, you will make the final decisions. Spring Crest stores usually occupy 1,200 to 1,600 square feet.

You will take your two-week training course at Spring Crest's home office in Brea, California. The $3,000 you pay the franchisor for training, store design, and business setup includes the travel and lodging expenses for two people at the training session. The course includes a comprehensive look at all aspects of the window covering industry. Later on, regional seminars and convention workshops will provide opportunities for updated training.

Your regional manager will help you set up your store and will work with you on the finer details of hardware installation. The manager will also see to it that your opening and first few days in business go smoothly.

Although you can buy equipment and supplies for your store from whomever you please, Spring Crest offers you an added incentive to purchase from its list of preferred suppliers. These vendors put 3 percent to 5 percent of the amount of your purchases into an advertising fund for your store. This does not constitute part of the advertising you are required to do under your franchise agreement.

Spring Crest advertises in publications such as *The Saturday Evening Post* and *House Beautiful*. It will run a grand opening advertising campaign on your behalf, for which you pay $3,000. And it will make available to you an audio-visual promotional program to help build sales from within your store. Your franchise agreement requires you to spend 1 percent of your sales on local advertising.

For further information contact:
Jack W. Long, President, Spring Crest Company, 505 West Lambert Rd., Brea, CA 92621, 714-529-9993

Wicks 'N' Sticks

Initial license fee: $27,500
Royalties: 6%
Advertising royalties: None at present, but franchise agreement states that company may collect 2% in the future
Minimum cash required: $45,000
Capital required: $150,000 to $200,000
Financing: The company will finance up to 75% of total investment.
Length of contract: 10 years

In business since: 1968
Franchising since: 1968
Total number of units: 290
Number of company-operated units: 9
Total number of units planned, 1990: 500
Number of company-operated units planned, 1990: NA

"The U.S. life-style is changing, and many Americans are returning to their homes as the center of family activity," says Harold R. Otto, president and cofounder of Wicks 'N' Sticks. He sensed this trend coming in 1968, when he started the company. Back then, candle stores catered mostly to tourists, and none had thought of merchandising candles as inexpensive home decorations and items for everyday use. By placing its stores in regional malls, Wicks 'N' Sticks positioned itself among other stores that sold products for the home, and introduced to customers the idea that they could use candles every day and not just for special occasions.

Wicks 'N' Sticks stores appeal to all the senses. As shoppers walk in, fragrances envelop them, varied shapes tempt them to touch, and a rainbow of colors delights their eyes. The names of some candle scents—piña colada, french vanilla—suggest a multiflavor ice cream store. Company buyers always search for new candle shapes to add to the product mix, which includes everything from small items costing a few dollars to two-foot high owl candles costing several hundred dollars. The stores also stock a variety of elegant glass candle holders. According to Newington, New Hampshire, franchisee Mary Jane Maglione, "the concept of Wicks 'N' Sticks stores is unique—no other chain has ever duplicated it."

Wicks 'N' Sticks offers you a week of training at its Houston headquarters, where you pay only for out-of-pocket costs. Subjects covered in the course include merchandising, selling, purchasing, promotion, inventory control, bookkeeping, pricing, and personnel. The training also includes hands-on experience in a company store.

The company will make setting up your operation relatively easy, since it will do most of the preliminary work. Wicks 'N' Sticks picks a promising regional mall location, negotiates the lease, and supervises construction of your store. The company's new store team stocks your shop, trains your employees, and spends the first week on the premises, easing you into your business. Thereafter a regional franchise director will visit you four times a year, and you can call the home office for advice on specific problems. Workshops and seminars, given at regional meetings and the annual convention, provide you with further ongoing assistance.

Wicks 'N' Sticks has taken special pains to build up a network of suppliers, many of whom sell exclusively to the company. This enables the company to secure big discounts for its franchisees as well as constantly supply them with new products.

For further information contact:

Houghton B. Hutcheson, Wicks 'N' Sticks, 7915 FM 1960W, Suite 300, Houston, TX 77070, 713-890-5900

Rental Stores

Colortyme, Inc.

Initial license fee: $10,000
Royalties: 3%
Advertising royalties: 3%
Minimum cash required: $38,000
Capital required: $38,000 to $73,000
Financing: The company has contracted with a third-party lender to provide financing to franchisees.
Length of contract: 5 years

In business since: 1980
Franchising since: 1982
Total number of units: 455
Number of company-operated units: None
Total number of units planned, 1990: NA
Number of company-operated units planned, 1990: NA

In recent years, consumers have taken an interest in a method of purchasing known as rent-to-own. Often the down payment required by retailers for the outright purchase of major household items is prohibitively high, so people come to rental centers like Colortyme for furniture and appliances. Through Colortyme Rental Centers, customers can rent items for a day or two—for instance, if they need folding chairs or punch bowls for a party—or long term, and apply their rental payments toward the ultimate purchase of a VCR, washing machine, or dining room set. Colortyme Rental Centers across the United States offer a specialized inventory of products, such as televisions, audio-visual equipment, appliances, and furniture.

Before you can become a Colortyme franchisee, you must find a company-approved site for your rental center, typically in a downtown storefront or suburban shopping center. For the term of your franchise contract, Colortyme will loan you the various signs and fixtures that will identify your store as a Colortyme outlet. The company will also provide you with plans and specifications for both the interior and exterior of your store, which you are required to follow. If you like, you can obtain office supplies and advertising materials from Colortyme, which makes a small profit on these sales, but you are free to purchase your office supplies from any source that meets the company's standards.

Every Colortyme offers a line of quality products, each of which has passed the company's rigorous controls. You can purchase these items from any source, but you may not offer unapproved products in your Colortyme Rental Center.

Before your grand opening, you and your franchise manager must participate in the company's five-week training program. Two weeks of this training takes place at a designated training center before you have signed the franchise agreement. Once you have actually signed the agreement, you will attend a week of classroom training at the company's headquarters in Athens, Texas. This training stresses basic operating principles and prepares you to train your own employees. You will learn general management skills, the principles of managing rental accounts, sales, ordering, delivery, equipment installation, and customer relations. Then, to test your newly acquired skills, Colortyme gives you two weeks of on-the-job training. In cases where the company feels your previous experience has adequately prepared you to run a Colortyme Rental Center, it may not require you to train formally.

If you need help in opening your Colortyme Rental Center, a company supervisor will come to your store and provide the necessary assistance. The company will also provide you with opening promotional and advertising materials and will supply you with an operating manual that you will use through out the term of your contract. You will be able to review samples of promotional materials developed by Colortyme and choose those most appropriate for use in your region. Colortyme's list of approved products contains a wide selection of merchandise from which you can build an inventory with the right product mix. And if at any time you have questions abut your Colortyme franchise, the company will provide consultation and advice.

For further information contact:

Wayne Atchison, Vice President, Franchising, Colortyme, Inc., P.O. Box 1781, Highway 175 West, Athens, TX 75751, 214-675-9291

Curtis Mathes Corporation

Initial license fee: $25,000
Royalties: None
Advertising royalties: 6%
Minimum cash required: $125,000
Capital required: $125,000
Financing: Certain third-party lenders have agreed to provide financing to qualified franchisees.
Length of contract: 1 year

In business since: 1920
Franchising since: 1982
Total number of units: 642
Number of company-operated units: 42
Total number of units planned, 1990: 850
Number of company-operated units planned, 1990:NA

Remember when VCRs first came out? Even the most expensive, sophisticated unit could only perform the simplest functions, and those not all that well. Now VCRs are not only more versatile and reliable, but more affordable as well. Consider personal cassette players, pocket calculators, compact disc players, or personal computers: The rule of thumb in home electronics seems to be that each year technological advances provide more entertainment or work capability per dollar. Many turn to rental or leasing of home entertainment systems while they wait for the price of their favorite gadget to come down and its abilities to go up. Others rush out to buy all the latest gizmos, only to trade up when new, improved versions are introduced.

Whether they rent or buy, Americans are hooked on high tech. Curtis Mathes Home Entertainment Centers rent, sell, and lease a broad line of high-quality electronic home entertainment products with extended warranties to serve this market. The stores also offer video movie rental clubs, satellite antenna systems, and complete service capability. Founded decades before electronics revolutionized everyday life, Curtis Mathes originally marketed other types of home accessories. In 1982 the company adopted franchising in order to expand more quickly in all regions of the U.S.

Four weeks of training will prepare you to operate your Cutis Mathes Home Entertainment Center. The first two weeks take place in Dallas, Texas, and will familiarize you with the Curtis Mathes system. The second two weeks are held at a designated training center near your location and cover the nuts and bolts of operating your business. "A strong point of the initial training," says Michael Rutledge, a Curtis Mathes franchisee in Ocala, Florida, "was that it was goal oriented. The training in each area of the business—retailing, management, and such—lasted a week or more. We trained in all fields of the business to prepare for success." The comprehensive business and management instruction includes bookkeeping, sales, and hiring and training personnel.

Outside the classroom, your preopening support continues with managerial and technical assistance in such areas as site selection, lease negotiation, store design and layout, financing, inventory control, advertising, and promotions—in short, the company will help you through every stage of your store opening. As Michael Rutledge puts it, "The open-door policy Curtis Mathes maintains toward franchisees is second to none. And there is ample coordination between dealers in helping each other out in times of need. Anyone can get in trouble, but we are a team. Between the company and the store owners, a total team effort is put forth for each dealer."

Part of that team effort is the company's program of follow-up training, held several times a year. The company will sometimes require you to take these refresher courses, and at other times it will leave the decision up to you. Some of the courses offered provide instruction in rental sales, account management, advertising and promotions planning, satellite receiver installation and troubleshooting, basic retail skills, motivational skills, and audio sales, among other things. "All of our people go through any training offered by Curtis Mathes," says Michael Rutledge, "and the ad-packs are great for planning advertising."

In your daily operations you can find the answers to many of your questions in your operating or technical manuals. You can also call on the technical service manager in your region, your district manager (there are fifty throughout the country), or for bigger problems you can contact your region manager, who is one of four in the U.S. "I have been a member of the franchise group for a long time, and Curtis Mathes has always been there. Each day is a better day for my business, and I don't think it could have worked out this well without Curtis Mathes," says Michael Rutledge. He concludes: "I couldn't ask for a finer group of people to work with."

For further information contact:
Rolland Barron or Reese Davis, Curtis Mathes Corporation, 1411 Greenway Drive, Irving, TX 75038, 214-550-8050

Nation-Wide General Rental Centers, Inc.

Initial license fee: None
Royalties: None
Advertising royalties: None
Minimum cash required: $7,000
Capital required: $25,000
Financing: The company offers 100% financing for inventory you buy after your initial purchase of rental goods.
Length of contract: 3 years

In business since: 1976
Franchising since: 1976

Total number of units: 143
Number of company-operated units: None
Total number of units planned, 1990: NA
Number of company-operated units planned, 1990: None

Nation-Wide has built its business on a simple idea. Many people occasionally need tools and equipment of various kinds for specific jobs. It doesn't pay for them to buy, so renting without having to worry about maintenance does make sense. A business that could meet the needs of such do-it-yourselfers, contractors, party givers, convalescents, and campers, all from one location, could turn a healthy profit. Customers who rent for one occasion or task would see the wide variety of tools and equipment available and might return in the future when their rental needs changed.

Nation-Wide franchised distributors run just such businesses; they have something in stock for just about everybody. Their inventory includes reversible drills, sod cutters, toboggans, wheelchairs, folding cots, torque wrenches, party tents, staple guns, dollies, paving breakers, wallpaper steamers, typewriters, pipe threaders, sanders, sleeping bags, and cement mixers. They also rent Santa Claus suits.

As a Nation-Wide franchisee, you can choose what kinds of equipment to rent in your business. The company ensures that you won't have to take a loss on unprofitable stock by offering a buy-back guarantee. Nation-Wide will take back for full credit any equipment that does not produce income in the first year.

If a Nation-Wide franchise appeals to you, you will need a building with at least 2,000 square feet inside and 15,000 square feet of securely fenced area outside. Some Nation-Wide centers occupy buildings as big as 7,000 square feet. You will need good traffic flow in the area and parking for six to ten cars.

Nation-Wide will train you to run an equipment rental center at its Columbia, South Carolina, rental center. Your five-day training course will cover equipment maintenance, the company's computerized accounting system, advertising and promotion, rental rates, insurance, and inventory control. Your accounting system will generate an itemized inventory report detailing monthly rental income per item, in addition to a balance sheet and income and cash flow statements.

Your Nation-Wide business preparation package, included in your licensing fee, contains a grand opening pennant, decals, 10,000 flyers, 10,000 rental contracts, and stationery. Nation-Wide supplements your local promotions with national advertising in magazines like *Popular Science* and *Popular Mechanics*.

For further information contact:
Ike Goodvin, Nation-Wide General Rental Centers, Inc., 1684 Highway 92 West, Suite A, Woodstock, GA 30188, 404-924-0057

Remco Enterprises, Inc.

Initial license fee: $15,000
Royalties: 3% to 6%
Advertising royalties: None
Minimum cash required: $60,000
Capital required: $60,000 to $200,000
Financing: The company helps arrange inventory loans and computer and vehicle leases.
Length of contract: 10 years

In business since: 1968
Franchising since: 1981
Total number of units: 163
Number of company-operated units: 56
Total number of units planned, 1990: 340
Number of company-operated units planned, 1990: NA

The number of stores that rent merchandise to consumers has doubled since 1970. Especially popular in the Sunbelt and Midwest, these stores have flourished by renting out items like washers, dryers, air conditioners, televisions, VCRs, and furniture. Remco, founded and still headquartered in Houston, has units in seventy cities, which focus on renting appliances to a young, predominantly blue-collar market. Its customers rent rather than buy because they move frequently and also may not be able to afford to pay one lump sum to purchase what they want.

The Remco rental plan offers several options to the customer. Through the rental/ownership program, rental customers own the appliance at the end of the rental term. In effect, the customer buys the item on time—with free service if it malfunctions during the rental period. Alternately, they can buy the appliance at any time during the rental term, or their third option is to return it and end the rental whenever they wish. The company creates a wide customer base by keeping the rental terms reasonable: It requires no down payment, just the first week's or month's payment in advance.

Remco will help you select a shopping center site for your store. In fact, the company puts so much emphasis on this process that it includes a preliminary location evaluation form in the first information package it sends prospective franchisees. It also helps you to negotiate the lease. Once you have leased the premises and have made improvements to prepare it for business, Remco will deliver its prefabricated modular store display components to display your rental merchandise to its best advantage. Remco calls this installation the "Store-in-a-Box."

You will probably need a staff of two or three, including a manager, to begin operations. Remco will help you hire a manager and will test him or her during a mandatory training session in Houston, reporting the results to you. The training, which is also open to you, covers general management, sales, cash control, bookkeeping, and credit. You will pay for any living and transportation expenses associated with the training.

Training developed specifically for owner-investors takes place over an extended period of time and will include instructional printed materials and videotapes as well as classroom training conducted by Remco personnel. This training covers real estate, staffing, purchasing, legal problems, financial planning and management, advertising and marketing, and product service.

A Remco operational manager will visit your store periodically to analyze your business and also to advise you on subjects like sales, hiring, and collections. You or your manager file regular reports through your computer system (which you buy or lease), and the operations manager will discuss these reports with you. The computer system will also enable you to keep tabs on your business from a distance, facilitating absentee ownership, since you can tap into Remco's mainframe computer from anywhere in the country to review the reports your store has been filing.

You will select stock in consultation with the franchisor. Remco will supply only top brands, including GE, Zenith, Pioneer, JVC, Sharp, Whirlpool, Kenwood, and Marantz. You will not have to maintain a huge inventory, since Remco promises easy availability of all rental items.

Remco will help you work out an advertising budget and will develop an advertising plan for your store that makes use of local television when available. It will also place your yellow pages advertisement at a lower cost than you could obtain if you did it yourself.

For further information contact:
Victor Beale, Remco Enterprises, Inc., 10703 Stancliff, Houston, TX 77099, 713-561-3319

Taylor Rental Corporation

Initial license fee: $20,000
Royalties: 2.75%/year up to $200,000 gross sales; 2.5% from $200,000 to $500,000; 2% over $500,000
Advertising royalties: None
Minimum cash required: $80,000
Capital required: $255,000
Financing: None
Length of contract: NA

In business since: 1949
Franchising since: 1962
Total number of units: 415
Number of company-operated units: 30
Total number of units planned, 1990: NA
Number of company-operated units planned, 1990: NA

Taylor Rental, the largest general rental chain in America, is a subsidiary of The Stanley Works, a manufacturer of building tools for professionals and do-it-yourselfers. Taylor franchisees rent out champagne fountains, cement mixers, popcorn machines, jack hammers, baby cribs, carpet cleaners, typewriters, pitchers and serving platters, wheelbarrows, lanterns—and just about everything else. Offering a broad line of rental merchandise has the advantage of partially insulating Taylor stores from recessions, since they draw customers from every walk of life.

When you buy a franchise, Taylor's staff will help you select a site for your rental center and will advise you on construction if you decide not to rent an already existing building. Your facility will occupy about 4,500 square feet indoors and include a fenced outdoor area of approximately 1,500 square feet. A bigger building can compensate if you can't find a store with outside space. You also need parking space for at least six cars.

You will train to run your rental store at one of Taylor's company-owned centers. The program lasts two weeks and covers personnel, advertising, customer relations, cash control, financial systems, inventory management, loss prevention, and the operation and maintenance of equipment. You can have future employees trained by the company for a minimal charge. Once in business, you will receive informal ongoing training from your regional director.

The company will work with you to determine the right product mix for your location. If you buy at least 60 percent of your inventory from Taylor, it will send a representative to your store to help you assemble and display your stock. Similarly, your purchase of display fixtures from the company entitles you to the services of a Taylor fixture installer, who will do the work for a competitive fee.

The company offers several optional computer programs to help franchisees manage their businesses. In 1980 it developed TOPIC, the first general rental industry computer system, in consultation with an advisory group of franchisees. With this system, you can track your inventory and handle your accounting. Other available software enables you to communicate your rental sales data to company headquarters and receive from the company an analysis of your inventory utilization. Through the company you can also buy liability insurance for your business.

Taylor has a co-op advertising program, through which it refunds to you 25 percent of your advertising expenditures up to 1 percent of your gross revenue. Its advertising department will also help you place your yellow pages advertisements and will provide you with direct mail and other types of promotional materials.

For further information contact:
Taylor Rental Corporation, 1000 Stanley Drive, New Britain, CT 06050, 203-229-9100

Specialty Retailing

Annie's Book Stop

Initial license fee: $25,000
Royalties: $50 to $100/month plus 2%
Advertising royalties: $25 to $100/month
Minimum cash required: $35,000
Capital required: $35,000 to $40,000
Financing: The company does not offer any direct financing, but a bank plan and loan application are included in the franchise package.
Length of contract: 5 years

In business since: 1974
Franchising since: 1981
Total number of units: 72
Number of company-operated units: None
Total number of units planned, 1990: 140
Number of company-operated units planned, 1990: None

Most book lovers dreams of owning their own bookstore. What could be more appealing than spending each day in the company of your favorite books and bibliophiles like yourself—and making a profit from it? But running a bookstore is also a business, and enormous numbers of independent bookstores fail each year because their owners know more about the Brontës than they do about bookkeeping. If you've always wanted to own a bookshop but never knew quite where to start, franchising can provide you with the know-how and experience you need.

Annie's Book Stop is a network of bookstores specializing in "upscale" paperbacks. The stores carry all kinds of books, from the biggest best-sellers to the most obscure titles. As a franchisee you will be able to offer discounts of up to 50 percent off the price of new juvenile and coffeetable books, and up to 20% off new best-sellers. Annie's shops also carry other discounted gift items. The company's marketing strategy features a number of decorative, display, and sign approaches designed to enhance name recognition and appeal to affluent young book buyers. Plans for expansion focus on the South, West, and Midwest.

If you feel you need it, you can train for up to a week at a company-owned store before opening your own Annie's Book Stop. The company will help you select your shop location and negotiate a lease and will provide a week of training and preopening assistance at your site. Store design and installation of fixtures takes up the first few days of the preopening training week, followed by three days of instruction in book categorization and shelving systems. On the day before opening, your company representative will help you with the remaining operational and decorating details. By the time you open your doors (with the complete assistance of your company representative), you will be fully trained in bookstore operations.

After opening day, you have the freedom to operate your bookstore according to your own managerial style. Your purchases of supplies and equipment, however, must meet the corporate guidelines, to ensure that your Annie's Book Stop contributes positively to the company's carefully planned image. An operations manual, updated regularly, provides guidance on daily administrative issues, and the home office is always available by telephone to answer any other questions you might have. The company publishes quarterly newsletters designed to keep you informed about developments in the company and the industry and provides directories of Annie's Book Stop locations for distribution in all shops.

Elected from among all active franchisees, an advisory board meets three or four times a year to review current franchise operations and to address franchisee relations and other topics of concern. Each year, Annie's Book Stop holds its two-day convention, which provides a forum for owners to meet with one another and with corporate staff and to share ideas and problems.

For further information contact:
Annie Adams, Annie's Book Stop, 15 Lackey St., Westborough, MA 01581, 617-366-9547

Docktor Pet Centers

Initial license fee: $15,000
Royalties: 4.5%
Advertising royalties: None
Minimum cash required: $50,000
Capital required: $149,000 to $192,000
Financing: Available
Length of contract: NA

In business since: 1967
Franchising since: 1967
Total number of units: 219
Number of company-operated units: 14
Total number of units planned, 1990: NA
Number of company-operated units planned, 1990: NA

This $5 billion industry's jargon may sound strange, unless you often refer to dogs and cats as "livestock." Docktor Pet Centers sell the pets familiar to everyone. Working on the theory that pet stores sell not only animals but love, Docktor Pet Centers encourage potential purchasers to handle animals in the store. And if you go into this business, it should be for love of animals as much as for love of profits, since you will spend your days surrounded by dogs, cats, fish, birds, and other kinds of pets.

Of course, any pet store is more than fur and fins. There are also combs, cages, flea collars, and food. The Docktor Pet Center merchandising system will make it possible for you to sell more than 1,800 items, 617 made under the company's own brand. Supplies and accessories make up a good part of the business of Docktor Pet Centers, the largest chain of shopping center-based pet department stores in the country. Accessories constitute the bulk of the chain's repeat business, and Docktor Pet Centers focus on developing merchandising techniques designed to make the hard goods pay off for each store. Sometimes that means taking an unusual approach like displaying sweaters for dogs on hangers instead of in bags on shelves. It also means pricing to fit the market. Your judgment of your local market comes into play here, because you will set your own selling prices.

If you love animals but worry that you don't know a cockatiel from a cockatoo and have real familiarity only with cats and dogs (your store will sell forty breeds), you'll feel reassured once you realize that Docktor Pet Center store owners range from former automobile industry executives to salespeople to teachers. The company's three-week training course, given in Wilmington, Massachusetts, will teach you every facet of the business, from management to animal care. Through your regional consultant and in national and regional seminars, Docktor Pet Centers will continue its assistance and instruction once you open for business.

Docktor Pet Centers will help you select a site for your pet store, negotiate the lease, and design your store's layout. The franchisor provides a computerized bookkeeping system to help you manage your money, and a variety of promotional materials to help you build sales volume.

For further information contact:
Docktor Pet Centers, Inc., 355 Middlesex Ave., Wilmington, MA 01887, 1-800-325-6011

Flowerama of America, Inc.

Initial license fee: $17,500
Royalties: 5% to 6%
Advertising royalties: None
Minimum cash required: $20,000
Capital required: $50,000 to $90,000
Financing: None
Length of contract: 10 years

In business since: 1967
Franchising since: 1972
Total number of units: 98
Number of company-operated units: 12
Total number of units planned, 1990: 156
Number of company-operated units planned, 1990: 20

Somewhere between luxuries and necessities lie the things that brighten our lives. Much of the thriving home-decoration business is based on people's desire to make attractive things part of their daily life-style. Flowers used to be a luxury; now growing numbers of Americans, especially those between the ages of twenty-five and forty-five, are thinking of them as an integral part of good living, something they buy as a matter of course.

For most people, flowers used to be reserved for special occasions—

birthdays and anniversaries, for example. Now flowers are as likely as a bottle of wine to be the gift you bring when invited to a friend's house for dinner. And many people buy fresh-cut flowers for their home as a regular practice—simply because flowers bring with them a sense of graciousness at a reasonable price.

So it is not only people with high incomes that the florist business caters to now—it is just about anybody. That's why you shouldn't be surprised to learn that Flowerama confines its operations to regional enclosed shopping centers, where its stores operate alongside those selling shoes, records, housewares, and the thousands of other things people buy regularly.

Flowerama units, whether 450-square-foot kiosks or 1,000-square-foot in-line stores, aim to attract a wide public and sell flowers at popular prices. Flowerama wants people to get into the flower-buying habit. And the company wants to do this throughout the country, although currently they do not offer franchises on the West Coast.

If selling fresh-cut flowers, floral arrangements, plants, and related accessories appeals to you, Flowerama will give you a considerable amount of help getting into the business. Not only does Flowerama take charge of selecting a site and negotiating your lease, the company actually signs the main lease agreement and then sublets the location to you at no profit to itself.

The company will teach you the ins and outs of the retail flower business at its Waterloo, Iowa, headquarters. Your nine-day training seminar at Waterloo covers everything you will need to know about floral design as well as store operational procedures and accounting. You will also receive on-the-job training at a Flowerama store.

Flowerama will have somebody on hand to help you open your business, and a company representative will drop in several times a year after that. You can get further training at Waterloo in seminars offered about five times a year. Blooming plants, hard goods, packaging, professional signs, and how to create successful promotions are subjects likely to be covered.

Flowerama assures potential franchisees that help is never more than a telephone call away. Greg Heid, who with his wife, Pat, operates the Flowerama franchise at the University Square Mall in Tampa, Florida, tells us that they are more than satisfied with that aspect of their franchising experience. "The company provides us with any help we ask for," he says, "whether it be legal, accounting, or merchandising techniques."

You do not have to buy your equipment and inventory from Flowerama, although franchisees generally opt for the convenience of purchasing from the company.

For further information contact:
Chuck Nygren, Flowerama of America, Inc., 3165 West Airline Highway, Waterloo, IA 50703, 319-291-6004

Petland

Initial license fee: None
Royalties: 4%
Advertising royalties: 0.5%
Minimum cash required: $60,000
Capital required: $150,000 to $450,000
Financing: The company helps franchisees prepare bank loan applications.
Length of contract: 20 years

In business since: 1967
Franchising since: 1971
Total number of units: 100
Number of company-operated units: 6
Total number of units planned, 1990: 200
Number of company-operated units planned, 1990: 2

To get an idea of the potential market for pets, pick up a copy of your local white pages and point to any listing at random. The odds are better than even that at least one pet lives at that number. A recent pet census shows that Americans own something like 250 million tropical fish, 48 million dogs, 27.2 million cats, and 25.2 million birds. People have to buy many of these creatures someplace, and all the animals need food and supplies—continually.

Petland wants to put you in the business of providing people with animal companionship and the supplies they need to keep their pets healthy and happy. This franchisor usually provides its franchisees with a turnkey operation: Petland will locate a site, build your store, install the prefabricated fixtures, and stock it with animals and accessories. In many cases, franchisees sublease their stores from Petland when the company has found and set up their store for them. If you sublease your premises, you will receive the same terms that Petland gets from the landlord. Petland stores range in size from regional mall or strip center stores of 2,500 to 4,500 square feet to "super" stores that occupy as much as 8,000 square feet. Sometimes franchisees can select their own site and build their own store to Petland's specifications.

You can operate one of these franchises even if you don't have animal expertise. The company will teach you everything you need to know, from how to work with a veterinarian to how to tame a bird by thinking like one. Petland will train you at its headquarters in Chillicothe, Ohio. In addition to animal care, the company's instruction will cover store management, personnel, accessories, inventory, merchandising, bookkeeping, and community relations.

Several days before you open for business, Petland's merchandising team will come to work at your side while you stock your store and get it ready for your grand opening. Company representatives will stay with you for up to ten days after you open, guiding you through the new experience of operating your own pet store.

Not only can you call Petland for advice on specific problems, it will call you regularly with advice and encouragement, and to review your monthly financial statement. This close attention generally enables the company to spot any trouble before it becomes a big problem. You will also receive regular visits from a Petland representative, who will follow a 1,000-point checklist to inspect your store and make sure that everything is up to company standards.

You have your choice of buying supplies from the Petland distribution network or from company-approved local suppliers. Petland ships by truck from its 18,000-square-foot warehouse in Chillicothe, Ohio, or it can drop ship directly from the manufacturer to you, in which case you receive the same discounts that you get when you buy directly from the franchisor. Even if you choose to buy from local sources, your supplier will have to match the low prices available to you through Petland. You can also purchase a line of private-label Petland supplies.

Each year when you begin to think about purchasing your Christmas inventory, Petland's distribution network sponsors an annual fall trade show at which manufacturers and distributors show animals as well as new products. There you can further your education in the business and also get together with your fellow franchisees to exchange information.

Petland runs several seasonal and year-round promotions through its franchisees. The company also provides giveaway calendars and sponsors contests and fish and bird clubs with membership cards and publications.

The best opportunities to open a Petland franchise now exist in the Sunbelt states of California, Florida, and Texas, and in Colorado, Illinois, Wisconsin, Michigan, Pennsylvania, Ohio, Illinois, North Carolina, Virginia, and Maryland.

For further information contact:

L. H. Heuring, Franchise Sales Coordinator, Petland, Inc., 195 North Hickory St., Chillicothe, OH 45601-5606, 1-800-221-5935; in Ohio: 1-800-221-3479

Video

Adventureland Video, Inc.

Initial license fee: $15,500
Royalties: 4.5%
Advertising royalties: None
Minimum cash required: $15,500
Capital required: $55,000 to $65,000
Financing: None
Length of contract: NA

In business since: 1981
Franchising since: 1982
Total number of units: 693
Number of company-operated units: 40
Total number of units planned, 1990: NA
Number of company-operated units planned, 1990: NA

Not since the advent of television in the 1950s has the entertainment industry seen such extraordinary change as that brought on by the video revolution. Americans have purchased more than 20 million video cassette recorders to date, and experts predict that half of the 80 million television households in the U.S. will own VCRs within the next two years. Many of these VCR owners and owners-to-be are families concerned about the quality of entertainment that comes into their homes. Adventureland Video meets their demand for wholesome video entertainment.

Adventureland has quickly become one of the country's largest and fastest-growing video stores. Franchisees benefit from national recognition of the Adventureland name, which the company fosters with distribution of a consumer video newsletter (200,000 copies per printing), high-profile press coverage of Adventureland activities, and nationwide promotions like vacation and cash giveaways. The company's officers, though, attribute Adventureland's explosive success to its policy of offering only family-oriented video and the best service in the industry. William Erickson, an Adventureland franchisee in Lehi, Utah, feels that his own success is due to "name recognition, shared ideas, and cooperative advertising."

Despite the company's youth, it offers franchisees the full complement of home office support services, from comprehensive basic training to exclusive territorial rights to a toll-free WATS line for instant assistance. Basic training covers management, merchandising, personnel administration, market analysis, technical background, and everything else involved in opening and operating your Adventureland store. The corporate field support staff offer professional direction in your advertising and promotional campaigns and information on new company developments, recommended products, and titles. The Adventureland operations manual, newsletters, bulletins, and seminars cover just about everything else relevant to your business.

Special features of the Adventureland franchise program are its distribution service center, through which you can order merchandise and supplies (and cash in on the company's purchasing power), and monthly store analyses and semiannual performance audits designed to ensure that your business operates at its full potential. The company supplies you with standardized accounting forms, legal data, inventory selection recommendations, and employee training tapes to help you maintain Adventureland's standards and image.

The company's guidelines for franchise operation include proven retailing and marketing methods that will help you enhance sales. Every Adventureland store features the same familiar signs, window graphics, and contemporary interior design, as well as a special area in which customers can learn to operate equipment. This standardization offers "strength in numbers," notes William Erickson, that can help you "make a lot of money in a very competitive environment."

For further information contact:
Michael F. Manning, Director of Sales, Adventureland Video, Inc., 4516 South 700 East, Suite 260, Salt Lake City, UT 84107, 1-800-227-0143; 801-266-9679

National Video, Inc.

Initial license fee: $35,000
Royalties: 4.9%
Advertising royalties: 3%
Minimum cash required: $39,500
Capital required: $39,500 to $350,000
Financing: None
Length of contract: NA

In business since: 1977
Franchising since: 1981
Total number of units: 662
Number of company-operated units: 3
Total number of units planned, 1990: 1,600
Number of company-operated units planned, 1990: 25

"We wanted to be the McDonald's of the industry," says Ron Berger, National Video's founder, about his company's beginnings. "And like

McDonald's we intended to provide the tools and backup that would allow the store owner to do what he does best, run his store successfully." Ron Berger had an idea of where he was going because in a way he had already been there. In 1974 he started the Photo Factory, which became a fifty-seven store chain spanning eight states.

The stores in his current chain feature the sale of prerecorded and blank video cassettes, accessories, and related products, as well as VCR and tape rentals (there is no "club membership" charge). In fact, according to Ron Berger, "the key to staying in business is sales," not just rentals of videotapes, and the company pushes that idea with its franchisees.

National Video Stores handle adult videos, but with discretion. Ron Berger states: "Under no circumstances do we allow our retailers to advertise, promote, or display adult products. Although they are allowed to carry adult tapes, the only way a consumer is going to know it's there is if he or she asks."

The company will guide you in every aspect of constructing or leasing and laying out your store. National Video trains its franchisees at company expense in Schaumberg, Illinois. "Most appropriately," notes Ron Berger, "it's located right near McDonald's Hamburger University." Classroom and hands-on instruction in a company store train new franchisees in the basics of running a National Video store. In addition, a company representative comes to your store for further training leading up to the opening of your new business. Regional operations managers provide assistance after that, and you can receive instant advice through the company hot line. For everyday advice, the franchisee can refer to the National Video operations manual—as thick as five Manhattan yellow pages directories, according to Ron Berger.

Once in business as a National Video franchisee, you can take advantage of numerous features of this company's franchising operations, like its extensive group buying program. National Video is an authorized distributor of Quasar and Sharp VCRs and Walt Disney films, as well as JVC and Scotch blank tape. National Video also sells its own brand of blank tape.

Because of its ties with various companies—some of them part of the Hollywood entertainment industry—National Video can also offer you numerous in-store promotional items, including free movie posters from Paramount, Warner Brothers, and MGM. You can also use Walt Disney characters to decorate your children's section. [Paul] Newman's Own Oldstyle Picture Show Popcorn is available exclusively to National Video franchisees to give away as a video promotional item. The franchisor has even developed its own mascot, the Viddy O. Bear, available as a toy or printed on T-shirts and other items.

National Video makes "coming attractions" preview tapes for soon-to-be available tape rentals, which you can play in your store. The company also issues its own credit card, currently held by 600,000 customers throughout the country. In addition, the company runs national contests and sweepstakes and promotional tie-ins with companies like Coca-Cola and Sears.

One of the company's greatest assets is its in-house advertising agency. Says Ron Berger: "If the dealer calls us up with an idea for an ad in the morning, we can have our art department design it, lay it out, and send it to the dealer the same day. It's as if the dealer had his own agency. Like an agency, we can actually track the effectiveness of the ad, and should it appear to work, we can share it with all our other operators." Nor does the company skimp on national advertising. You can find National Video ads in *TV Guide* and *People Magazine*, as well as on television.

Most National Video franchises are Class I stores designed for areas with populations over 10,000. Smaller Class II stores, targeted at rural areas, require a proportionately smaller investment. You can get information on this unit from the company.

For about $40,000, which includes the franchise fee, you could buy a National Video Movie Express Kiosk. This "store within a store," often found in a K-Mart, Sears, or Safeway retail store, begins with an initial inventory of 400 films, to which you add about 20 or 30 additional titles a month. The unit occupies about 200 to 300 square feet of space. Big retailers have been turning to National Video franchisees to open such businesses because they have had neither the personnel nor the expertise to run these operations successfully themselves.

For further information contact:
Franchise Development Department, National Video, Inc., P.O. Box 18220, Portland, OR 97218-0220, 503-284-2965

Network Video

Initial license fee: None
Royalties: None
Advertising Royalties: None
Minimum cash required: $37,900
Capital required: $37,900 to $60,900
Financing: None
Length of contract: Franchise is sold outright

In business since: 1981
Franchising since: 1981

Total number of units: 172
Number of company-operated units: NA
Total number of units planned, 1990: NA
Number of company-operated units planned, 1990: NA

Network Video sells a hybrid operation—not quite a franchise but more than an independent business. People with a strong entrepreneurial instinct and a desire to call their own shots, but who also want start-up help and the benefits of volume purchasing in a competitive field, might find this business just right for them.

Network Video sells you a turnkey operation containing all the inventory and promotional material you need to set up a rental video business. The package also includes assistance with site selection and lease negotiation, ongoing advice via the telephone, and the opportunity to purchase tapes and equipment through the company at prices lower than those paid by independent stores. Network Video only sells one store in each area, hence you receive, in effect, a protected territory. In the near future, Network Video stores will probably run cooperative advertising. For these goods and services you pay a one-time fee—and no royalties of any kind.

You choose between two packages, according to the size of your market. The "Basic" package, at $37,900, covers operations in small towns, where your store will probably have little or no competition. It includes 400 movies, plus rental equipment, promotional items, and fixtures. The "Competitive" outfit, sold in markets where franchisees will have to compete with other stores, includes 800 movies, in addition to everything contained in the less expensive package. Currently, Network Video sells about an equal number of each package.

While you have the final say on the size of your facility, Network Video, based on the results of its own research, has determined that 1,200 square feet is the ideal size for the seventeen company-owned competitive-level stores that it plans to build soon. The company will locate its units in strip shopping centers and staff each with two full-time and two part-time workers. Most of the units that Network Video has sold to franchisees have been opened in Ohio, Pennsylvania, New York, and Florida, and the company welcomes expansion in other states.

The company will train you and your employees at your location and will supervise your grand opening promotion, and it will provide ongoing support through its telephone hot line.

For further information contact:
Network Video, 8320 South Tamiami Trail, Sarasota, FL 33583, 813-966-3626

Sounds Easy International, Inc.

Initial license fee: $15,000
Royalties: 5%
Advertising royalties: None
Minimum cash required: $30,000
Capital required: $100,000 to $150,000
Financing: None
Length of contract: 10 years; two 5-year renewals

In business since: 1980
Franchising since: 1981
Total number of units: 93
Number of company-operated Units: 1
Total number of units planned, 1990: NA
Number of company-operated units planned, 1990: NA

Sounds Easy is an ancient company by the standards of the video industry. With six years of experience renting video cassettes, it can trace its roots almost back to the industry's beginnings. And it made what turned out to be a shrewd decision right at the beginning: rent only VHS tapes, the format that was to virtually chase Beta off the field. According to the company, it was the first to confine its stock to VHS. It also decided at the beginning to stay away from steamy X-rated films. Sounds Easy stores have, as the company puts it, "strictly a family-type atmosphere."

Sounds Easy has set a high goal for itself: to place one of its video cassette rental stores "in every community in America!" Currently, its operations are concentrated in the West and Midwest, with Utah and Minnesota leading other states in numbers of franchises. If you decide to own the Sounds Easy video store in your area, you'll tap into a segment of the home entertainment market whose growth has been strong and steady. Within a few years, there will probably be a VCR in most American homes. Meanwhile, to serve homes that still don't have one of these addictive gadgets, Sounds Easy stores also rent the machines.

Compared to most franchises, Sounds Easy's licensing fees and minimum required capital are on the low end. The company has deliberately kept the financial requirements low to achieve quick expansion and market penetration. But you will have to invest plenty of energy and determination, if not a lot of money. Initial training lasts five days at the Sounds Easy national training center in Minneapolis. You are responsible for the lodging, food, and travel expenses related to your training.

Your training in Minneapolis will be intensive, with frequent quizzes and a comprehensive final exam to make sure you're absorbing everything. None of the company's franchises have ever failed, and it doesn't want you to be the first. One of the teaching methods, appropriately enough, is the videotaping of trainees as they practice skills such as telephone communications, handling reservations, and meeting with and instructing employees. The course also covers maintenance of VCRs and videotapes, and standard business practices, including bookkeeping, budgeting, and inventory control. Sounds Easy will also teach you how to plan a profitable ad campaign and develop effective in-store promotions.

The company will also guide you through the launching of your enterprise. Sounds Easy helps you select a site for your store and negotiate the lease. You can figure on having to purchase about forty VCRs and spending at least $50,000 on your initial inventory of films. Sounds Easy will have a representative at your grand opening, and that person will stay for a couple of days afterwards to make sure you get a good start.

The company gives a refresher training seminar annually at regional locations. It covers advertising, personnel policies, and updates on developments in the industry. There's also a monthly newsletter, periodic special seminars and conferences, and an advisory council for consultation and advice.

This franchise offers a maximum of independence for the franchisee who wants to mold a business to his or her tastes. Sounds Easy provides expertise, research, and guidance for every major decision you'll have to make. For equipment and fixtures, the company gives you an approved list of vendors. But you will have the final decision regarding which movies you will carry in your store.

For further information contact:

David Meine, Sounds Easy International, Inc., P.O. Box 989, Orem, UT 84057, 1-800-437-4363

Video Biz

Initial license fee: $55,000
Royalties: 2.5%
Advertising royalties: 2.5%
Minimum cash required: $85,000
Capital required: $85,000
Financing: None
Length of contract: 35 years

In business since: 1981
Franchising since: 1983
Total number of units: 250
Number of company-operated units: 1
Total number of units planned, 1990: 1,200
Number of company-operated units planned, 1990: NA

Ray Fenster and Robert Moffett, cofounders and still principals of Video Biz, pioneered videotape-rental stores and franchising for Video Station in 1978. Their experience with franchising, they say, is the key to their success. Robert Moffett states: "Some of the other chains that have had problems were run by good retailers but not good franchisors. It's not just a matter of training your store owners how to rent and sell tapes. It's providing them with the tools and know-how that can enable their Video Biz franchises to become almost one-stop convenience centers. Hardware, software, blank tapes, tape cases, etc.—a good franchisor makes the carrying of these items a potentially profit-making situation for the stores."

The company's franchise fee may seem high, but the figure is all-inclusive. Video Biz sells a turnkey operation, so the fee includes the cost of your opening inventory of rental tapes, equipment, and promotional materials, as well as training, which you receive at your store.

While you will find your own location, negotiate your own lease, and make store alterations, Video Biz will provide advice on site selection, since the company considers this a crucial decision. Your fee includes the company's fixture and decor package. A typical Video Biz store has a striped awning, track lighting, and glass display cases, with promotional material set out alongside rental tapes.

When you buy a Video Biz franchise, you buy the company's purchasing clout as well as the merchandise and assistance included in its franchise package. In 1985 *Venture* ranked Video Biz number thirty among the fastest-growing franchisors in America, and it has continued to grow at a rapid rate, making it capable of negotiating some of the lowest wholesale prices in the industry on films and equipment. The company passes on these savings. In an industry where competition has reached a fever pitch, that price edge could mean the difference not only between modest and substantial profits, but also between surviving or failing, as many less competitive independent video stores have.

Video Biz promotes its name through national advertising, which includes full-page advertisments in *Video Review*. It also sponsors a variety of promotional events, such as contests, in franchisee stores.

For further information contact:
Ed Fainelli, Video Biz, 2981 West State Rd. 434, Longwood, FL 32779, 305-774-5000

Video Update, Inc.

Initial license fee: $19,500
Royalties: 5%
Advertising royalties: 3%
Minimum cash required: $60,000
Capital required: $120,000 to $150,000
Financing: None
Length of contract: 7 years

In business since: 1981
Franchising since: 1982
Total number of units: 94
Number of company-operated units: 3
Total number of units planned, 1990: 674
Number of company-operated units planned, 1990: 24

This rapidly growing chain of video-rental stores has ambitious goals for further expansion, geographically as well as in the number of its franchises. It seeks new franchisees all over America, but if you would like to open a store in Europe, Australia, or Malaysia, the company would also like to hear from you.

A typical Video Update store covers about two thousand square feet, and it has a special kids' section known as the "kiddie corner," where kid-size fixtures, puppets, and balloons encourage children to browse. The company will help you select the site for your store and will advise you on exterior and interior design.

Video Update will train you at its headquarters in Saint Paul, Minnesota, and at your store. The course covers retailing, accounting, customer and employee relations, and advertising, as well as Video Update store operations. Later on, periodic visits from company representatives and phone contact with the franchisor will keep you up to date on company policies and programs.

Your initial stock ranges from 1,000 to 1,500 VHS rental tapes. Although the company distributes new videotapes to most franchisees, you do not have to purchase your movies from the company. Your franchise package includes ten VCR rental units, and Video Update's exclusive computer software will help you control your inventory and keep up-to-date customer records.

Among the kinds of advertising run by Video Update, one stands out as particularly appropriate to its business. The company has cross-promotional agreements with the makers of major motion pictures like *Poltergeist II, Crazywheels,* and *Datenight,* to include the Video Update logo in their movies. Video Update also arranges more conventional cooperative advertising with distributors, can run a direct mail campaign for you, and will assist you in your own advertising efforts.

For further information contact:

Richard P. Bedard, Video Update, Inc., 261 East 5th St., St. Paul, MN 55101, 612-222-0006

18. The Travel Industry

Contents

Travel Agencies

International Tours, Inc.

Initial license fee: $34,000
Royalties: .75% on revenues up to $500,000; 0.5% on higher amounts
Advertising royalties: None
Minimum cash required: $40,000
Capital required: $70,000 to $90,000
Financing: None
Length of contract: 20 years

In business since: 1968
Franchising since: 1970
Total number of units: 263
Number of company-operated units: 2
Total number of units planned, 1990: 600 to 800
Number of company-operated units planned, 1990: NA

The number of travel agencies has doubled over the past decade, and their average annual volume has tripled. Travel costs less than it used to, so more people can afford to travel. We have an older population, and older people often travel for leisure. But the intense competition from airline deregulation has promoted bigness among the agencies as much as among airlines. The discounts available to volume purchasers emphasize economies of scale in the travel business. In this atmosphere, the little guy gets squeezed.

International Tours suggests that travel agents caught in this squeeze, or people interested in getting into the field in the first place, would do well to link their fortunes to the oldest and largest franchisor of travel agencies. But although International aims for growth, it intends to grow under closely controlled conditions. Only in the past few years has the company begun to expand out of the Midwest.

Particular about its choice of franchisees, International prefers somebody with successful managerial or sales experience, although it does not insist on this. More than half of its franchisees owned a business previously, but no more than 20 percent of these were travel agents.

The company's national sales manager, Larry Davidson, once said of International's franchise selection policy: "Honesty and their standing in the community are big factors in the approval process. After every meeting Ron Blaylock [International's president], other staff members, and I discuss whether a prospect is right for us, and we actually turn down quite a few applicants who have the financing for the franchise package but just don't fit our criteria."

If you do pass muster, the company will evaluate potential sites for your agency and will negotiate a lease. It will also offer advice on office layouts, the purchase of furniture and office equipment, and color schemes. Subscriptions to basic industry publications also come with the franchise package. And International will help you choose a qualified manager for your first agency.

At a five-day training session in Tulsa, Oklahoma, the company will teach you its way of conducting a business—all costs except meals included. Topics you will study include accounting, budget review, sales and marketing, and travel agency computerization. In the course of your training you will receive manuals totaling almost fifteen hundred pages, which detail the operations of your agency. Those new to the field may also want to take advantage of the course offerings of the International Travel Institute, an International Tours subsidiary. Also located in Tulsa (with additional facilities in Houston), this school trains people for work in all segments of the travel industry. Franchisees pay no tuition, and their employees get reduced rates.

International will send a representative to your agency for a week of start-up help. You can call for additional support on the company's toll-free number. Frequent follow-up training seminars in Tulsa cover subjects such as how to train outside sales personnel and how to secure and retain commercial accounts.

Other parts of the company's assistance program include uniforms for your staff and a ready-to-use bookkeeping system with monthly balance sheets and profit-and-loss statements for the first six months. They will also guide you through the process of getting approval for your business from the various airline regulatory groups.

International Tours runs several special programs that benefit its franchisees. Travel-Trac, a computer software package, aids in budget forecasting. The company maintains travel planning facilities for the handicapped unmatched by any other agencies, according to International. And the company travel club, instituted in 1986, involves a direct marketing campaign featuring discounts and other promotions. The first promotional mailing was sent to 350,000 people.

International Tours prides itself on being a company with a rock solid reputation and a policy of steady but conservative growth. The company's management, employees, and franchisees own most of its stock, and the company boasts of never having lost a franchise to bankruptcy.

Klara Bley owns the International franchise in Hickory, North Carolina. When asked if she would change any part of her relationship with the franchisor, she replied that "it is perfect the way it is. If we need help in management, we get it, but otherwise our business is as good as we are. If we work hard, we're doing great, and if I don't want to do anything, nobody forces me." "Terrific," is how she summed up the relationship. "I trust them totally."

For further information contact:
Peggy Hurley, International Tours, Inc., 5001 E. 68th, Suite 530, Tulsa, OK 74136, 918-494-8721

Travel Agents International

Initial license fee: $24,500
Royalties: $750/month
Advertising royalties: $400/month
Minimum cash required: $39,000
Capital required: 76,000
Financing: None
Length of contract: NA

In business since: 1980
Franchising since: 1982
Total number of units: 166
Number of company-operated units: 1
Total number of units planned, 1990: NA
Number of company-operated units planned, 1990: NA

Travel Agents International points to the numbers to make its case for the future of the travel agency business, and its franchise system in particular. It reports that more than 68 percent of all airline tickets sold in America in 1985 were sold through travel agents—and Travel Agents International did $220 million of that business. Every day, at least 15 million Americans travel at least 100 miles. In 1985 that added up to $242 billion spent on travel. And yet half of Americans who travel do not yet use a travel agent. Moreover, 20 million people in this country who could afford to take a cruise have never taken one.

According to Travel Agents International, people with no previous experience in the industry can conquer such markets. It says that most of its franchisees have never owned an agency, yet none of its franchises have ever failed. The company stays competitive by constantly upgrading its client services. The first travel franchisor to mail a monthly promotional newspaper directly to all franchise clients, Travel Agents International pioneered in sending management reports to commercial clients and was the first to operate its own tour company.

The company will help you hire a second-in-command for your agency, whose background in the industry will lend your business instant respectability and experience. Travel Agents International's two-week training course, which you take in Clearwater, Florida, starts you on the road to travel industry savvy with units on marketing and advertising, incentive plans, government regulation agencies, computer training, travel insurance, and vacation and commercial travel sales, as well as standard business topics like accounting and employee relations. Quarterly regional seminars will continue your education, and any employees you hire during the term of your contract can take the company's regional orientation seminar for new staff members.

Travel Agents International will help you find the right site for your agency and negotiate the lease. It will assist you in establishing working relationships with suppliers of travel products and will give you a flowchart that details your preopening tasks and the sequence in which you should do them. The furniture and supply package the company requires you to buy includes everything from wall posters to chairs to credit memos. You also get fifty flight bags and a safe as part of the package. A company representative will spend two days at your agency just before you open for business, giving you last-minute instructions, answering your questions, and making sure that your employees are fully prepared to serve your customers.

Travel Agents International will plan your local television advertising campaign, which is timed to coincide with your opening. It will conduct a market profile study of your area and will help you prepare direct mail advertising. The company also arranges co-op advertising with product suppliers and offers you promotional items at a discount.

In 1986 the company accelerated its growth by instituting a conversion franchise program, permitting independent travel agents to enter the company's system. It also started the Travel Training Academy, a school that offers classes on various aspects of the travel business taught by senior company staff at franchise locations.

For further information contact:
Travel Agents International, Inc., 8640 Seminole Blvd., Seminole, FL 33542, 1-800-237-1258; in Florida: 1-800-282-4817

Uniglobe Travel [International] Inc.

Initial license fee: $42,500
Royalties: 1%
Advertising royalties: $582/month
Minimum cash required: $55,000
Capital required: $150,000
Financing: Varies by region
Length of contract: 10 years

In business since: 1979
Franchising since: 1980
Total number of units: 375
Number of company-operated units: None
Total number of units planned, 1990: 1,550
Number of company-operated units planned, 1990: None

One of the top five international travel organizations after only a few years in existence, Uniglobe accounts for about 2 percent of all retail travel outlets in America. The company has zeroed in on the corporate travel market, pursuing commercial contracts by using aggressive sales techniques. To date, this strategy has landed as many as 15,000 corporate accounts. Uniglobe's business strategy for the next few years calls for marketing vacation packages as aggressively as it has sold commercial travel.

Uniglobe sells conversion franchises to independent travel agents for a fee of $15,000. For brand new start-up businesses, it charges $42,500 and assists with site selection and lease negotiations. The company also offers a custom layout and design for your agency and will help you staff your business and obtain any necessary licenses.

You must take the company's four-day management training course, which it holds in Vancouver, British Columbia. Uniglobe encourages you to bring your manager along, too. Your franchise fee covers tuition for both of you. The course topics include commercial and group sales, the vacation market, cash flow, and personnel.

Uniglobe believes in continuous training. To increase the knowledge and skills of you and your staff, the company offers an extensive selection of regional courses on advanced topics in the travel business. These courses cover subjects like closing commercial sales, vacation sales, employee motivation, promotions, the convention business, special incentive programs, customer relations, and budgeting.

Your regional office will provide guidance during your start-up period, beginning with a fifty-step checklist that will help you systematically do everything you need to do to get off to a strong start. The regional office will also put you in touch with your travel products suppliers and will help coordinate your opening promotion. Thereafter, the regional office will serve as your travel consultant, just as you perform this function for your customers.

Your franchise package includes exclusive computer software, initial office supplies, stationery, and business forms imprinted with your company name. Uniglobe will give you a list of "preferred suppliers" for your future purchases.

Uniglobe advertises on television and currently spends about $2 million dollars a year to promote its image.

For further information contact:

Michael Levy, Senior Vice President, Uniglobe Travel, Inc., 90-10551 Shellbridge Way, Richmond, B.C., Canada, V6X 2W9, 604-270-2241

Part III

Tables and Indexes

Table 1: Franchisor Data

Companies Listed in Order of Total Number of Units in Operation

Company Name	*Total Units*	*Company-Owned*	*Founded*	*Franchising Since*
H & R Block, Inc.	9,000	4,100	1946	1958
McDonald's Corp.	8,500	2,500	1955	1955
Kentucky Fried Chicken	8,200	1,800	1930	1952
7-Eleven	7,323	4,526	1927	1964
Help-U-Sell, Inc.	6,500	0	1976	1978
Intl. Dairy Queen, Inc.	4,805	7	1940	1944
Jazzercise, Inc.	3,275	0	1976	1983
ServiceMaster	3,250	0	1948	1952
Baskin-Robbins Ice Cream Co.	3,225	68	1945	1948
Wendy's Intl., Inc.	3,120	1,150	1969	1971
Budget Rent a Car Corp.	3,100	75	1958	1960
Domino's Pizza, Inc.	2,826	796	1960	1967
Hardee's Food Systems, Inc.	2,546	875	1960	1962
Taco Bell Corp.	2,200	1,150	1962	1964
Uniroyal Goodrich	2,200	0	1870	1920
Diet Center, Inc.	2,090	0	1972	1972
Ben Franklin Stores, Inc.	1,537	0	1925	1946
Midas Intl. Corp.	1,508	40	1956	1956
Arby's, Inc.	1,500	200	1964	1965
Church's Fried Chicken, Inc.	1,445	1,218	1952	1952
Long John Silver's Seafood	1,378	838	1969	1970
Dunkin' Donuts of America	1,350	65	1950	1950
American Intl. Rent A Car Corp.	1,300	0	1969	1969

Company Name	*Total Units*	*Company-Owned*	*Founded*	*Franchising Since*
Convenient Food Mart, Inc.	1,276	10	1958	1958
Pearle Vision Center, Inc.	1,130	450	1962	1980
Martin Franchise, Inc.	1,100	0	1949	1949
Postal Instant Press	1,072	5	1965	1968
Fantastic Sam's	1,064	3	1974	1976
Coast to Coast Stores, Inc.	1,058	0	1928	1928
Rainbow Intl. Carpet	975	2	1981	1981
Kwik-Kopy Corp.	972	0	1967	1967
Sonic	931	80	1973	1975
AAMCO Transmissions, Inc.	920	0	1963	1963
Computerland Corp.	852	1	1976	1977
Dial One Intl., Inc.	833	0	1982	1982
Jani-King Intl., Inc.	825	0	1969	1974
Jack in the Box	813	671	1950	1983
Bob's Big Boy Restaurant System	800	200	1936	1954
Packy the Shipper	800	0	1976	1981
Subway Sandwiches and Salads	800	11	1965	1975
RE/MAX	783	0	1973	1976
Orange Julius	768	33	1926	1963
Chem-Dry Carpet Cleaning	759	0	1977	1977
Pizza Inn, Inc.	725	280	1961	1963
Meineke Discount Muffler Shops	704	1	1972	1972
Mister Donut	704	2	1955	1956
General Business Services, Inc.	700	0	1962	1962
Adventureland Video, Inc.	693	40	1981	1982
Nutri/System	683	133	1971	1972
National Video, Inc.	662	3	1977	1981
Curtis Mathes Corp.	642	42	1920	1980
Ponderosa Steakhouses	630	430	1965	1966
Cutco Industries, Inc.	612	52	1955	1967
Goodyear Tire Centers	610	0	1898	1968
Servpro Industries, Inc.	600	0	1967	1967
Sir Speedy, Inc.	600	0	1968	1968
Western Sizzlin Steak House	582	3	1962	1966
Bonanza Restaurants	551	NA	1962	NA
Hickory Farms of Ohio, Inc.	550	300	1959	1960
Roy Rogers Restaurants	546	359	1968	1968

Company Name	*Total Units*	*Company-Owned*	*Founded*	*Franchising Since*
Dollar Rent A Car	540	10	1966	1969
Tastee-Freez International	537	0	1950	1950
Minuteman Press	524	0	1973	1975
A & W Restaurants, Inc.	515	7	1919	1925
Gallery of Homes, Inc.	500	0	1950	1950
Thrifty Rent-A-Car System, Inc.	491	1	1962	1964
Rax Restaurants	486	153	1978	1978
Decorating Den Systems Inc.	485	0	1969	1970
Captain D's Seafood Restaurants	484	270	1969	1975
Round Table Pizza	481	10	1959	1962
Sizzler Restaurants Intl., Inc.	472	144	1957	1961
The Athlete's Foot	469	102	1972	1973
*ISU Intl.	465	0	1979	1980
Carl's Junior Restaurants	458	381	1956	1984
Colortyme, Inc.	455	0	1980	1982
Intl. House of Pancakes	450	115	1958	1958
Mr. Build Intl.	450	0	1981	1981
Snelling and Snelling	445	0	1951	1955
Taylor Rental Corp.	415	30	1949	1962
Maaco Auto Painting	405	5	1972	1972
Taco John's Intl.	400	5	1969	1969
Swensen's	386	18	1948	1963
Personnel Pool of America	381	103	1946	1956
American Speedy Printing	375	0	1977	1977
Uniglobe Travel [Intl.] Inc.	375	0	1979	1980
Ziebart Corp.	371	14	1954	1962
Bojangles'	369	169	1977	1979
Command Performance	352	10	1976	1976
Rent-A-Wreck	350	3	1969	1980
Bressler's 33 Flavors, Inc.	335	5	1963	1963
Popeyes Famous Fried Chicken	333	170	1972	1976
Insty-Prints, Inc.	330	4	1965	1967
Merry Maids, Inc.	325	1	1980	1980
Money Concepts Intl., Inc.	319	1	1979	1982
Lawn Doctor	301	1	1967	1969
Clentech/Acoustic Clean	300	0	1976	1984
Pioneer Take Out Corp.	300	45	1961	1961

Company Name	*Total Units*	*Company-Owned*	*Founded*	*Franchising Since*
Precision Tune, Inc.	295	2	1976	1977
Wicks 'N' Sticks	290	9	1968	1968
Original Great American Cookie	288	39	1977	1978
Dunhill Personnel Systems, Inc.	284	2	1952	1961
TCBY	281	18	1981	1982
Spring Crest	275	0	1955	1968
Shakey's Pizza Restaurant	271	11	1954	1958
Village Inn Pancake House	266	132	1958	1961
Intl. Tours, Inc.	262	15	1979	1979
Stained Glass Overlay, Inc.	260	0	1974	1981
Entré Computer Centers	256	15	1981	1982
Stanley Steemer Intl., Inc.	253	20	1947	1972
Norrell Services	252	160	1961	1967
Video Biz	250	1	1981	1983
Intl. Blimpie Corp.	240	1	1964	1977
Western Temporary Services, Inc.	236	145	1948	1984
The Hair Performers	234	7	1967	1977
Taco Time Intl., Inc.	234	17	1959	1961
Gingiss Intl., Inc.	228	23	1936	1968
Molly Maid, Inc.	226	1	1984	1984
RainSoft Water Conditioning	220	0	1953	1963
Docktor Pet Centers	219	14	1967	1967
Dahlberg Electronics, Inc.	214	14	1948	1984
Homes & Land Publishing Corp.	208	0	1973	1984
The Ground Round, Inc.	207	167	1969	1970
Mr. Transmission	207	2	1962	1978
Mail Boxes Etc., USA	205	0	1980	1980
Steamatic	202	12	1948	1967
Victory Intl., Inc.	202	0	1969	1982
Gymboree	201	5	1976	1980
Athletic Attic Marketing, Inc.	200	0	1972	1973
Frontier Fruit & Nut Co.	196	89	1977	1978
The Peanut Shack	196	39	1975	1975
Physicians Weight Loss Centers	195	20	1979	1980
Western Steer Family Steakhouse	191	25	1975	1975
Deck the Walls	190	31	1979	1979
TV Focus, Inc.	190	0	1980	1980

Company Name	*Total Units*	*Company-Owned*	*Founded*	*Franchising Since*
Quik Print	185	60	1963	1966
Lindal Cedar Homes, Inc.	178	4	1945	1962
David's Cookies	176	1	1979	1983
Dynamark Security Centers, Inc.	172	0	1977	1984
Network Video	172	0	1981	1981
Corp. Invest. Bus. Brokers, Inc.	169	0	1979	1982
MicroAge Computer Stores, Inc.	167	4	1976	1980
Po Folks, Inc.	167	56	1975	1975
First Choice Haircutters	166	82	1980	1981
Travel Agents Intl.	166	1	1980	1982
Four Seasons Greenhouses	165	4	1975	1985
Remco Enterprises, Inc.	163	56	1968	1981
The Maids Intl., Inc.	161	0	1979	1981
Del Taco, Inc.	160	134	1965	1981
One-Hour Moto Photo	160	3	1981	1982
Tuff-Kote Dinol, Inc.	160	8	1964	1967
Langenwalter Carpet Dyeing	152	0	1972	1981
Marcoin Business Services	151	15	1952	1956
Holiday-Payless Rent-A-Car System	150	0	1971	1971
Sbarro	147	93	1977	1977
Dry Clean-USA	145	51	1977	1977
Coustic-Glo Intl., Inc.	143	0	1977	1980
Nation-Wide Gen. Rental, Inc.	143	0	1976	1976
Video Data Services	142	2	1980	1981
Lee Myles Associates Corp.	140	0	1947	1964
Sylvan Learning Corp.	136	3	1979	1982
Mazzio's Pizza	134	45	1961	1968
Maid Brigade	133	0	1982	1982
Freedom Rent-A-Car	130	2	1981	1981
Noble Roman's Pizza	127	55	1972	1973
Great Clips, Inc.	123	7	1982	1983
AAA Employment	121	88	1957	1977
Sparks Tune-Up	120	0	1980	1981
Primo's/Jan Drake's	119	16	1972	1976
Spring-Green Lawn Care Corp.	118	3	1977	1977
Just * Pants	116	0	1969	1969
Paul W. Davis Systems, Inc.	115	0	1966	1970

Company Name	Total Units	Company-Owned	Founded	Franchising Since
Champion Auto Stores, Inc.	113	10	1956	1961
NuVision, Inc.	113	77	1950	1983
Sales Consultants Intl.	111	24	1957	1965
D'Lites of America, Inc.	110	35	1981	1982
State Wide Real Estate Services	110	NA	1944	1944
El Chico Corp.	106	81	1940	1960
Money Mailer, Inc.	102	0	1979	1979
CAR-X Service Systems, Inc.	101	0	1971	1973
K-Bob's, Inc.	101	3	1966	1968
National Financial Co.	101	1	1970	1970
Petland	100	6	1967	1971
Scandia Down Corp.	100	0	1980	1980
Flowerama of America, Inc.	98	12	1967	1972
TriMark Publishing Co., Inc.	96	0	1969	1978
Video Update, Inc.	94	3	1981	1982
Sounds Easy Intl., Inc.	93	1	1980	1981
American Advertising Distributors	92	2	1975	1977
Bathtique Intl., Ltd.	92	36	1969	1969
Earl Keim Realty	92	0	1958	1968
New England Log Homes	87	1	1969	1970
All American Hero	84	4	1980	1980
Endrust Industries	81	1	1969	1969
Playful Parenting	79	0	1971	1984
CHROMA Intl.	77	1	1983	1983
California Closet Co., Inc.	74	3	1978	1982
Annie's Book Stop	72	0	1974	1981
HouseMaster of America	72	0	1971	1979
Print Shack Intl., Inc.	71	0	1982	1983
Everything Yogurt	70	18	1976	1982
Interstate Auto. Transmission	69	2	1973	1974
Mifax Service and Systems, Inc.	68	0	1969	1979
American Vision Centers, Inc.	67	24	1977	1977
Grease Monkey Intl., Inc.	63	0	1978	1978
Pilot Air Freight	59	1	1970	1978
Software Galeria, Inc.	59	1	1982	1983
Coit Drapery and Carpet Cleaners	54	8	1950	1962
CHEM-CLEAN Restoration	52	0	1966	1968

Company Name	*Total Units*	*Company-Owned*	*Founded*	*Franchising Since*
Sportastiks	50	1	1979	1985
Benihana of Tokyo	44	37	1964	1970
F-O-R-T-U-N-E Franchise Corp.	37	0	1959	1973
Gelato Classico Italian Ice Cream	35	5	1976	1982
Duds 'n Suds Corp.	34	8	1983	1984
Cuco's Restaurantes	30	10	1981	1984
Homeowners Concept, Inc.	21	0	1982	1985
Lewis of London	21	5	1950	1977
Ben & Jerry's Ice Cream	16	1	1978	1981
Bryant Bureau	NA	NA	1977	1977

Table 2: Start-up Expenses

Franchises Listed in Order of Minimum Capital Required

Company Name	*Minimum Capital*	*Maximum Capital*	*Minimum Cash*	*Init. License Fee*
	$	**$**	**$**	**$**
General Business Services	variable	variable	variable	24,500
Packy the Shipper	995	1,295	995	995–1,295
H & R Block, Inc.	1,500	3,000	1,500	0
Gallery of Homes, Inc.	2,000	100,000	2,000	7,000
Jazzercise, Inc.	2,000	NA	500	500
TV Focus, Inc.	2,500	7,500	5,000	2,500
Molly Maid, Inc.	4,000	NA	4,000	12,900
CHEM-CLEAN Restoration	4,500	40,000	4,500	4.5–24,000
Dahlberg Electronics, Inc.	5,000	50,000	25,000	12,500
Dial One Intl. Inc.	6,000	20,000	10,000	6,500
AAA Employment	7,000	18,000	4,000	5–13,000
TriMark Publishing	7,000	NA	7,000	24,900
Homes and Land Publishing	7,600	NA	7,600	7,500
NuVision, Inc.	8,000	100,000	25,000	8,000
Chem-Dry Carpet Cleaning	9,900	NA	4,900	9,900
American Advertising Dist.	10,000	50,000	10,000	19.5–34,500
Coustic-Glo Intl., Inc.	10,000	28,000	8,750	8.75–25,000
Earl Keim Realty	10,000	25,000	8,500	8,500
*ISU Intl.	10,000	NA	10,000	3,000
Merry Maids, Inc.	10,000	15,000	17,500	17,500
Nutri/System	10,000	75,000	10,000	49,500
Rainbow Intl. Carpet	10,000	13,000	10,000	15,000

Company Name	*Minimum Capital*	*Maximum Capital*	*Minimum Cash*	*Init. License Fee*
	$	**$**	**$**	**$**
RE/MAX	10,000	20,000	5,000	7.5–17,500
Thrifty Rent-A-Car System	10,000	75,000	10,000	9,000
Western Temporary Services	10,000	NA	10,000	10–50,000
ServiceMaster	10,700	19,800	5,350	5.45–11,500
Jani-King Intl., Inc.	11,000	11,500	13,500	8,500
Marcoin Business Services	11,000	30,000	11,000	20,000
Maid Brigade	14,000	NA	14,000	7,900
Lindal Cedar Homes, Inc.	15,000	20,000	5,000	0
Mr. Build Intl.	15,000	35,000	20,000	6–12,900
Servpro Industries, Inc.	15,000	20,000	13,000	17,800
Steamatic	15,000	50,000	10,000	10–50,000
CHROMA Intl.	16,000	18,000	16,000	5,000
Video Data Services	16,950	NA	16,950	14,950
Money Mailer, Inc.	17,000	200,000	4,500	15–150,000
Dunhill Personnel Systems	17,500	116,000	17,500	15–25,000
National Financial Co.	18,000	NA	18,000	18,000
Sales Consultants Intl.	18,000	36,000	35,000	16–25,000
Clentech/Acoustic Clean	19,700	29,000	10,000	10,000
Decorating Den Systems	20,000	NA	18,500	15,500
Freedom Rent-A-Car	20,000	NA	20,000	11,000
Gymboree	20,000	38,000	20,000	7–14,000
Langenwalter Carpet Dyeing	20,000	NA	15,000	15,000
Mifax Service and Systems	20,000	30,000	8,500	16–22,150
Money Concepts Intl., Inc.	20,000	28,000	7,000	10,000
The Peanut Shack	20,000	130,000	60,000	5–20,000
Playful Parenting	20,000	25,000	7,500	12,500
RainSoft Water Cond.	20,000	50,000	10,000	0
Stanley Steemer Intl., Inc.	20,000	50,000	10,000	34–200,000
State Wide Real Estate	20,000	30,000	20,000	9,500
Diet Center, Inc.	22,000	39,000	12,000	12–24,000
Homeowners Concept, Inc.	22,000	NA	22,000	7,500
HouseMaster of America	22,000	34,000	27,000	17–35,000
Minuteman Press	22,500	32,500	22,500	22,500
Help-U-Sell, Inc.	25,000	60,000	25,000	4,500/up
Nation-Wide Gen. Rental	25,000	NA	7,000	0
Pearle Vision Center, Inc.	25,000	35,000	25,000	20,000

Company Name	*Minimum Capital*	*Maximum Capital*	*Minimum Cash*	*Init. License Fee*
	$	**$**	**$**	**$**
Tuff-Kote Dinol, Inc.	25,000	35,000	25,000	4–11,000
American Intl. Rent A Car	30,000	350,000	30,000	5–175,000
Coit Drapery and Carpet	30,000	1 mill	35,000	7.5–150,000
Endrust Industries	30,000	NA	30,000	30,000
Insty-Prints, Inc.	30,000	NA	30,000	28,500
Pilot Air Freight	30,000	50,000	25,000	10–30,000
Sonic	30,000	50,000	30,000	7,500
Spring-Green Lawn Care	30,000	35,000	10,000	13,500
Subway Sandwiches	30,000	80,000	15,000	7,500
The Maids Intl.	30,000	10,000	30,000	7.5–11,500
Dynamark Security Centers	31,000	NA	18,000	12,000
Lawn Doctor	31,500	NA	26,500	26,500
Annie's Book Stop	35,000	40,000	35,000	25,000
Command Performance	35,000	NA	35,000	21,500
Dry Clean-USA	35,000	70,000	35,000	0
Frontier Fruit & Nut Co.	35,000	120,000	23,000	15,000
Holiday-Payless Rent-A-Car	35,000	125,000	35,000	12–75,000
Norrell Services	35,000	65,000	45,000	0
Snelling and Snelling	35,400	45,300	35,400	29,500
Bryant Bureau	37,000	55,000	19,000	29,500
7-Eleven	37,300	NA	30,000	30,000
Network Video	37,900	60,900	37,900	0
Colortyme, Inc.	38,000	73,000	38,000	10,000
National Video, Inc.	39,500	350,000	39,500	35,000
Meineke Discount Muffler	45,000	NA	45,000	25,000
Physicians Weight Loss	45,000	50,000	45,000	18,500
Stained Glass Overlay, Inc.	45,000	60,000	45,000	34,000
Tastee-Freez Intl.	45,000	NA	45,000	10,000
Victory Intl., Inc.	45,000	62,000	65,000	25,000
Spring Crest	49,000	NA	20,000	10,000
Sylvan Learning Corp.	49,550	107,000	25,000	20–30,000
Flowerama of America, Inc.	50,000	90,000	20,000	17,500
F-O-R-T-U-N-E Franchise	50,000	NA	60,000	0
Four Seasons Greenhouses	50,000	200,000	25,000	30,000
The Hair Performers	50,000	125,000	15,000	15,000
Mail Boxes Etc., USA	50,000	65,000	50,000	15,000

Company Name	*Minimum Capital*	*Maximum Capital*	*Minimum Cash*	*Init. License Fee*
	$	**$**	**$**	**$**
Paul W. Davis Systems	50,000	NA	50,000	25–45,000
Print Shack Intl., Inc.	50,000	NA	50,000	34,500
Ziebart Corp.	50,000	60,000	50,000	15,000
Adventureland Video, Inc.	55,000	65,000	15,500	15,500
Fantastic Sam's	55,000	67,000	55,000	25,000
Postal Instant Press	58,500	NA	32,500	40,000
California Closet Co., Inc.	60,000	95,000	60,000	25,000
Convenient Food Mart, Inc.	60,000	NA	45,000	5–15,000
Domino's Pizza, Inc.	60,000	135,000	60,000	4–6,250
First Choice Haircutters	60,000	NA	35,000	15,000
Remco Enterprises, Inc.	60,000	200,000	60,000	15,000
Goodyear Tire Centers	65,000	NA	65,000	0
Intl. Blimpie Corp.	70,000	110,000	50,000	15,000
Sportastiks	70,000	NA	30,000	20,000
Taco John's Intl.	70,000	500,000	21,000	16,500
Cutco Industries, Inc.	72,000	155,000	50,000	18,000
Quik Print	72,500	NA	72,500	10,000
Great Clips, Inc.	74,000	NA	74,000	12,500
Lee Myles Associates	75,000	78,000	45,000	20,000
Pizza Inn, Inc.	75,000	NA	75,000	17,500
Rent-A-Wreck	75,000	250,000	75,000	5–50,000
Long John Silver's Seafood	76,000	NA	76,000	15,000
Travel Agents Intl.	76,000	NA	39,000	24,500
Kwik-Kopy Corp.	78,200	NA	46,500	41,500
Corp. Invest. Bus. Brokers	80,000	NA	50,000	22.5–35,000
Grease Monkey Intl., Inc.	80,000	160,000	80,000	20,000
Village Inn Pancake House	80,000	NA	80,000	25,000
Jiffy Lube Intl., Inc.	84,000	NA	35,000	35,000
Video Biz	85,000	NA	85,000	55,000
Sir Speedy, Inc.	86,000	NA	86,000	17,500
Interstate Auto. Trans.	88,000	NA	73,000	20,000
American Speedy Printing	90,000	100,000	30,000	37,500
Athletic Attic Marketing	90,000	180,000	25,000	7,500
Bathtique Intl., Ltd.	90,000	100,000	25,000	25,000
TCBY	93,000	155,000	93,000	20,000
Intl. Dairy Queen, Inc.	95,000	NA	95,000	30,000

Company Name	*Minimum Capital*	*Maximum Capital*	*Minimum Cash*	*Init. License Fee*
	$	**$**	**$**	**$**
AAMCO Transmissions, Inc.	100,000	110,000	42,000	25,000
Ben & Jerry's Ice Cream	100,000	NA	80,000	15,000
Bressler's 33 Flavors, Inc.	100,000	130,000	50,000	10,000
Gelato Classico	100,000	150,000	50,000	25,000
Personnel Pool of America	100,000	200,000	80,000	15,000
Rax Restaurants, Inc.	100,000	500,000	100,000	25,000
Sounds Easy Intl., Inc.	100,000	150,000	30,000	15,000
Uniroyal Goodrich	100,000	NA	50,000	0
Precision Tune, Inc.	102,000	118,000	35,000	15,000
Mr. Transmission	103,000	NA	35,000	19,500
Dunkin' Donuts	110,000	544,000	39,000	30–40,000
Orange Julius	110,000	160,000	110,000	17,500
Taco Time Intl., Inc.	110,000	175,000	110,000	15,000
Original Great American	115,000	140,000	115,000	20,000
Gingiss Intl., Inc.	120,000	160,000	60,000	15,000
Sparks Tune-Up	120,000	NA	32,000	20,000
Video Update, Inc.	120,000	150,000	60,000	19,500
Captain D's Seafood	122,000	NA	122,000	10,000
The Athlete's Foot	125,000	150,000	50,000	7,500
Curtis Mathes Corp.	125,000	NA	125,000	25,000
David's Cookies	125,000	NA	25,000	25,000
Just * Pants	125,000	201,500	65,000	0
Ponderosa Steakhouses	125,000	NA	125,000	15,000
Martin Franchise, Inc.	127,000	216,000	50,000	16,000
Champion Auto Stores, Inc.	130,000	NA	70,000	0
Primo's/Jan Drake's	132,000	216,000	46,200	20,000
Maaco Auto Painting	134,900	NA	45,000	15,000
All American Hero	140,000	NA	140,000	25,000
Baskin-Robbins Ice Cream	140,000	NA	60,000	0
Docktor Pet Centers	149,000	192,000	50,000	15,000
CAR–X Service Systems, Inc.	150,000	NA	40,000	12,500
Deck the Walls	150,000	200,000	45,000	27,500
Del Taco, Inc.	150,000	450,000	150,000	20,000
Intl. House of Pancakes	150,000	600,000	50,000	50,000
Mister Donut	150,000	300,000	60,000	15,000
New England Log Homes	150,000	NA	50,000	7,500

Company Name	*Minimum Capital*	*Maximum Capital*	*Minimum Cash*	*Init. License Fee*
	$	**$**	**$**	**$**
One-Hour Moto Photo	150,000	250,000	37,000	35,000
Petland	150,000	450,000	60,000	0
Pioneer Take Out Corp.	150,000	300,000	75,000	25–150,000
Scandia Down Corp.	150,000	NA	60,000	25,000
Uniglobe Travel	150,000	NA	55,000	42,500
Wicks 'N' Sticks	150,000	200,000	45,000	27,500
Duds 'n Suds Corp.	160,000	210,000	50,000	27,500
Everything Yogurt	165,000	450,000	80,000	20,000
American Vision Centers	170,000	220,000	60,000	10,000
Midas Intl. Corp.	170,000	NA	75,000	10,000
Shakey's Pizza Restaurant	175,000	212,000	175,000	20,000
Jack in the Box	190,000	NA	160,000	25,000
Ben Franklin Stores, Inc.	200,000	300,000	80,000	1,390
Church's Fried Chicken	200,000	NA	100,000	15,000
Coast to Coast Stores	200,000	700,000	100,000	3,000
Computerland Corp.	200,000	450,000	40,000	15–75,000
K-Bob's, Inc.	200,000	350,000	125,000	25,000
Lewis of London	200,000	NA	150,000	40,000
Taco Bell, Inc.	200,000	NA	100,000	35,000
Western Steer Steak House	200,000	300,000	200,000	20,000
Hickory Farms of Ohio, Inc.	215,000	327,000	215,000	20,000
Sbarro	217,000	550,000	108,500	35,000
Software Galeria, Inc.	225,000	275,000	125,000	30,000
Arby's, Inc.	235,000	304,500	100,000	20–32,500
Noble Roman's Pizza	235,000	375,000	70,000	12,500
Bonanza Restaurants	250,000	1 mill	90,000	30,000
Budget Rent a Car Corp.	250,000	750,000	250,000	15,000
The Ground Round, Inc.	250,000	NA	30,000	30,000
Taylor Rental Corp.	255,000	NA	80,000	20,000
Entré Computer Centers	280,000	950,000	90,000	40,000
Round Table Pizza	280,000	300,000	80,000	20,000
Cuco's Restaurantes	300,000	500,000	275,000	20–30,000
MicroAge Computer	300,000	550,000	150,000	30,000
Kentucky Fried Chicken	360,000	NA	360,000	10,000
Swensen's	390,000	520,000	150,000	25,000
McDonald's Corp.	400,000	NA	200,000	12,500

Company Name	Minimum Capital	Maximum Capital	Minimum Cash	Init. License Fee
	$	$	$	$
Western Sizzlin Steak House	425,000	800,000	125,000	15,000
A & W Restaurants, Inc.	450,000	NA	100,000	10,000
Dollar Rent A Car	550,000	1 mill	50,000	7,500
Wendy's Intl., Inc.	627,000	1.3 mill	627,000	25,000
Po Folks, Inc.	650,000	900,000	100,000	37,000
Hardee's Food Systems, Inc.	675,000	1.3 mill	150,000	15,000
Bojangles'	694,000	858,000	120,000	25–35,000
D'Lites of America, Inc.	740,000	1 mill	150,000	35,000
El Chico Corp.	750,000	1.4 mill	300,000	40,000
Roy Rogers Restaurants	750,000	1 mill	175,000	25,000
Sizzler Restaurants Intl., Inc.	750,000	NA	200,000	30,000
Mazzio's Pizza	800,000	NA	200,000	20,000
Carl's Junior Restaurants	850,000	NA	175,000	35,000
Bob's Big Boy Restaurant	897,500	1.4 mill	100,000	25,000
Benihana of Tokyo	1 mill	2 mill	375,000	50,000
Popeyes Fried Chicken	1.5 mill	NA	65,000	65,000

Table 3: Royalty Expenses

Franchises Listed in Order of Royalties Charged

Company Name	*Royalties*	*Advertising Royalties*	*Total Royalties*
No Royalties:			
Champion Auto Stores	0	0	0
CHEM-CLEAN Restoration	0	0	0
David's Cookies	0	0	0
Endrust Industries	0	0	0
Lindal Cedar Homes, Inc.	0	0	0
Mifax Service and Systems	0	0	0
Money Mailer, Inc.	0	0	0
National Financial Co.	0	0	0
Nation-Wide Gen. Rental	0	0	0
Network Video	0	0	0
TriMark Publishing	0	0	0
Uniroyal Goodrich Co.	0	0	0
Percentage of Gross:	%	%	%
Intl. Tours, Inc.	.5–.75	0	.5–.75
Gelato Classico	0	1	1
Western Sizzlin	2	0	2
Dynamark Security	1–4	1	2–5
Sonic	.5–1	1.5	2–2.5
Taylor Rental Corp.	2–2.75	0	2–2.75
Four Seasons Greenhouses	2.5	0	2.5

Company Name	*Royalties*	*Advertising Royalties*	*Total Royalties*
Paul W. Davis Systems	2.5	0	2.5
Dunhill Personnel System	2–7	.5–1	2.5–8
Goodyear Tire Centers	3	0	3
Remco Enterprises, Inc.	3–6	0	3–6
The Athlete's Foot	3	.5	3.5
Athletic Attic Marketing	3	.5	3.5
Baskin-Robbins Ice Cream	.5	3	3.5
Ben & Jerry's Ice Cream	0	4	4
Docktor Pet Centers	4	0	4
Mazzio's Pizza	3	1	4
Clentech/Acoustic Clean	3–4	1	4–5
ServiceMaster	4–10	0	4–10
Adventureland Video, Inc.	4.5	0	4.5
Petland	4	.5	4.5
Convenient Food Mart	4.5–5	0	4.5–5
Freedom Rent-A-Car	3.5	1–2	4.5–5.5
Bathtique Intl., Ltd.	5	0	5
Captain D's Seafood	3	2	5
Everything Yogurt	5	0	5
The Ground Round, Inc.	3	2	5
K-Bob's, Inc.	3	2	5
Noble Roman's Pizza	5	0	5
Personnel Pool of America	5	0	5
Quik Print	5	0	5
Sounds Easy Intl.	5	0	5
Spring Crest	3	2	5
Video Biz	2.5	2.5	5
Village Inn Pancake House	5	0	5
Flowerama of America	5–6	0	5–6
Software Galeria, Inc.	4.5–6	.5–1.5	5–7.5
Lawn Doctor	0	5–10	5–10
Tastee-Freez Intl.	4.25	1	5.25
Benihana of Tokyo	5	.5	5.5
Sales Consultants Intl.	5	.5	5.5
Taco Time Intl., Inc.	5	.5	5.5
Swensen's	5.5	0–3	5.5–8.5
Colortyme, Inc.	3	3	6

Company Name	*Royalties*	*Advertising Royalties*	*Total Royalties*
Command Performance	6	0	6
Coustic-Glo Intl., Inc.	5	1	6
Curtis Mathes Corp.	0	6	6
Cutco Industries, Inc.	6	0	6
Earl Keim Realty	5	1	6
Frontier Fruit & Nut Co.	6	0	6
Gallery of Homes, Inc.	4	2	6
Kentucky Fried Chicken	4	2	6
Minuteman Press	6	0	6
The Peanut Shack	5	1	6
Taco John's Intl.	4	2	6
Western Steer Steakhouse	4	2	6
All American Hero	5	1–3	6–8
Sir Speedy, Inc.	4–6	2	6–8
Wicks 'N' Sticks	6	0–2	6–8
Homes & Land Publishing	6–9	0	6–9
Kwik-Kopy Corp.	4–8	2	6–10
Cuco's Restaurantes	4	2.5	6.5
Insty-Prints, Inc.	4.5	2	6.5
One-Hour Moto Photo	6.	.5	6.5
Shakey's Pizza Restaurant	4.5	2	6.5
American Intl. Rent A Car	7	0	7
American Speedy Printing	5	2	7
Bob's Big Boy Restaurant	3	4	7
CHROMA Intl.	5	2	7
El Chico Corp.	3	4	7
Gen. Bus. Services, Inc.	7	0	7
Mail Boxes Etc., USA	5	2	7
Merry Maids, Inc.	7	0	7
MicroAge Computer	6	1	7
Nutri/System	7	0	7
Orange Julius	6	1	7
Original Great American	7	0	7
Pizza Inn, Inc.	4	3	7
Rainbow Intl. Carpet	7	0	7
Round Table Pizza	4	3	7
Stained Glass Overlay, Inc.	5	2	7

Company Name	*Royalties*	*Advertising Royalties*	*Total Royalties*
TCBY	4	3	7
Carl's Junior Restaurants	3–4	4	7–8
Intl. Dairy Queen, Inc.	4	3–5	7–9
Postal Instant Press	6–8	1	7–9
The Maids Intl.	5–7	2	7–9
Servpro Industries	7–10	0–3	7–13
Arby's, Inc.	3	4.2	7.2
Intl. House of Pancakes	4.5	3	7.5
Po Folks, Inc.	4	3.5	7.5
Primo's/Jan Drake's	6	1.5	7.5
National Video, Inc.	4.9	3	7.9
A & W Restaurants, Inc.	4	4	8
Bryant Bureau	7	1	8
Computerland Corp.	7	1	8
Corp. Invest. Bus. Brokers	6	2	8
D'Lites of America, Inc.	4	4	8
Deck the Walls	6	2	8
F-O-R-T-U-N-E Franchise	7	1	8
Gymboree	6	2	8
Holiday-Payless	5	3	8
Jack in the Box	4	4	8
Just * Pants	5	3	8
Popeyes Fried Chicken	5	3	8
Rax Restaurants, Inc.	4	4	8
Rent-A-Wreck	6	2	8
Sbarro	5	3	8
Scandia Down Corp.	5	3	8
Sizzler Restaurants Intl.	4.5	3.5	8
Snelling and Snelling	7	1	8
State Wide Real Estate	5	3	8
Thrifty Rent-A-Car	3	5	8
Video Update, Inc.	5	3	8
Wendy's Intl., Inc.	4	4	8
Sportastiks	6–8	2	8–10
Mister Donut	5.4	3	8.4
Domino's Pizza, Inc.	5.5	3	8.5
Hardee's Food Systems	3.5–4	5	8.5–9

Company Name	*Royalties*	*Advertising Royalties*	*Total Royalties*
Bojangles'	4	5	9
Dollar Rent A Car	9	0	9
Entré Computer Centers	8	1	9
Grease Monkey Intl., Inc.	5	4	9
Intl. Blimpie Corp.	6	3	9
Long John Silver's Seafood	4	5	9
Maid Brigade	7	2	9
Playful Parenting	6	3	9
Roy Rogers Restaurants	4	5	9
Spring-Green Lawn Care	7	2	9
Gingiss Intl., Inc.	6–10	3	9–13
Budget Rent a Car Corp.	7.5–10	2	9.5–12
Pioneer Take Out Corp.	5.9	3.9	9.8
AAA Employment	10	0	10
Bressler's 33 Flavors, Inc.	6	4	10
Church's Fried Chicken	5	5	10
Del Taco, Inc.	5	5	10
The Hair Performers	6	4	10
HouseMaster of America	6	4	10
Molly Maid, Inc.	8	2	10
Print Shack Intl., Inc.	5	5	10
Taco Bell, Inc.	5.5	4.5	10
Jani-King Intl., Inc.	10	0–.5	10–10.5
Money Concepts Intl., Inc.	8–10	2	10–12
CAR–X Service Systems	5	5–10	10–15
Steamatic	5–10	5	10-15
Subway Sandwiches	8	2.5	10.5
First Choice Haircutters	10	1	11
Great Clips, Inc.	6	5	11
California Closet Co., Inc.	6	6	12
Hickory Farms of Ohio	6	6	12
Physicians Weight Loss	10	2	12
Sylvan Learning Corp.	8–10	4	12–14
Decorating Den Systems	11	2	13
Tuff-Kote Dinol, Inc.	8	5	13
Ziebart Corp.	8	5	13
Jiffy Lube Intl., Inc.	5–6	8	13–14

Company Name	*Royalties*	*Advertising Royalties*	*Total Royalties*
Help-U-Sell, Inc.	7	7	14
Pilot Air Freight	13	1	14
American Vision Centers	8.5	6	14.5
McDonald's Corp.	11.5	4	15.5
NuVision, Inc.	8.5	7	15.5
Stanley Steemer Intl., Inc.	6–10	10	16–20
Pearle Vision Center, Inc.	8.5	8	16.5
Precision Tune, Inc.	7.5	9	16.5
Meineke Discount Muffler	8	10	18
Mr. Transmission	8	10	18
Midas Corp.	10	10	20
Jazzercise, Inc.	25	0	25
H & R Block, Inc.	30–50	0	30–50
7-Eleven	50	0	50
Norrell Services	60	0	60
Flat Weekly Fee:	***$***	***$***	***$***
TV Focus, Inc.	90–250	0	90–250
Mr. Build Intl.	90	70	160
Fantastic Sam's	136.50	167.68	304.18
Flat Monthly Fee:	***$***	***$***	***$***
Coast to Coast Stores	50	0	50
Langenwalter Carpet	0	100	100
Chem-Dry Carpet Cleaning	103	0	103
RE/MAX	60	50	110
Ben Franklin Stores, Inc.	125	0	125
Dry Clean-USA	250	300	550
*ISU Intl.	300	500	800
Travel Agents Intl.	750	400	1,150
Flat Yearly Fee:	***$***	***$***	***$***
Video Data Services	500	0	500
Dial One Intl., Inc.	400–2,000	300–800	700–2,800
Martin Franchise, Inc.	1,500	0	1,500
New England Log Homes	3,000	0	3,000
RainSoft Water	4–7,000	0	4–7,000

Company Name	*Royalties*	*Advertising Royalties*	*Total Royalties*
Fee per Unit Sold:	***$***	***$***	***$***
Packy the Shipper	.50/package	.05/package	.55/package
Dahlberg Electronics, Inc.	33/instr.	0	33/instr.
American Advert. Dist.	163/10,000	0	163/10,000
Miscellaneous:			
Dunkin' Donuts	NA	NA	NA
Homeowners Concept, Inc.	NA	NA	NA
Diet Center, Inc.	variable	variable	variable
Western Temp. Svc.	variable	variable	variable
Ponderosa Steakhouses	4%	variable	variable
AAMCO Transmissions	9%	variable	variable
Uniglobe Travel	1%	$582/m	1% + $582/m
Annie's Book Stop	2% + $50–100/m	$25–100/m	2% + $75–200/m
Duds 'n Suds Corp.	$450/m	2%	2% + $450/m
Interstate Auto. Trans.	6%	$250/week	6% + $250/w
Bonanza Restaurants	4.8%	2% + $1,150/y	6.8% + $1,150/y
Marcoin Business Services	6.5% + $100/m	.5%	7% + $100/m
Sparks Tune-Up	7%	$420/m	7% + $420/m
Lee Myles Transmissions	8%	$300–400/w	8% + $300–400/w
Maaco Auto Painting	8%	$500/w	8% + $500/w
Lewis of London	5–10%	$2.5K/y	5–10% + $2.5K/y
Victory Intl., Inc.	7% or $350/m	3%	10%; 3% + $350/m
Coit Drapery and Carpet	5–7%	10% + $55/m	15–17% + $55/m

Table 4: Alphabetical Index of Companies